T0185816

Practical Mono

Mark Mamone

apress®

Practical Mono

Copyright © 2006 by Mark Mamone

ISBN : 978-1-4842-2018-4

ISBN : 978-1-4302-0097-0 (eBook)

DOI 10.1007/978-1-4302-0097-0

Lead Editor: Jason Gilmore
Technical Reviewer: Marcus Fletcher
Editorial Board: Steve Anglin, Dan Appleman, Ewan Buckingham, Gary Cornell, Tony Davis, Jason Gilmore, Jonathan Hassell, Chris Mills, Dominic Shakeshaft, Jim Sumser
Project Manager: Pat Christenson
Copy Edit Manager: Nicole LeClerc
Copy Editors: Kim Wimpsett, Ami Knox
Assistant Production Director: Kari Brooks-Copony
Compositor: Susan Glinert
Proofreaders: Lori Bring, Kim Burton, Linda Seifert, Dan Shaw, Nancy Sixsmith
Production Editing Assistant: Kelly Gunther
Indexer: Ann Rogers
Artist: Kinetic Publishing Services, LLC
Cover Designer: Kurt Krames
Manufacturing Director: Tom Debolski

Distributed to the book trade worldwide by Springer-Verlag New York, Inc., 233 Spring Street, 6th Floor, New York, NY 10013. Phone 1-800-SPRINGER, fax 201-348-4505, e-mail orders-ny@springer-sbm.com, or visit http://www.springeronline.com.

For information on translations, please contact Apress directly at 2560 Ninth Street, Suite 219, Berkeley, CA 94710. Phone 510-549-5930, fax 510-549-5939, e-mail info@apress.com, or visit http://www.apress.com.

The source code for this book is available to readers at http://www.apress.com in the Source Code section.

Contents at a Glance

Contents

About the Author

MARK MAMONE is a senior solutions architect with British Telecom (BT) and is currently the chief technology officer for the enterprise solutions group whose focus is on a major program within BT. Mark has been involved in .NET since its inception and has delivered solutions based on numerous technologies including .NET, J2EE, Linux, Windows, and more. When he's not writing books and spending what precious spare time he has with his family, Mark researches leading-edge technologies and looks for practical applications for them.

About the
Technical Reviewer

MARCUS FLETCHER is a systems integration engineer with British Telecom (BT) and has used Mono since Beta 1. He has worked on nationwide projects involving .NET solutions and is currently evangelizing Linux-based technologies within the BT group. In his spare time, he likes to investigate computer security—in general, finding new technologies and breaking them.

Preface

I've been involved in the information technology industry for more than 18 years, and I've seen many technologies come and go. However, having tackled and survived various approaches to systems architecture and the multitude of language and technologies that are out there, nothing excites me more than .NET and open source. Therefore, when I had the opportunity to develop and write a book based on a combination of these topics in the form of Mono and Linux, how could I say no? However, I couldn't have done it without the unrelenting support of my wife, Rachel, and the less than helpful support of my nine-month-old son, Oliver. I'd also like to say a big thank you to everyone at Apress, especially Jason and Marcus for their constructive criticism during reviews and Pat and Kim for their help in ensuring the project went to press on time. I hope you enjoy the book.

CHAPTER 1

■ ■ ■

Introducing .NET and Mono

Ever since the .NET initiative launched in January 2000 and the Visual Studio .NET beta subsequently launched in October 2000, the .NET train has been gaining speed; it now is the number-one development platform for the Windows operating system. However, you may have noticed a key point in that statement: for the Windows operating system! Yes, you guessed it: Microsoft targeted the .NET technology suite at the Windows operating system only; therefore, at the time of its launch, .NET was not available on other platforms such as Unix, Mac OS X, or Linux. This is not surprising, as Microsoft develops the Windows operating system and doesn't want to invest time in creating versions for competing operating systems; however, in the corporate world, other operating systems exist and for good reasons.

In this chapter, you'll learn exactly what .NET is and what it consists of; it's important to note that Microsoft made a key decision that acted as the catalyst for the Mono project and ultimately enabled .NET to run on operating systems other than Windows. This decision was to submit the specification for a core component of the common language runtime (CLR) and the Common Language Infrastructure (CLI) to the international standards body ECMA International, an industry association "dedicated to the standardization of information and communication systems." What does this mean? It means that anybody can obtain the specification for core .NET components and in doing so develop their own implementation of that specification, effectively writing their own .NET Framework components.

In addition, this chapter will introduce Mono and its associated elements including its tools and configuration. You'll also take a brief look at integrated development environments (IDEs), which are graphical applications that make developing your application as little easier. Finally, this chapter will cover what you need to know about the sample application you'll develop throughout this book, which is a fully functional RSS aggregator.

Microsoft Introduces .NET

In 2000, use of the Microsoft Windows operating system was widespread on desktop and laptop PCs, both at home and at work. In addition to the numerous other desktop products (such as Microsoft Office) and server products (such as SQL Server, Exchange, and so on) Microsoft produces, it had achieved success with development technologies such as C++, Visual Basic, Active Server Pages (ASP), the Common Object Model (COM), and so on. However, Java was starting to gain steam, and Microsoft needed to evolve its technology stack to help combat this threat and others in the open-source community (such as Python and PHP). After hiring the lead designer of Borland Delphi, Microsoft announced .NET 1.0 in the summer of 2000 for a 2001 launch (see http://www.pcworld.com/news/article/0,aid,17397,00.asp). Thereafter, Microsoft launched version 1.1 of the .NET Framework in April 2003, and more recently, it announced version 2.0, which is to be launched late in 2005.

What Is .NET?

Microsoft .NET is, according to Microsoft, "a strategy for connecting systems, information, and devices through Web Services." This is true; however, it doesn't do justice to the power of the .NET Framework, so I'll describe it in a slightly different way.

.NET is a software platform that provides several technologies that benefit corporate organizations, individuals, and the development community. Its aim is to provide a set of technologies that will offer ubiquitous interoperability through the standards it embraces and defines. At a high level, .NET consists of several elements, such as the .NET Framework and class library. I'll introduce each of these in the following sections.

The .NET Framework

As its name implies, the .NET Framework is an all-encompassing framework or environment for constructing, deploying, and running applications that leverage the features of .NET, including Extensible Markup Language (XML), Web Services, Windows Forms, ADO.NET, and so on. In addition, the .NET Framework also encompasses a companion framework, called the .NET Compact Framework, that is targeted at mobile devices or indeed any device that can run the CLR, including set-top boxes.

Common Language Runtime (CLR)

The CLR is the foundation that underpins all .NET applications; it's the engine that drives the vehicle. The CLR is an execution environment (hence the term *runtime*) that supports the execution of applications written in Intermediate Language (IL), the product of compiling your .NET application. The CLR is standards based; therefore, it is possible for you to develop your own version for your favorite operating system, which is exactly what has happened with the Mono environment (although it is no simple task!). The CLR offers a *managed* environment that supports a number of advanced features, including the following:

- Multiple library versions

- Just-in-time (JIT) compilation

- Automatic memory management

It would be easy to assume what some of these features offer without fully understanding their benefits, so I'll provide a brief overview of what benefit these advanced features offer in the following sections.

Multiple Library Versions

A well-known problem on the Windows platform, and to a lesser extent on other operating systems, is the complexities associated with deploying multiple versions of the same components. This problem manifests itself by stopping working applications from running correctly, because a new version of a component has been installed on which the application relies. The .NET Framework solves this by allowing different versions of the same component to be installed side by side; applications simply continue using the version of component against which they were built. These libraries in the .NET world are also known as *assemblies*, which are something I cover in Chapter 5.

Just-in-Time Compilation

One trait of the managed environment that the .NET Framework offers is the compilation of code into an intermediate language that is then executed by the CLR. This compilation happens *just-in-time*, which means the code is compiled when first referenced and thereafter the already compiled code can be executed. This offers the benefits of an interpreted language whilst reducing the performance impact.

Automatic Memory Management

One of the features of a managed environment is the automatic memory management that the CLR provides. This memory management allocates and releases memory automatically without your application's code having to explicitly do it—although some best practices (discussed in Chapter 12 of this book) can help the CLR perform to the best of its ability.

Note This memory management is associated only with *managed code*, that is, code running under the control of the CLR. The .NET Framework allows you to still write and execute code written in unmanaged languages such as C++, which does not run under the control of the CLR but can interact with managed code through features within the .NET Framework.

Class Library

The CLR alone would not constitute an easy development environment in which to build. You'd need to know the complexities of IL, and you'd be going back to the days of assembler programming. This is obviously still something you can do, should you want to harness all the power possible at the lowest level; however, it's time-consuming and largely unnecessary.

The class library that accompanies the .NET Framework is a set of comprehensive classes, interfaces, and value types that provide access to the system's functionality and services. They are the building blocks on which you create .NET applications, components, and custom controls.

.NET As an Open Industry Standard

Microsoft made an important decision early on in the development of the .NET Framework: to submit the specifications for key components of the .NET Framework to the international standards organization ECMA International. The result is that the specifications are now standard and available to anyone who wants to implement their own version of the .NET Framework. You can view the final standards on the ECMA International Web site at http://www.ecma-international.org.

Command Language Infrastructure (CLI)

The CLI is the overarching specification (ECMA 335) that allows you to write an application in a high-level programming language and execute it on any platform that provides an implementation of the CLR. The CLI consists of the following:

- A file format

- A common type system (CTS)

- An extensible metadata system

- IL code

- Access to the native operating system services

- A base class library

For clarity, in the following sections, I'll provide a brief overview of what some of these key components of the CLI actually mean.

Common Type System (CTS)

The CTS provides a number of guiding principles to enable the .NET Framework to support multiple but interoperable languages. It provides a set of rules that a .NET language must follow in order to interact with other languages; these include how to handle types (both *reference* and *value*) and how to provide a model for object orientation. This is a key feature of the .NET Framework and means that you could write your application using one or more of the languages supported by the .NET Framework, including C#, Visual Basic .NET (VB .NET), Python, and more.

For a list of the languages supported (although it's not exhaustive), see `http://www.dotnetlanguages.net/DNL/Resources.aspx`.

■ **Note** Your application could have different parts written in different languages. These could be one of the managed languages available such as C# or an unmanaged language such as C++, which you could then integrate.

Intermediate Language (IL)

Once you have written your application in one (or more) of the languages mentioned, you then compile the application (using the JIT compiler) into an intermediate language known as IL. The CLR then executes the IL. This language is platform independent though its definition is a standard file format that an implementation of the CLR can understand. It's this file format that offers the ability for you to run any .NET code on any platform, provided it has an implementation of the CLR available.

Note You can even write your applications directly in IL if you want!

To summarize, the file format provides a standard for representing files, the CTS provides the interoperability of languages and applications, IL provides platform interoperability and allows further compilation in native systems, and finally the metadata system and base class library complete the features necessary for component-based development.

Other Technology Support, Such As Extensible Markup Language (XML)

In addition to defining standards for adoption and supporting interoperability with other technologies and platforms, the .NET Framework embraces other well-known standards such as XML and Web Services (the provision of functionality over the common HTTP channel).

While this does not guarantee interoperability, it promotes it, and provided that both parties in communication observe the standards present, code can now happily coexist and talk regardless of the language it was written in (in other words, Java, C#, and so on), the runtime it executes under (that is, the Java Runtime Environment [JRE] or CLR), and the platform it runs on (that is, Windows, Linux, and so on).

Technologies

In addition to the foundation provided by the CLR and all its components, .NET provides you with several other technologies and services for you to embrace within your applications. The following sections describe some of these technologies.

Active Server Pages .NET (ASP.NET)

The ASP technologies implemented by previous versions of Windows and Internet Information Services (IIS) received wide adoption by the information technology (IT) industry, and Microsoft rearchitected the concept of server-side, dynamic scripting code when it introduced ASP.NET. This allows you to implement your Web site using all the power and features of the .NET Framework and class libraries when developing powerful, server-side browser-based applications and\or Web sites. Another key architectural feature is the implementation of code-behind pages, where the graphical user interface (representing the content) and the back-end code (representing the business logic) is separate.

ADO.NET

The implementation of Active Data Objects (ADO) for .NET is an evolutionary step in providing a common framework for accessing disparate sources of data. It provides four key advantages:

- *Interoperability*: You gain interoperability, because the data format underpinning ADO.NET is XML, an industry standard understood by most platforms.

- *Scalability*: You achieve scalability through the support of advanced features such as disconnected datasets and connection pooling.

- *Productivity*: You gain productivity through the adoption of standard data components that use abstraction to connect to any data source but that are strongly typed for improved reliability.

- *Performance*: You achieve productivity through the support of features that also benefit scalability. Connection pooling reduces the overhead of establishing connections; data classes are provided to inherit the native speed of database libraries or the interoperability of concepts such as Open Database Connectivity (ODBC).

Safe, timely, and easy access to data is critical to the success of a framework, and the power of ADO.NET makes these tasks easy without sacrificing other important factors such as speed.

.NET Tools

The .NET tools are necessary to create, execute, and debug .NET applications; they include the categories of tools described in the following sections.

Command-Line Tools

Providing command-line based tools as part of the .NET Framework allows developers to start developing .NET applications straightaway. You don't need to purchase expensive commercial, off-the-shelf (COTS) packages, although you can if you want some of the advanced functionality these typically offer. The .NET Framework ships with a compiler, runtime environment, assembler, disassembler, class viewer, and much more. I'll cover these in more detail in Chapter 2.

Commercial, Off-the-Shelf (COTS) Packages

In addition to the command-line tools and open-source tools such as MonoDevelop, you also have the option to purchase (or write!) COTS packages that often provide functionality that is more advanced than that available in the open-source community (although this is becoming less true; take a look at MonoDevelop!). The most obvious candidate for this is Microsoft Visual Studio, an extremely powerful development environment that runs on the Windows platform only. It is on this product that the MonoDevelop tool is modeled (although it was born as the SharpDevelop tool). Another IDE is Eclipse (see http://www.eclipse.org/), which can provide support for the .NET Framework and C# through a downloadable plug-in (see http://www.improve-technologies.com/alpha/esharp).

The COTS products in the Windows world are big business. In the open-source community, though, the driver is "sharing" rather than "the bottom line," so fewer COTS products are sold. However, commercial products are sold that are built upon Mono and other open-source technologies; Novell's iFolder is a good example.

The History of Mono

Launched in mid-2001 by Ximian cofounder Miguel de Icaza, Mono is an open-source initiative that brings .NET technologies to operating systems other than Microsoft Windows. At the time of this writing, the Mono project has .NET distributions available for Linux, Windows, Mac OS, Berkeley Software Distribution (BSD), and Solaris operating systems. It also includes support for the x86 (32-bit and 64-bit) and PowerPC (PPC) processors. In doing so, this allows you to use Mono to develop cross-platform applications simply and easily.

Icaza started the GNU Object Model Environment (GNOME) project in August 1997 with a friend, Federico Mena. Although the project was successful, Icaza was becoming frustrated with the complexity of developing component-based solutions and liked Microsoft's .NET platform. It was a "good platform to innovate from."[1] He also wanted to promote the concepts introduced as part of the Bonobo project (see http://developer.gnome.org/arch/component/bonobo.html), a Microsoft COM–influenced component model but on the .NET platform. Hence, the Mono project was born.

Icaza cofounded Ximian with the aim of producing and marketing Linux-based productivity software. GNOME featured at the core of this software suite, and it included additional value-add applications such as Evolution (http://www.novell.com/products/evolution), a comprehensive calendar/e-mail client and contact management application.

Icaza is now the vice president of development at Novell (http://www.novell.com); Novell acquired the Ximian group in 2003, so Mono is now a fundamental part of the Novell strategy, with a number of its core applications and services, such as Novell Linux Desktop 9, being based on the Mono development environment.

What Is Mono?

So, you should now have an idea of what .NET is. If not, don't worry too much, but a key message to take away from the previous sections is that the .NET Framework, as written by Microsoft, is available for the Windows platform only. But people often ask the question, Is .NET available for the Unix operating system? What about Apple's Mac OS? What about Linux? The answer to all of these questions was "no!"—until the advent of Mono, that is.

Mono is an open-source (community-built) implementation of the .NET Framework and associated components for platforms other than Windows. The Mono environment can be classified as the "core Mono" environment and "additional components" that offer enhanced functionality that will often be built upon the core Mono environment. Let's look at what is typically contained within these elements.

Core Mono

The core Mono environment is where you should start; it provides key components that are required to create and host .NET applications. Chapter 5 covers the key topics introduced in the following sections.

---

1. From "GNOME's Miguel de Icaza on .NET: The New Development Environment for the Next 20 Years" at http://www.ondotnet.com/pub/a/dotnet/2001/07/09/icaza.html

Common Language Runtime (CLR) Implementation

This provides an implementation of the CLR through an executable that invokes your .NET application within the bounds of the CLR.

C# Compiler

A core part of the Mono development environment, the C# compiler comes standard with the option of downloading compatibility options for both Java and Visual Basic, although the compilers are still in development. For example, at the time of writing, MonoBasic (mbas) is still heavily in development, although I recommend keeping an eye on the Mono Web site for the latest details. For example, check out http://mono-project.com/Visual_Basic for the latest Visual Basic news.

.NET Class Library Implementation

The Mono environment also includes a set of libraries that constitute the .NET class library implementation, which is the Mono implementation of the .NET class library explained previously. As you can imagine, this is a big task, and you can check the status of the various classes available at http://www.go-mono.com/class-library.html. Of course, the nature of the open-source environment means there's always work to do and contributions are always welcome.

GNOME, Mono, or Unix Libraries

In addition to the .NET implementations provided through Mono, the fact that Mono lives on platforms other than Microsoft means that embracing other technologies is a natural enhancement. One such example is the provision of a GNOME toolkit called Gtk#, which provides a set of C# bindings that can be used to develop GNOME-based applications.

Development Tools

In addition to some of the tools mentioned, other tools are provided that are covered in Chapter 2. Some examples include assemblers and disassemblers for IL, digital certification utilities, assembly cache utilities, and more.

Additional Mono Components

In addition to the core Mono components, Mono 1.0 includes support for other components. Figure 1-1 shows a high-level view of the Mono components, and I should stress that this functionality is being extended on a daily basis.

The following sections describe some of the components, and I'll cover the other elements in more detail in Chapter 5. For now it's important only that you understand the concepts.

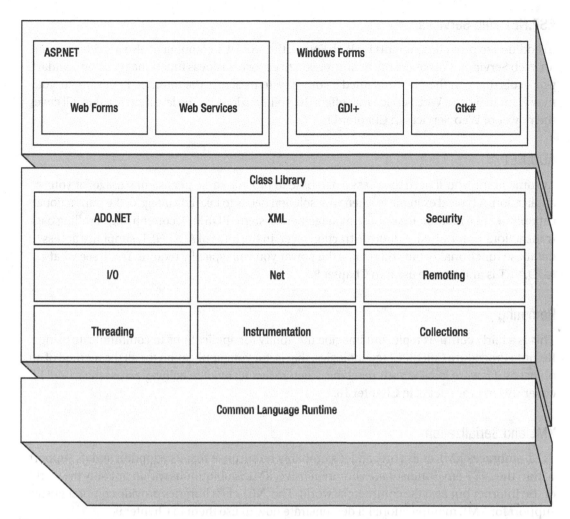

Figure 1-1. *High-level view of the Mono components*

ASP.NET Web Forms

The ability to create dynamic server-side Internet applications that provide the rich function-ality normally associated with rich client applications is the forte of the ASP.NET Web Forms technology. It allows you to design and construct Web pages (or *Web Forms*, as they are termed) using a graphical user interface (GUI) designer that are then transformed into a Hypertext Markup Language (HTML)–based implementation that can be viewed through a standard Web browser. This component provides the environment and functionality to interpret the Web Forms and allows you to provide business logic in a .NET-compliant language such as C#. Chapter 11 describes how to harness some of the functionality within ASP.NET.

ASP.NET Web Services

In addition to providing support for Web Forms, the ASP.NET component also provides support for Web Services. This offers the ability for you to expose business functionality using standard protocols that can then be consumed by other systems across the Internet. For example, you may want to write a Web Service that offers the ability to look up the latest stock value. I'll cover the power of Web Services in Chapter 11.

ADO.NET

At some point, you'll need to access a database to provide some persistent storage for your application. A typical example is when your solution needs to take advantage of the transactional capabilities of a relational database management system (RDBMS), committing or rolling back transactions as required. A data abstraction layer, in the form of ADO.NET, simplifies access to database functionality but still retains the power you will typically require. You'll see what ADO.NET is and how to use it in Chapter 8.

Remoting

This is a fairly complex topic, but imagine the ability for applications to communicate using Remote Procedure Call (RPC) technologies, that is, for your application to call the method of an object as if it were local to your machine, when in fact it could be halfway across the world! I'll cover this in more detail in Chapter 10.

XML and Serialization

.NET embraces XML at its core, and it's probably no surprise that its adoption and its support within the .NET environment are comprehensive. XML is ubiquitous within not only the world of the Internet but also the commercial world. The .NET class libraries provide comprehensive support for XML manipulation; I'll demonstrate how to use them in Chapter 9.

In addition to the aforementioned elements, .NET provides many other cool features with powerful capabilities, including Web Services, language neutrality, mobile development, and much more.

How to Get Involved with Mono

As Mono is part of the open-source community, your contributions are always welcome, and how you choose to contribute is pretty much up to you. The community is coordinated via the Mono home page (http://www.mono-project.com/); for example, you could fix a bug or complete an unfinished class from a list. In either case, your source code is then booked back into source code control and integrated into the Mono code base through controlled build and testing procedures.

How to Obtain Mono

You've been introduced to Microsoft .NET, and you've learned the story of how Mono started and what Mono is. Now you'll learn how you obtain the software, install it, and start using the powerful features I'll explain within this book.

One method is to ensure that you have a suitable host operating system on which to run. A native installation such as this involves installing the software onto a supported platform such as one of the approved Linux distributions, and—hey, presto!—you're off and running.

Another method, and one that is ideal if you want to start to learn Mono with the minimum amount of impact to your desktop, is to use Monoppix, which makes Mono available on a distribution of Linux that is based on Knoppix and that boots and runs entirely from CD. You can find it at http://www.monoppix.com/.

However, for the purpose of this book, I'll show native installations. So, the first step is to ensure that you download the components appropriate to the platform you are running. At the time of writing, these are split into those considered stable (older but tested versions) and those considered unstable (newer but not fully tested):

- Linux

- Microsoft Windows 2000 and above

- Mac OS X

For Linux, the following x86 processor distributions are recognized:

- Red Hat 9.0 and Fedora Core 3.0

- SUSE Linux Enterprise Server 9, SUSE Linux 9.0, and SUSE Linux 9.1 (see http://www.novell.com/linux/suse/)

Some of the "unstable" releases include a version for the Mac OS X operating system and 64-bit processor implementations. The source code is also available as a separate download from the packages discussed next.

You can find all these versions on the Mono home page under Downloads (http://www.mono-project.com/Downloads). I'll show how to implement the solution in this book on the Fedora Core 3 distribution, and you can download the packages for this as appropriate. Figure 1-2 shows the downloads section for Fedora Core 3.

Note The Microsoft Windows download is slightly different in that the download offered is a single installation module that includes Gtk# and the XSP Web server.

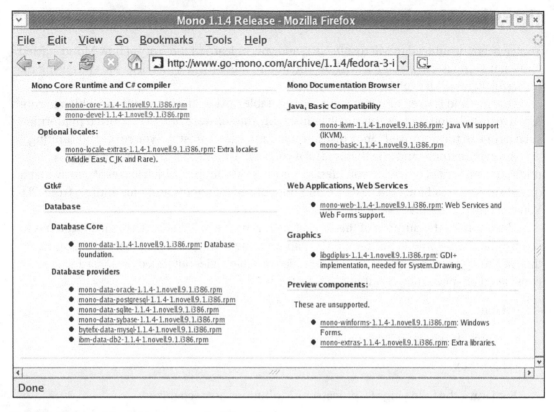

Figure 1-2. *Sample archive page at the Mono home page*

The next step is to download the required components, which may be listed either individually or grouped; in either case, you won't need all the packages, but I'll briefly explain what some of the components do before continuing:

- *Mono core runtime and C# compiler*: This provides the CLI implementation and a C# compiler, along with some other core command-line tools such as an assembler, disassembler, and global assembly cache (GAC) utility.

- *Mono development tools*: As fun as the command-line may be, the Mono development tools provide a comprehensive IDE, similar to that provided by Microsoft Visual Studio.

- *Gtk#*: This provides the necessary libraries to write applications that utilize the GNOME toolkit.

- *Java, basic compatibility*: These packages provide support for other languages and basic compatibility; for example, if you're more comfortable using the Java language, this is the package to download.

- *Web applications and Web Services*: This provides support for Web-based applications and Web Services, including ASP.NET technologies that are contained within these packages.

- *Database core*: This provides the ADO.NET implementation, allowing your .NET applications to connect to external data sources using the appropriate data provider.

- *Database providers*: These data providers provide access to well-known external data sources such as industry-standard relational databases. An example of a data provider is the MySQL data provider.

- *Graphics*: These packages provide the implementation of GDI+, the .NET graphics layer, allowing you to write complex graphical applications.

- *Preview components*: This package provides components that are currently undergoing development and so are considered "preview" components. It can be fun to experiment with the up-and-coming components found in these packages.

How to Install Mono on Linux

To get started, I'll ask you to download the following packages for now, and then you can download further packages as I introduce the topics that require them throughout this book. So, to start, download the Mono Core Runtime, Mono Development Tools, and C# Compiler packages.

You can install Mono using other methods (for example, using the Novell Red Carpet FTP service, compiling from source code, and so on), but I'll focus on the simplest, albeit more laborious, method.

Note If you are new to Linux, Red Hat Package Manager (RPM) and is a standard method for deploying software on the Linux platform using the RPM Package Manager module. This is usually used for installing and removing Linux software packages (although it's not the only option by any means).

Once you've downloaded your files, you need to install them. You'll need to ensure that you're logged in as the root user and then can install all the RPM packages in the current directory by using the following command line:

```
rpm -Uvh *.rpm
```

Or, you can install them individually, if you want to be more specific, using the following command line:

```
rpm -i mono-core-*.rpm
rpm -i mono-devel-*.rpm
```

Tip The filename downloaded will reflect the version number, so to avoid confusion I've used an asterisk. However, you must ensure that you either have only one version present before installation or explicitly reference the filename.

I chose the former option, which should install the packages successfully. Figure 1-3 shows how your screen should look.

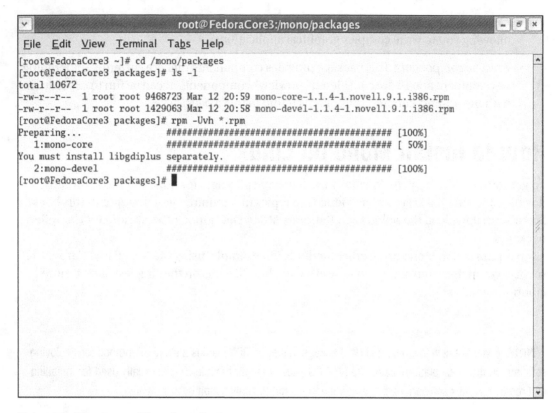

```
root@FedoraCore3:/mono/packages

File  Edit  View  Terminal  Tabs  Help

[root@FedoraCore3 ~]# cd /mono/packages
[root@FedoraCore3 packages]# ls -l
total 10672
-rw-r--r--  1 root root 9468723 Mar 12 20:59 mono-core-1.1.4-1.novell.9.1.i386.rpm
-rw-r--r--  1 root root 1429063 Mar 12 20:58 mono-devel-1.1.4-1.novell.9.1.i386.rpm
[root@FedoraCore3 packages]# rpm -Uvh *.rpm
Preparing...              ####################################### [100%]
   1:mono-core            ####################################### [ 50%]
You must install libgdiplus separately.
   2:mono-devel           ####################################### [100%]
[root@FedoraCore3 packages]# █
```

Figure 1-3. *Linux core Mono installation*

■Tip You may find you're missing some dependent files. For example, a vanilla Fedora Core 3 installation will be missing some files that you can find within the `libicu-3.2-1.i386.rpm` file; this is provided with the Fedora `Extras` folder on the Fedora site. Another good source of missing RPMs is the RPMforge site at `http://www.rpmforge.net`.

You can check whether the installation was successful by executing the following command line:

```
mono --version
```

This should report the version of Mono that was installed; in addition, you can double-check by looking for some key tools that are provided as part of the Mono command-line utilities in the `/usr` folder (see Table 1-1). I'll briefly categorize these, but I'll discuss these and more comprehensive tools throughout the book as appropriate and primarily within Chapter 2.

Table 1-1. *Common Command-Line Utilities*

Executable Name	Description
monodis	Disassembler
ilasm	Assembler
mcs	C# compiler
mono	CLI runtime implementation
gacutil	GAC utility

Tip Once you have finished installing Mono as the root user, I recommend switching to your standard user profile to avoid problems through mistakes.

Now let's try a really simple C# program just to make sure everything is in order and the installation has worked. Enter the example shown in Figure 1-4 using your favorite editor, taking care to ensure you copy it exactly, as the C# language is case-sensitive. When done, save this in a folder called /mono/Samples/Chapter1 under the name helloworld.cs. The .cs extension signals this is a C# file.

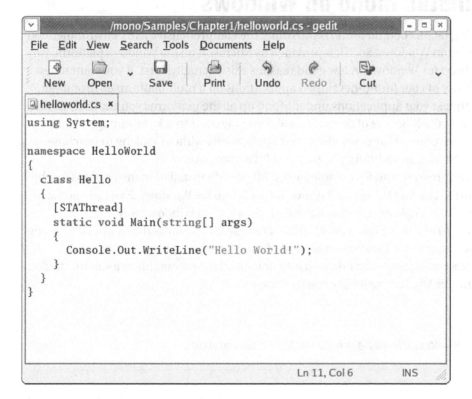

Figure 1-4. *The HelloWorld C# application*

Don't worry about trying to understand the syntax at this point; I'll provide a C# primer as part of the book. If you do understand the general notation, well done—you'll have a head start. Once you have saved the file, you can compile this into an executable and try executing it. So, first compile the file using the C# compiler. Enter the following line at a command-line prompt:

```
mcs helloworld.cs
```

As is often the case in the Linux world, no news is good news, and if you return to the command prompt with no further output, chances are it has worked. You can verify this by looking for the helloworld.exe file in the same folder. Now try running the executable by entering the following line:

```
mono helloworld.exe
```

The output should look similar to the following; in summary, you've written and implemented your first C# application—the infamous HelloWorld application:

```
[root@FedoraCore3 Chapter1]# mono helloworld.exe
Hello World!
```

How to Install Mono on Windows

One of the driving factors behind Mono is providing the comprehensive .NET environment on a platform other than Windows. So, if it is provided by Microsoft on the Windows platform, why bother to use Mono for Windows? A few good reasons exist, actually! First, if you want to test the interoperability of your Mono-developed applications on a multiplatform environment, it makes sense to test your applications under Mono on all the platforms you support—and Windows will most likely be one of them. Second, you may want to take advantage of the MonoDevelop environment for developing your applications without looking to purchase Microsoft Visual Studio. In addition, you may just love open source!

Whatever your reason, and for completeness, I'll provide installation instructions for the Windows platform. The first thing you'll notice is that Mono for Windows does not consist of lots of packages; it's a single executable that installs in a typical Windows way.

I'll show how to install the latest development release for Windows that is available, along with all other versions in the Downloads section of the Mono home page, at http://www.mono-project.com/Downloads/. The first step is to download the executable to a suitable folder; in my case it's under \My Documents\My Mono\Packages.

Note Mono for Windows is available only for Windows 2000 and above.

Once downloaded, you can start the process of installing Mono by simply executing the setup executable. This will start the setup process, and you should see an installation screen similar to the one shown in Figure 1-5.

Figure 1-5. *Mono for Windows setup screen*

At this point, you will be guided through the installation wizard, being prompted to answer questions along the way, such as the location of the program files. I suggest you accept the default values, as I will be assuming this throughout the book. You are free to provide your own answers to questions, but bear this in mind when you progress through the book, as the samples may assume the default values. I'll indicate that this is the case as you progress.

Once you've completed the wizard successfully, you should see a completion screen similar to Figure 1-6.

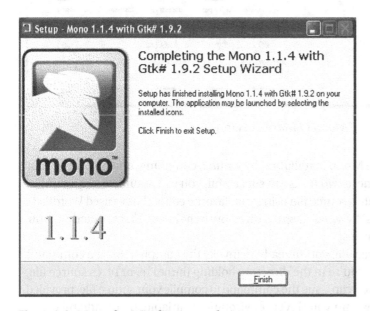

Figure 1-6. *Mono for Windows completion screen*

You can go through similar tasks as you did with the Linux version to see whether the installation was complete. The first step is to check that the command-line utilities have been installed; if you've accepted the default details as suggested, you should see a large number of files in the C:\Program Files\Mono-1.1.4\bin directory. These files are not only utilities but also runtime dynamic link libraries (DLLs) necessary to run Mono. You can check this by looking at the installation folder using Microsoft Windows Explorer; your screen should look something like Figure 1-7.

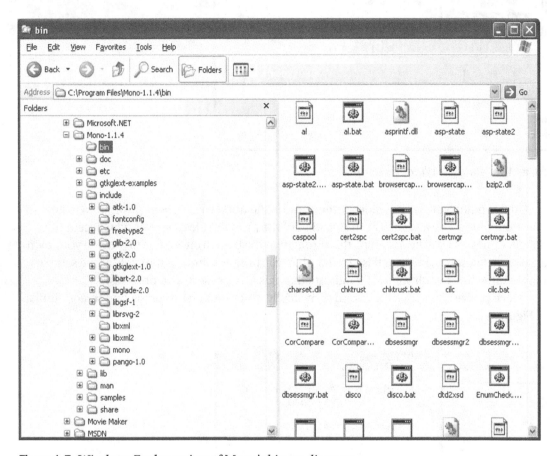

Figure 1-7. *Windows Explorer view of Mono's binary directory*

The second step is to test the Mono installation by writing, compiling, and executing your test application, HelloWorld. If these two tasks are successful, you can assume a successful installation and continue. So, create a source file using your favorite editor (I have used WordPad), and save this in the My Documents\My Mono\Samples directory as helloworld.cs, exactly as you would do (or did do) for the Linux test.

Once you've create this source file, you're ready to invoke the compiler. Start a command prompt window, and ensure that you're in the directory holding the helloworld.cs source file, as defined previously. From here you can issue the command to compile your source file, provided you have Mono's \bin directory within your PATH environment variable. If not, add this to your PATH environment variable before you start a command prompt window.

After changing to the directory and issuing the compile command, your window should look something like Figure 1-8. This demonstrates a successful compilation, and running the application will execute the application and display "Hello World!"

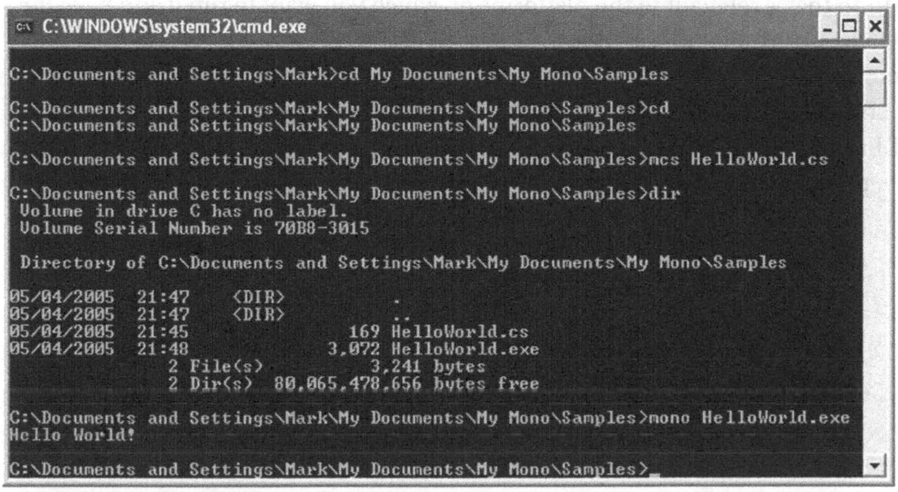

Figure 1-8. *Successful compiler from the Windows command line*

The Book's Project

Throughout the book, you will not only be introduced to what Mono consists of, and what the .NET Framework consists of, but you'll also be progressively taken through using your newfound knowledge to write a Really Simple Syndication (RSS) aggregator. RSS is a format for syndicating news headlines by using XML as its means of representing the information. During the book, you'll build a Windows Forms–based application that will allow you to subscribe to a list of RSS feeds and view the contents in an easy-to-read manner.

In addition to simply reading RSS feeds, the application will allow you to manage a list of your favorite feeds and will store the information offline in a MySQL database, allowing you to view the information when not connected to the Internet.

You can find the simple design for the application in the code download for this book. Refer to the Source Code section of the Apress Web site at http://www.apress.com.

Mono Support of .NET 2.0

So, where does that leave you with Mono? The Mono implementations defined within this book will work on versions 1.0, 1.1, and 2.0 of the .NET Framework with the latest Mono distri-bution, including support for version 2.0 elements of the .NET Framework and associated technologies. However, for clarity, most chapters will have a "What's New in Version 2.0?" section that will detail the key new features in the .NET Framework that will eventually (or may already be) supported by Mono.

Summary

In this chapter, I introduced the .NET Framework, its associated technologies, and the industry standards it has either embraced or defined. You should now have obtained and downloaded the version of Mono that is relevant to the platforms on which you want to run it and have the necessary knowledge to install and test Mono on your platform. You are now ready to begin Mono development!

In the next chapter, I'll introduce and discuss some of the tools that are either provided as part of the .NET Framework or provided as part of the open-source community, specifically an IDE, to make the process of developing applications easier and more graphical.

CHAPTER 2

■ ■ ■

Introducing Development Tools and MonoDevelop

Completing Chapter 1 should mean that you now have the core .NET components installed and everything you need to develop great .NET-based applications—almost. It's true that opening a terminal session and typing commands on the command line to achieve your goal has a certain gratification. It's almost as if you're not a *real* programmer unless you're working in a black window with an 8-point, white (or green) font, but of course this is nonsense. Why battle with command-line prompts when an IDE and other tools can make day-to-day tasks faster and more efficient? In this chapter, you'll explore some tools that can make your life easier and help you develop enterprise-scale applications using Mono and .NET.

What IDEs Are Available?

Those of you who have seen Microsoft's development tool Visual Studio or have seen the Eclipse environment will know how lucky those developers are. Gone are the days when you had a few disjointed tools and only your command-line tools to write code. These days, the whole experience of writing applications is easier, at least in part, because of comprehensive developments tools with GUIs known as IDEs. I'll cover some of the options available to you when writing code using the Mono platform, specifically the following IDEs:

- MonoDevelop

- Eclipse

  The decision about which IDE to use depends on a number of factors:

- Operating system

- Cost

- Ease of use

- Flexibility and functionality

- Personal choice

  I'll cover how to download and install the MonoDevelop environment, but that doesn't mean it's the only IDE on the market—far from it! On the Windows platform I've already mentioned Visual Studio; in fact, Visual Studio 2005 is expected to ship in late 2005. Another example is Eclipse (see `http://www.eclipse.org`), which is available on a number of platforms and is not only becoming the standard for Java 2 Enterprise Edition (J2EE) development but is proving popular on other platforms with its ability to extend its functionality through plug-ins, as has been done with the .NET plug-in (see `http://www.improve-technologies.com/alpha/esharp/`). Figure 2-1 shows an example of the Eclipse IDE with the .NET plug-in installed.

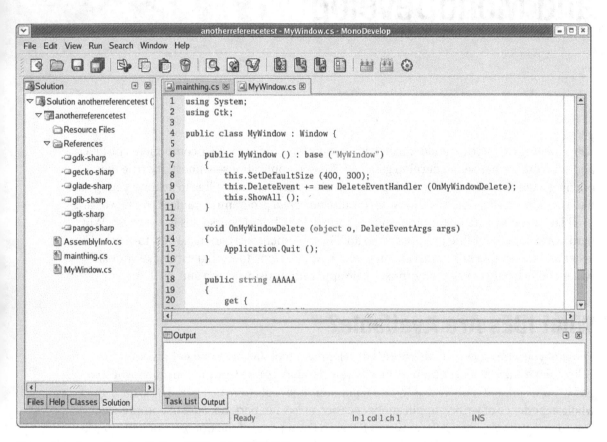

Figure 2-1. *Opening the Eclipse IDE with .NET C# support*

Note The Eclipse IDE is a Java-based installation with the .NET plug-in and also requires the Java 2 runtime environment to be installed.

In general, you should experiment with these IDEs and decide which one to use based on personal choice and experimentation. You can find more in-depth information about the available IDEs on the Mono Web site (see `http://www.mono-project.com/Development`➥ `_Environments`). As you progress through the book, I recommend you experiment with one of the IDEs mentioned to enhance your productivity and make your life a whole lot easier. This chapter will provide you with sufficient knowledge to obtain, install, and begin to use MonoDevelop for its ease of development.

Introducing MonoDevelop

The MonoDevelop tool should suit your needs nicely as the ideal IDE.

The History of MonoDevelop

The MonoDevelop application (http://www.monodevelop.com/) is based upon a previous open-source IDE called SharpDevelop (also known as #develop).[1] This was a C# and VB .NET development environment available as a free download. Its source was taken and ported to use the GNOME toolkit (Gtk+) framework and to use the Mono development platform for compilation. It's not the only IDE available to you, though; you could continue to use #develop, you could use the command line and a GUI editor, or you could use a commercial offering such as X-develop (http://www.omnicore.com/). However, for the remainder of the book, the examples we use will either be the command line or MonoDevelop.

Downloading MonoDevelop

You can find the current version of MonoDevelop at http://www.monodevelop.org/ under the Releases section. If you'd prefer to obtain a older, packaged version, you can navigate to the archive page at http://www.mono-project.com/OldReleases. Here you will need to navigate to the release appropriate for your distribution and level of stability; it's here that you'll find the packages corresponding to a given Mono release number. The examples in this book will use Mono for Fedora (http://www.go-mono.com/archive/1.0.6/fedora-3-i386/). You'll notice that rather than downloading the latest release of MonoDevelop, as you did for the Mono core runtime and C# compiler, you may find a different release available here; for example, you may want to avoid a version with a known problem, although the latest version will usually be the most stable. The following sections cover the required packages, in the order in which you should install them.

■**Note** I've used MonoDevelop version 1.0.6 in these examples, but your version may differ.

International Components for Unicode 2.6 or Greater

For those of you old enough to remember, American Standard Code for Information Interchange (ASCII) used to be the standard way (and one of the only ways) of representing text, using 8 bits to define all the characters required. However, this was insufficient to represent characters required for some languages such as those used in the Far East. So, an international standard was created with the goal of representing all text that people would want to see on a computer, therefore making it a global standard. This consequently requires 16 bits to store the data necessary to represent all the characters required.

As mentioned in Chapter 1, this Unicode component may not be installed on your distribution, so you may have to look for it. In the case of Fedora, you can find it within the /Extras folder on the Fedora download site (see http://fedora.redhat.com/download/). For other

---

1. SharpDevelop is available for download from http://www.icsharpcode.net/OpenSource/SD/.

distributions this will vary, and using some of the other resources available to your distribution will be necessary.

Core Mono Runtime

The core Mono runtime and its associated components, as discussed in Chapter 1, provide an open-source implementation of the .NET Framework, with complementary tools and components such as unit testing tools. You can obtain the runtime from the Mono Web site (see `http://www.mono-project.com`) in both stable and unstable (the latest) releases. It represents the core components required by a Mono application, the runtime environment, the class libraries, and the associated command-line tools.

gtk-sharp 1.0 or Greater

The GNOME graphical environment provides all the power of a Windows-based operating system and can be embraced by the applications that are written to use it. This is possible via the GNOME toolkit, a set of libraries and interfaces that allow GNOME-based applications to be written. The `gtk-sharp` package is a set of .NET bindings (or *hooks* for lack of a better word) for the Gtk+ toolkit and allows you to build applications that are 100 percent native to GNOME using .NET. You can obtain this from the Mono Web site at `http://www.mono-project.com/GtkSharp`.

monodoc-core 1.0

MonoDoc is a documentation system written specifically for Mono and .NET and includes not only the ability to create the documentation to accompany your application but also a documentation browser written entirely in C#. You can obtain this from the Mono Web site (see `http://www.mono-project.com/Downloads`) in both stable and unstable (the latest) releases.

gtksourceview-sharp.0.5

The `gtksourceview-sharp` package is a text widget (and text-editing component) that enhances the existing Gtk+ text widget to provide the features that have come to be expected in programming language editors of modern times. For example, the implementation of syntax highlighting is the kind of feature that is now standard for source editors. You can obtain this at `http://gtksourceview.sourceforge.net/` as well as at the Mono Web site.

gecko-sharp-0.5

Gecko is Mozilla's layout engine (also used in Netscape and other products), which was originally written by Netscape Communications Corporation but is now overseen by the Mozilla Foundation. It includes browser components that form the foundation for building Internet-enabled applications with user interfaces that therefore require content presentation and layout management. You can obtain this at `http://www.mozilla.org/newlayout/` as well as at the Mono Web site.

So, the introductions have been made; you should at least have an overview of the components (and packages) required by the MonoDevelop application and should now be in a position to start downloading these packages.

You've already started to download some of the packages within Chapter 1; for instance, the international components for Unicode were contained in `libicu*.rpm`, and the Mono core installation was in the `mono-core*` and `mono-devel*` RPMs. So, the next step is to download the remaining packages and store them in the /Mono/Packages folder.

Installing MonoDevelop on Linux

The next step is to install MonoDevelop. It may have already been installed if you chose to install Mono using one of the prebuilt binary installation packages that is available for Windows and Linux, or you may have decided to be more selective and downloaded only the required packages. In either case, once you have downloaded all the packages required (an installation from binaries is recommended), if you haven't already done so, you can create a terminal session and move all the packages required into the /Mono/Packages folder. You can then proceed to install all the packages individually using the following command, replacing <package name> with the name of the Mono package downloaded. You can find a tutorial for installing MonoDevelop at http://www.monodevelop.com/tutorials/package_install.aspx, but I'll walk you through the steps anyway.

```
rpm -uvh --nodeps <package name>
```

On the Fedora Core 3 distribution, I encountered a problem with package versioning and dependency, something you may encounter on some of the other Linux distributions (or any other package for that matter). When trying to install the gtksourceview-sharp package, it reported the following error message:

```
file /usr/share/gtksourceview-1.0/language-specs/vbnet.lang ➥
from the install of
gtksourceview-sharp-0.5-1.novell.9.1 conflicts with the file ➥
from package gtksourceview-1.1.0-3 [
```

Tip A number of package managers can help you identify and resolve problems that occur because of package dependencies. The recommendations typically vary depending on the operating system, but Linux examples include Yum and Up2date. See http://www.brennan.id.au/07-Package_Management.html for more information.

This basically means that the gtksourceview-sharp package I'm trying to install has a conflict with a file called gtksourceview-1.1.0-3. To rectify this, the quickest method was to remove this package and attempt the installation of the Mono-provided package again. I achieved this using the following command:

```
rpm -e gtksourceview-1.1.0*
```

But this failed because of a dependency with another package on the gedit application, namely, the GNOME editor. The error reported was as follows:

```
Error: failed dependencies:
libgtksourceview-1.0.so.0 is needed by (installed) gedit.2.8.1.1.i386
gtksourceview >= 1.1 is needed by (installed) gedit.2.8.1.1.i386
```

So, as I don't need the GNOME editor for my source code because I'll be using the MonoDevelop environment, I decided to remove the gedit package by using the following command:

```
rpm -e gedit-2.8.1-1.i386
```

I was then able to install the Mono-provided gtksourceview-sharp.0.5 package and the other remaining packages.

When you have installed all the prerequisite MonoDevelop packages listed previously, you can run the MonoDevelop executable by changing to the /usr/bin directory and entering the following command line:

```
./MonoDevelop
```

■ **Note** You may notice that this has already appeared in your Start application menu, so you can run it from here too.

This fires up the MonoDevelop IDE, so you are ready to begin. Running the MonoDevelop IDE application should present you with a screen similar to Figure 2-2.

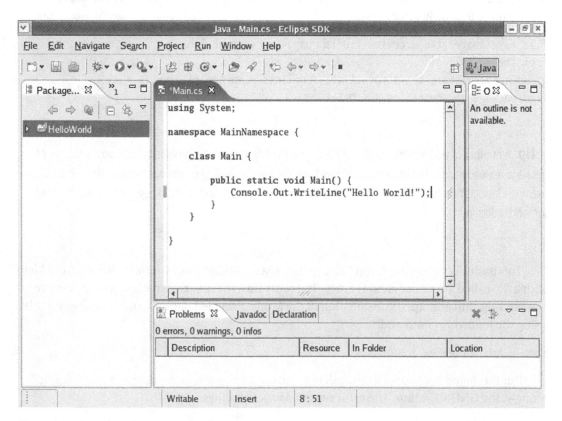

Figure 2-2. *Opening the MonoDevelop IDE*

You are now ready to start using the tool for developing your .NET applications, saying "goodbye" to a terminal shell forever—well, at least for building and deploying .NET applications anyway.

I'll now provide you with an overview of the MonoDevelop IDE by taking you on a brief tour. I won't give you a comprehensive description of all the features of the MonoDevelop application; space simply wouldn't permit it, and I'd need an entire book dedicated to the topic. However, I will present the basics and enough for you to feel comfortable using the environment.

Introducing the MonoDevelop Layout

As a precursor to showing how to use the MonoDevelop application, I will introduce its structure and features. MonoDevelop (and most other IDEs) consists of a main application window and a number of internal windows and tabs that present various pieces of functionality. Figure 2-3 shows a rough view of the main MonoDevelop windows that will open by default, although more will become available depending on the state your development is in.

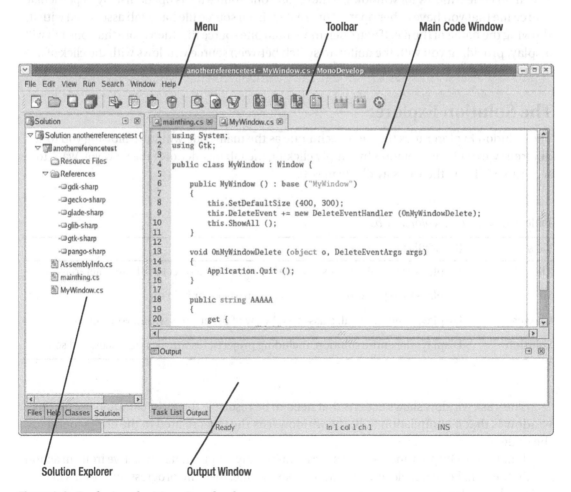

Figure 2-3. *Exploring the MonoDevelop layout*

I'll explain some of the IDE elements in the following sections.

The Menu

The menu represents the functionality available to you through the IDE, with elements becoming enabled or disabled as appropriate. You won't be surprised to hear that keyboard shortcuts are available for most menu-based operations, allowing you to access commonly used pieces of functionality quickly and easily.

The Toolbar

The toolbar represents commonly used pieces of functionality that, like a keyboard shortcut, are presented on the toolbar for ease of use. Whilst the toolbar cannot be customized in the current version of the IDE, you can add useful tools to the Tools menu through an option within the File ➤ Preferences menu. This allows you to reference external tools that can then be launched from within the MonoDevelop environment.

The Main Source Window

The main code window (or windows, if more than one source file is open) displays a particular source file that you have either opened or created. Each source file has a tab associated with it, showing the name of the file. If you open more than one source file, then more than one tab will display, providing you with the ability to switch between source windows with the click of a button. In Figure 2-3, note three source files have been loaded.

The Solution Explorer

The Solution Explorer uses the same technique as the main code window, allowing you to see different views of your solution by simply clicking the tab that denotes the view you want to see. Table 2-1 lists the views available to you.

Table 2-1. *Solution Explorer Tabs*

View	Description
File	Displays a view of the files within the solution in a directory-based hierarchy
Help	Displays help pages related to topics you asked for help on
Classes	Displays a hierarchical, class-based view of the entities within your project
Solution	Displays the entire solution, including projects, resources, references, and so on

The Task window shows actions that need to be resolved; the most common use for this window is that if compilation fails, the window lists the tasks related to the errors found in the code.

Finally, the Output window shows the results of any output that may derive from an action within the IDE. For example, if you compile a source file, then the progress and results of this will display in the Output window.

Creating a Project

The first step in using your IDE is to create a project that can then be used to target a specific application type, compile the source files contained within it, and build the target executable. In this case, I'll show how to use MonoDevelop to create a project for the HelloWorld application from Chapter 1. You should be mindful that this method will change depending on the IDE you are using, but conceptually the same concepts are likely to be used.

The first step is to create your solution, that is, combination of files. Select File ➤ New Solution/Project from the menu. The New Solution dialog box will open (see Figure 2-4). You need to select the type of project you're creating, so in this instance select C# and then choose C# Console Project from the options available.

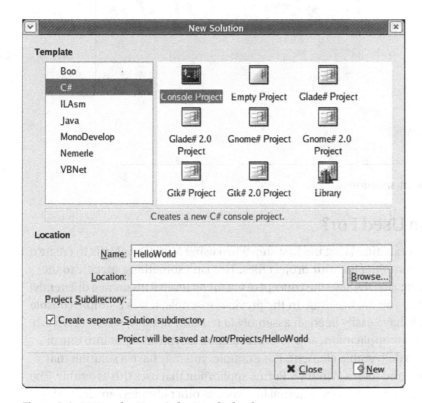

Figure 2-4. *Using the New Solution dialog box*

You'll need to assign a name for the combine file, a location on your file system, and any subdirectory you want to use. A default subdirectory is offered (which you can use if acceptable), which in this case is HelloWorld. I suggest you use /Mono/Samples/Chapter2/HelloWorld again and create your solution there. The idea is that you can have a default location for your solution files, and the subdirectory allows a cleaner organization of files.

When you are ready, click the New button on the dialog box, and your combine solution will be created, albeit an empty one. You should see a screen similar to the one in Figure 2-5.

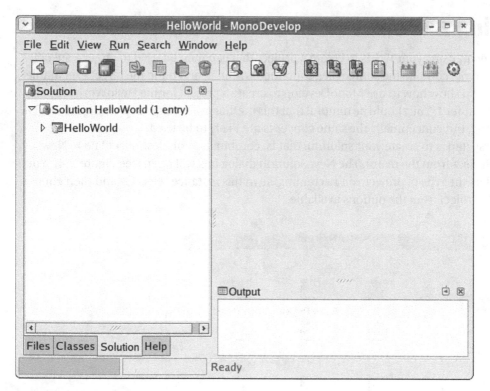

Figure 2-5. *Viewing an empty solution*

What's a Solution Used For?

In the previous example, I explained that the first step when using MonoDevelop is to create a solution, which acts as a container for your project files. This isn't something specific to the MonoDevelop environment; all IDEs have the concept of a *solution* (even if it's named differently) to represent the target type you are building. In the previous example, it was a simple console application, but this could have easily been an assembly (a reusable library), a Web Service, a Web page, a Windows Forms application, and so on. A solution is typically split into one or more *projects* that define a deliverable element. For example, you may have a solution that builds a reusable assembly and then a Windows Forms application that uses this assembly. The dependencies between these projects (and external files such as other libraries) are defined within the solution, and the IDE uses this information when building the solution's outputs.

In addition, the concept of a project not only acts as a container for files that are used within the solution but also stores other attributes that are used to build the target. These attributes are usually represented by parameters that can be given to the compiler; for example, the /target option dictates the target type for its output. Therefore, a solution is your friend; if you select the assembly solution type, you can expect this to automatically apply the /target:library option. You should remember, though, that you have the ability to override these defaults and the solution attributes in order to build your application in the way you want it to be built! I'll cover this in more detail in the "Configuring Your Target Output" section.

Adding Project Files

So, you have your solution created with a single project called HelloWorld, although at the moment no source files are present. Let's add a single source file that represents the application. You can achieve this in a number of ways: you can choose the Add Files icon depicted in Figure 2-4, or you can use the context-sensitive menu by right-clicking when over the HelloWorld project and selecting Add ➤ Add New File, as shown in Figure 2-6.

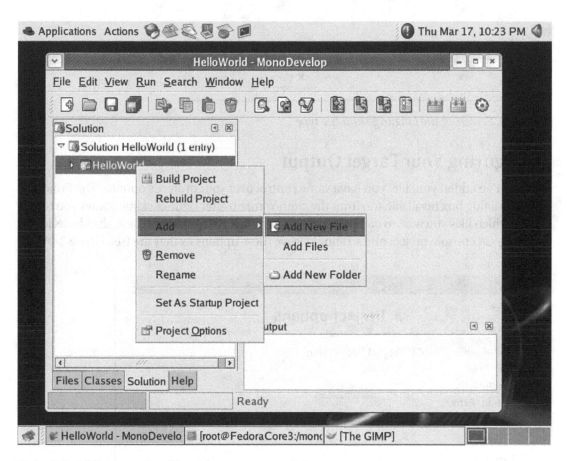

Figure 2-6. *Adding a project file with a context-sensitive menu*

In either case, the Add New File dialog box will display, showing a list of support languages in the left pane; after selecting your chosen language, you'll see a list of recognized file types on the right side. In Figure 2-7, you can see that I've selected C# as the language and Empty File as the file type.

Figure 2-7. *Selecting the language and file type*

Configuring Your Target Output

Once you've added your file, you have some control over your project's options. The Project Options dialog box (available too from the context menu after right-clicking) allows you to choose which files you want to compile and how, although at this stage you have already decided to build a C# console project and so should leave these options as they are (see Figure 2-8).

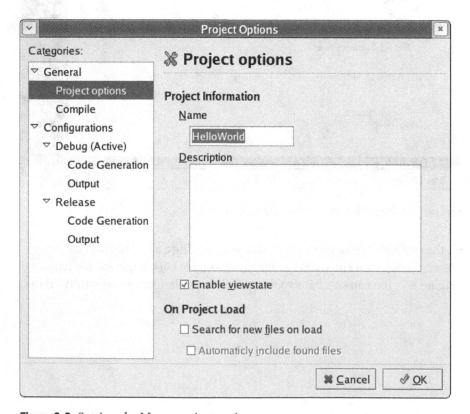

Figure 2-8. *Setting the Mono project options*

Building Your Target

Once you have created your solution, added a project, and included the necessary file, you are ready to compile the main application source code and build your target executable. As usual, you have a number of options. You can choose Run ➤ Compile or Run ➤ Compile All; alternatively, you can select either the solution or the project and choose Build Solution or Build Project, respectively. In this example, this will compile the console application using the source file added. If the process is successful, it will leave an executable on disk.

After you have chosen to compile the project using one of these methods, the Output window should show the results of the compilation process. If you have copied the code correctly, this should successfully compile, as shown in Figure 2-9.

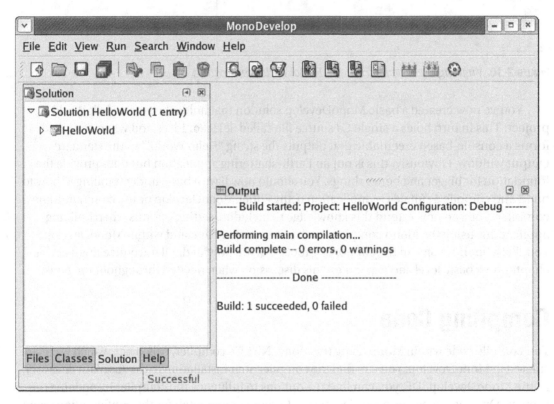

Figure 2-9. *Viewing the successful build results*

Testing Your Target

Finally, you've created the project, added the source file, and successfully built your first application using MonoDevelop. You can now test this by selecting Run ➤ Run or by clicking the Run icon. In either event, this will execute the application in a separate window, as shown in Figure 2-10.

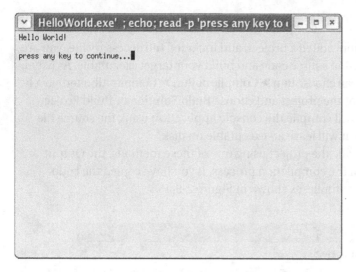

Figure 2-10. *Viewing the output from the HelloWorld application*

You've now created a basic MonoDevelop solution that holds the single HelloWorld project. This in turn holds a single C# source file called HelloWorld.cs and when compiled, forms a console-based executable that outputs the string "Hello World!" to the standard Output window. Obviously, this is not an Earth-shattering application but does provide the foundation for bigger and better things. You should now have a basic understanding of how to build and compile a simple C# application using either MonoDevelop or the command-line compiler. You can now extend this knowledge to including setting options when building applications using the Mono compiler, both at a command line and within MonoDevelop. You'll also look as some of the supporting tools that are provided; I'll introduce them in this chapter on a basic level and expand on this discussion when needed throughout the book.

Compiling Code

You compile code within Mono using the Mono .NET C# compiler, called mcs, which is encapsulated in MonoDevelop. You can find the compiler after installation in the /usr/bin directory. In the MonoDevelop IDE, you can find the options to influence the compiler by opening the Projects Options dialog box and selecting the Code Generation tab for the configuration being used (by default this is Debug), as shown in Figure 2-11.

You can influence the code produced by enabling or disabling optimization, automatically generating overflow checks, and so on. You can also target different outputs and change the level of warnings produced. Notice in Figure 2-11 that a Compile Target option also exists; this simply allows you to choose which files you want to include in the compilation.

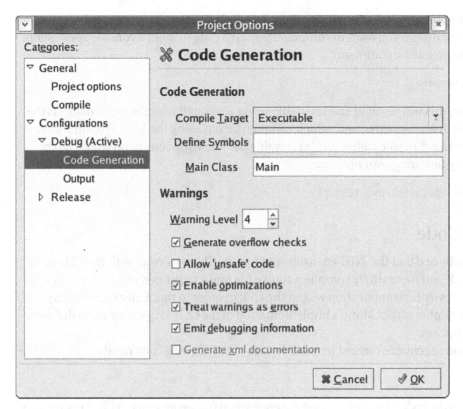

Figure 2-11. *Viewing the typical code generation options*

However, these are not the only options available to you. The compiler has a plethora of built-in options that can be switched on or off using command-line options. You can view the options available by using the -help flag or the -help2 flag. Table 2-2 lists some of the more commonly used options.

Table 2-2. *Common C# Compiler Flags*

Option	Description
--about	Displays information about the C# compiler.
-doc:FILE	Indicates that you want XML documentation to be created in the file specified by FILE.
-g	Generates debugging information.
-out:FILENAME	Specifies the name of the output file as noted by FILENAME.
-target:KIND	Specifies which type of target you want to build. By default this is exe for executable.

Many more options exist, but for the moment I'll concentrate on those required to compile your code. For example, if you want to compile the source code to build a console application, you can issue the following command:

```
mcs <source filename>
```

If successful, this will result in an executable being generated with the same name as the source file but with an .exe extension, which can then be run using the Mono runtime interpreter. If you had a source file called test.cs, issuing the following command would be the same as explicitly declaring your options:

```
mcs -target:exe -out:test.exe test.cs
```

Executing Code

I've already mentioned that the .NET environment has the CLI at its core, with the CLR as its runtime engine. If you successfully compile a source file into a target executable, you will need to execute your newly built application within the CLR in order to run. You can do this by running the executable within Mono's implementation of the CLR, implemented as the mono command-line option.

So, to test the executable created previously, issue the following command:

```
mono test.exe
```

This executes the code with the CLR, and the code should run as expected. This of course isn't magic; a lot of hard work is going on behind the scenes, some of which can be explained by describing the .NET execution model.

Examining the Execution Model

So far, you've compiled you code, you've executed it, and it has most likely worked. Figure 2-12 shows what's happening in the background.

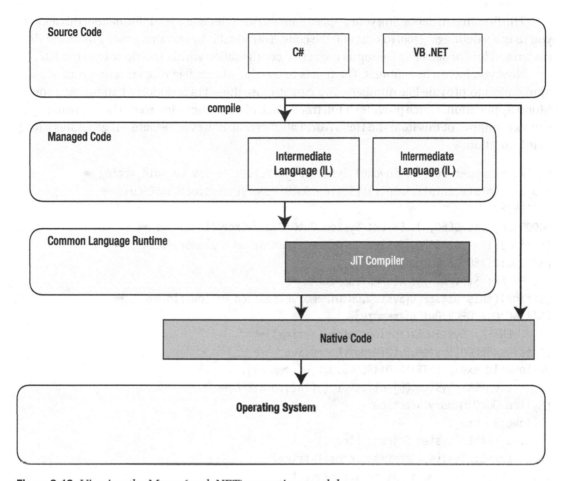

Figure 2-12. *Viewing the Mono (and .NET) execution model*

Debugging Your Projects

The command line is not very forgiving, especially when it comes to debugging your applications. A common and old favorite is to embed text output statements to a console or debug window that provides hints on how your code is doing. This is effective but cumbersome and not appropriate for anything other than simple applications—certainly not for complex applications that may involve running different components on different physical machines. I'll cover a more comprehensive approach to debugging in Chapter 12, but in this section I'll provide some advice on debugging simple applications that will help you diagnose problems you may encounter in the meantime.

The first step in debugging your application is to include debugging information; this allows you to use a debugging tool to examine the code. You add this by specifying the -g option at the command line or selecting Debug as the active configuration within the MonoDevelop IDE.

Now you have a few options. The first is to use the --debug flag when running your Mono application to provide line numbers. You can also use the --trace option when running your Mono application, which provides a full trace stack of all methods invoked. The following shows a snippet of this from the HelloWorld application; however, beware—it generates a lot of information:

```
ENTER: (wrapper runtime-invoke) System.Object:runtime_invoke_void_string ➥
(object,intptr,intptr,intptr)([System.OutOfMemoryException:0148EFC0], ➥
0022FE38,
00000000, 016A0E60, ). ENTER: System.OutOfMemoryException:.ctor ➥
(string)(this:0148EFC0[System.OutOfMemoryException HelloWorld.exe], ➥
[STRING:0148DFC8:Out of memory], )
. . ENTER: System.SystemException:.ctor ➥
(string)(this:0148EFC0[System.OutOfMemoryException HelloWorld.exe], ➥
[STRING:0148DFC8:Out of memory], )
. . . ENTER: System.Exception:.ctor (string) ➥
(this:0148EFC0[System.OutOfMemoryException
HelloWorld.exe], [STRING:0148DFC8:Out of memory], )
. . . . ENTER: System.Object:.ctor ()(this:0148EFC0➥
[System.OutOfMemoryException
HelloWorld.exe], )
. . . . LEAVE: System.Object:.ctor ()
. . . LEAVE: System.Exception:.ctor (string)
. . . ENTER: System.Exception:set_HResult ➥
(int)(this:0148EFC0[System.OutOfMemoryException HelloWorld.exe], -2146233087, )
. . . LEAVE: System.Exception:set_HResult (int)
. . LEAVE: System.SystemException:.ctor (string)
. . ENTER: System.Exception:set_HResult (int)(this:0148EFC0➥
[System.OutOfMemoryException
 HelloWorld.exe], -2147024882, )
. . LEAVE: System.Exception:set_HResult (int)
. LEAVE: System.OutOfMemoryException:.ctor (string)
LEAVE: (wrapper runtime-invoke) System.Object:runtime_invoke_void_string➥
 (object,intptr,intptr,intptr)[OBJECT:00000000]
```

The other options are to use the MonoDevelop environment, something that is highly recommended because of its pure simplicity.

Using the Class Viewer

The class viewer provides a graphical representation of your classes, demonstrating the inheritance and interface components of the C# (and object-oriented) language. The class viewer can be useful for providing a holistic view of your code without you being blinded by the detail that exists within code. Figure 2-13 shows the class viewer within MonoDevelop.

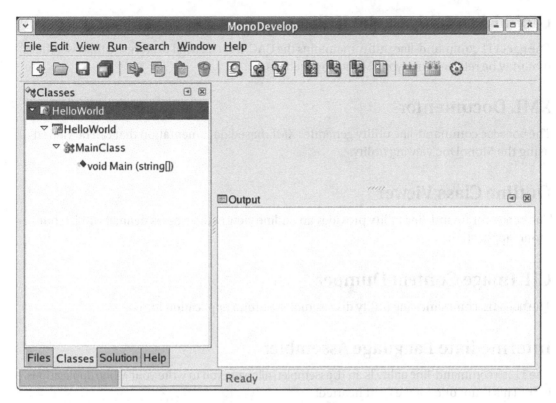

Figure 2-13. *Viewing the class hierarchy for the HelloWorld application*

You'll notice that within the HelloWorld project is a class named MainClass; this has a single method called Main that returns void and takes a single string array as an argument.

Using Other Tools

I'll also cover a number of other tools not mentioned within this chapter in more detail throughout the book, introducing them when required. However, in the following sections, I'll introduce most of the tools available as part of the core Mono framework and MonoDevelop IDE, as well as a few value-added extras you'll be using.

C# Compiler

As introduced in Chapter 1, the mcs command-line utility is the C# compiler that is provided as part of the core Mono installation and is used to compile your C# source code. You downloaded this as part of the installation instructions in Chapter 1, so this should already be installed and working on your system.

Mono's CLR Implementation

The mono command-line utility is Mono's implementation of the CLR and is used to invoke your Mono applications.

Global Assembly Cache Utility

The gacutil command-line utility maintains the GAC, a cache used to store central assemblies that may be referred to in your Mono applications.

XML Documentor

The monodoc command-line utility generates XML-based documentation that can be viewed using the MonoDoc viewing utility.

Outline Class Viewer

The monop command-line utility provides an outline view of the classes defined within your Mono application.

CIL Image Content Dumper

The monodis command-line utility disassembles a Mono application into IL.

Intermediate Language Assembler

The ilasm command-line utility is an IL assembler, allowing you to write your Mono applications in IL. This is not one for the faint hearted!

Certification Creation

The makecert command-line utility creates x.509 certificates for testing purposes, allowing you to create certificates that can then be used to digitally sign your code for authenticity.

Certificate Manager

The certmgr command-line utility allows you to manage the digital certificates that may exist on your machine. Several other security-related command-line utilities are beyond the scope of this chapter, so I'll cover these in more detail in Chapter 11.

Summary

In this chapter, I introduced a comprehensive but user-friendly IDE in the form of MonoDevelop and touched on some of the other IDEs on the market such as Eclipse. These allow you to build enterprise-class applications but in a more user-friendly and productive environment. I also introduced some of the development tools provided as part of the core Mono environment. I encourage you to use these throughout the book, as it will improve your productivity, even though you can build all the applications presented throughout this book using the command-line tools.

The next two chapters will introduce the C# language, which is the default programming language used throughout this book and one of the most common in the industry. This will provide the foundation necessary to start building the book's project application, the RSS aggregator.

CHAPTER 3

■■■

Introducing C#

One of the most powerful features in .NET is its language neutrality, and I don't mean its support for languages other than English! If you look at most other programming environments, such as Java, C++, and so on, you'll see they all have one feature in common. They are fixed to the language mandated; for example, in the case of the Java runtime environment, you have no choice but to use the Java language.

The .NET runtime can support multiple languages; in fact, it can support *any* language that conforms to two main specifications, the Common Language Specification (CLS) and CTS. These standards ensure interoperability in the .NET Framework and also mean that your .NET application could in fact be implemented in as many different languages as you want! If you want to see how many languages the .NET Framework currently supports, refer to http://www.dotnetpowered.com/languages.aspx.

This chapter will introduce the C# language and its key concepts. I've chosen to use C# in this book because it is a language that has influences from Java and C++, combining the best of both worlds. It's a fully object-oriented language, with features that enable you to write code that doesn't suffer from some of the problems that can arise in languages such as C++ because of typing mistakes or oversights on the programmer's part. Beware, though—this doesn't mean you can't write poor code!

In subsequent chapters, I'll expand on these topics and discuss other advanced C# topics while showing how to build some of the core objects you'll use in this book's RSS aggregator application.

■**Note** Those of you who have used other languages such as Java or C++ will notice a similarity in the C# syntax. If you are familiar with the Delphi platform, you'll also notice some similarities. C#'s influences are the languages that came before it and the experience of its key architect, Anders Hejlsberg. C# is fast becoming an industry-standard language because it combines the power of C++ with the syntax simplicity of Java.

Exploring the Structure of a C# Program

In this section, you'll examine the structure of the C# code written in Chapter 1. This will demonstrate some of the key concepts introduced in this chapter and will be expanded upon in subsequent chapters. Let's take a look at the key elements of the example shown in Chapter 1.

Namespace: A namespace defines scope with an associated unique identifier; this is an arbitrary name and allows you to organize code into namespaces for clear lines of responsibility. In the Chapter 1 HelloWorld application, the namespace was (unimaginatively) called `HelloWorld`; I'll cover the implications of not using namespaces in Chapter 4.

File: All code must exist in a file that is then compiled. In the HelloWorld example, you stored the code in a file called `helloworld.cs`. The `.cs` extension denotes that the file contains C# code.

Class: A class is a template for an entity that you want to exist in your code; in the HelloWorld example, the entity was the executable itself. A class has a name and belongs in a namespace. In Chapter 1, the class was `Hello`. (By the way, this name is not too creative—let's hope my imagination improves as the book progresses!)

Figure 3-1 demonstrates the scope of a particular concept by bounding it within a box. In this example, the HelloWorld application represents a .NET application in its (almost) simplest form, which is a single file with a single namespace within a single class.

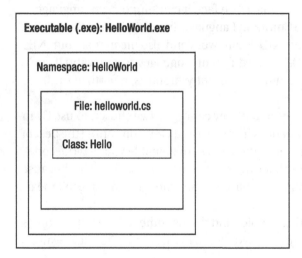

Figure 3-1. *Scope within a Mono application*

Now that I have set the scene and explained the key concepts behind the structure of the HelloWorld application, I'll start the C# tutorial in earnest and explain these and additional concepts in more detail.

Introducing Variables and Types

One of the keystones of any programming language is the ability to store data and then reference and manipulate it. You do this in C# by using variables and types. Specifically, you associate a variable with a given type that defines the category of data stored. You also give a variable a name that you can then use when you want to access this data. The variable name can consist of alphanumeric characters but must not clash with any of the language's keywords; for example, you cannot have a variable called `namespace`.

Introducing the Unified Type System

I've already touched on the elements that make up the *unified type system* at the start of this chapter; the unified type system is a holistic name for the CLS and CTS, the two specifications that ensure compatibility between .NET language implementations. The unified type system is a fairly complex topic but one that is directly applicable to types. However, don't worry if you don't understand it at this point—as I explain some of the other concepts involving types, all should become clear (or clearer).

The C# language type system contains the following categories:

- Value types

- Reference types

- Pointer types

I'll cover each of these categories in turn with the exception of pointer types; pointer types are an advanced topic and are related to languages that run in an "unmanaged" environment, which does not include C#. You should also note that *all* value types are compatible with the object type defined within the C# language. This means all objects descend, or *inherit*, from the base object type within C#, which allows your objects to take core functionality and properties from this object and further extend them. Chapter 4 covers this in more detail.

Value Types

As its name suggests, a *value type* is associated with a value of a given type based on the types available; for example, an integer value type may hold any value that is valid for the integer type it represents. Table 3-1 lists the available value types, also called *simple types*.

Table 3-1. *Value Types Available Within .NET*

Value Type	Description	Class Type	Range
bool	Typically used as a flag to indicate true or false	System.Boolean	True or false
char	Unicode character	System.Char	Unicode
sbyte	Signed single byte	System.SByte	-128..127
byte	Unsigned single byte	System.Byte	0..255
short	Signed 16-bit integer	System.Int16	-32768..32767
ushort	Unsigned 16-bit integer	System.UInt16	0..65535
int	Signed 32-bit integer	System.Int32	-2147483648..2147483647
uint	Unsigned 32-bit integer	System.UInt32	0..4294967295
long	Signed 64-bit integer	System.Int64	-263..263-1
ulong	Unsigned 64-bit integer	System.UInt64	0..264-1
float	Single-precision floating-point number	System.Single	+1.5E-45..+3.4E38

Table 3-1. *Value Types Available Within .NET (Continued)*

Value Type	Description	Class Type	Range
double	Double-precision floating-point number	System.Double	+55E-324..+1.7E308
decimal	Decimal number	System.Decimal	+1E-28..+7.9E28

You may have come across similar value types in other languages such as C or C++ and therefore may be familiar with how to use them. If not, don't worry—I'll demonstrate how to use the C# value types throughout the book.

For now, I'll show a simple example of how to use the int value type. Let's say you want to store somebody's age. You can achieve this by defining a variable of a given value type and assigning it a name. The following example defines an integer value called age and leaves it uninitialized:

```
int age;
```

All value types are initialized to a default value depending on the type, in this instance zero. However, I recommend you *always* initialize all variables, whether they are reference or value types, to avoid any possible confusion and to avoid introducing errors through the ambiguity that can surround default values. So, rewrite the previous declaration like so:

```
int age = 0;
```

You are then free to reference the variable by its name, assign it values, and manipulate it as required. Assign the variable a value of 26, like so:

```
age = 26;
```

The other nuance of value types is what happens when you assign one value type the value of another. Consider the following example:

```
int his_age = 26;
int her_age= his_age;
```

In this example, a variable called his_age is assigned the value of 26. When you then create a variable of the same type called her_age and assign it his_age, the value is copied across, and therefore both his_age and her_age hold the value of 26.

Type Conversion

You can convert one variable type to another using the C# language. In some cases this is handled automatically, but in other cases you may need to manually indicate the conversion you want with something called a *cast*. Table 3-2 lists the valid conversions that are handled automatically within the C# language.

Table 3-2. *Type Compatibility*

Type	Compatibility
Unsigned	byte ➤ char ➤ ushort ➤ uint ➤ ulong ➤ float ➤ double
Signed	sbyte ➤ short ➤ int ➤ long ➤ float ➤ double
Other	char ➤ ushort

If you want to convert a variable of type double to a variable of type decimal, you require an explicit conversion, or a cast. Therefore, you indicate this in the code, as follows:

```
double dbl = 36.12;
decimal dcm = (double)dbl;
```

The (double) notation indicates a cast on the part of the programmer when converting the value. When performing a cast operation, you should make sure you understand the consequences of casting from one type to another. For example, consider the following example:

```
double floating = 10.45;
int casted_float = (int)floating;
```

In the previous example, the casted_float integer variable will lose its precision as a result of the cast because the int type doesn't support precision. A similar effect is true of reference types; for example, if you create an object with a member variable and cast it to an object that isn't of the same type, the object will take on the behavior and attributes of the new type, and you may be unable to access the member variable. (I'll cover reference types next.)

Reference Types

In contrast to value types, *reference types* are user-defined types and do not hold values but merely point to a location where a value is held in the computer's memory. You should note that when declared but left unassigned, reference types (unlike value types) are not initialized to a value and point to nothing, also called *null*. The following example demonstrates this:

```
string nme;
```

This creates a reference type using a user-defined C# type called string, but you have not assigned it to anything. Therefore, if you tested the value of nme, it would be null. If you change the example slightly, you can assign it a value at the same time you define the variable, as follows:

```
string nme = "Mark Mamone";
```

This example creates the reference type and assigns a value indicating my name. This value is stored in memory and is pointed to by the nme reference. To see this in action, you can create another reference type of a different name but assign its value to that of the variable nme. In the following code, you can see that both variables now point to the same area of memory, holding the same information:

```
int nme = 10;
int cpy = nme;
```

If you then change the value of nme, this will change the memory location that held the data, so the variable cpy will also change. A word of caution: because the string reference type is immutable (explained in the "Strings" section), the same behavior does not apply, and once referenced, any further changes are not reflected in any other reference types. You can replicate the previous code but use the string type as follows:

```
string nme = "mark";
string cpy = nme;
```

At this point, both strings would hold the same value; however, if you assign the variable nme a new value, this will *not* be reflected in the variable cpy. The nme variable will still hold the original value.

Enumerations

An *enumeration* is a special kind of reference type and one of my favorite methods for representing data within the C# language—and for good reason. A universally accepted best practice in the world of software development is to make your code readable, also called *self-documenting*. Using enumerations is a good way to help ensure your code is self-documenting, as well as to ensure type safety (discussed in a moment).

The following example shows how to declare an enumeration that represents weekdays:

```
enum weekdays {monday, tuesday, wednesday, thursday, friday};
```

You can then use this as a variable and assign it values that *must* be part of the enumerated constants defined. Consider the following example; the first statement is legal, but the second statement is illegal and will cause the code to not compile:

```
weekdays    BestDayOfWeek = weekdays.friday;        // OK
weekdays    WorstDayOfWeek = weekdays.sunday;       // Error
```

Earlier I mentioned *type safety*, and you may be wondering what this actually means. In essence, type safety means you can assign a value only to a variable that is valid, given the type defined. For example, in the enumeration example, you couldn't assign a value of sunday to a variable of type weekdays, because sunday is not recognized within the list of constants specified. This ensures that variables can hold only valid types, and it helps to ensure the accuracy of your program.

C# provides a System class that allows you to apply certain operations to your enumerated types. The class is System.Enum from the System namespace, and it can, for example, return you the string representation of the constant that is assigned to an enumerated variable. For example, the following example would return friday:

```
string nme = System.Enum.GetName(BestDayOfWeek);
```

Arrays

An *array* allows you to group variables of the same type in a collection that can then be accessed by an *index*, a numeric value representing the position in the array. An array can be single-dimensional (that is, be a number of elements in a list vertically), or it can be multidimensional where the list can then expand horizontally as well as vertically. I'll discuss each type in turn and represent an array as it would appear in memory to help solidify your understanding.

Single-Dimensional Arrays

Single-dimensional arrays can represent a list of elements held in memory and can be referenced by an index.

```
char[] nme = new char[4];
```

■**Note** The new keyword creates an *instance* of a reference type.

In memory, the previous array will logically look similar to the following:

```
nme    ➤    nme[0]    ➤    M
       ➤    nme[1]    ➤    A
       ➤    nme[1]    ➤    R
       ➤    nme[1]    ➤    K
```

I'll walk you through the example: the variable points to an area of memory that is defined as holding an array of four characters, which in C# always start at zero (the same as the C/C++ and Java languages). You can then access each of these elements' values using its index.

Multidimensional Arrays

So, you've looked at a single-dimensional array, but what if you wanted to use an array to store data that may require more than one dimension? For example, what if you wanted to store a list of strings? One option would be to use a *multidimensional array*. For example, to store my full name, you need three array elements: one for my Christian name, one for my middle name, and one for my surname. Even in this scenario, you have two options, both of which work but have different benefits in terms of performance:

- Nonregular-shaped array

- Regular-shaped array

Nonregular-shaped arrays are more efficient in terms of space but are slower in terms of access performance. I will demonstrate these two examples in action using code. First, the following shows a nonregular-shaped array where each element can stretch out horizontally to a size that's appropriate for the data.

```
char[][] nme = new char[3][];
nme[0] = new char[4];
nme[1] = new char[6];
nme[2] = new char[6];

nme[0]="mark";
nme[1]="thomas";
nme[2]="mamone";
```

Second, the following example demonstrates the use of regular-shaped arrays, which sacrifice space for the sake of speed:

```
char[,] nme = new char[3,6];
nme[0]="mark";
nme[1]="thomas";
nme[2]="mamone";
```

Collections

In addition to the ability to declare and manipulate arrays in the native C# language, the .NET Framework provides a number of powerful *collection classes* that enable you to declare and manipulate collections of objects such as strings in the same fashion. However, it is often the case that these classes offer far more advanced functionality and are faster in terms of performance than writing your own implementations, purely because they have been optimized to do so.

The .NET Framework provides you with a number of collection classes in both the `System.Collections` and `Systems.Collections.Specialized` namespaces. Too many exist to list here, but these are some of the common ones:

- `ArrayList`

- `Hashtable`

- `SortedList`

- `StringCollection`

For example, the `StringCollection` class is a strongly typed `ArrayList` class that contains a list of objects that must be of type `string`. This is flexible when frequent changes are required and has a fast lookup method (although at the expense of the ability to search by value).

You'll be using some of these collection classes in this book's RSS aggregator project, so I will expand upon how to use them at that time.

Strings

The `System.String` class is worth special mention; applications typically tend to use it frequently. You can use the `System.String` class or the standard type `string` interchangeably.

An important notion regarding strings is that they are *immutable*, which means their contents cannot change. Surely, this is limiting, you're probably saying. Well, that's not really true; I'll show you why by explaining how strings work.

If you create a string using the following command, an instance of an object of type `System.String` is created and held in memory:

```
using System;
class    markstest
{
  static void Main(string[] args)
  {
    string nme = "Mark Thomas Mamone";
```

```
    Console.Out.WriteLine("nme[" + nme + "]");
  }
}
```

If you compile and run this program using an executable, the output is as follows:

```
nme[Mark Thomas Mamone]
```

So, what if you reset this string to something else? Let's say you added this piece of additional code after you output the string:

```
nme = "Mark Mamone";
Console.Out.WriteLine("nme[" + nme + "]");
```

The output in this instance is as follows:

```
nme["Mark Mamone"]
```

How does this work? I just said that a string is immutable, and it can't change! Well, this is true, but it's the processing going on behind the scenes that has probably confused you. When you assign a string another value, or indeed append something to it, you create a new copy of the string, and the reference variable points to this new string. The old piece of memory that held the string's previous contents is now marked for deletion, and this will be cleaned up later. (This is part of the automatic garbage collection provided by .NET and discussed in Chapter 5.)

So, what else can you do with a string? I'll demonstrate some code that allows you to build a string using the + operand, appending data to the end of an existing string. You will then return its length and return the second-to-last character by accessing it as if it were an array—these are all topics you should be familiar with or I have discussed. So, here's some code:

```
using System;
class    markstest
{
  static void Main(string[] args)
  {
    string nme = "Mark ";
    nme = nme + "Thomas ";
    nme = nme + "Mamone";

    int lgth = nme.Length;

    Console.Out.WriteLine("nme[" + nme[lgth-1] + "]");
  }
}
```

What character did you get? Were you expecting n? The reason this doesn't return n is because the Length method returns 18 characters (its length), but an array is zero based, so the index range is from 0 to 17, with 17 being the last character and the reason that e is returned.

You can compare strings in the same way you can compare numerical values; for example, you can issue a comparison such as (if nme == "Mark Thomas Mamone"), or you can use one of the many useful methods provided by the String class such as CompareTo().

Rather than exhaust the features of the String class, I'll leave it up to you to experiment with what's possible using the System.String class and some of the other mentioned classes.

Introducing Statements

I won't belabor the point of what constitutes a statement in the C# language, instead assuming you have some basic programming knowledge; this section will revolve around syntax.

A statement in C# terminates with a semicolon, in the same way as C and C++ do, like so:

```
int value=0;
```

A method call is in the form of <object>.<method>. For example:

```
string mystr = value.ToString();        // calling the ToString() method
```

And as you can see, both of the previous statements terminate with a semicolon. This means complex lines can actually span more than one physical line, as shown here:

```
if (value == 0)              // statement starts here
  value = value + 1;         // and finishes here
```

Note Line placement is not the same for all languages, so you will need to stick to the syntax of the language you are using to avoid errors. Examples of programming languages where this may differ include Python and VB .NET.

Conditional Flow

The if statement is similar to a number of other languages, including Java. It takes the following form:

```
int value = 0;
if (value == 1)
  // value equals 1
else if (value ==2)
  // value equals 2
else
{
  // value is not 1 and
  // value is not 2
}
```

Note The curly braces (defining a *block*) are optional if you have only one statement but compulsory if you have more than one statement following the condition.

You could streamline this notation by using the switch statement, a concept that will be familiar to Java programmers and that shares similarities with other languages. You can rewrite the previous example using the switch statement, as shown in the following code, which in my opinion is far more elegant:

```
int value=0;
switch (value)
{
  case 1:
    // value equals 1
    break;
  case 2:
    // value equals 2
    break;
  default:
    // value is not 1 and
    // value is not 2
    break;
}
```

Unconditional Flow

You probably noticed in the previous example that the flow of code is dealt with on a conditional basis. In other words, the statements execute only if a given expression is true. You may have also noticed the use of the break keyword to terminate a flow of execution when you were using the switch statement. This is because if you did not use the break command, flow would have continued into the next statements. However, in the C# language, the compiler traps this and throws an error.

However, you can use other commands to direct the flow of your code in an unconditional manner, as listed in Table 3-3.

Table 3-3. *Direct Flow Control Keywords*

Statement	Action
continue	Continues with the next loop interaction
goto case <case label>	Jumps to the <case label> within a switch statement
goto <label>	Jumps to a label, provided it is not within a different block and does not cause you to jump out of a try..finally statement

I won't cover these keywords in detail because using them is generally considered to be bad programming practice.

Loops

You can repeat a sequence of commands using a *loop* command, which will typically start at a known value and repeat until a condition is met. You can use three methods for performing loop-type functionality. The first is the for command, which typically covers a range. The second is do..while, which will loop until a condition has been met; the last is the while command, which again loops until a condition has been met.

The following example demonstrates how to use the for command to print the numbers from 1 to 10:

```
for (int idx=1; idx<=10; idx++)
  Console.Out.Write(idx + ",");
```

In contrast, you can perform the same operation but use a while statement that loops until the condition is met; in the following case, that condition is idx <=10;:

```
int idx=0;
while (idx++ <10)
{
  Console.Out.Write(idx+",");
}
```

You'll notice that this example needed some adjustments to ensure the same output.

For completeness, the following shows the do..while statement:

```
int idx=1;
do
{
  Console.Out.Write(idx+",");
} while (idx++ <10);
```

You may notice that you need to further adjust this code, but this resembles the for statement more closely, including the terminating semicolon.

Introducing Classes

Object-oriented programming encompasses using an object-oriented (OO) language such as C# to model your environment using objects or entities with behavior (methods) and attributes (using either variables or properties). You typically create your object or entity through a class. This promotes encapsulation, which in turn improves code readability and security.

If you are not familiar with OO concepts, then I suggest you read *Beginning C# Objects: From Concepts to Code* (Apress, 2003) or another Apress book (http://www.apress.com). Alternatively, check out the Internet for many valuable resources. To attempt to discuss and explain OO analysis and design within one chapter is not feasible; it's a topic that justifies a whole book, and for this reason I will assume a certain level of prior OO experience.

In the following sections, I'll introduce the elements that typically make up an object.

Methods

A *method* represents the functionality of an object, which can often be identified as the "verb" describing an object's action. For example, if you had a Person object, Talk() may be a method implementing an action.

A class also allows the definition of two special methods called *constructors* and *destructors*, which are inherent within any class object. These methods allow you to execute custom code when constructing (also known as *initializing*) or destroying an object; however, the signature for these methods must conform to a specific notation. This is to aid the compiler in identifying the constructors and destructors for a given class. The syntax is as follows:

```
modifier name (parameters)
{
  // constructor or destructor body
}
```

The modifier in this code can be one of the valid modifier values that define its scope; these are private, public, protected, and internal. The name must be the same as the class name, and a constructor can take zero or more arguments, passed as the parameters.

Properties and Attributes (or Fields)

You can define an *attribute* (also known as a *field*) of an object as either a member variable or a field; an attribute is a variable that belongs to ("is a member of") an object. In addition to this, you can support additional functionality by using a concept known as a *property*, which allows you to define Get and Set methods that return a value that may be a simple member variable or may involve running custom logic. I'll discuss these in more detail in Chapter 4.

To introduce you to the concept of classes and structures, I'll start by describing the high-level concepts. To continue with the Person object, you can define this as a class using the following syntax:

```
class Person
{
}
```

The class keyword defines that the object is a class type object, and the curly braces define the class representation. It is within the braces that you define methods, properties, and attributes. So, let's extend the Person class by adding some common attributes and a few methods. First, add some attributes, like so:

```
class Person
{
  // Attributes
  int       age = 0;
  string    Christian="";
  string    Surname="";
}
```

Second, add a few methods, like so:

```
string SpeakName()
{
  return (Christian + " " + Surname);
}

int GetAge()
{
  return age;
}
```

This example defines the complete class, both with attributes and with methods that you can now reference.

Introducing Structures

I've covered the class keyword, but what about the struct keyword? On the face of it, the struct type definition seems to encompass all the features of a class. However, it has some subtle differences:

- Value types, which include a struct, are created on the *stack* (an area of memory for storing and passing values).

- The struct keyword does not support inheritance.

- The struct keyword does not support destructors.

In contrast, a class is constructed on the *heap*, a larger area of memory than the stack for .NET to use; in addition, a class supports inheritance and supports destructors and constructors. My general rule of thumb is that by default a struct's or class's members have private scope, and therefore you should base your decision about which one to use on the desired scope of your entities' members.

Note The stack and heap are memory concepts that are explained in more detail in Chapter 4.

Introducing Declarations

I've already touched on the concept of declarations; specifically, you've already seen how to declare classes, structs, fields, and methods. You can group declarations by using the C# entities, as shown in Table 3-4.

Table 3-4. *Declaration Matrix*

Entity	Allows the Declaration of...
namespace	Classes, *interfaces*, structs, enums, *delegates**
class, struct	Fields, methods, properties, *events*, *indexers*
enum	Enumeration constants
Block (curly braces)	Local variables

* The italicized items are concepts I haven't covered yet but will do so through the course of the book.

You can see a number of these entities in action within the following code snippet, which defines a namespace entity that holds a field that is visible only within this namespace:

```
namespace ANamespace { int aField; }
```

Some conditions exist when defining entities: basically, you can't use a name twice, and you can't use a reserved keyword for a name. Also, declarations can be in an arbitrary (any) order, with the exception of local variables, which must be declared before they are used.

Defining Scope

You can define *scope* (the visibility an object or variable has) within your code in a number of ways that vary depending on the item to which you are trying to apply scope. Also, you can limit the scope of a class or the scope of class members such as methods and attributes. This is an important concept to grasp, because the least scope an object has, the better. This allows you to be specific about what is visible and therefore what can be used. The first method encountered by the compiler will be its location, relative to its declaration. This means an object is visible only within its declaration area; for example, local variables defined within a block are visible only within that block.

The second method for applying scope is to use scope keywords, known as *modifiers*, such as private, public, and protected. You apply these before object or type definitions and thus define the scope of the object they precede.

Private

As its name suggests, the private modifier limits the scope of an object to the lowest level, and therefore it's visible only to the object that owns the methods or attributes within it. Consider the following example:

```
class Person
{
  private int age = 0;            // Private access by this object only
}
```

This limits the scope of age to only those methods that belong to the Person object. This means if you created an instance of the object and tried to access it, you would receive a compilation error indicating that it was inaccessible because of its protection level.

■**Note** The absence of a keyword denotes private membership by default, although it is considered good practice to explicitly define the scope of your objects.

Public

In contrast to the previous example, the public keyword applies global scope to an attribute or method and allows any access to it. In the following example, using the public keyword will allow anybody to access the variable age, either internally or externally to the object:

```
class Person
{
  public int age = 0;            // Any access, internal or external
}
```

Protected

So, internal access only and any access may lead you to think that these are the only two options available to you. Think again! The protected keyword is reserved for use by an object-oriented concept called *inheritance*. The ability for an object to inherit the attributes and methods of another object is one of the most powerful concepts in OO analysis and design. It is here that the use of the protected keyword comes into play; it allows the scope of an object's attributes or methods to be visible in any object that inherits from it, as well as in the object itself.

If you created another object called Man that is a type of person and so inherits from Person, you could mark the age member variable as protected and therefore make it visible to not only the Person object but also to the Man object. The variable, however, would *not* be visible to objects that do not conform to either of these restrictions.

Namespaces

You can also limit the scope of your classes using the namespace keyword. By default, if you omit a namespace, your class is placed within a default namespace. So, consider the following example:

```
class NoNamespace
{
  string nme = "Mark Thomas Mamone";
}
```

This will create a class that exists within the default namespace because you failed to define one.

The following example introduces some of the concepts that I have discussed so far:

```
using System;

// Class encapsulating my name
class NoNamespace
{
  public string nme = "Mark Thomas Mamone";
}

// Class acting as the entry point for the executable
class Entry
{
  static void Main(string[] args)
  {
    NoNamespace def = new NoNamespace();
    Console.Out.WriteLine("nme[" + def.nme + "]");
  }
}
```

If you run the previous example, you should see the following output:

```
nme[Mark Thomas Mamone]
```

This is because the NoNamespace class and the Entry class are both in the default namespace, because the code failed to indicate otherwise. Therefore, it is perfectly acceptable for the Entry class to create an instance of the NoNamespace class and use it. However, if you change the code so that the declaration of the NoNamespace class indicates it belongs to a specific namespace, you will have the following code:

```
// Class encapsulating my name
namespace MyUniqueNamespace
{
  class NoNamespace
  {
    public string nme = "Mark Thomas Mamone";
  }
}
```

When attempting to recompile the application, the following error should occur:

```
c3ex2.cs(17) error CS0246: Cannot find type 'NoNamespace'
Compilation failed: 1 error(s)  0 warnings
```

This indicates you attempted to reference a type object called NoNamespace but it didn't have visibility—and hence couldn't be found. However, you can specify where this type is using a fully qualified name and therefore specifying the namespace in which the type is contained. For example:

```
MyUniqueNamespace.NoNamespace def = new MyUniqueNamespace.NoNamespace();
```

Alternatively, you can use the using keyword at the start of the file to indicate the namespaces that should be searched, thus importing the objects within. In the examples so far, you have been using the System namespace by default, as this gives you access to the console object for outputting text to the console window.

In either case, the code will now compile and run. Which do I use? The former is more long-winded but far more specific, but typically I use the latter option for simplicity.

Introducing Operators

Finally, I'll introduce *operators*. The C# language introduces a number of operators that, when used in code, form *expressions*. I'll focus on the key expressions in this section and allow you to dig a little deeper on your own for those that are not explained.

Table 3-5 defines the most commonly used operators.

Table 3-5. *Operator Definitions and Usage*

Operator	Description
+	Addition
-	Subtract
*	Multiple
/	Divide
%	Percentage
&	And
|	Or
<<	Bit shift left
>>	Bit shift right
()	Priority
=	Assignment

In most cases, you can use the operator either *prefix* (before) or *postfix* (after), which has the effect of applying the operator either before or after output. For example, if you were to use a variable in an equality test, you would impact how the expression would be evaluated. For example, the following snippet of code, if compiled, would find the equality expression to be true and output the string x is equal to 1:

```
int x=0;
if (++x == 1)
  Console.Out.WriteLine("x is equal to 1");
```

However, if you changed the addition operator to be postfix, as follows, and then you recompile and run the code, you'd find that the equality expression would be false and no string would be output:

```
int x=0;
if (x++ == 1)
  Console.Out.WriteLine("x is equal to 1");
```

Table 3-6 defines the priority of these operators and more.

Table 3-6. *Operator Priorities*

Type	Operator
Primary	(x) x.y f(x) a[x] x++ x--new typeof sizeof checked unchecked stackalloc
Unary	+ - ~ ! ++x --x (T)x * &
Multiplicative	* / %
Additive	+ -
Shift	<< >>
Relational	< > <= >= is as
Equality	== !=
Logical bitwise (AND, XOR, OR)	& ^	
Logical boolean (AND, OR, and conditional)	&& || c?x:y
Assignment	= += -= *= /= %= <<= >>= &= ^= |=

I'll briefly explain how to use these operators in the following sections.

Primary

The *primary* operators access and manipulate the value of a single variable. For example, the following operator increases the value of the variable by 1:

```
int a=0;
a++;        // same as doing a=a+1
```

Unary

A *unary* operator is one that manipulates a single variable's value; for example, the following example increases the variable's value by 1:

```
int a = 2;
int b = ++a;    // 'b' holds 3 after being incremented before being assigned
```

Multiplicative

The *multiplicative* operators are mathematical operators that multiple, divide, or find the percentage of a value. For example:

```
int a = 2;
a = a * 2;          // 'a' would now equal 4
```

Additive

The *additive* operators are again mathematical operators that can add or subtract values. For example:

```
int a = 5;
a = a -1;           // 'a' would now hold 4
```

Shift

The *shift* operator performs a bitwise shift of bits that form a variable such as an int; in the following example, shifting the following bits left by 1 would mean that c holds 128:

```
int c = (64 << 1);
```

Relational

The *relational* operators perform relational comparisons; for example, the following comparison is false:

```
bool a = (2 > 3);    // 'a' would hold false as 2 is less than 3
```

Equality

The *equality* operators compare the equality of two variables or values; for example, the following condition is true:

```
bool same = (1 == 1);        // same would equal true
```

Logical Bitwise

The *logical bitwise* operators apply the bitwise condition to the variable and return the results. For example, the following AND condition returns true where the bits match and so returns the value 32:

```
int b = 32 & 34;
```

Logical Boolean

The *logical boolean* operators perform a logical conditional comparison; in the following example, the variable is true:

```
bool both_same = (1==1 && 2==2)
```

Assignment

The *assignment* operators assign values after first applying the operation that has been declared, as shown in the following code:

```
int a = 0;
a+= 1;       // Same as doing a=a+1;
```

Summary

In this chapter, I introduced the fundamentals of the C# programming language available with the .NET Framework while touching on some of its influences. I also described the high-level structure of the C# language and how a C#-based application may look.

You learned how to use variables, value types, statements, classes, and structures. This knowledge can supplement any existing development knowledge you have or can act as an introduction to C#. In either case, you should now understand the fundamental constructs of the C# language needed for developing C#-based applications. In the next chapter, I'll elaborate on some of the concepts discussed here and introduce more features of the C# language.

CHAPTER 4

■ ■ ■

Learning C#: Beyond the Basics

In Chapter 3, I introduced some of the basic concepts surrounding the C# language, for example, how you can define the state of an object through variables based on types. In addition, I explained the different types available such as value types, reference types, and enumerated types, as well as how code is represented using statements and is organized into flows of execution. I also introduced operators, demonstrating how you can use these to alter the value of a field, either prefix (before) or postfix (after) it has been evaluated in an expression. Finally, I introduced classes and structs and how to define their visibility, thus specifying their scope.

Now that you've been introduced to the fundamentals, I'll elaborate on these concepts and introduce a few more that will complete the C# primer and leave you ready to tackle the book's project and write your own .NET-based Mono code. The majority of this chapter will focus on the features and syntax surrounding the definition of objects using either the class keyword or the struct keyword. As explained in Chapter 3, few differences exist between the two, so I'll cover the features that are applicable to both and highlight the differences as you encounter them throughout this book. To save duplication, I'll hereafter focus on classes, but you should apply the concepts to both classes and structs unless told otherwise.

What's Contained Within a Class or Struct?

So, what's in a class or struct? Well, these structures contain quite a lot! Both classes and structs define the specification for an object that includes its state (its attributes) and operations (its methods). A class does not exist in the runtime environment, which is why you cannot create an instance of a class. Instead, you define an object as being based on a (type of) specific class and instantiate (or create) an instance of the object. It is after being successfully created that the object exists within the .NET runtime until it is automatically destroyed.

A class is the most important concept within C#; it forms the foundation for the class library, which is a set of rich functional classes encapsulating functionality that you can then use in your application. Some good examples of functionality provided by the classes included in the .NET Framework's class library are the ability to draw graphics (see the System.Drawing namespace) and the ability to access files (see the File class in System.IO). You can start to develop your own classes that may contain or enhance the existing classes, or you can define new functionality. So, without further ado, I'll cover the contents of a class and explain how you can embrace this power.

Instance Construction and Destruction

As mentioned previously, a class is a template or specification for an object. You cannot create an instance of a class; you can create only objects that are based on a class. The same is true of structs. However, a difference exists in how you actually create an instance of a struct. I'll walk you through some examples. First you'll define a simple class for a Person object, and then you'll create an instance of this object using the new keyword. The new keyword creates an instance of an object based upon a class. So, define the class with a single attribute named age, like so:

```
class Person { public int age; }
```

Then create an instance of this class using an object named mark, like so:

```
Person mark = new Person();
```

In this example, you're creating an object in memory (in an area called the *heap*, which you'll learn more about in Chapter 5) based on the Person class, and you can then use this instance object, referenced by the mark variable, to interact with the object.

The struct has different semantics for creating an instance that don't require the new keyword. As such, you can rewrite the previous example by creating a struct to represent the object and then creating an instance of an object using this reference type. So, create the struct reference type first, like so:

```
struct Person { public int age; }
```

Then create an instance of this class using an object named mark, like so:

```
Person mark;
```

You'll notice an immediate difference in that you don't need to explicitly indicate the creation of an instance using a keyword; instead, this is automatically implied, and the object is created in an area of memory called the *stack*.

So, you've created instances, but how do you destroy them? Well, the answer is simple—you don't! I'm encroaching on the topic of garbage collection, which is the memory management facility of the .NET runtime that is covered in more detail in Chapter 5, but the principle in .NET is that every object that is referenced within code has a *count*. This is also known as an object being *reference counted*. This is an internal counter associated within an object that the automatic memory management facility within .NET uses to see whether it can reclaim the memory used by that object. Therefore, when an object is no longer referenced, it's no longer required and can be destroyed. However, you can ensure that an object is destroyed as soon as possible by indicating that it's no longer required by using a null assignment, although this is not applicable for structs. For example, to destroy the instance of the Person class called Mark, you could do the following:

```
Mark = null;    // Null class assignment signals the object can be garbage collected
```

Method Signatures

In this section, I'll explain what a *signature* is in the world of .NET (which is also applicable to other programming environments), as it's something that is important in object-oriented languages. A signature describes the characteristics of the method being called. The following example shows a simple method for adding two numbers:

```
int add(int a, int b)
{
  return a+b;
}
```

The signature consists of a number of components, including the following:

- Return value and type

- Method name

- Parameters passed, in terms of numbers, type, and order

When a method call is made, and the components of the signature you pass match the components of a signature found in any of the methods defined, then this will be the method called. In the case of a constructor, if a matching signature cannot be found, the default constructor will be called, which is one with no parameters and no return type.

Constructors and Destructors

Constructing objects (when an instance of an object is physically created) and destructing objects (when an instance of an object is reclaimed by the garbage collector) allow you the opportunity to execute custom code that you define. When you create an object, the .NET runtime will search for a constructor whose signature matches that used when creating the instance.

Constructor

A *constructor* is called when an object is instantiated, which is when you create an object using the new keyword. The signature you use to create the object will dictate the constructor called. This feature is inherent in object-oriented languages and is known as *operator overloading*. It's also used in *polymorphism*, something I'll discuss in more detail in the "Generalization, Specialization, and Initializers" section of this chapter. This is the ability to define a number of methods of the same name but with different signatures (that is, using a different combination of the components mentioned) and for the compiler to call the most appropriate method. All constructors have a method name that matches the name of the class; the following code defines two different constructors:

```
class Person
{
  private int age;
  private string firstname;
  private string surname;

  Person(string firstname, string surname) {}            // Constructor 1
  Person(string firstname, string surname, int age) {}   // Constructor 2
}
```

In this scenario, you have defined two constructors that take different parameters. This would allow you to use those parameters during the construction call to perform object initialization; for example, you could set some internal member variables to the value of the parameters passed. The following code examples provide the implementation for the constructors that do precisely that:

```
// Constructor 1
Person(string firstname, string surname)
{
  age=0;
  this.firstname = firstname;
  this.surname = surname;
}

// Constructor 2
Person(string firstname, string surname, int age)
{
  this.age= age;
  this.firstname = firstname;
  this.surname = surname;
}
```

These implementations are rudimentary, although you may notice the use of the this keyword. The this keyword differentiates the variables that are defined within the class (and so are available within the object) and the parameters passed. This is because both have the same name and allow the compiler to differentiate. You can use the this keyword to denote the object instance that's implementing the code, or you could change the parameter names being passed.

■**Note** When defining attributes for a class or struct, a naming convention that is often used (although isn't mandatory) is to precede all attributes with an underscore.

I'll now show how to implement some code to demonstrate how to create three objects based on the same class but using different constructors. Try to see whether you can decide which constructor would be called by the compiler.

```
{
  // Construct three Person objects
  Person    mark = new Person("mark", "mamone");
  Person    callum = new Person("Callum","Hibbert",65);
  Person    johndoe = new Person();
}
```

The declaration of the constructors and the code used to construct the objects should make the decision pretty easy; however, what about the last example (highlighted in bold for clarity)? Which constructor would be called in that case?

Perhaps this is a trick question, because this code doesn't explicitly define a constructor that takes no parameters. The .NET compiler will always create a default constructor that takes no parameters when no constructors are explicitly defined, and the .NET runtime will then use this when no parameters are passed in the construction of an object, as is the case when constructing the third object in the previous example. However, because the code defines some custom constructors, the compiler decides that in this instance you must define all constructors called. Therefore, in this case, the compiler will produce a compile error.

Destructor

A *destructor* is similar in nature to a constructor but at the other end of the object's lifetime; that is, it is called only when an object is destroyed and no longer being referenced (and is eventually reclaimed by the garbage collector). This means it has a number of key differences when compared to constructors. First, you cannot specify multiple signatures for a destructor; only one signature exists, and it's one that doesn't take any parameters. Second, you don't define the visibility of the method, because the garbage collector calls it automatically. Finally, the method will automatically call the Object.Finalize method on the object's base class. Using the class from the previous section, you would define your destructor as follows, but instead of using the previous method you could use the Close() method, which is associated with an arbitrary TextReader object:

```
~Person()
{
  // Call any tidy-up methods associated with objects being used
  if (myTextReader != null)
    myTextReader.Close();
}
```

■**Note** You cannot use destructors with structs, only classes. Destructors are called automatically and cannot be invoked. They return no value and take only parameters, they can have only one destructor per class, and the tilde (~) denotes a destructor's signature.

Scope Using Visibility Modifiers

You can define scope explicitly in both a struct and a class using visibility modifiers, which, as their name suggests, modify the scope of visibility for the member with which they are associated. Table 4-1 lists the available visibility modifiers.

Table 4-1. *Visibility Modifiers*

Modifier	Description
private	Visible only to internal members of the class
public	Visible to all, both internally and externally
protected	Visible internally and to methods that are inherited

By using these modifiers, you can restrict the scope (visibility) of your class's contents and in doing so build more reliable code. How? You avoid misusing your class or struct through accidental exposure to its "internal workings" (that is, attributes and operations) by explicitly defining the scope of these members and exposing only those elements you want exposed. This ensures that only those members that you give access to are permitted access and therefore reduces the opportunity for error.

Let's look at some examples of using these keywords and how they affect a sample application. Consider the following snippet of code that defines and instantiates a class and struct of the type you have defined. You'll then modify elements to observe the result.

```
using System;

class Test
{
  // Define a structure
  struct MyStruct    {    int age;    }

  // Define a class
  class MyClass    {    int age;    }


  [STAThread]
  static void Main(string[] args)
  {
    // Create and initialize my struct
    MyStruct s;    // No instance creation; therefore it's on the Stack
    s.age = 36;

    // Create and initialize my class
    MyClass c = new MyClass();    // Create an instance on the heap
    c.age=36;
  }
}
```

Note To ensure that the code examples are easy to follow, I've sometimes reduced code onto a single line when my preference would be to use separate lines. A good example is in the previous code; general best practice suggests that braces and the contents of a class/struct/operation as defined within the curly brace block should be on separate lines.

The first thing to notice with the previous code is that it will not compile! This is for a good reason: by default all member variables and methods are private. This causes the compilation process to produce errors whenever you try to access the age attribute, complaining that the "attribute is inaccessible due to its protection level."

Using Public Modifiers

This is a good thing, as a default scope of private means you must explicitly state that an attribute or operation is visible to entities other than itself. So, if you want the age variable to be visible outside the class so that other entities based on the class can see it, use the public visibility modifier. Consider the following modifications to the code:

```
// Define a structure
struct MyStruct    {    public int age;    }
```

In this revised example, you explicitly change the visibility of the age attribute to public for the struct. You can observe the effect this has: the compilation no longer complains that you cannot access the age attribute of the struct. This is because its visibility has clearly been defined as public with the appropriate visibility modifier, meaning it can be seen and accessed from either inside or outside the class.

Using Protected Modifiers

As touched on earlier, in addition to the private and public modifiers, you can use the protected modifier to indicate that a method or attribute is not only visible to the class but its decedents as well. The following code demonstrates how to use the protected modifier:

```
// Define a structure
struct MyStruct    {    protected int age;    }
```

In this example, the compiler still complains that you are attempting to access an attribute that is inaccessible because of its protection level. This is because while private is visible only inside the class, and public is visible both outside and inside the class, protected dictates that only the class and its descendants (through inheritance, something I'll cover in the "Generalization, Specialization, and Initializers section") can access it.

Attributes

An *attribute* is a declarative tag (enclosed within square brackets) that informs the compiler how to handle the statement to which it applies. For example, in one of the examples so far, you may have noticed the [STAThread] attribute. This attribute tells the compiler that the method uses the single-threaded apartment model (see the following note for more details) where only one thread can be entered and executed at a time. The .NET Framework provides this attribute automatically, along with a number of other attributes that are pertinent to the namespace and classes in which they are defined. Too many exist to list here, but Chapter 11 contains a good example; you'll look at the definition of a method that is actually exposed as a Web Service! For the moment, let's look at a simple example that allows you to signal to the compiler that a method has been deprecated and a new method should be used. Consider the class AttributeTest defined in the following example code:

```
using System;

class AttributeTest
{
```

```
[Obsolete("This method has been deprecated, please use ➡
NewMethod() instead", true)]
  public void OldMethod()
  {
    // Does something
  }

  public void NewMethod()
  {
    // Does something
  }

}
```

You can then define the Test class to use the previous class and create an instance, calling the method (that is, OldMethod) that has been marked as obsolete using the Obsolete attribute. The following example code shows this:

```
class Test
{
  static void Main(string[] args)
  {
    AttributeTest t = new AttributeTest();
    t.OldMethod();
  }
}
```

If you attempt to compile this, it will return a compilation error stating that the method is obsolete and then output the string you defined, informing the user they should use an alternative method instead. If you then modify the code to use the alternative method (that is, NewMethod), this will successfully compile. More adventurous developers can even define their own attributes, although to cover this in depth is beyond the scope of this chapter and will provide maximum benefit when used in conjunction with reflection, something I'll cover in Chapter 12.

Note The [STAThread] attribute is a complex subject but succinctly allows an object within an apartment (a multithreading concept) to communicate synchronously. For more information, see http://msdn. microsoft.com/library/default.asp?url=/library/en-us/com/html/ 2f345ae2-8314-4067-a6d6-5a0275941ed4.asp.

Operations

The operations that you can apply to both reference and value objects vary but can primarily be classified into the following groups:

- Primary

- Unary

- Arithmetic

- Relational and logical

- Type operators

Each group has distinct but related capabilities that I will cover over the next few pages.

Primary

Primary operators can access or manipulate single-variable operators using the available operators defined within Table 4-2.

Table 4-2. *C# Primary Operators*

Operator	Description
(a)	Denotes the precedence in an operation, meaning evaluate a first.
a.b	Denotes a member of a class or structure. For example, b is a member of a.
a[b]	Denotes an array index. For example, access array a using index number b.
a++	Post-increment operator following a variable. For example, a++ is the same as a=a+1.
a--	Post-decrement operator following a variable. For example, a-- is the same as a=a-1.
new	Denotes the instantiation of a reference type object.

Listing 4-1 demonstrates some of these examples.

Listing 4-1. *Primary Operators*

```
using System;
public class PrimaryOperators
{

  public static void Main(string[] args)
  {

      Person p = new Person("mark", "mamone");  // Instantiates our Person object
      p.age = 35;  // Sets the age member of object p to 35
      p.age++;  // Increments the age member variable by 1
      p.age--;   // Decrements the age member variable by 1

      Console.Out.WriteLine("1st character of First Name is " + p.firstname[0]);
```

```
    if (p.age==35)  // Precedence for expression evaluation
        Console.Out.WriteLine("…must be getting old at over 30!");

  }

}
```

Unary

Unary operators can manipulate single-variable operators using the operators defined within Table 4-3.

Table 4-3. *C# Unary Operators*

Operator	Description
+	Returns its value in its original form. For example, +a is the same as 0+a.
-	Returns its value in a negative form. For example, -a is the same as 0-a.
!	Returns the NOT value, so !false is equal to true, and !true is equal to false.
~	Returns the NOT value but using 1's complement. For example,!0000 equals 1111.
++a	Pre-increment operator following a variable.
--a	Pre-decrement operator following a variable.

Listing 4-2 demonstrates some of these examples.

Listing 4-2. *Unary Operators*

```
using System;
public class UnaryOperators
{

  public static void Main(string[] args)
  {

    int a = 1;
    Console.Out.WriteLine("+a = " + +a);  // would output '+a=1'
    Console.Out.WriteLine("-a = " + -a);  // would output '-a=-1'
    Console.Out.WriteLine("!false=" + !false);  // would output '!false = true'
    Console.Out.WriteLine("~a=" + ~a);  // would output '~a=-2'
    int b;
    b = ++a;  // b would equal 2, a would equal 2
    Console.Out.WriteLine("b=" + b);
    b = --a;  // b would equal 1, a would equal 0
    Console.Out.WriteLine("b=" + b);
  }

}
```

Arithmetic

Arithmetic operators can manipulate a single variable using the operators listed in Table 4-4.

Table 4-4. *C# Arithmetic Operators*

Operator	Description
*	Multiplication operator. For example, a*b multiples a by the value b.
/	Division operator. For example, a/b divides a by the value b.
%	Modulus operator. For example, a % b returns the modulus of a divided by b.
+	Add operator. For example, a+b adds b to the value of a.
-	Subtract operator. For example, a-b subtracts b from the value a.
<<	Bitwise left Shift. For example, a << 2 shifts the bits in a 2 bits to the left.
>>	Bitwise right shift. For example, a >> 2 shifts the bits in a 2 bits to the right.
=	Assignment operator. For example, a=b would assign a the value of b. See the previous example in Listing 4-2.

Listing 4-3 demonstrates some of these examples.

Listing 4-3. *Arithmetic Operators*

```
using System;
public class ArithmeticOperators
{

  public static void Main(string[] args)
  {

      int a;
      a = 1;                    // a would equal 1
      a = a * 10;               // a would equal 10
      a = a / 2;                // a would equal 5
      a = a % 2;                // a would equal 1
      a = a + 4;                // a would equal 5
      a = a - 1;                // a would equal 4
      a = a >> 2;               // a would equal 1
      a = a << 2;               // a would equal 4

  }


}
```

Relational and Logical

Relation and logical operators involve the relational and logical comparison of variables using the operators listed in Table 4-5.

Table 4-5. *C# Relational and Logical Operators*

Operator	Description
==	Equality comparison. For example, a==b will return true if the value of a equals the value of b.
<	Less than comparison. For example, a<b will return true if the value of a is less than the value of b.
>	Greater than comparison. For example, a>b will return true if the value of a is greater than b.
<=	Less than or equals to comparison.
>=	Greater than or equals to comparison.
&	Logical AND operator.
^	Logical XOR operator.
|	Logical OR operator.
&&	AND comparison.
||	OR comparison.
?:	Similar to the if statement but should be avoided because of lack of readability.

Listing 4-4 demonstrates some of these examples.

Listing 4-4. *Relational and Logical Operators*

```
using System;
public class LogicalOperators
{

  public static void Main(string[] args)
   {

      int a =1;
      Console.Out.WriteLine("a==2"+ (a==2));   // False
      Console.Out.WriteLine("a<2"+ (a<2));     // True
      Console.Out.WriteLine("a>2"+ (a>2));     // False
      Console.Out.WriteLine("a<=1"+ (a<=2));   // True
      Console.Out.WriteLine("a>=2"+ (a>=2));   // False
      Console.Out.WriteLine("a & 1"+ (a&1));   // 1
      Console.Out.WriteLine("a ^ 1"+ (a^1));   // 0
      Console.Out.WriteLine("a | 1"+ (a|1));   // 1
```

```
        Console.Out.WriteLine("(a<2) && (a>0)"+ ((a<2)&&(a>0))); // True
        Console.Out.WriteLine("(a<2) || (a>0)"+ ((a<2)||(a>0))); // True


    }

}
```

Type Operators

Type operators work on type-based objects (see Table 4-6).

Table 4-6. *C# Type-Based Operators*

Operator	Description
typeof	Denotes reflection operation.
sizeof	Returns the byte size of a value type but only in code marked as unsafe.
is	Reference type comparison. For example, a is b would return true for the same reference types.
unchecked	Denotes that overflow checking should not be performed for the evaluation following it.
checked	Denotes that overflow checking should be performed for the evaluation following it.

Listing 4-5 demonstrates some of these examples.

Listing 4-5. *Type-Based Operators*

```
using System;
public class TypeOperators
{

    public static void Main(string[] args)
    {

        Person p = new Person("mark", "mamone");
        bool result = ( p is Person );
        int size_of_age = sizeof(p.age); // Returns the size of 'age'
        short a = 32767; // a cannot hold more than 32767 as a value
        short b = checked( a + 1 ); // checked, overflow will raise an exception
        short c = unchecked( a + 1 ); // unchecked, no exception is raised
        Console.Out.WriteLine("{0}", a.GetType());  // return 'System.Short'


    }


}
```

Constants

An important aspect of programming is to ensure that your code is safe; by this I mean it should work as you intended and is not open to misuse. I won't describe the intricacies of writing secure code—many good books do that already. Using constants, however, can ensure that a value type is immutable and its use in expressions is as intended. It also aids in producing self-documenting code.

For example, let's assume you wanted to use an expression in a value that defines the age limit that a child is considered an adult for the purpose of buying cinema tickets. You could represent this condition as follows:

```
if (age > 16)
  // process as adult
else
  // process as child
```

If you consider this example, you can make a few observations. The first one is that 16 isn't descriptive. What would that mean without the context that surrounded it? The second is that the value represented in a variable could change by mistake. To address these issues, you can use constant values. You can rewrite the previous example as follows:

```
const int child_age_limit = 16;
if (age > child_age_limit)
  // process as adult
else
  // process as child
```

The difference should be obvious; you can use constants in conjunction with a meaningful named variable to ensure its value is fixed and descriptive, thus achieving some of the qualities of self-documenting code.

Enumerated Types

Continuing the discussion of constants and the mantra of achieving self-documenting code, I'll introduce *enumerated types*. An enumerated type is a value type that holds values with associated names. Let's use an example whereby you associate a day index (as a numeric value) with each day of the week, Sunday being 0, Monday being 1, and so on.

```
public enum DaysOfWeek
{
  Sunday, Monday, Tuesday, Wednesday, Thursday, Friday, Saturday
}
```

By default, the first value is assigned 0, and then each named member has a value that is incremented by 1. You can, however, specifically assign values. The following shows the same example with the same values but explicitly defined:

```
public enum DaysOfWeek
{
  Sunday=0, Monday=1, Tuesday=2, Wednesday=3, Thursday=4, Friday=5, Saturday=6
}
```

You can then use an enumerated type as if their values were constants, thus implementing well-structured, descriptive code. The following shows how you could use the previous example:

```
DaysOfWeek day = 2;
if (day == DaysOfWeek.Tuesday)
  // it's tuesday
else
  // it's not Tuesday
```

As you can see, the numeric value is constant, and the semantics used to reference the enumerated value are constant. This also means that the variable being compared is not just a number; you can clearly see that it's a DayOfWeek, which helps people who may be reading the code to more clearly understand it.

Fields and Properties

A *field* is associated with class definitions; it's a variable that is encapsulated by a class and can therefore be accessed only through methods provided by the class. This can be direct access if its visibility modifier allows it or indirect access using a property to conduct access.

I'll use the following example to explain. A field, or *member variable*, is a variable that is encapsulated by a reference type such as a class. Therefore, the following example demonstrates three fields that are members of the Person class, all directly accessible because of the public visibility modifier:

```
class Person
{
  public int age-0;
  public string firstname=""'
  public string lastname="";
}
```

Another method is to encapsulate the fields and provide access only through a property construct, also known as a *smart field*. These are nothing more than methods that allow access to the field for either reading or writing. Listing 4-6 duplicates the age field's accessibility.

Listing 4-6. *Using Properties*

```
class Person
{

    private int _age = 0;

    public int age
    {
        get { return _age; }
        set { _age = value; }
    }

}
```

In Listing 4-6, the private age field is denoted by an underscore that prefixes the variable name. Using the underscore character is a personal preference and is not compulsory. The syntax is similar to the declaration of a field; however, you can define methods called set and get to represent the read and write methods, respectively. In Listing 4-6 the property implementation is limited to simply either returning or setting the internal age member variable. The following code demonstrates how to use the class defined in Listing 4-6 and its age property:

```
using System;

class Test
{
  static void Main(string[] args)
  {
    Person p = new Person();
    p.age = 36;
    Console.Out.WriteLine("Person.age = " + p.age);
  }
}
```

In the previous example, after creating an instance of the Person class, you simply assign the age value that will call the implicitly set method, passing the value assigned, and then you output the value of the age property using the get property. Another benefit of using property declarations is the ability to provide read-only fields, which are similar to constant fields but with intelligence. For example, if you wanted to return the full name using the concatenation of two fields, you could use a property for this, as shown in Listing 4-7.

Listing 4-7. *Dynamic Properties*

```
class Person
{

  public string firstname="";
  public string lastname="";

  public string fullname
  {
    get
    {
      return firstname + " " + lastname;
    }
  }

}
```

This allows you to refer to a property as if it were another variable, but internal processing may have been undertaken to return its value. The following application that uses this class demonstrates this:

```
using System;

Class Test
{
  static void Main(string[] args)
  {
    Person p = new Person();
    p.firstname = "Mark";
    p.lastname = "Mamone";
    Console.Out.WriteLine("Fullname = " + p.fullname);
  }
}
```

Overloaded Operators

In the previous chapter, I discussed how to use operators within expressions, something that is typified through arithmetic type operations. However, an extremely powerful feature is the ability to overload an operator and, in doing so, provide your own implementation for handling the expression. This means using the polymorphic ability of truly object-oriented languages such as C#, which provides more meaningful code.

For example, if you continue to use arithmetic as an example, you could hold a date value within a class by using some kind of internal numeric representation such as the Julian calendar (see http://en.wikipedia.org/wiki/Julian_calendar) or .NET's internal representation. Using this context, it would be far more readable if you could perform addition, using the + operator, on a date value with an elapsed number of days and have it return the date value that takes into account leap years, and so on. The following example uses an object, called MyDate, that encapsulates a date value:

```
MyDate    dob = new MyDate(22,8,1969); // DD.MM.YYYY
```

You could then perform some arithmetic operations on the date in one of two ways. You could either use the + operator or use a custom-provided method. Consider these options in the following example, and you'll probably agree that the + operator is more meaningful:

```
MyDate    dob_next_year = dob + 365;          // + operator
MyDate    dob_next_year1 = dob.AddDays(365);       // AddDays() method
```

So, how do you do it? You already learned how to create a method in the previous chapter, and in this instance the Date class already implements the AddDays method, so I'll demonstrate how you can create an overloaded method for the + operator to implement functionality that holds a calendar's Month value that obviously cannot go beyond month 12 and in this case wraps around.

To start, create a Month class that holds an internal integer representation of the month, provides a default constructor, and also provides a read-only property that returns the Month value as an integer. For example:

```
public class Month
{
    int _month;     // Internal month representation

    // Default Constructor
    public Month(int month)
    {
        _month = month;
    }

     // Read-only 'monthValue' property
    public int monthValue { get { return _month; } }

}
```

Then define the overloaded + operator, which *must* be public and static. It can also take only those parameters that are of the same type; this is true for all unary operations, and in the case of operator overloading, the parameters represent the values on either side of the operator.

```
public static Month operator + (Month month1, Month month2)
{
    // Add our two month values together
    int newMonth = month1.monthValue + month2.monthValue;

    // Check for a month 'overflow' and wrap around if found
    if (newMonth>12)
        newMonth = newMonth % 12;    // Modulus to wrap around

    // Return the new month value
    return new Month(newMonth);
}
```

Finally, to test this, you can embed this in a Test class with its own Main entry point, as shown here:

```
using System;

// Month class definition would go here

class Test
{
  [STAThread]
  static void Main(string[] args)
  {
    Month feb = new Month(2);
    Month dec = new Month(12);

    Month new_month = feb + dec;
    Console.Out.WriteLine("new_month="+new_month.monthValue); // shows 2 = Feb
  }
}
```

Nested Types

I won't dwell on the topic of nested types, primarily because I've already introduced them (the more observant of you may have already noticed it). The C# language, and others, provides the ability for you to nest one type within another. In the examples shown so far, you created a class for demonstrating a specific technique and then embedded this within another class that provides the Main entry point for testing. To recap, define the Person class again, as follows:

```
class Person
{
    // Some implementation
}
```

If you then wanted to create further classes that encapsulated behavior or attributes, and their visibility was not required outside the Person class, you could embed these within the Person class. This would mean the Person class is also known as a *container class*, and it demonstrates nested types. This of course is not limited to reference types such as classes; encapsulating value types such as integers is also a demonstration of nested types, albeit one that's a little more simplistic.

Create a reference type for a Face class that encapsulates the characteristics of a face and a value type that represents the hair color.

```
class Person
{

    // Class visible only within Person
    class Face
    {
        int _numberOfTeeth;
    }

    // Internal reference type instance called face
    Face _face;

    // and an encapsulated value type called hairColor
    String _hairColor;
}
```

Generalization, Specialization, and Initializers

The next few sections will focus on what is probably one of the most powerful features of object-oriented languages; these are generalization and polymorphism. We'll cover these in turn, starting with generalization.

Let's imagine the scenario where you want to create classes that model objects in the real world that have a certain amount of commonality. They may be distinct objects in their own right but share behavior or attributes with a more general object. To continue the Person example, you could model human beings (nothing like starting easily!), noting that instances of a human being can also be referred to as more specialized types of a *human* object such as a *man* or *women*. Yes, the gender would be different, but certain aspects would be common such as the facial attributes or the ability to perform actions such as talking (assuming that no disability is present).

So, let's start to model these classes in C#, as follows:

```csharp
enum Gender { Male=0, Female=1 }

class Male
{
    // Some common attributes
    int numberOfLegs;
    int numberOfArms;

    // Some specialized attributes
    Gender gender = Gender.Male;

}

class Female
{
    // Some common attributes
    int numberOfLegs;
    int numberOfArms;

    // Some specialized attributes
    Gender gender = Gender.Female;

}
```

If you can imagine the two classes being far more complex, you can see the amount of duplication that may occur. This is because, fundamentally, the Male and Female class instances share commonality with a more *generalized* object called Human. So, using the object-oriented features of C#, you could represent the previous classes by first embracing the common elements into a generalized class called Human.

```csharp
public enum Gender { Unknown=0, Male=1, Female=2 }

public class Human
{
    // Default constructor
    public Human() {}

    // Specialized constructor
    public Human(Gender gender){ this.gender = gender; }

    // Some common attributes
    int numberOfLegs;
    int numberOfArms;
    public Gender gender;
}
```

You've now created the Human class with a default constructor that allows you to pass the gender of the human as a parameter, setting the internal gender attribute to the value passed. You now need to create the *specialized* Male and Female classes by denoting that the object inherits from the Human class. You do this on the class declaration line using the colon notation, like so:

```
public class Man : Human
{
}    // Man inherits from Human

public class Female : Human
{
}    // Female inherits from Human
```

Do you notice anything wrong? You have not told the class instances what gender they should be. (If you created an instance and output the value of the gender attribute, it would default to Unknown.) Semantically the two classes are the same, just as the objects instantiated from them would be, albeit they are based on different classes. But how do you indicate the gender when you aren't instantiating the class? In this instance, you can specify the constructor to use when creating an instance of this class—something called an *initializer*, or *instance constructor*. An instance constructor is added to a constructor method within your classes, so let's add a default constructor to the Male class but add an instance constructor with it by using a similar notation to inheritance, the colon. The syntax for the default instance constructor is as follows:

```
public Male() : base(Gender.Male) {}
```

I've highlighted in bold the instance constructor notation, which instructs the .NET runtime to call the class's base default constructor with the parameters passed, before the default constructor to which it is associated is called; this builds hierarchical objects from the ground up.

This example will call the Human(Gender) constructor first, passing Gender.Male as the enumerated value, after which the Male() default constructor will then be called. In addition to the obvious code rationalization benefits, this opens the door to polymorphism, which I'll discuss next.

Dynamic Method Behavior Through Polymorphism

The ability for a child class (a specialized or subclass) to inherit from a parent class (the generalized or superclass) provides the foundation for a method's behavior to reflect the class to which it belongs while still being associated with the parent class. This feature is called *polymorphism*, and as its names suggests, it allows a method's behavior to be polymorphic, depending on the context of the class. It's a difficult concept for some to grasp, so I'll demonstrate this using some concrete examples.

To continue with the Male and Female classes, you can identify some common behavior against these object types. For example, a human can speak and can get dressed. These are behavioral attributes normally associated with human beings, so you could create methods to represent these attributes, as shown here:

```
public void speak()
{
}

public void getdressed()
{
}
```

However, this is a good point to introduce some attributes that decorate methods for enabling the functionality discussed. Table 4-7 introduces these at a high level, and I'll elaborate in the sections following the table.

Table 4-7. *Method Decoration*

Keyword	Description
virtual	Declares that a method supports polymorphic behavior
override	Declares that you want to provide your own derived polymorphic behavior
new	Declares that you want to hide a virtual method
abstract	Declares that no implementation is provided within the class and thus cannot be instantiated

So, let's start at the beginning: in the Human class, you identified two methods that reflect behavior found in humans and that you want to support in your class. You can declare these within the Human class as shown previously; however, this would not allow you to provide a specific implementation in derived classes, namely, the Male and Female classes. To do this, you need to indicate that the methods have the ability to be polymorphic; that is, you can provide your own implementation in a derived class. Such methods are also referred to as *virtual* methods, and thus a C# keyword is provided for you to decorate your method with, indicating to the .NET runtime that a derived method may exist. The following code shows how to rewrite your methods as virtual methods:

```
public virtual void speak()
{
}

public virtual void getdressed()
{
}
```

Simple, eh? This will now allow derived classes to *override* the default behavior and provide their own behavior based on the context of the class, thus demonstrating the power of polymorphism. But what if it doesn't make sense for the parent class—in this case, the Human class—to provide a default implementation for a method? For example, in the example scenario, the default behavior for the speak() method may be to utter sounds, but the getdressed() method would not know what to do!

For the previous scenario, you can use the abstract keyword to indicate that no implementation is provided, although the behavior must be supported. This effectively means you have to derive from the class and provide your own implementation, and you cannot create an instance of an object based on the Human class. This is because it doesn't make sense, within the context of the base class, to provide any default implementation, and hence it's marked as abstract. The following code shows how to rewrite the virtual methods to indicate this:

```
public virtual void speak()
{
}

public abstract void getdressed()
{
}
```

You should notice that you replace the virtual keyword with the abstract keyword for the method that doesn't have a default implementation. By its nature, this means the method is virtual and *must* be overridden in derived classes.

The following is the Human class implementation, complete with the methods discussed and default behavior where appropriate:

```
public abstract class Human
{
  // Some common attributes
  int numberOfLegs;
  int numberOfArms;
  public Gender gender;

  // Default constructor
  public Human()
  {
  }

  // Specialized Constructor
  public Human(Gender gender)
  {
    this.gender = gender;
  }

  // Methods
  public virtual void speak()
  {
    Console.Out.WriteLine("make some sounds");
  }

  public abstract void getdressed();

}
```

As you can see from the changes, you provide a declaration for the nonabstract method, decorating each method as appropriate. You also indicate that the class is abstract because it contains one (or more) abstract methods. If you don't make this decoration, the compiler will refuse to compile the code, stating that the class is not abstract. So, you can continue to provide specific implementations for these methods using the override keyword as follows for the Male class:

```csharp
public class Male : Human
{

  public Male() : base(Gender.Male)
  {
  }

  public override void speak()
  {
    Console.Out.WriteLine("Hello! << in a gruff male voice >>");
  }

  public override void getdressed()
  {
    Console.Out.WriteLine("Put on shirt, boxers, and trousers.");
  }

}
```

And you can use the same for the Female class:

```csharp
public class Female : Human
{

  public override void speak()
  {
    Console.Out.WriteLine("Hello! << in a soft feminine voice >>");
  }

  public override void getdressed()
  {
    Console.Out.WriteLine("Put on bra, blouse, knickers, and ➡
skirt (or trousers).");
  }

}
```

If you test this by instantiating objects of type Male and Female and calling the methods in turn, you should see the specific behavior being called. You can use some test code similar to this:

```
public void main(string[] args)
{

  Male mark = new Male();
  Female rachel = new Female();

  // First MARK
  Console.Out.WriteLine("mark's gender is " + mark.gender);
  mark.speak();
  mark.getdressed();

  // Then RACHEL
  Console.Out.WriteLine("rachel's gender is " + rachel.gender);
  rachel.speak();
  rachel.getdressed();

}
```

The output should look something like this:

```
mark's gender is Male
Hello! << in a gruff male voice >>
Put on Shirt, Boxers, and Trousers.
rachel's gender is Female
Hello! << in a soft feminine voice >>
Put on bra, blouse, knickers, and skirt (or trousers).
```

Another powerful feature associated with polymorphism is that you could create an array of objects that are of type Human but that point to specialized instances of a Human such as a Male or Female. You could then cycle through your array-calling methods, which would actually exhibit the behavior of the specific class. The method name would be the same, but the behavior, because of its specific implementation, is different. Play with this!

Implementing and Using Interfaces

In the same way that methods denote behavior and usually (with the exception of abstract methods) provide an implementation, an *interface* is a reference type that declares behavior but exclusively through abstract methods—its provides *no* implementation.

It has other restrictions: an interface cannot contact constants, data fields, constructors, destructors, or static members. It is a pure definition of behavior—a kind of contract that states any class that subscribes to it will realize its implementation. I'll now discuss a real-world example before attempting to define this within code. If you take electronic devices that can play music (MP3, cassettes, and CDs) and video (VCR, MP4, DVD, and so on), then you can define some collective behavior that they all share. For example, they would all support the following behavior: Play, Fast Forward, Rewind, and Stop. So, you could group this behavior in an interface for any class to inherit and implement. The following is the example code:

```
interface IPlayer
{
    void Play();
    void Stop();
    void Rewind();
    void FastForward();
}
```

First, you are able to call the class whatever you want, but an "unofficial" industry standard is to prefix your interface name with a capital *I*. Hence, this class is called IPlayer. Second, you'll notice the declaration of methods but with no implementation; this is because the implementation is provided within the class that inherits from the interface and implements it.

You are now able to inherit from the interface and provide implementation (remember, this is also called *realizing*) relative to the class, like so:

```
public class MP3Player : IPlayer
{
    public void Play()
    {
        // Play music here
    }

    public void Stop()
    {
        // Stop music from playing here
    }

    public void Rewind()
    {
        // MP3s may not support rewinding, so this may go to the previous track
    }

    public void FastForward()
    {
        // MP3s may not support rewinding, so this may go to the next track
    }
}
```

Another benefit of using interfaces is that your class can inherit from more than one interface, thus achieving *multiple inheritance* but in a controlled and structured manner. Table 4-8 summarizes some of the key differences between using interfaces and classes for inheritance.

To summarize, you can group a collection of associated behavior and refer to the group by name. This creates a contract that an object may subscribe to and implement and therefore offer its own implementation. Imagine consequently that a collection of objects may all exhibit similar behavior and so realize a specific interface, allowing your classes to automatically detect this and utilize it or for you to programmatically detect this using reflection (covered in more detail in Chapter 12).

Table 4-8. *Interface and Class Comparison*

Functionality	Supported in Class?	Supported in Interface?
Provide implementation	Yes	No
Multiple inheritance	No	Yes
Static members	Yes	No
Constructors/destructors	Yes	No
Data fields	Yes	No
Defines behavior	Yes	Yes

Understanding Events and Delegates

Events and delegates are a complex topic, and therefore this section of the book introduces the concepts for you to then experiment with in more detail. I'll be using these concepts within the book project, the RSS aggregator.

An *event* is a way in which a class can provide notifications to a user of a class; this is called *firing* an event. As you are probably aware, thousands of events are being fired on your machine right now. Every time you move your mouse, an event is fired indicating that your mouse has moved and its on-screen location should be updated. A *delegate* is a reference type that has a specific signature and return type; it acts as a middleman (an intermediary) between the event source (from where it is being fired) to the event destination (from where it is received). You will notice that events and delegates are therefore related; the method that is called when an event is fired can be encapsulated using a delegate, and the event provides the mechanism for the methods to be invoked.

The best way to visualize the two is via an example; let's start with a simple example that defines a delegate. The delegate simply accepts a method that can display a string, and you use this to call the method, outputting the string accordingly. (After this example, I'll then demonstrate the concept within a more detailed example.) For the simple example, define the delegate's declaration and implementation as follows:

```
// Declaration
public delegate void StringOutputDelegate (string name);
```

This example therefore reflects a method with a signature that returns nothing and receives a string as a parameter. This delegate declaration could be defined to point to *any* method, provided it has a matching signature. This is similar to a function pointer in a language such as C or C++. In a simple example, you could define a method with the following matching signature:

```
// Implementation
public static void SayHelloToSomebody (string name)
{
    Console.Out.WriteLine("Hello {0}", name);
}
```

Using this delegate, you can define an instance of a delegate, passing the previously defined method and invoking it, which will execute the method's implementation.

```
// Define and instantiate an instance of our delegate
StringOutputDelegate  hello;
hello = new StringOutputDelegate(SayHelloToSomebody);

// and invoke it
hello("mark");
```

The output will look something like this:

```
Hello mark
```

You can even use the + notation to chain delegates together; for example, you can create a delegate that will actually invoke the same method twice, as follows:

```
StringOutputDelegate  sayhellotwice;
sayhellotwice = hello + hello;

// invoke it
Hello("mark");
```

This will repeat the output, as follows:

```
Hello mark
Hello mark
```

Now that I've touched on delegates, I'll cover how to integrate events into the equation. I'll elaborate on the concept of delegates with a more comprehensive example by still using a delegate but creating an event that fires the delegate. In this scenario, you'll create a new delegate that allows you to implement a change notification system. First, define the delegate as follows:

```
public delegate void ChangedEventHandler(object sender, EventArgs e);
```

Then define the following event that a client can use to inform you of a change:

```
public event ChangedEventHandler changed;
```

Then, in the client code, you can declare the following method that is used to fire the event:

```
public void OnChange(EventArgs e)
{
    if (changed != null)
        changed(this, e);      // Pass the client reference
}
```

And finally within the code, you can fire the event when appropriate:

```
OnChange(EventArgs.Empty);
```

The topic of events and delegates is fairly complex, so I suggest you refer to the documentation and examples in order to help solidify your knowledge. In addition to this, the book's project will include examples of events and delegates for its user interface component; this will provide a valuable context around which you can validate your knowledge. Listing 4-8 provides a practical example of how events and delegates are used within .NET, especially for user interfaces that want to trap the user interaction.

Listing 4-8. *News Channel Example*

```csharp
using System;



// Delegate for the news channel
public delegate void NewsChangeEventHandler(string news);



// Class that records the latest news headline
public class NewsChannel
{

  // Last news item (stops repeats)
  private string newsHeadline;

  // Event fired on a change of news
  public event NewsChangeEventHandler LatestNewsChange;

  // News property
  public string LatestNewsHeadline
  {
    // Set the news headline
    set
    {
      if (newsHeadline != value)
      {
        LatestNewsChange(value);
        newsHeadline= value;
      }
    }
  }
}
```

```csharp
// A class representing somebody watching the channel
public class NewsChannel_Watcher
{
  private string _name;

  public NewsChannel_Watcher(NewsChannel  nh, string name)
  {
    _name = name;
    nh.LatestNewsChange += new NewsChangeEventHandler(NewsChanged_Event);
  }

  // Event fires, show latest news
  private void NewsChanged_Event(string news)
  {
    Console.Out.WriteLine(_name + " is informed of " + news);
  }
}


// Testbed
class Test
{
  static void Main(string[] args)
  {
    // A single news channel
    NewsChannel n = new NewsChannel();

    // Setup all of the viewers
    NewsChannel_Watcher nick = new NewsChannel_Watcher(n, "nick");
    NewsChannel_Watcher ashley = new NewsChannel_Watcher(n, "ashley");
    NewsChannel_Watcher emma = new NewsChannel_Watcher(n, "emma");
    NewsChannel_Watcher megan = new NewsChannel_Watcher(n, "megan");

    // Publish a news item
    n.LatestNewsHeadline = "mark buys a drink";

  }

}
```

The example starts by defining a delegate that represents the publication of a news headline, which simply receives the news headline as a string. You then set up a NewsChannel class, which has an event that is fired when a new headline is published using the property LatestNewsHeadline. A person watching the news channel is then represented by the NewsChannel_Watcher class, which records the name of the person but also passes a pointer to the NewsChannel class. You can then add a pointer to an event that is fired by the news channel whenever the news headline changes.

In this example, the NewsChannel class is created and four arbitrary viewers are created, passing the NewsChannel instance in its constructor along with a name to identify each class instance. You then change the NewsChannel class's latest headline, which fires the event for all the news watchers. This is a well-known concept called *publish-subscribe*, allowing multiple subscribers to watch a publication and be informed of changes.

Handling Your Errors Through Exceptions

It's a fact of life in the development world—at some point your carefully crafted code will encounter an error. This may be of your own making or be because of circumstances beyond your control, but in either case your code should behave defensively and handle errors as elegantly as possible. In such circumstances, the code you are writing or using will often use *exceptions* to signal that an error has been encountered. In the next sections, I'll discuss the method for catching and handling such exceptions, plus the ability to throw your own exceptions to signal an error.

Catching Exceptions

The first step is to understand how you intercept (or *catch*) an exception and handle it. Therefore, consider this fragment of code:

```
try
{
  // Execute code here
}
catch(Exception e)
{
  // Exception-handling code here
}
finally
{
  // Exception tidy-up code here
}
```

I'll discuss each section in turn, starting with the try {} block. This block encapsulates the code that is to be executed and for which exceptions should be trapped. If an exception is raised, this will first be presented to the catch() {} block and then lastly to the finally {} block, if present (note that the finally {} block is optional).

If an exception is encountered, the code will jump to the catch() {} block and look for an exception that matches (or is related to the hierarchy of) the exception being thrown. For example, if your exception is a derived exception such as DivideByZeroException and your catch() {} block specifically looked for this type, the catch() {} code would be implemented. If your exception was not directly defined within the catch() {} block but was related by inheritance, then this would also be caught in the appropriate block. For example, if you caught exceptions of type Exception, because all exceptions inherit from this base class, all would be caught. Finally, an empty catch() {} block with no exception reference would catch all exceptions. To confirm this, the following catch() {} blocks would all catch a divide-by-zero exception:

```
catch(DivideByZeroException e)
{}

catch(Exception e)
{}

catch
{}
```

The ability to capture more than one exception in a block is possible by defining more than one catch() {} block. In this instance, you would define your more specialized catch() {} blocks first, and these are then checked in order, defaulting to a matching generalized catch() {} block if no specialized blocks exist. If you consider the previous catch() {} blocks as part of a single try{} statement, the program would check each block in turn and eventually fall into the catch() {} block at the end if no matches are found.

The last feature to discuss is the finally {} block, which allows you to provide cleanup code associated with the exception that has been caught. A good example of its use is when you are dealing with a connection, whether that be for a file, a database, or any resource that should be cleaned up in the event of an error. If you attempt to open a database, then you should always remember to close the database connection, even if an exception was thrown and you were unable to complete the processing required. You can use the finally {} block to good effect in this scenario, as follows:

```
sqlconnection conn = null;
try
{
    // open database connection
    conn = new sqlconnection("dsn");

    // do some work that may thrown an exception
}
catch
{
    // handle exceptions
}
finally
{
    // close the network connection
    if (conn != null)
        conn.dispose();    // this will automatically close the connection
}
```

Throwing Exceptions

The process of throwing an exception is pretty straightforward and should be used to indicate an error in exceptional cases only. In fact, exceptions should not be raised for problems that you may expect and mitigate. For example, if your code checks for the existence of a file and will do one of two actions depending on whether it exists, then you shouldn't use exceptions to indicate it doesn't exist. You should use simple programmatic tests to look for the existence of a file. If, however, your code expects a file to exist and it doesn't, then something has seriously gone wrong. Therefore, the inability for your code to continue would be considered exceptional, so you should raise an exception.

Raising an exception is known as *throwing* an exception and is done using the throw keyword. All exceptions inherit from the base Exception class, and this includes the .NET Framework–provided exceptions such as DivideByZeroException or OutOfMemoryException and your own. The .NET Framework exceptions will be thrown automatically by the .NET Framework class library. You can choose to handle the exception, or you can choose to rethrow the exception back to a higher context using the throw keyword on its own or leave it to be automatically passed up the stack if you haven't caught it. Listing 4-9 demonstrates this last scenario.

Listing 4-9. *Exception Example*

```
using System;

class Dummy
{
  public void DivideBy(int val)
  {
    try
    {
      // If I pass a value of 1, throw a custom exception
      if (val == 1)
          throw new Exception("My Custom Exception");

      // Perform a division
      int aValue = 10 / val;
      Console.Out.WriteLine("10 / " + val + " = " + aValue);
    }
    catch(DivideByZeroException e)
    {
      Console.Out.WriteLine("In Dummy.DivideBy() (Level 1): Exception [" + ➥
e.Message + "]");
    }
  }
}

class Test
{
  static void Main()
  {


    Dummy d = new Dummy();
```

```
    try
    {
        // Main Loop
        d.DivideBy(2);  // Should be OK
        d.DivideBy(0);  // Should throw a divide-by-zero exception, caught ➡
higher up in a custom
        d.DivideBy(1);  // Should throw a custom exception but catch it ➡
within the Dummy class

    }
    catch (Exception e)
    {
        Console.Out.WriteLine("In Main() (Level 0): Exception [" + e.Message + "]");
    }
  }

}
```

In Listing 4-9, you have a class that exposes a method for performing division by the number passed. You can make this throw a DivideByZero error by passing a zero value or a delta value that triggers a custom exception, as done in the example. The DivideByZero exception is handled locally, because there is an exception block for it; however, any unhandled exception is passed back up the stack and caught with the higher exception block. This is shown by calling the Dummy class method three times: once successfully, a second time to simulate a local exception, and a final time to trigger a locally unhandled exception. So, the output is as follows:

```
10 / 2 = 5
In Dummy.DivideBy() (Level 1): Exception [Division by zero]
In Main() (Level 0): Exception [My Custom Exception]
```

If you want to be able to define and throw your own exceptions for other people to trap and use, then you can simply define your own exception but inherit from the existing Exception class or one of its children or indeed wrap some simple text within the System.Exception class's custom constructor. An example of throwing a custom exception is shown here:

```
// Declare your own exception
class MyException : Exception
{
}

public static void Main(string[] args)
{
    int x = 1;
    int y=2;
```

```
    // Perform some comparison (obviously this will fail) and throw an exception
    if (x != y)
        throw new MyException();
}
```

Setting Scope Through Namespaces

Finally, I'll cover scope, something I touched on in the previous chapter through visibility modifiers. In this chapter, I'll cover how to set scope through *namespaces*. A namespace defines scope and allows you to organize your code into a block (referred to by the namespace's name) that is identified by a unique name. The name associated with a namespace can be any legal identifier and can include periods. If you don't define a namespace, then one is provided by default; therefore, at a semantic level, all your type declarations belong to a namespace that is either the default one or one defined by you.

You can use the namespace, once defined, to encapsulate the following types:

- Class

- Interface

- Struct

- Enum

- Delegate

- Another namespace

Defining a Namespace

In a way, a namespace is similar to an Internet domain name. It's a unique identifier, so you could create a namespace related to the domain you own, knowing that it will be unique. The following example uses the namespace keyword to create a namespace based around my domain name:

```
namespace mamone.org
{
  // Declarations go here
}
```

You can nest namespaces, defining one within this namespace, which is referred to as a *nested namespace*. For example:

```
namespace mamone.org
{

  // Declarations go here
 namespace AnotherNamespace
  {
    // or here
  }
}
```

A more common approach to namespaces is to use a period to define the individual blocks; a good example is for those that exist within the .NET Framework. Let's say I want to create a framework of code that implements a multiple-tiered architecture with the following tiers:

- User interface tier

- Business tier

- Data tier

I could use the following namespace convention in conjunction with my domain name to ensure uniqueness and to provide a logical separation of scope:

```
namespace userinterface.mamone.org
{
    // User interface-based components and namespaces would go here
}

namespace business.mamone.org
{
    // Business-based components and namespaces would go here
}

namespace data.mamone.org
{
    // Data-based components and namespaces would go here
}
```

Using a Namespace

Once you have defined your own namespace, or you know of a namespace you want to use, you then need to reference the types that exist within it. You can do this in one of two ways, explicitly or relatively. The explicit method involves the need to fully qualify each type that you want to access, so in the example of the previous namespace for data-based components and the existence of a DataAccessLayer type, you could use the following notation:

```
data.mamone.org.DataAccessLayer dal = new data.mamone.org.DataAccessLayer()
```

This is long-winded and, as you can imagine, does not lead to readable code. Therefore, the C# language introduces a keyword called using that allows you to define a namespace that the .NET runtime should automatically look for by default in order to resolve a type declaration. Instead of the previous example, you could use this keyword to save typing a lot of code, as follows:

```
using data.mamone.org;
DataAccessLayer dal = new DataAccessLayer();
```

And it's almost certain that you will have more than one namespace you'll want to use, so you can use more than one using keyword at the beginning of your code. If I assume you want to use the system namespace as well as my own namespace, the code would be as follows:

```
using System;
using data.mamone.org;

DataAccessLayer dal = new DataAccessLayer();
Console.Out.WriteLine("finished");  // from the System.Console type
```

What's New in .NET 2.0?

Now I'll provide a brief overview of some of the features introduced within the latest version of C# in .NET, version 2.0. This will, however, mean that some of the elements may still be in development within the open-source community and therefore may not be fully implemented when you attempt to use them. Therefore, you should always check that the feature has been implemented and works to your satisfaction.

Partial Types

One of the new features in .NET 2.0 is the ability to split the definition and implementation of classes across multiple files using partial types (in this example, a partial class). If a class has two methods that are physically implemented within two different files, you can bring them together at compilation time to present a single class. Listing 4-10 and Listing 4-11 present a part definition and implementation for a method; the class is also marked as partial.

Listing 4-10. *Partial Class Segment 1*

```
using System;

public partial class MyClass
{
  public void MethodA()
  {
    Console.Out.WriteLine("MethodA called");
  }
}
```

Listing 4-11. *Partial Class Segment 2*

```
using System;

public partial class MyClass
{
  public void MethodB()
  {
    Console.Out.WriteLine("MethodB called");
  }
}
```

You could then define these classes within different physical files and resolve the references at compilation time. This can then use all the methods defined within the partial class, as shown in Listing 4-12.

Listing 4-12. *Using a Partial Class*

```
using System;

class Test
{
  static void Main(string[] args)
  {
    MyClass aClass = new MyClass();
    aClass.MethodA();
    aClass.MethodB();
  }
}
```

This feature adds little more than convenience and is particularly used to encapsulate all the automatically generated code into a custom file, which would then leave you with another file with only your code within it.

Generics

The concept of a *generic* is similar to the concept of templates within the C++ language. Generics allow you to generalize the implementation within code at design time and then allow the compiler to specialize the code depending on the types being used at runtime. For example, you could write a generic collection class to handle an array of objects using the generics feature, as shown in Listing 4-13.

Listing 4-13. *Generics Example*

```
using System;

class MyCollection<ItemType>
{
    private const int MAX = 10;
    private ItemType[] items = new ItemType[MAX];
    private int count = 0;

    public void Add(ItemType item)
{
        if (count < MAX)
            items[count++] = item;
        else
            throw new Exception("Error: Collection is Full");
    }
```

```
public ItemType GetItem(int index)
{
        if (index < count && index >= 0)
            return items[index];
        else
            throw new Exception("Error: Invalid index");
    }
}
```

You could then extend this to provide specialized collections for different types (that is, int, string, and so on) at runtime. The following example shows how you can use this to provide specialized implementations of the generic template:

```
Using System;

class Test
{
  static void Main(string[] args)
  {
    MyIntCollection<int> ic = new MyIntCollection<int>();
    c.Add(4);
    c.Add(102);


    MyStringCollection<int> sc = new MyStringCollection<int>();
    sc.Add("Mark");
    sc.Add("Mamone");

  }
}
```

■**Note** To use generics in the version of Mono available at the time of writing, you must compile your code using the gmcs command line rather than the usual mcs command line.

Other Features

The following sections introduce some (but not all) of the other features introduced in version 2.0 of the framework.

Nullable Types

A *nullable type* is new to version 2.x of .NET; it allows a value type to hold a null value, which is something that wasn't possible within .NET 1.x. For example, you may want to make a boolean selection, either true or false, but also allow an undecided value, which could be null. This is possible by simply adding ? after the type and before its definition. Listing 4-14 shows how to implement the boolean concept described.

Listing 4-14. *Nullable Type Example*

```
using System;

class Test
{
  static void Main(string[] args)
  {

    bool? aChoice;
    aChoice = true;
    aChoice = false;
    aChoice = null;
  }
}
```

Static Classes

A *static class* is now supported and defines a class whose members are all static and is not instantiated. A good use for static classes is for a helper class that continues utility methods or attributes. Listing 4-15 demonstrates this.

Listing 4-15. *Static Class Example*

```
using System;

public static class MathematicsHelper
{
  // Simple method to return highest value
  // of two value passed
  public static int returnHigher(int a, int b)
  {
    if (a>b)
      return a;
    else
      return b;
  }
}

class Test
{
  static void Main(string[] args)
  {
```

```
    // The next line will not compile, comment
    // it out to test the next bit
    MathematicsHelpera = new MathematicsHelper();

    // This next block will work
    int b = 10;
    int c = 20;
    int highest = MathematicsHelper.returnHigher(b,c);
    Console.Out.WriteLine("Highest between {0} and {1} is {2}.", b,c,highest);

  }
}
```

This example demonstrates how the compiler will prevent a static class from being instantiated at compile time and will also automatically apply a static declaration to any member where a class is defined as static. Using static classes is useful for helper classes, as you've seen by defining and using a simple method to return the highest number of any two numbers passed.

Accessor Accessibility

You may remember that when defining accessor methods (that is, set and get) within a class, they both have a scope of public (its default accessibility value) and cannot be changed. However, you are now able to define the scope for these accessor methods individually, providing a far more flexible property system. So, you can have the following scenario:

```
public int Age
{
  get { return _age; }
  protected set { _age = value; }
}
```

This will mean that *any* object could access the Age property value, but only the class and its descendants could set its value.

Anonymous Methods

Anonymous methods are useful when dealing within delegate methods; they allow your class to define a method using the delegate keyword and not commit to a specific method name, just its implementation. So, in version 1.*x* of C#, you need to define a delegate and then a method by using the same signature, creating an instance of the delegate and passing the method's name. In version 2.*x* of C#, you can define the delegate with an implementation and not provide a method name, as follows:

```
class Test
{
  delegate void ADelegate();
  ADelegate d = delegate() { return "Anonymous Delegate"; }
}
```

Iterators

The *iterator* feature enables your application to loop through user-defined data types with the C# using the foreach loop keyword. In version 1.*x* of .NET, to achieve this you'll need to implement the IEnumerable interface, which contains only a single method, GetEnumerator(). This method returns an object of type IEnumerator. The IEnumerator interface contains one public property, Current, and two public methods, MoveNext() and Reset(). Whilst this isn't too time-consuming, it's even easier in version 2.0; you just need to write a method named GetEnumerator() with the IEnumerator return type in your class, and your class will be eligible to be iterated through the foreach loop. It will iterate the foreach loop the number of times the runtime finds the yield return keyword. Listing 4-16 demonstrates this.

Listing 4-16. *Iterator Example*

```
using System;

public class MyCollection
{

  string name = "Mark";
  string surname = "Mamone";
  string age = "36";

  public IEnumerator<string> GetEnumerator()
  {
    yield return name;
    yield return surname;
    yield return age;
  }

}

class Test
{
  static void Main(string[] args)
  {

    MyCollection m = new MyCollection();
    foreach (string s in m)
    {
      Console.Out.WriteLine(s);
    }

  }
}
```

In Listing 4-16, you simply create a class that contains some arbitrary members, in this case my first name, surname, and age. You can then write an Iterator method that will enable the user of the class to iterate through its members; I've highlighted in bold this method for clarity. As you can see in the Test class, you can instantiate an instance of the class and iterate through its members using the foreach keyword, outputting the values. The results are code that is fast, easy to read, and elegant.

Summary

In this chapter, I discussed some advanced topics and constructs within the C# language, although I have still only scratched the surface. As you can imagine, this is a huge topic that is covered by a plethora of books and documentation.

I introduced the concept of class and struct reference types, exploring the possibilities within them, such as member variables, fields, attributes, and properties. You learned how you can implement behavior using operations or methods. You looked at operators, including the ability for you to customize the behavior associated with them. I introduced the advanced topic of generalized and specialized classes and touched on the ability to define polymorphic operations. In addition, I introduced contractual behavior through interfaces that define abstract behavior in relation to polymorphic operations. Finally, I discussed how exceptions could be thrown, trapped, and handled to produce safe and defensive code. I also described the purpose and usage of namespaces to define and limit scope, extending the topic of visibility modifiers that I previously discussed.

You should now have a foundation in the C# language, and I encourage you to experiment with the features discussed. The next chapter will introduce the core features of the .NET Framework, completing the foundations necessary to start using this knowledge in developing the RSS aggregator, which is this book's project.

Summary

CHAPTER 5

■ ■ ■

Exploring the .NET Core

Chapter 1 introduced the core components in the .NET Framework, including the compiler, the class library, and the framework tools. You then learned how to install both Mono and the MonoDevelop IDE, and you received a thorough introduction to the C# language. In this chapter, I will complete your fundamental course in .NET by delving into some of these core components, and some additional ones, in more detail. This will leave you with sufficient knowledge to explore .NET on your own and will allow you to use this knowledge to start developing the RSS aggregator using some of the framework features available for graphical user interfaces, data access, networking, and much more.

Specifically, in this chapter, you'll closely examine the CLR's purpose. I'll describe how applications consist of assemblies and how they all run within the confines of the CLR and benefit from the features it provides. You'll learn how .NET handles memory management, how code is executed within the CLR, and ultimately how you use the .NET Framework to build applications, including this book's RSS aggregator project (which you'll start in Chapter 6).

Going Deeper into the Common Language Runtime (CLR)

Chapter 1 briefly introduced the CLR. You'll now delve deeper into exactly what the CLR is and what it encompasses. Essentially, the CLR is an engine that is responsible for runtime services such as managing and executing code, implementing security, managing memory, and more. Figure 5-1 shows some of the main CLR components and the path of a .NET executable once the system has been asked to execute it.

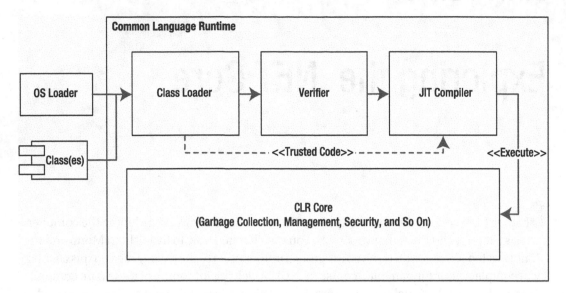

Figure 5-1. *The CLR*

I'll now elaborate on the key components of the CLR, discussing the role they play and how they work in tandem to provide a rich runtime environment. The key components within the CLR are as follows:

- Portable Executable (PE) file format

- Metadata

- IL

- Class loader

- Verifier

- JIT compiler

- CLR core

After providing an overview of these elements, I'll cover how you can create your own assembly and execute it using these components. In doing this, I'll describe how an application is loaded, how references are resolved, and how memory is managed. These are complex topics and ones that for the most part are handled automatically for you by the .NET Framework and its components. However, a good understanding and appreciation of the work that is being performed for you will help you design applications that are respectful of the tasks being carried out by the CLR and that ultimately perform more efficiently and with greater speed.

Portable Executable (PE) File

The Windows operating system enforces a standard known as the Common Object File Format (COFF) from which the PE file format is derived. This provides a standard through which the operating system can load and run executables (EXEs) and DLLs. The PE file contains a number of sections that hold resources, data, and code, and it is by extending these sections that the CLR now includes additional sections for metadata and IL. The CLR uses these two additional sections to provide support information for loading and compiling the platform-independent IL code into native (machine-specific) executable code.

The fact that Mono is targeting operating systems other than Windows may cause you some confusion; for example, how are executables invoked in a non-Windows environment? Despite being derived from a Windows-based format, the PE file is in fact pretty platform neutral. It does include a specific byte sequence for its entry point that allows Windows operating systems to execute the code; however, this is being phased out in favor of the operating system knowing how to support, or installing extensions to support, the execution of .NET-based code, as is the case for Mono on Linux and the PowerPC.

This is a fairly advanced topic, so don't be too worried if you don't grasp this concept the first time. A deep understanding is not necessary, but background information on why the CLR uses the PE file format is useful and so is provided for that reason only.

Metadata

Metadata is a description of data that the .NET Framework uses to provide information about components and their resources. For example, an assembly contains types that are exposed by the assembly, and metadata provides information about the types the assembly exposes. This information includes the modules contained within an assembly; the classes and interfaces it may contain; the methods, properties, fields and events, and so on, within these classes; and much more. An example of a .NET Framework component that requires, seeks, and uses this information is the class loader for when classes are loaded into the framework. In this respect, metadata is not a new concept; the Interface Definition Language (IDL) has been describing components and their interfaces/types for some time with Microsoft's COM and the Common Object Request Broker (CORBA) technologies. The same is true of *type libraries*, which describe the types that are exposed within a given library, but for both IDLs and type libraries, one thing is common—they all require an external resource that is in addition to the resource being described. So, taking the example of a type library, you not only need the library itself (such as a DLL) but also need a type library to understand its concept. This is not the case with .NET. The metadata is stored with the actual data, so the two go hand in hand.

The presence of metadata also helps the .NET Framework overcome a common problem that existed within the Windows operating system known as *DLL hell*. This demonstrated the problem of different applications requiring external code held in DLLs (similar to shared objects in Unix/Linux). These DLLs often had the same filename but could contain different versions of code, so applications failed to work because they depended on a specific version of code that had changed.

Associating metadata with an application and its assemblies means that these components can be installed side by side (with different names and/or locations, though). The CLR will load the appropriate files based on the version information it also contains. This has helped solve DLL hell in the Windows operating system and made deploying applications with their associated components far easier. The presence of this information also provides the following benefits:

- Promotes self-describing applications

- Enforces component versioning

- Isolates applications

I'll now elaborate on these benefits.

Promotes Self-describing Applications

An application that holds information about itself and its dependency on external components means that it no longer relies on external information stores such as the Windows registry. This also helps simplify installing and removing applications.

Enforces Component Version

Providing versioning control and descriptions within the framework avoids the mismatch of components whilst loading. The .NET Framework provides this version enforcement.

Isolates Application

The ability to install applications and components side by side means that applications can be isolated from one another, with changes made to one while not impacting the other. This is a common problem when deploying components that may be in use by one or more applications or components.

Intermediate Language (IL)

IL, sometimes called *MSIL code* (pronounced "missile" because of its connotations with speed), is a high-level, platform-agnostic language. This isn't a new concept; for instance, the Java language has *bytecode* that is an intermediate language that the Java Virtual Machine (JVM) understands and can execute. In this context, the CLR is similar in nature to the JVM but is far more powerful in terms of functionality and speed, with IL providing the ability for it to be compiled to native code and executed. This *abstraction* is documented within the ECMA CLI specification and provides a language that supports true object-oriented features such as abstraction, inheritance, and overloading. The .NET compilers take any language that has been written for the .NET environment (including C#, C++, Visual Basic, Java, Pascal, Cobol, among others) and compiles it into IL and then to executable native code by the JIT. This allows you to write your .NET application in any .NET-conformant language, including directly into IL (which is somewhat similar to x86 assembler).

The .NET Framework ships with the Microsoft Intermediate Language Disassembler (ILDASM), which can interpret IL code and disassemble it into a textual representation that is more easily understood. In the Mono framework, the ILDASM tool is called monodis and behaves similarly; it can be executed at the command line, as shown here using the HelloWorld example from Chapter 1:

```
monodis --output=helloworld.asm helloworld.exe
```

If successful, this will then produce a file called helloworld.asm, which will contain the disassembled HelloWorld executable that shows the textual representation of IL. Listing 5-1 displays the contents of helloworld.asm.

Listing 5-1. *helloworld.asm*

```
.assembly extern mscorlib
{
  .ver 1:0:5000:0
  .publickeytoken = (B7 7A 5C 56 19 34 E0 89 ) // .z\V.4..
}
.assembly 'helloworld'
{
  .hash algorithm 0x00008004
  .ver  0:0:0:0
}
.module helloworld.exe // GUID = {3BC6A1DB-5173-44A4-8AA4-E290A5C99C66}


  .class public auto ansi beforefieldinit HelloWorld
                 extends [mscorlib]System.Object
  {

    // method line 1
    .method public hidebysig  specialname  rtspecialname
          instance default void .ctor ()  cil managed
    {
        // Method begins at RVA 0x20ec
        // Code size 7 (0x7)
        .maxstack 8
        IL_0000:  ldarg.0
        IL_0001:  call instance void object::.ctor()
        IL_0006:  ret
    } // end of method HelloWorld::instance default void .ctor ()

    // method line 2
    .method public static  hidebysig
          default void Main (string[] args)  cil managed
    {
        // Method begins at RVA 0x20f4
        .entrypoint
        // Code size 16 (0x10)
        .maxstack 8
        IL_0000:  call class [mscorlib]System.IO.TextWriter class [mscorlib]➥
        System.Console::get_Out()
        IL_0005:  ldstr "Hello World!"
        IL_000a:  callvirt instance void class [mscorlib]➥
        System.IO.TextWriter::WriteLine(string)
        IL_000f:  ret
    } // end of method HelloWorld::default void Main (string[] args)


  } // end of class HelloWorld
```

I won't delve into the inner workings or representation of IL, but even with little knowledge of the subject, it's not too difficult to follow. Those of you with some assembly background may notice the similarities; I've highlighted in bold the implementation within the `Main()` function to help.

So, once you have written your application and it has been compiled into an assembly whose code is written in IL, it's the job of the class loader to physically load the files referenced into memory and get them ready for execution where appropriate.

Class Loader

The *class loader* component of the .NET Framework manages the loading of IL code and its associated metadata. It also manages when the JIT compiler will execute the containing code. This is an important and complex task, so the class loader is dedicated to performing this job as part of the .NET Framework. It is therefore responsible for loading the actual code and loading dependent classes such as those referenced in external assembles and those inherited through the use of object-oriented features.

Let's look at a specific example of an application executing on the Windows operating system (OS). The OS automatically loads this into memory before beginning execution at the specified entry point. The limitation of the OS loader for these operating systems is, as you would expect, limited to PE files specific to the Windows operating system. This OS loader has been updated for these operating systems to support the .NET Framework and as such the .NET PE file format. In this instance, control passes to the CLR, which locates the executing assembly's entry point and thus is able to start executing the assembly. To do this, though, the classes referenced, including the one containing the entry point, must be loaded into memory and, if being referenced for the first time, must be compiled. The JIT compiler handles this compilation, but the class loader must first be able to locate the class, ensure it has the knowledge of the memory required to instantiate the class, and insert some code stubs to ensure that types that have been referenced more than once are subsequently loaded from the cache for performance.

Once the class has been loaded and security verified, including the verification of access rules for classes and interfaces, the next step is to ensure that the code is valid and type safe. This is the job of the verifier, the component of the CLR I'll describe next.

Verifier

Historically, type safety has varied among programming languages. Chapter 3 introduced *type safety*, which ensures that the use of a given type, either reference or value, is as intended and thus helps avoid errors introduced as a result. As mentioned, the class loader is responsible for loading the class and its code, and the *verifier* is then responsible for checking that the code is type safe and the metadata contained within it is valid. It isn't until the code passes these checks that the JIT compiler then takes control and compiles the code.

You may wonder whether this feature affects the performance of .NET code, especially as this takes place at runtime. It does in part, but several features are responsible for reducing this load. With the advances in JIT compilation, managed code running under .NET can often be just as fast as natively compiled code. These features include the ability for code to be compiled and verified only when first referenced, which results in delivering the performance of native code execution for code that has already been through this process. An additional feature is the ability to mark code as trusted and therefore avoid the verification process altogether.

Once the code has been verified, if necessary it is compiled using the JIT compiler, prior to being handed to the CLR core for execution. I'll cover the JIT compiler next.

Just-In-Time (JIT) Compiler

The JIT compiler is arguably the most important component within the CLR; its primary role is to compile the code as represented in IL into native code for execution. The JIT compiler will receive the code to compile only once it has been passed through the verifier for untrusted code or directly from the class loader in the case of trusted code. In either case, the performance of the JIT is further improved beyond its own optimization (which is extremely good) to include the ability to cache compiled code. This results in the JIT incurring the performance penalty associated with compiling code only when the IL code is first referenced; thereafter, the native code is provided from the cache, delivering near native execution speeds in a managed environment.

The JIT also has two other advantages:

- Performance

- Portability

I'll now provide a brief overview of why these are important.

Performance

A key benefit of using a JIT compiler is that your application is executed using native code, which on the Intel platform would be the x86 instruction set but with the benefits of being derived from portable IL, which is platform agnostic. You can further improve the performance of the JIT by precompiling the code during installation; doing this means the JIT wouldn't have to compile any code at all and would behave in the same manner as a native executable does today. In both cases, once the code is no longer needed and references to it have been destroyed, the garbage collector will automatically reclaim the memory used and then be ready for the next process. It should be noted, however, that the garbage collection is not immediate; unreferenced memory will be collected only when the garbage collector next runs.

Portability

The JIT compiler also promotes portability. The JIT compiler is platform/hardware specific because it takes the portable IL and compiles it into native code. Therefore, a JIT compiler is provided for a number of platform (such as Linux, Unix, Windows, and Mac OS) and CPU (such as Intel and Risc) combinations. This allows your IL code to be compiled to a native language and executed, with the caveat that the other CLR components are still required for tasks such as memory management.

Now you're at the point where your application code has been loaded, verified, and compiled (if necessary), so you are ready to start executing the code and performing all the tasks, such as memory management, associated with running an application. This is the responsibility of the CLR core.

CLR Core

Once the class loader has retrieved the necessary code, the verifier has ensured type safety (if required), and the JIT compiler has produced native code, then the CLR is ready to execute the code. This code is passed onto further processes that lie within the CLR and that implement other features required of .NET applications such as memory management, exception handling, and security. In addition to these, the CLR also provides you with the ability to debug your code and interoperability between managed code (.NET) and unmanaged code (non-.NET such as native C or C++). I'll start by introducing the two core units that form the foundation of any application written using .NET and for which the CLR is responsible for compiling:

- Assembly

- Module

An *assembly* is compiled code with a descriptive header associated with it known as a *manifest*; a *module* is a unit of executable code but without a manifest. A manifest contains metadata such as the assembly name, its version number, the culture (the international language it targets), and the security-related information such as an optional strong name (used by the CLR when loading code prior to its execution), exception handling, security support, debugging support, and interoperability.

Memory Management

A significant benefit of developing for and running within a managed environment such as .NET is the support for automatic memory management. This is provided within the CLR using the *garbage collector*, which manages objects and their memory for their lifetime within the CLR. This is in contrast to unmanaged languages such as C and C++, where it is the responsibility of the developer to ensure that all memory allocated is deallocated and thus made available to the system. A common problem in such environments is where memory is not deallocated because *memory leaks* occur, leading to memory being allocated and unable to be reallocated. Memory leaks are a thing of the past in managed environments! I'll discuss memory management in more detail in Chapter 12.

Exception Handling

In addition to being able to report errors by simply returning a known value that indicates the success or otherwise of a method, more recent languages such as C++ and Java have introduced exception handling as a standard part of the language. However, their implementations differ, and no single exception-handling mechanism exists for all of these languages. The .NET Framework includes exception handling that is standard across all .NET languages, allowing you to code in a standard manner and allowing exceptions to pass to and from code written in different languages within the CLR.

I covered the topic of exception handling in Chapter 4; refer to that chapter to understand how the .NET Framework, specifically the CLR, can enforce a common exception-handling framework across multiple languages.

Security

The security of your code is paramount, and the .NET Framework provides a number of features to help ensure this. One such feature I've already discussed is the verifier, which ensures all running code is type safe. In addition to this, .NET supports code access security, ensuring that entry to code can be secured against unauthorized access. This is built into the CLR and is a core part of the .NET Framework, not an add-on. You can also control security declaratively, which means you use attributes in code to indicate your intentions, or you can manage certain security features using configuration files.

Using Assemblies

An *assembly* supports a number of basic features, including versioning, deployment, security, and execution, through its ability to contain one or more units of IL code (called *modules*, covered in the next section). Each assembly includes metadata that provides information about the assembly and its contents. Collectively, this metadata is known as the *manifest*. An assembly can be private to a single application or can be shared by more than one application. In either case, an assembly that has been created at compile time is referred to as a *static assembly*. This is in contrast to an assembly that may have been created at runtime using reflection. These are called *dynamic assemblies*, although for the purposes of this book, I'll discuss only static assemblies.

This is an example of a manifest:

```
.assembly HelloWorld
{
    .hash algorithm 0x00008004
    .ver 1:0:0:0
}
```

■**Note** A dynamic assembly is created at runtime and so doesn't exist as an application on disk; you would need to remember to save this to disk if you wanted to keep it. A static assembly is, however, already on disk and can be reloaded at any time.

An application refers to its dependencies through its own manifest and therefore contains a section that lists the external references required by the code within it. The manifest also includes the following information:

- Identity information such as name, version, and culture

- Shared name in the case of shared assemblies

- Names of all modules contained within the assembly

- Encrypted hash to protect the assembly's integrity

- Information about classes their methods and properties

- Security details

The compiler automatically adds this information, and therefore these explicit references are not something you need to add yourself. In addition, the class loader automatically uses the manifest's information when the module is referenced.

Introducing Modules

A *module* is a subunit of an assembly, with an assembly containing one or more modules. A module is similar to a Windows DLL or a Linux/Unix shared library and contains executable code in the form of IL but not executable in its own right. An assembly therefore encapsulates one (a single-module assembly) or more modules (a multimodule assembly) and contains metadata describing itself and its contents (the modules). Like assembly metadata, this is known as a *manifest*. A module does not contain a manifest; this is reserved for the assembly. But this rule has an exception: if an assembly is executable rather than just dynamically loadable, the manifest will be located in the module that contains the entry point, which in turn is held within the assembly.

Creating an Assembly

You may not have noticed it, but you've already created an assembly. The infamous HelloWorld application written in Chapter 1 is probably one of the simplest .NET assemblies you'll ever create. Consider the following simplified HelloWorld code:

```
using System;
class HelloWorld
{
   public static void Main(string[] args)
  {
    Console.Out.WriteLine("Hello World");
  }
}
```

You can create a single-file assembly by using the command-line compiler, which will create an assembly with the same name as the source file but with an .exe extension. This is a single-file assembly because it is based on a single source file (or module) and has an entry point, in this case the Main() function. The following command line will achieve this:

```
mcs helloworld.cs
```

So, creating a single-file assembly that represents an executable application and exists within a single file is pretty straightforward. What if you wanted to create an assembly that wasn't executable? Instead, it simply acts as a library of code that could be referenced and used in your applications. This kind of assembly is referred to as a *library assembly* and is synonymous to Windows DLLs and Linux/Unix shared libraries. You can create it on the command line using the target flag (/t) with an option of library. So, you can use the simplified Human and Man class introduced in Chapter 4 as the code base and store it in a file called human.cs, as follows:

```
using System;

public abstract class Human
{
    public abstract void Speak();
}

public class Man : Human
{
    public override void Speak()
    {
        Console.Out.WriteLine("Hello <in a gruff voice>\n");
    }
}
```

You can compile this using the command-line option mentioned previously to create your own library assembly. The following command line demonstrates this:

```
mcs /t:library human.cs
```

This will create a file with the extension .dll for a dynamic link library, with the same filename as the source file. You may notice through the mcs help (using man mcs or mcs /? at the command line) that other target types exist, which the mcs compiler can produce (see Table 5-1).

Table 5-1. *Compiler Target Types*

Type	Description
exe	Executable assembly (.exe)
library	Library assembly (.dll)
module	.NET module (.netmodule)
winexe	Windows executable (.exe)

■ **Note** On Windows, the /t:winexe option causes the application to run as a Windows process and not within a console window. At the time of this writing, this does nothing on the Mono platform but may be extended to handle GUI support.

Finally, you can create a multifile assembly; in this instance, at least one file must contain the manifest for the assembly, and any assembly that starts the application must have an entry point through which to do so, such as Main(). To create a multifile assembly, the first step is to compile the assembly source files using the /t:module flag to create modules. (Remember, these do not contain a manifest and can be used only to build assemblies.) So, taking the same source code as used previously and still storing this in the human.cs file, you can use a different target option to denote that you want to create a .NET module. For example:

```
mcs /t:module human.cs
```

This will create the .NET module with a filename of human.netmodule. The second step is to add this to a library assembly that can be referenced by another application (executable assembly) or add it to an executable assembly in its own right without referencing it externally. So, with the .NET module created previously and added directly, you would create the simple executable (in a filename called mantest.cs) with its entry point like so:

```
class Test
{
    public static void Main(string[] args)
    {
        Man m = new Man();
        m.Speak();
    }
}
```

Next, compile it using the /addmodule option, like so:

```
mcs /t:exe /addmodule:human.netmodule mantest.cs
```

This will result in an executable assembly called mantest.exe that has brought in the human .NET module code, resolving references to form an executable application. The alternative is to create the human.dll library assembly and still create the mantest application as before but now reference the human library assembly, allowing the executable to resolve this reference at runtime. This would result in a multifile assembly, with the mantest.exe assembly referencing the human.dll assembly. You can do this by first creating the library assembly (human.dll) and then creating the executable assembly (mantest.exe) but referencing the library assembly that contains the classes required. For example:

```
mcs /t:library human.cs
mcs /t:exe /reference:human.dll mantest.cs
```

This will produce two files, the human.dll library assembly and the executable mantest.exe, which is dependent on human.dll for its referenced code. You can prove this by renaming the human.dll library assembly and then executing the application again. This will fail because of its inability to load the referenced assembly required. If you rename the human.dll assembly to its true name, the code will begin executing normally again.

Finally, I'll demonstrate how to create a library assembly from multiple files by storing the Woman class implementation in a separate source code file called woman.cs. This file would contain the following implementation:

```
using System;

public class Woman : Human
{
    public override void Speak()
    {
        Console.Out.WriteLine("Hello <in a soft voice>");
    }
}
```

The compilation of this file depends on the ability to resolve the reference to the Human class. To create a multifile library assembly using the human.cs file, which contains definitions for both the Human and Man classes, you can use the following command line:

```
mcs /t:library /out:people.dll /addmodule:human woman.cs
```

For completeness, I'll briefly break down this command line and each option's effect, even though I already discussed these topics in this chapter. The /t:library option indicates you're building a library assembly, the /out:people.dll option indicates you want the resulting file to be called people.dll, and finally the /addmodule:human option indicates you want to include the human.netmodule module created previously to resolve dependencies within the Woman class. This library assembly will then contain the Human, Man, and Woman class definitions and implementations for the executable code to use.

Finding an Assembly

In the previous sections, I discussed an assembly's manifest and how the class loader within the CLR uses this to find an assembly. It is obvious that a lot of work is going on "under the hood." In fact, your code will seem to work as if by magic. For example, how does it find an assembly? The CLR looks in these three places in order to resolve references necessary to execute their dependent assembly:

- The same directory as the executing assembly.

- The directories specified in the MONO_PATH environment variable, with each directory separated by a colon. You could set this using the method appropriate to the operating system on which you're running, for example, bash with Linux.

- Finally, the GAC (more on this shortly).

You can see the second option, the MONO_PATH feature, in action by moving the hello.dll assembly to another location. For example, move it to the /temp directory. Then set the MONO_PATH accordingly (for example, to /temp), and rerun the helloworld.exe application. However, you will need to recompile the HelloWorld application to reference (using the /reference: flag) the hello.dll library because its location has changed. After you do this, it will then work correctly.

Finally, the option to install the library assembly into the GAC is more involved because the hello.dll library needs to be signed in order for it to be installed. This is a matter I'll cover a little later in the "Adding Assemblies to the Cache" section of this chapter.

Introducing the Global Assembly Cache (GAC)

At this point, I've introduced assemblies as units of deployable code that can contain an entry point for an executable application, with the exception of a *library assembly*, which is used as a reference. These are typically located on disk, and the manifest describes their version number, which is then resolved at runtime by the class loader within the CLR. I've also discussed how you go about referencing one or more assemblies and how the Mono framework locates a referenced assembly using a number of predefined methods, such as an Executables directory, environment variable, and the GAC. The GAC is a single repository on disk for all assemblies that can then be referenced at runtime by your application. The class loader will handle this automatically, referring to the GAC only when its previous search patterns have failed. The GAC is a great place to install common assemblies that may be used by one or more applications.

It's worth noting that while the CLR has knowledge of the GAC for resolving referenced assemblies, the compiler does not. The compiler will therefore need to be told of the existence of an assembly in the GAC through the use of packages that are then referenced by the compiler using the -pkg command-line option. I'll now cover the GAC in more detail, discussing its purpose, benefits, and the gacutil tool for manipulating assemblies within it. Table 5-2 lists the command-line options supported by the utility.

Table 5-2. *gacutil Options*

Flag	Description
-i	Installs an assembly into the GAC
-il	Installs assemblies using a list of assembly names
-l	Lists the contents of the GAC
-u	Uninstalls an assembly from the GAC
-us	Uninstalls assemblies using a specified name
-ul	Uninstalls assemblies using a list of assembly names

Adding Assemblies to the Cache

You can use the -i flag in conjunction with the assembly name to indicate you want to install the specified assembly into the GAC. An important prerequisite for all assemblies installed in the GAC is that they are *strong named*. If you create an assembly that contains the abstract Human class and the specialized Male and Female classes, you can then install this into the GAC for all applications to reference.

The first step is to create a public key for signing the assembly; you do this by using the sn.exe utility. This utility can create a random public/private key pair by using the -k option. The following command line demonstrates this:

```
sn -k my.key
```

If successful, this will create a strong-named key pair using a 1024-bit RSA key pair file that you can use to digitally sign the assembly and thus ensure its integrity and authenticity within the GAC. Once you have the strong-named file, you can use it to indicate to the compiler that the assembly should be strong named. You do this using the -keyfile command-line option for the compiler. Using the assembly source code and strong-named file, you can create the digitally signed library assembly and get it ready for installation into the GAC. Use the following command line:

```
mcs -keyfile:my.key /t:library human.cs
```

This will result (pending no errors) in a static library assembly that is strong named and thus meets the prerequisites for installation into the GAC. To add this to the GAC, you use the gacutil command-line program with the -i option as follows:

```
gacutil -i human.dll
```

If no errors are reported, then you should receive a message indicating that this has been completed successfully and the assembly now resides in the GAC. You can, however, verify this using another command-line option that I'll discuss next. The output from a successful installation should look like this:

```
human installed into the gac (/usr/lib/mono/gac)
```

Verifying the Contents of the Cache

I've discussed the role of the GAC within the .NET Framework, and as you can imagine, a number of assemblies exist within it, ranging from those that form part of the core .NET Framework to custom assemblies that have been added specifically. The human.dll assembly is an example of a custom assembly, targeted at applications that specifically reference it. Therefore, it makes sense to provide the ability to view the contents of the GAC, either in part or as a whole. This is why the -l option has been provided as part of the gacutil utility; it provides a way of listing the entire contents of the GAC or the details of a specific assembly using its name.

To list the entire contents of the GAC, you simply use the following command line:

```
gacutil -l
```

As you watch a list of assembly names and their versions, culture, and public keys scroll by, you'll realize that searching for one assembly amongst them is not a simple task. Therefore, if you want to verify that a specific assembly exists within the GAC, then you simply specify the assembly name after the -l flag, like so:

```
gacutil -l human
```

This will list the assembly details if found, including the installed assembly's version, culture, and public key. The text should look something like this:

```
human, version=0.0.0.0, Culture=neutral, PublicKeyToken=13d9b9e8beca5908
```

If more than one version of the assembly is installed, then you will see multiple versions with the different version numbers being reported.

Note When specifying the assembly name, you will need to omit its extension (in this case `.dll`). Otherwise, the assembly will not be found.

Removing Assemblies from the Cache

I've covered installing assemblies into the GAC and verifying the contents of the GAC. But what if you wanted to remove an assembly from the GAC? For example, you may want to tidy up the GAC after uninstalling an application to remove its associated assemblies. As you would expect, an option exists to remove an assembly from the GAC; you can use the same `gacutil` command-line application but with a `-u` option. A key difference here is that you specify the assembly display name rather than the assembly name, because you may want to qualify the assembly using its version, culture, or combination. The following code demonstrates this by removing the assembly that was installed and verified in the previous sections:

```
gacutil -u human
```

This command will remove all assemblies whose display names start with the text `human`. Therefore, you should be aware that this may remove more than one assembly; in other words, be very careful when using this command. In addition to these options, you can also use the `-us` and `-ul` options to remove assemblies using the assembly filename or a list of assemblies, respectively. These are more specific and are not based on the *greedy removal* method used for the `-u` option.

Managing Memory with the Garbage Collector

As mentioned, the CLR provides automatic memory management for the lifetime of objects that exist within the CLR. This memory management avoids allocating memory that is no longer referenced but unable to be reclaimed, also known as a *memory leak*. It also means that arguably the developer needs to be less concerned about ensuring that objects are destroyed; however, it's still important to understand how memory is managed within the .NET environment and understand the best practices for helping the CLR do its job. The automatic nature of garbage collection has often led to criticism regarding its inefficiency in terms of both performance and memory usage. This criticism is often because of a lack of knowledge of the subject, and while trade-offs do exist, .NET applications are far more reliable and equal in performance in a lot of cases.

Reference-Counted Objects

So, how does it work? The objects you create using the new keyword are stored on the heap, so when you create your object, it is stored within an area of memory that is managed by the CLR (the *managed heap*) and associated with your application when it is first initialized. An object has two pieces of information stored against it, its *reference count* and its *generation number*. The reference count is the number of times this object is being referenced within a piece of code, so every time you create a reference to the object, the reference count is incremented. The reverse is true: whenever an object is destroyed, the reference count for the objects it references is decremented. This means when an object is no longer being referenced by any other object, its reference count will be 0, and it will be a candidate for garbage collection.

Generations of Objects

The other piece of metadata associated with an object is its *generation number*, which when first created will be 0. The purpose of generation numbers is to enable the garbage collector to be more efficient when reclaiming memory. Typically, the garbage collector will attempt to reclaim only the memory associated with generation-0 objects. However, if this fails to reclaim sufficient memory, it will then attempt to reclaim generation-1 objects. In the unlikely event that this is not enough, the garbage collector will reclaim objects in generation 2, which currently is the highest generation. This staggered distribution of objects into the different generations allows objects to have a short life span, so objects that may come and go often are kept at a generation level that allows them to be tidied up sooner rather than later, freeing important memory. It also has the effect of ensuring that garbage collection is fast and efficient, not trying to reclaim the memory associated with objects that may still be in use and avoiding long delays whilst the garbage collection is taking place.

You may be wondering how an object moves from one generation to another. This is pretty simple; the garbage collector will focus on objects within a certain generation first, which is by default only generation 0. If objects within this generation are still being referenced and therefore cannot be reclaimed, then they are said to have *survived garbage collection*, and their generation numbers are incremented by 1. The current maximum generation cycle for an object is 2. Figure 5-2 shows this process.

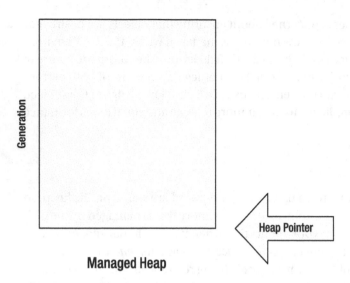

Figure 5-2. *An empty memory allocation on the heap*

When you initially execute your application, an area of memory is reserved on the heap, as shown in Figure 5-2, with the empty box representing unallocated heap memory and the heap pointer starting at the bottom.

This clearly shows an empty memory allocation on the heap with the pointer located at the start of this area for newly created objects. So, if you created two objects based on the defined Man and Woman classes, these would be created on the heap as generation-0 objects, and the heap pointer would be incremented accordingly, as shown in Figure 5-3.

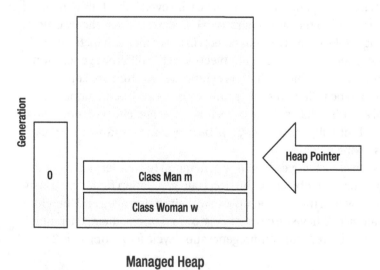

Figure 5-3. *Newly created generation-0 objects on the heap*

And then if garbage collection were to occur and these objects were still referenced and so survived the collection, their generation number would be incremented. If another object was then created, the heap would look like Figure 5-4.

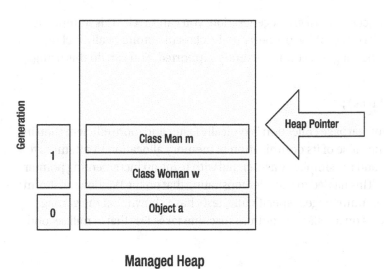

Managed Heap

Figure 5-4. *Objects on the heap after a garbage collection*

This shows that the objects at generation 0 are promoted to generation 1 if they survive the garbage collection, and newly created objects are created at generation 0.

A Good Garbage-Collecting Citizen

Just because garbage collection within the CLR is automatic doesn't mean you cannot write code to help the garbage collector in its ongoing tasks and therefore improve your application's performance. The most important aspect of a managed application's code is that you should structure your code so that memory is allocated only when needed and is made available to be reclaimed at its earliest point, by setting its reference to null. In addition, you can use the Dispose() method to indicate to the CLR that an object is no longer required (by internally setting its reference count to 0) and so is ready for the next garbage collection run. This method closes or releases unmanaged resources such as files, streams, and handles that are encapsulated within an object. The invocation of this method doesn't start an immediate garbage collection and won't affect the frequency at which the next garbage collection is performed.

If you are implementing the Dispose() method yourself, you must ensure that this is propagated to all objects within your hierarchy. For example, if the object inherits from another object, then the base class's Dispose() method should also be called within the Dispose() method.

Direct Control of the Garbage Collector

Your application can have limited access to and control of the garbage collection process by referencing the System.GC type. This class provides few features, although it does provide a Collect() method that can force the garbage collection to occur immediately. This method provides two implementations, one that takes a generation number and one that doesn't. If you want to force the garbage collection to occur immediately but use its normal collection method of searching only for generation-0 objects, then you would call it as follows:

```
GC.Collect();
```

If you want to collect all objects up to a given generation, you can specify this number as a parameter, or you can use the MaxGeneration property of the class to automatically reclaim all objects for the maximum number of generations currently supported. You can do this using the following statement:

```
GC.Collection(GC.MaxGenerations);
```

In a managed environment, garbage collection is typically faster and more efficient than in an unmanaged environment because of its optimization of memory allocation (it attempts to avoid memory fragmentation) and the simplicity associated with using an incrementing pointer rather than complex structures. This has led to tests demonstrating that on the Windows platform managed memory is faster than unmanaged; specifically, tests have shown that the garbage collection of generation-0 objects on a 200MHz Pentium machine takes less than a millisecond.

Note You should leave the CLR to call the garbage collector manually, and you should avoid using the Collect() method directly. Also, calling the Dispose() method of an object in some cases will simply set the object to a null value and thus reduce its reference count.

Using Application Domains

An *application domain* is similar to a namespace. However, instead of working on the isolation and scope of reference and value types, it defines the isolation level and scope of an application. It's both a logical boundary and a physical boundary that is created by the CLR to host your .NET application and typically maps onto a *physical process* within which one or more applications can run. The benefit of this isolation is that each application can be isolated from one another and therefore prevent one application from affecting another. For example, the level of granularity for isolating an application has been the process; this was true of early versions of Microsoft Internet Information Services (IIS). This means that numerous ASP applications would effectively run within a single process, and if one of these applications caused a problem, it would bring down not only the application concerned but also *all* other Web applications within it. The ability for .NET to define a finer level of isolation via application domains means that your application can run explicitly in its own domain. Because it's isolated from all other applications, it is therefore able to benefit from the security and reliability this brings. This feature is not limited to just IIS. The existence of application domains is a standard feature of the .NET Framework and so is beneficial to all applications, regardless of the operating system and associated technologies used.

Understanding Domain Sharing

You can use an assembly in multiple domains; however, this can prove inefficient if the assembly is loaded for every domain within which it's referenced. When an assembly is being used within multiple domains, the code of the assembly would be loaded only once and shared between domains. It's important to note that this is not the data associated with the assembly, and therefore the application instance is still isolated and safe from rogue applications.

Defining and Using Your Own Application Domain

I'll now take you through the basics of creating and using a custom application domain so that you will gain an understanding of the work involved and will be able to research the subject further should you have the need to use them. The first step is to create your own application domain using the CreateDomain() method that exists within the System namespace. It makes sense to use a namespace to define the scope for all objects within that domain, because this will ensure that your code is easier to read. The CLR host will automatically create an application domain for your process, but if you want a finer level of control, then you can define and manage your own domain as shown here:

```csharp
using System;

namespace MyDomain
{
   class Test
   {
      public static void Main(string[] args)
      {
         AppDomain mydomain = null;
         try
         {
            // Create our domain
            mydomain = AppDomain.CreateDomain("MyDomain", null);

            // Code can now be loaded and executed from this domain
         }
         catch(Exception e)
         {
            Console.Out.WriteLine("The following exception ➡
            occurred: " + e.Message);
         }
         finally
         {
            // Ensure the domain is unloaded
            AppDomain.Unload(mydomain);
         }
      }
   }
}
```

You can see in the bold lines of code that an application domain is created and given a "friendly" name. The second step is to use this domain to load and execute assemblies and finally unload them from memory when complete.

Using the Class Library

I've defined the features of the CLR, and touched on support for multiple languages such as IL and C#, but in order for you to develop feature-rich applications in a reasonable amount of time, you'll need to use the .NET Framework's *class library*. This is a set of classes that support a number of functions, including the following:

- Concrete and user-defined data types

- Exception handling

- Input and output operations on streams

- Data access

- Network communications

- Windows-based GUI support

- Client-server and fat-client architecture models

- Web and Web Service application support

In addition to supporting these core .NET Framework class libraries, Mono supports several other libraries that provide application programming interfaces (APIs) for open-source technologies such as the GNOME toolkit (Gtk#) and more. Those of you who have built applications using products from Microsoft, Borland, or Sun will have come across the Microsoft Foundation Classes (MFC), the Visual Class Library (VCL), or the Java Standard Edition, all of which are or contain class libraries for use by these products. The .NET Framework is no different in that respect, although the class library is one of the most powerful and complete on the market.

You'll use a number of core class libraries during the book to build the RSS aggregator. I'll cover them in the following sections. However, far more classes exist within the .NET Framework and are provided by various other groups, both commercial and noncommercial, than can be covered in this chapter. Figure 5-5 indicates some of the core namespaces provided by the .NET Framework, some of which I described in the following sections and some of which I'll leave for you to discover and use.

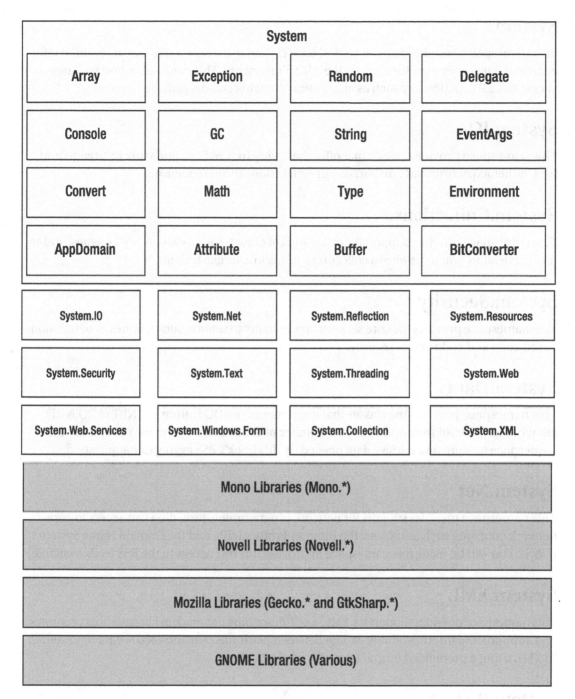

Figure 5-5. *Some of the class libraries available to the Mono environment*

System

This namespace contains core classes and base classes that define a number of common reference and data types used throughout the .NET Framework. This namespace also includes access to CLR functionality such as application domains and the garbage collector.

System.IO

This namespace provides classes that offer the ability to read from and write to streams and files, either asynchronously (in parallel) or synchronously (in sequence).

System.Collections

This namespace provides support for collections of objects such as lists, arrays, queues, and so on. These allow you to traverse a collection's items in a simple fashion.

System.Security

This namespace provides the core security functionality to support such features as permission-based code and code access security.

System.Data

This namespace provides the classes that implement the ADO feature for .NET (ADO.NET), allowing you to read from and write to a number of different data sources. You will use this namespace to store and retrieve data needed by this book's RSS aggregator application.

System.Net

This namespace provides support for network programming, providing you access to core network concepts such as sockets, the Internet Protocol (IP), and the Domain Name System (DNS). You will be using this namespace to provide Internet access to the RSS feeds available.

System.XML

This namespace provides support for XML, a self-describing text markup language that promotes and supports the interoperability of data between platforms. The RSS feed is data represented in XML using a predefined format known as an *XML schema*.

System.Web

This namespace provides classes to support the ASP technology for .NET (ASP.NET), allowing you to write and implement dynamic Web sites through a supported Web server. This was traditionally the foundation on which Microsoft IIS was built, but you are now able to host ASP.NET applications outside IIS using alternative technologies such as Apache and the `mod_aspdotnet` addition (see `http://httpd.apache.org/cli/`).

System.Windows.Forms

This namespace provides classes that support the creation of form-based GUIs using a variety of user interface concepts. You'll use these classes to develop the user interface to your applications. This namespace provides similar functionality to that provided by the GNOME toolkit, also known as Gtk#.

Summary

This chapter introduced some of the core concepts within the .NET Framework, including the CLR, the garbage collector, and the class libraries. The CLR provides a sophisticated runtime environment with advanced features such as memory management, security, exception handling, and so on. This provides the framework within which you can deploy and execute your managed and unmanaged applications. The garbage collector, a component of the CLR, provides automatic memory management such that the performance of the CLR is on par with native compilers and their executable code. Often, skeptics dismiss the improved performance of runtime environments, which has led to tests demonstrating that on the Windows platform, memory management is faster than unmanaged code. The garbage collection of generation-0 objects on a 200MHz Pentium machine takes less than a millisecond.

The power and the scale of the .NET Framework allow you to develop commercial, enterprise-scale applications much more quickly than was previously possible. You can now put the knowledge you have accumulated to good use—in the following chapters, you'll learn how to develop a RSS aggregator using the Mono environment and the .NET Framework's class library.

System.Windows.Forms

Summary

CHAPTER 6

■■■

Creating Windows Forms

The user interface is arguably one of the most important elements of any application incorporating interface elements into its design. It represents the conduit between the user of the system and the functionality exposed by the application. The user interface can make or break an application through usability and presentation alone. If users cannot access the functionality they require, or if the functionality is exposed but accessing it requires negotiating a nonintuitive interface, then users will become frustrated with the entire process, which ultimately detracts from the application's success!

In an effort to help you avoid such dilemmas, throughout this chapter I'll discuss sound user interface design and introduce some of the options at your disposal. I'll present this material in the context of the .NET Framework's Windows Forms technology, which is one of the technologies available to you when defining your GUI. Specifically, I'll show how to use Windows Forms to implement your user interface, both by using readily available graphical components and by defining your own. I'll also discuss how you can use the Graphical Display Interface Plus (GDI+) to provide the rendering capability for your own custom user interface controls. In addition, you'll look at alternatives to Windows Forms for designing and developing a GUI; you'll learn how to use the GNOME toolkit (Gtk#) for Mono, which fuses the open-source toolkit with .NET and Mono.

Graphical User Interface (GUI) Overview

You have a number of options for building a user interface within the Mono environment. These include (but are not limited to) the following:

- *Windows Forms*: A .NET-based set of GUI components

- *Gtk#*: An open-source GNOME-based set of GUI components

- *Cocoa#*: A .NET interface to Apple's Cocoa suite of GUI components

This chapter will discuss Windows Forms. The Windows Forms technology is implicit within the .NET Framework, so code development using user interface components will work on all Mono-supported platforms, assuming that the Windows Forms application's classes have been implemented fully.

Hunkering down to the actual code level is not necessary to build your user interfaces, as numerous open-source and commercial IDEs such as MonoDevelop (http://www.monodevelop.com/), Eclipse (http://www.eclipse.org/), and X-develop (http://www.omnicore.com/) can make your life far easier. However, while the IDEs help automate the code generation for developing your own user interface, throughout this chapter and the next I will show how to write the code to create user interfaces without relying on these IDEs. My experience has shown that it's far more beneficial for you to know how the code works and let the IDE support you rather than to depend on the IDE to write the code.

The following sections provide an overview of the options available, together with some of their advantages and disadvantages. This will provide you with sufficient information to make an informed decision regarding which programming interface to use during design and implementation.

Graphic Display Interface Plus (GDI+)

The GDI+ layer is an API that is implemented as a set of detailed interfaces that are more complex to understand than some of the other components such as Windows Forms and Gtk#. For example, the Windows Forms programming interface actually consists of a set of components that utilize the GDI+ API through classes within the System.Drawing namespace (see http://www.mono-project.com/Drawing). Therefore, Windows Forms applications are completely dependent on the functionality offered by GDI+ but hide the details in easy-to-understand .NET components. The System.Drawing namespace contains the programming interface for a number of graphical concepts that will be familiar to those of you who have delved into the depths of Windows, Linux, or Mac OS windowing technologies. It exposes concepts such as brushes, color, images, points, pens, rectangles, and more, allowing you to directly manipulate the graphical display and create user interface components such as list boxes, trees, panels, and so on.

The GDI+ programming interfaces exposes two drawing subsystems. The first is Microsoft's System.Drawing API (which acts as a C# wrapper around the C-based API exposed for GDI+), and the second is an implementation of the Cairo vector graphics library (see http://www.cairographics.org/download) whose purpose is to provide high-quality display and print outputs. Figure 6-1 shows these two components graphically.

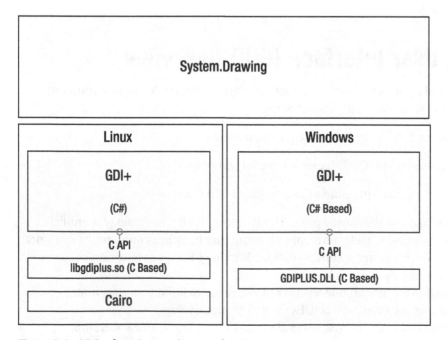

Figure 6-1. *GDI+ drawing options under Mono*

■**Note** Cairo is a 2D graphics library with support for multiple output devices; see `http://www.cairographics.org/introduction` for more details.

Windows Forms

In this section, I'll discuss the Windows Forms (also known as WinForms) set of user interface components provided as part of the core .NET Framework and more recently incorporated into the standard Mono distribution. The WinForms components are provided within the `System.Windows.Forms` namespace, providing readily available user interface components that are built upon the drawing capabilities of the `System.Drawing` namespace. Thus, they provide a fully managed API with which to develop your application. The WinForms components allow you to create and manipulate windows and controls using the predefined base classes provided under the relevant namespace with relative ease.

The disadvantage of using this technology is that, at the time of this writing, the code base is still under heavy development and therefore is subject to change. In addition to this, the layout mechanism associated with Windows Forms development under Mono is poor. In fact, it's often the case that you will need to manually adjust your layout depending on factors such as font size changes or internationalization.

Windows Forms vs. Web Forms

In the Windows world of .NET, you can create Windows Forms–based applications or Web Forms–based applications. The similarity of their names provides a clue as to what the differences are, but in summary the Windows Forms technology is for building rich clients that are stand-alone applications and that require the .NET Framework to be present in order to run. A Web Forms application is one that is delivered to the user using a browser-based interface but nonetheless delivers Windows Forms–type functionality. You achieve this by generating HTML-based code (including using XML and scripting technologies) to drive the controls and by delivering this code as a thin-client application.

Using Web Forms applications has its advantages and disadvantages, and it will obviously mean that the requirements on your target environment are few—just a Web browser. On the server, however, this will consume resources in the production of the code. Further, the limitations of HTML ultimately mean that the user experience will not be as rich.

Implementing Good User Interface Design

Taking time to plan your user interface is imperative if your application is going to be intuitive, easy to use, and pleasing to the eye. Therefore, you should take care in how you design your user interface, determining how your application will be used by putting yourself in the shoes of a potential user. Specifically, you should consider the following when designing your user interface:

- *Standards*: Adopting standards such as those defined by your host operating system not only helps ensure that your application looks like other native applications but also can support key concepts such as the Web Accessibility Initiative (see http://www.w3.org/WAI/).

- *Audience*: If your audience wants to achieve fast data entry, ensure that your user interface makes it as easy as possible. Alternatively, you may want to create a separate, easy-to-use interface for beginners.

- *Simplicity*: The style for your user interface is your choice, but a recent trend is that a clean, simple user interface is preferred over a busy, heavily graphical user interface.

Remember that simple features such as the alignment of controls and the consistent use of user-friendly colors can make or break a user interface design. Numerous articles on the Web explain techniques to employ when designing a user interface; for example, you can find GNOME's user interface guidelines at http://developer.gnome.org/projects/gup/hig/.

Creating the User Interface for the RSS Aggregator

As mentioned, the project you'll tackle throughout this book is an RSS aggregator that allows you to subscribe to RSS feeds and view the corresponding articles published on the Internet. The code download includes the design notes about the functionality required of such an application, and it is from this point forward that I'll start showing how to build the application and start demonstrating the techniques, tools, and technologies used.

The first step is to define the user interface that will be presented to the user; I'll cover this in a step-by-step manner over the next few sections. The main screen fits into a few discrete sections, as shown in Figure 6-2.

The mock-up of the screen depicts a number of graphical controls that will be displayed on the main screen:

- *Main menu*: This provides a key method for interaction, offering important functionality for the application such as exiting the application or adding a new subscription feed.

- *List box for subscribed feeds*: This will display feeds that have currently been subscribed to by users.

- *List of threads for each feed*: This lists all the threads of conversation available for the highlighted subscription feed.

- *Text for highlighted thread item*: This displays the text associated with the particular thread highlighted.

- *Status bar for general information*: This displays general information such as the number of feeds or threads.

I'll now show how you can implement these features using the Windows Forms technology, which is included as part of the .NET Framework.

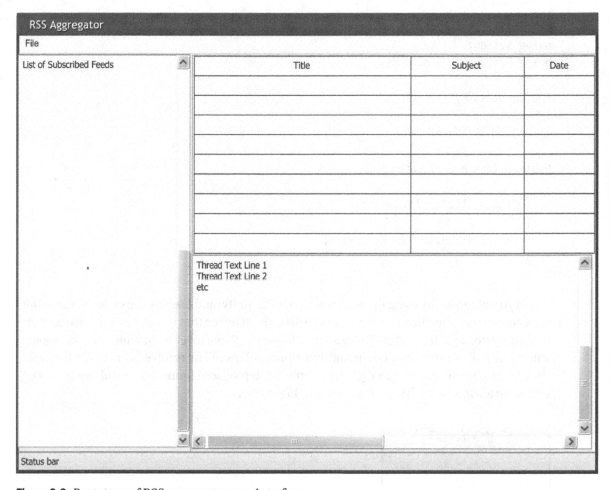

Figure 6-2. *Prototype of RSS aggregator user interface*

Creating a Form

Creating a Windows Forms application is a pretty simple task; the Form class within the System.Windows.Forms namespace represents the functionality associated with a single form. Therefore, to create a local instance of a form, you simply need to create your own class that inherits the functionality from the Form class and extends or uses its functionality as required. The following code defines a reference type for just such a class:

```
class myform : form
{
}
```

You'll notice that this requires little code. This is because the core features are inherited from the Form class, which provides you with basic window functionality, such as displaying the window, responding to events, resizing and minimizing the window, and so on. You can now include this class within your application and create an instance of an application that uses this form as its main window, as shown in Listing 6-1.

Listing 6-1. *Creating a Simple Form*

```
using System;
using System.Windows.Forms;

public class MyForm : Form
{
}

public class MyApplication
{
   public static void Main(string[] args)
   {
      Application.Run(new MyForm());
   }
}
```

If you compile (by using the mcs command-line utility) and execute the code (by using the mono command-line utility) shown in Listing 6-1, you'll notice that it won't compile without an explicit reference to the System.Windows.Forms assembly. (Remember to omit the .dll extension when using the /reference: command-line option.) This will be resolved at runtime through the GAC. If you execute the executable assembly that is produced from a successful compilation, you'll see a window similar to that shown in Figure 6-3.

Figure 6-3. *A default Windows Forms window*

Note Chapter 1 discusses how to compile and execute your Mono-based applications. The mcs command line will compile your code and, if successful, leave you with a resulting executable that you can then execute using the mono command line.

If you study the window in Figure 6-3, you'll notice that you can resize it, minimize it, maximize it, and close it, all without writing a single line of code. This is because this function-ality is provided as standard within the Form class. However, it doesn't make for an interesting window and sure doesn't constitute an application, so I'll now show how to adjust some of its properties to customize its behavior.

The first thing I'll show you is how to change the window's title to something that reflects your application's purpose, which is an RSS aggregator. You can also set the size of the default window 800×600 pixels. To set these values, the most appropriate place is within your derived Form class constructor, as shown in Listing 6-2.

Listing 6-2. *A Customized Windows Form Example*

```
public class MyForm : Form
{
  public MyForm ()
  {
    this.Text = "RSS Aggregator";
    this.Height = 600;
    this.Width - 800;
  }
}
```

After you've modified the class and compiled the assembly, the resulting executable assembly should produce a window like Figure 6-4.

Figure 6-4. *Your window with the defaults changed*

As you can see, the window is far larger, measuring 800×600 pixels, and the window's title is RSS Aggregator. An alternative method is to set the Size property, which encompasses both the width and the height, to form a single reference type. You do this simply by constructing an instance of the System.Drawing.Size reference type, passing the width and height to the constructor like you did in Listing 6-2. For example:

```
this.Size = new System.Drawing.Size(800,600);
```

You should also note that this references a class called Size within the System.Drawing namespace, so you'll need to explicitly import that namespace with the following statement:

```
using System.Drawing;
```

Setting the Client Size

In the examples so far, you've been dealing with the size of the overall window, which includes window elements such as the caption, borders, and so forth. This doesn't truly reflect the actual space available for you to add user interface components, such as list boxes, textboxes, and so on, to your form. This is because the actual *canvas* available for laying out controls is reduced by the window elements mentioned previously. To overcome this, you can use the ClientSize property to modify the size of the *client* dimensions of the form, which is where you're able to place content. This has the same reference type as the Size property, so you can set it in the same way. Although I won't adjust the form shown in this chapter, if you wanted to change the canvas size for user interface components to be the full 800×600 pixels, you would use a statement similar to the following:

```
this.ClientSize = new System.Drawing.Size(800,600);
```

Setting the Border Type

You may notice from the border of the forms displayed that while using any graphical environment, the border of a window often denotes the behavior of a form. An example is an application splash screen. This type of form has no need to be resized, minimized, or maximized; therefore, these controls never appear on the form. Alternatively, the default is a resizable form with all the controls mentioned previously. You can control the border type by setting the FormBorderStyle attribute, which has a number of valid values; these are held in an enumerated type of the same name and are listed in Table 6-1.

Table 6-1. *Window Border Styles*

Border Style	Description
None	This creates no border or border elements.
Fixed3D	This is like the default setting, but the border is raised, creating a 3D effect.
FixedDialog	This creates a border that is not resizable and is recessed. This is typically used for dialog boxes.
FixedSingle	This creates a border that is not resizable and has a thin width. This is common for toolbars.
FixedToolWindow	This creates a border that is not resizable, has a smaller font, and is not registered with the taskbar.
Sizable	This is the default. This creates a border that is resizable, and all border elements are included.
SizableToolWindow	This is like FixedToolWindow but is resizable.

To change the border, you simply need to set the FormBorderAttribute attribute. The following example creates a class that can be used for splash screens and contains no border or elements:

```
class MySplashForm : Form
{
  public MySplashForm(string title)
  {
    this.Text = title;
    this.FormBorderStyle = FormBorderStyle.None;
  }
}
```

Figure 6-5 shows a collage of windows that have been created with the FormBorderStyle values mentioned in this section, with the exception of the value None, which shows no border, as you would expect. Take some time to examine the different border styles (indicated by the window title) and to note the different border styles/widths and the effects they have on the icons/controls in the window's title bar.

Figure 6-5. *Various window border styles*

Modifying the Look of Your Form

Table 6-2 lists some other common attributes that affect the visual representation of a form.

Table 6-2. *Other Common Visual Attributes*

Attribute	Description
Width	Defines the width of the form in pixels
Height	Defines the height of the form in pixels
MinimizeBox	Shows the Minimized border element (true or false)
MaximizeBox	Shows the MaximizeBox border element (true or false)
ControlBox	Shows the ControlBox border element (true or false)
ShowInTaskbar	Shows the window in the taskbar (true or false)
TopMost	Always shows the form on top (true or false)
Font	Sets the default font attributes for the form
ForeColor	Sets the foreground color of the form
BackColor	Sets the background color of the form
BackgroundImage	Sets a background image for the form
Text	Sets the window title as a text string

It's beyond the scope of this book to cover every property and their options for the System.Windows.Forms assembly. I will therefore concentrate on key topics, focusing on the ones you'll need to implement the RSS aggregator.

Creating a Menu

The window you've created is basic and gives you no way to interact with it, apart from being able to perform fundamental actions such as minimizing it and closing it. You can address this by creating a main menu from which the user can access the application's functionality. The Form class has a Menu property, which provides read and write access to a window's main menu, which at the moment will be null, because you haven't created or assigned a menu yet. The System.Windows.Forms.Menu class provides the required menu functionality, which allows you to create your own class that inherits the functionality of the Menu class and allows you to add MenuItem class instances that represent individual menu items. The application's main menu will be pretty straightforward; it'll contain a single File menu item with the submenu items shown in Table 6-3.

Table 6-3. *Your Main Menu*

Menu Item	Description
Open	Opens the dialog box to capture the RSS URL
Close	Closes down an open RSS feed
<separator>	Visually separates menu items
Exit	Exits the application

I'll now show how to create your menu within a custom class that inherits from the System.Windows.Forms.MainMenu class and extends this to include your submenu items. Listing 6-3 shows the definition of the MyMenu class, complete with the constructor implementation to add the menu items discussed.

Listing 6-3. *The Main Window's Form*

```
public class MyMenu : System.Windows.Forms.MainMenu
{
  // Member variables
  public System.Windows.Forms.MenuItem miFile;
  public System.Windows.Forms.MenuItem miFileOpen;
  public System.Windows.Forms.MenuItem miFileClose;
  public System.Windows.Forms.MenuItem miFileExit;
```

```
//
// Default constructor
//
public MyMenu()
{
  // Create your File main menu item
  miFile = new MenuItem("&File");
  this.MenuItems.Add(miFile);

  // Create the File menu items
  miFileOpen = new MenuItem("&Open");
  miFileClose = new MenuItem("&Close");
  miFileExit = new MenuItem("E&xit");


   // ...and add them to the File menu item
  miFile.MenuItems.Add(miFileOpen);
  miFile.MenuItems.Add(miFileClose);
  miFile.MenuItems.Add(new MenuItem("-"));
  miFile.MenuItems.Add(miFileExit);
  }
}
```

The first thing to note is that you create three member variables that will refer to your menu items in the menu item array, defined by the MenuItem type. The declarations for these variables are in bold in Listing 6-3. The listing defines a constructor for the MyMenu class, and the first thing you do is create a File menu item (using the new keyword) and add it to collection of associated menu items (using the Add() method on the MenuItems collection), as follows:

```
// Member variables
public System.Windows.Forms.MenuItem miFile;
public System.Windows.Forms.MenuItem miFileOpen;
public System.Windows.Forms.MenuItem miFileClose;
public System.Windows.Forms.MenuItem miFileExit;
 // Create your File main menu item
miFile = new MenuItem("&File");
this.MenuItems.Add(miFile);
```

The next step is to create your menu items (again using the MenuItem reference types) and assign these instances of the MenuItem class with their respective menu captions. This takes place in the following code:

```
// Create the File menu items
miFileOpen = new MenuItem("&Open");
miFileClose = new MenuItem("&Close");
miFileExit = new MenuItem("E&xit");
```

And finally, you need to add these individual menu items to the main menu's File menu item, which will enable the user to collapse and expand the File menu item to reveal the individual menu items within—as per the usual GUI-type menu functionality:

```
// ...and add them to the File menu item
miFile.MenuItems.Add(miFileOpen);
miFile.MenuItems.Add(miFileClose);
miFile.MenuItems.Add(new MenuItem("-"));
miFile.MenuItems.Add(miFileExit);
```

Note You can define the separator simply by using a hyphen (-) as its caption.

To ensure that the menu is associated with your main form, the constructor for your form now needs to create an instance of the new MyMenu class; but first you need to define a member variable of type MyMenu that is held within the main Form class, which is held in the MyForm instance, as follows:

```
public MyMenu mainMenu;
```

Then you need to create an instance of MyMenu and assign it to the form's MainMenu property, as shown in the following code. This will result in the form displaying your menu as discussed previously and will allow the user to interact with it. The assignment is possible because your MyMenu class derives from System.Windows.Forms.MainMenu, the same reference type as the MainMenu property itself.

```
mainMenu = new MyMenu();
this.Menu = mainMenu;
```

This completes creating your main menu, so now you can assign some event handlers to invoke your menu handler code. Before you do that, though, take some time to compile your new source code, which should include a class definition for your menu called MyMenu and a class definition for your form called MyForm. Listing 6-4 shows the code so far, complete with event handler code (which I'll cover in the next section) and your application's test class to create and display the form.

Note The following example includes some event handlers, which are discussed in the next section.

Listing 6-4. *Main Window with Associated Menu and Application Class*

```
using System;
using System.Windows.Forms;

public class MyMenu : System.Windows.Forms.MainMenu
{
```

```csharp
  // Member Variables
  private System.Windows.Forms.MenuItem miFile;
  public System.Windows.Forms.MenuItem miFileOpen;
  public System.Windows.Forms.MenuItem miFileClose;
  public  System.Windows.Forms.MenuItem miFileExit;

  //
  // Default constructor
  //
  public MyMenu()
  {
    // Create your main menu item
    miFile = new MenuItem("&File");
    this.MenuItems.Add(miFile);

    // Create the File menu items
    miFileOpen = new MenuItem("&Open");
    miFileClose = new MenuItem("&Close");
    miFileExit = new MenuItem("E&xit");

    // ...and add them to the File menu item
    miFile.MenuItems.Add(miFileOpen);
    miFile.MenuItems.Add(miFileClose);
    miFile.MenuItems.Add(new MenuItem("-"));
    miFile.MenuItems.Add(miFileExit);


  }
}

public class MyForm : Form
{
  public MyMenu mainMenu;

  public MyForm()
  {
    this.Text = "RSS Aggregator";
    this.Width = 800;
    this.Height = 600;
```

```
    mainMenu = new MyMenu();
    this.Menu = mainMenu;

    // Assign your event handler
    mainMenu.miFileOpen.Click += new System.EventHandler(this.miFileOpen_Click);
    mainMenu.miFileClose.Click += new System.EventHandler(this.miFileClose_Click);
    mainMenu.miFileExit.Click += new System.EventHandler(this.miFileExit_Click);
  }

  public void miFileOpen_Click(object sender, System.EventArgs e)
  {
    // Implementation goes here
  }

  public void miFileClose_Click(object sender, System.EventArgs e)
  {
    // Implementation goes here
  }

  public void miFileExit_Click(object sender, System.EventArgs e)
  {
    // Implementation goes here
    Console.Out.WriteLine("File Exit clicked");
    this.Close();
  }

}


public class MyTest
{
  public static void Main(string[] args)
  {
    Application.Run(new MyForm());
  }
}
```

Once successfully compiled and executed, this should display a window similar to Figure 6-6.

Figure 6-6. *Your application's main window with menu*

■**Note** To compile this, you need to reference the Systems.Windows.Forms assembly with a command line of mcs listing6-3.cs /r:System.Windows.Forms.

Handling Events from Your Controls

If you compile and execute the executable assembly that results from its successful compilation, you should find a standard window with a main menu. The main menu has a single File item that, when expanded, shows the Open, Close, and Exit menu items, as shown in Figure 6-7.

Figure 6-7. *Your main menu*

As you can see, the functionality to expand, collapse, and highlight entries is provided by the base MainMenu class, but at the moment the window doesn't react to the user selecting an item. This requires an *event handler* to be registered with the menu item, which can then capture the menu items' click events and execute the code you define.

You may remember from Chapter 4 that I discussed events and covered how delegates can refer to methods in the definition of event handlers; this is the underlying principle for how events are handled in the .NET environment. An *event* is a type of delegate that points to one or more methods; it is also known as a *multicast delegate* because of its ability to fire the same event at multiple methods. You can see this when using your MenuItem controls; these use the MenuItem class that has an event called Click. This is a multicast delegate that references one or more event handlers that are to be called when the click event occurs. The event handled is defined within the MenuItem class as a member variable like so:

```
public event EventHandler click;
```

This in turn will have an associated delegate signature that corresponds to an event, as follows:

```
public delegate void EventHandler(object sender, System.EventArgs e);
```

So, to create an event handler method that can be referenced by a menu item's click event, you create a method with the same signature as your event handler, as shown previously. The following is the code for the Exit menu item:

```
public void miFileExit_Click(object sender, System.EventArgs e)
{
  // Implementation goes here
  Console.Out.WriteLine("Exit Clicked");
}
```

You then need to hook this event handler into the menu item's click event so that when the event is fired, your event handler is called. You do this by using the overloaded addition and assignment operation (+=) and assigning this operation an instance of EventHandler that points to the event handler defined. In this case, you'll do this within the form constructor, as follows:

```
mainMenu.miFileExit.Click += new System.EventHandler(this.miFileExit_Click);
```

If you now select File ➤ Exit and keep an eye on the console window that shows debugging output generated from your graphical form application, you'll notice that your miFileExit_Click event is being called, outputting the text File..Exit Clicked.

Your event handler has now been successfully installed and is working, so you can provide the correct implementation for this method, which is to call the Close() method on the form that contains the menu item, which can be accessed using the this member variable. You could have obtained the form by using the object passed to the event handler as the sender, which would be your MenuItem class; however, for simplicity simply use the this variable, as follows:

```
public void miFileExit_Click(object sender, System.EventArgs e)
{
    // Close the calling form
    this.Close();
}
```

You'll return to assign more event handler functionality during later sections (such as the "Interacting with the Dialog Box" section), but for now I'll show how to create the handlers and hook them up to the menu controls ready for implementation. First, define the event handlers like so:

```
public void miFileOpen_Click(object sender, System.EventArgs e)
{
  // Implementation goes here
}
public void miFileClose_Click(object sender, System.EventArgs e)
{
  // Implementation goes here
}
```

Second, assign them to their respective menu items, as follows:

```
mainMenu.miFileOpen.Click += new System.EventHandler(this.miFileOpen_Click);
mainMenu.miFileClose.Click += new System.EventHandler(this.miFileClose_Click);
```

This will provide you with placeholders for functionality to be added later in this chapter. If you want to test these, you can add a statement to output some debugging text to the console; you will then see the placeholders in the active console window, as shown in the following simple example:

```
public void miFileExit_Click(object sender, System.EventArgs e)
{
  // Implementation goes here
  Console.Out.WriteLine("Exit clicked");
  this.Close();
}
```

This is a good point in the chapter to suspend work on this book's RSS aggregator and introduce some other features available within Windows Forms. You'll return to this book's project in the "Creating a Dialog Box" section.

Exploring Form Types

The first part of this chapter focused on creating your application's main window. This section briefly introduces the types of window support within GUI environments such as Microsoft Windows and Linux.

These are the main concepts:

- Multidocument interface (MDI)

- Single-document interface (SDI)

- Modal

- Modeless

I'll briefly explain these concepts and their relationship in the following sections.

Multidocument Interfaces (MDIs) vs. Single-Document Interfaces (SDIs)

An MDI is usually found within an application where more than one document is required, often referred to as a *document-centric* approach, within a single window border. For example, word processing applications typically support one or more documents open at a time that are housed within different windows. Figure 6-8 shows an example of each document represented by a separate window and accessed by using the tabs.

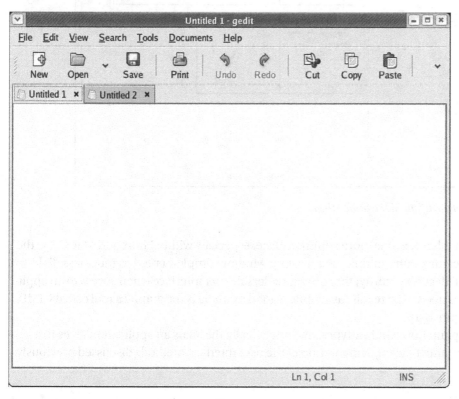

Figure 6-8. *Example of an MDI application*

By comparison, an SDI is where an application supports a single window, and the contents of this window are refreshed, are split, or contain dialog boxes (which I'll discuss shortly) that are displayed over the top or in addition to the window. This makes sense when an application is focused on a single view of information. For example, a calculator application deals with a single focus, and multiple views wouldn't really benefit you. Figure 6-9 shows a Linux image tool that presents you with a single view of your file system, displaying any graphical files that are present.

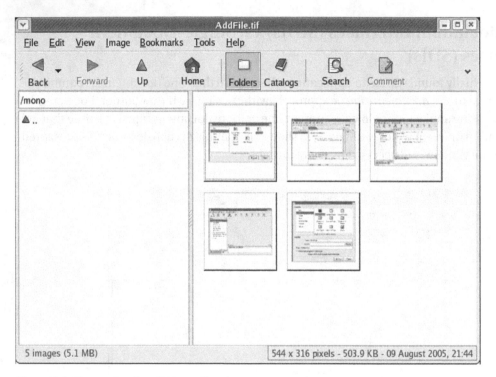

Figure 6-9. *Example of an SDI application*

Finally, what has become more commonplace, especially within Linux and Mac OS, is the use of an application with multiple, cooperating windows (implemented as modeless dialog boxes, which I'll describe shortly) that provide a flexible user interface when access to an application's features need to be readily available. A good example is the graphics tool called GIMP, as shown in Figure 6-10.

I'll now explain how window types, and specifically the focus an application gives to a certain window, affect the implementation of the user interface methods discussed previously.

Figure 6-10. *Example of multiwindow application*

Modal vs. Modeless

In addition to an application supporting one or more windows, a window can be *modal* or *modeless*. A modal window is where focus for that application is on a given window, and the application forces the user to make a decision regarding that window before being able to access any other part of the application. For example, if you select the option to open a file, then more often than not the application will force you to either choose a file to open or cancel the file open request. This is a modal form, and the application is forcing you to make a response. An alternative is a modeless form where the user may switch between one or more forms associated with the application without being forced to complete a task. A good example is a word processor or graphics application; you will normally choose from one or more open windows and then perform tasks related to the contents of that window.

In the Windows Forms environment, to open a form modally, you use the ShowDialog() method. To display modeless forms or dialog boxes, you use the Show() method. Throughout the book, you will be using a single modeless form for your main application window and will use modal dialog boxes to prompt the user for information.

Creating a Dialog Box

A *dialog box* is a window that retains focus until the user closes it. In terms of presentation, a dialog box has little to distinguish itself from a normal, default window. The differences are subtle but typically consist of it being a fixed, nonresizable window and being slightly recessed compared to a normal window. The dialog box passes control within an application to users, prompting them to make a decision that relates to the dialog box being shown. This decision usually involves taking an action that will cause the dialog box to close and processing to continue, and the options available are usually either positive or negative.

Let's consider the Open File (or File Open) dialog box that is common to most windows-based applications. Figure 6-11 shows the GNOME Open File dialog box within Linux.

Figure 6-11. *Example of a dialog box*

You notice that this dialog box presents various functional options, all of which are designed to support you when navigating to a chosen file. You can close the window using the Close button or using the close window border element, indicated as a cross, or you can open the file using the Open button. While this dialog box is open, the application to which it belongs is disabled, because the application gives focus only to the dialog box.

To continue with the previous RSS aggregator example, I'll show how to create a class that represents a dialog box whose aim is to prompt the user to enter an address (via a URL) for their desired RSS feed. At the moment, I won't show how to include any controls on the form and will leave the user to close the form using the close window border element. Listing 6-5 shows the code for the dialog box.

Listing 6-5. *An Example Dialog Box*

```
class MyDialog: Form
{
  // Default constructor
  public MyDialog(string title)
  {
    this.Text = title;
    this.FormBorderStyle = FormBorderStyle.FixedDialog;
    this.ClientSize = new System.Drawing.Size(362, 96);
    this.MinimizeBox= false;
    this.MaximizeBox = false;
  }
}
```

Next, you can use this dialog box instance within your code by implementing some code within the FileOpen event handler, which will create an instance of your dialog box and show it modally, like so:

```
public void miFileOpen_Click(object sender, System.EventArgs e)
{
  // Create and Display your File Open dialog box
  MyDialog dlgFileOpen = new MyDialog("File Open");
  dlgFileOpen.ShowDialog();
}
```

Take note of the ShowDialog() method, which shows the dialog box with modal focus and forces the user to make a choice. You also remove both maximize and minimize border elements, because these are not appropriate for a dialog box, as shown in Figure 6-12.

Figure 6-12. *The RSS aggregator's File Open dialog box*

Adding Functionality Through Controls

The ability to create and display windows within Mono is straightforward thanks in part to the wealth of functionality provided in the base Form class. However, any window is of limited use without any controls through which the user can interact and the application can present information. In this section, I'll cover how to create, place, and use various graphical controls that provide system functionality to the application.

I'll continue to focus on the dialog box and cover how to add the controls necessary to allow the user to type in a text field that holds the address of the RSS feed they want to open, and I'll show how to add two buttons, Open and Close. The Open button will return the RSS feed's address to the application and indicate that the user wants to open this feed. The Close button will simply close the window and return the user to the calling window, canceling the operation. The functionality described will require the following controls:

- *Label*: A control used for representing static text. This will inform the user what needs to be typed into the TextBox control.

- *TextBox*: A control used for supporting textual input by the user. This will allow the user to enter some free-form text to represent the URL of the RSS feed they want to open.

- *Button*: A control that denotes an action such as canceling a function. Two buttons will allow the user to open an RSS feed and close the window.

To implement this functionality, first create four reference types for the controls discussed previously, as shown here:

```
Label          label1;
TextBox        txtRssURL;
Button         btnOpen;
Button         btnClose
```

Then within your form constructor, create instances of these controls, and set their attributes as appropriate, as shown in Listing 6-6.

Listing 6-6. *An Example Dialog Box*

```
public MyDialog(string title)

{
  // Default attributes are set here, omitted for clarity

  // Label
  label1 = new Label();
  label1.Text = "Enter RSS URL:";

  // TextBox
  txtRssURL = new TextBox();
  txtRssURL.Top = label1.Top;
  txtRssURL.Left = label1.Left + label1.Width;

  // Open button
  btnOpen = new Button();
  btnOpen.Text = "&Open";

  // Close button
  btnClose = new Button();
  btnClose.Text="&Close";

}
```

Setting the Owner and Location of Your Controls

If you compile and execute the assembly that results from setting the previous code, you'll notice that the form doesn't look as expected; for example, where did the buttons go? They do exist, honestly! It's just that the controls have not been associated with the form, and even if they had, they would all have a default location of the top-left corner of the form and so would be overwritten by each other. To set the controls' locations, you need to specify exactly where you want the controls to be located using the Location property, which encapsulates the Top and Left properties. These properties affect the location of the control as you would expect: the Top property is the number of pixels from the top of the form's client area, and the Left property is the number of pixels from the left of the form's client area. Figure 6-13 shows these properties.

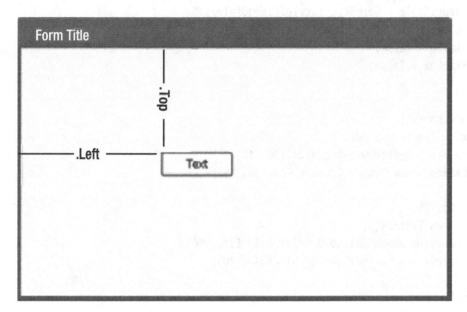

Figure 6-13. *How a control is located within a window*

So, I'll now show how to set the locations of your controls specifically by using the Location property. You'll create a new instance of the System.Drawing.Point reference type with the Left and Top values passed in the constructor and assign it to the Location property. As you can see in the following code, this is similar to setting the Size property:

```
label1.Location = new System.Drawing.Point(8, 19);
```

In a GUI environment such as that provided with Linux and Windows, all controls are essentially windows but with different attributes. A window can act as a container for other controls; this example shows the dialog box acting as a container for controls that support data entry. A parent window is responsible for drawing all the controls it contains that are marked as visible. The method for assigning a parent to the controls, and causing the parent (in this case the form) to *draw* them, is pretty straightforward. The Form reference type has a property called Controls that is a collection of controls that can be associated with and therefore drawn by the form. You simply need to use the Add method on this property to add your controls. You should add the following code after the control instantiation within the form constructor:

```
this.Controls.Add(label1);
this.Controls.Add(txtRssURL);
this.Controls.Add(btnOpen);
this.Controls.Add(btnClose);
```

Listing 6-7 shows the constructor for the dialog box.

Listing 6-7. *The Dialog Box's Completed Constructor*

```
public MyDialog(string title)
{
    this.Text = title;
    this.FormBorderStyle = FormBorderStyle.FixedDialog;
    this.ClientSize = new System.Drawing.Size(362, 96);
    this.MinimizeBox= false;
    this.MaximizeBox = false;

    // Label
    label1 = new Label();
    label1.Text = "Enter RSS URL:";
    label1.Size = new System.Drawing.Size(100, 16);
    label1.Location = new System.Drawing.Point(8, 19);

    // TextBox for URL
    txtRssURL = new TextBox();
    txtRssURL.Location = new System.Drawing.Point(112, 16);
    txtRssURL.Size = new System.Drawing.Size(240, 20);

    // Open button
    btnOpen = new Button();
    btnOpen.Text = "Open";
    btnOpen .Location = new System.Drawing.Point(192, 56);

    // Close button
    btnClose = new Button();
    btnClose.Text="Close";
    btnClose.Location = new System.Drawing.Point(275, 56);

    // Add the controls to the form
    this.Controls.Add(label1);
    this.Controls.Add(txtRssURL);
    this.Controls.Add(btnOpen);
    this.Controls.Add(btnClose);
}
```

When you include this in your application (which is then successfully compiled and executed), you should see the dialog box shown in Figure 6-14 (under Mono) or Figure 6-15 (under .NET) when selecting File ➤ Open.

Figure 6-14. *The File Open dialog box under Mono on Windows*

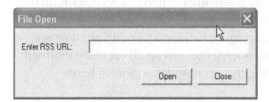

Figure 6-15. *The File Open dialog box using Microsoft's .NET on Windows*

Interacting with the Dialog Box

At the moment, the form lacks any implementation behind the controls on it; however, in the same fashion as you did for the menu, you can implement functionality by using event handlers. In this section, I'll show some code to implement the functionality behind the Close button. The principle is the same for the buttons as the menu-driven events. The first step is to attach an event handler that points to a method that is local to your dialog box class, as follows:

```
btnClose.Click += new System.EventHandler(btnClose_Click);
```

After this, you need to ensure that the event handler method exists, as shown in Listing 6-8. (You can find the full version in the code download available in the Source Code section of the Apress Web site.)

Listing 6-8. *Ensuring the Event Handler Exists*

```
public void btnClose_Click(object sender, System.EventArgs e)
{
  // Implementation goes here
  Console.Out.WriteLine("Close button clicked");
}
```

You are now in a position to provide an implementation for your Close button, which will use the sender object (which in this case will be a Button control and is represented by the Button class) to close the dialog box window. The implementation for the Close button's event handler is as follows:

```
public void btnClose_Click(object sender, System.EventArgs e)
{
  // Implementation goes here

using (sender as Form)
{
    Close();
}
}
```

First, the using statement, which was introduced in Chapter 4, sets the reference context for all commands within the block that follows it. For instance, in the previous example, the Close() method is being applied to the reference that is provided as part of the code within the using statement—in this case the dialog form object.

Second, the code within the braces of the using statement looks scary, but it's pretty simple once you break it down. The next statement's result is a reference to an object being returned. Let's consider the first element that will be evaluated by the compiler, as shown here:

```
(sender as Form)
```

This takes the sender argument as defined in the event handler method and *typecasts* it (tells the compiler what reference type it is) as a Form object. The sender in this instance is the owner of the object that is raising the event and so is the dialog box. You can now access the Form properties and methods. In this case, you're not implementing any core functionality, because it's the Close button and so will simply call the Close() method to close the dialog box, returning control to the main application form.

You could rewrite this in the following manner, which is perhaps clearer to beginners but more inefficient and long winded:

```
Form  frm = (sender as Form)  // Dialog box
frm.Close();  // Call the Close() method to close it down
```

Once control has returned to your main application form, you can then interact with the dialog box reference until it loses scope and is eventually destroyed. In this case, you want to be able to act upon the selection made by the user. For example, if the user clicks the Open button, you'll retrieve the RSS URL to display. You could do this in a number of ways. You could use the Tag property of the dialog box to store the RSS URL as typed by the user and set it to blank if the user clicks Close. A more elegant method would be to expose one or more properties/attributes that indicate to the calling code which action the user took. This is the method shown in the following bold code; it outputs the RSS URL entered in the console window:

```
public void miFileOpen_Click(object sender, System.EventArgs e)
{
  // Implementation goes here
  MyDialog dlgFileOpen = new MyDialog("File Open");
  dlgFileOpen.ShowDialog();
  if (dlgFileOpen.ChoseOpen)
  {
      Console.Out.WriteLine(dlgFileOpen.txtRssURL.Text);
  }
}
```

Before the previous code will work, you'll notice that you access an attribute of the dialog box called ChoseOpen. This is an addition to hold the state associated with your dialog box. Once you've provided a definition for this attribute, you'll simply set its Boolean value to true if the user clicks the Open button or to false if the user clicks the Close button. You can then use this by extending your Open menu's event handler to act on the user's request, which in this case is to simply output the URL entered.

I recommend that at this point you compile your RSS aggregator code, as shown in Listing 6-9. This now implements the dialog box's Open and Close buttons and sets the ChoseOpen state indicator variable (marked as public scope for access) to true for the Open button and to false for the Close button. You can then query this attribute after returning from the dialog box's ShowDialog() method call. If the ChoseOpen attribute is true, then the user has chosen the Open button, and you can simply output the context of the URL textbox, which can be accessed using dlgFileOpen.txtRssURL.Text. If your code won't compile, carefully check the code syntax by comparing it to the listing. If your code fails to run, examine carefully the trace information that will be sent to the console window from which you executed the application. This often provides error messages for the problems you encounter.

Listing 6-9. *The Dialog Box's Implementation So Far*

```
using System;
using System.Windows.Forms;

class MyDialog: Form
{

  Label label1;
  public TextBox txtRssURL;  // Public scope for access
  Button btnOpen;
  Button btnClose;

  // Define your new state variable
  public bool ChoseOpen = false;

  // Default constructor
  public MyDialog(string title)
  {
    this.Text = title;
    this.FormBorderStyle = FormBorderStyle.FixedDialog;
    this.ClientSize = new System.Drawing.Size(362, 96);
    this.MinimizeBox= false;
    this.MaximizeBox = false;

    // Label
    label1 = new Label();
    label1.Text = "Enter RSS URL:";
    label1.Size = new System.Drawing.Size(100, 16);
    label1.Location = new System.Drawing.Point(8, 19);
```

```csharp
    // TextBox for URL
    txtRssURL = new TextBox();
    txtRssURL.Location = new System.Drawing.Point(112, 16);
    txtRssURL.Size = new System.Drawing.Size(240, 20);

    // Open button
    btnOpen = new Button();
    btnOpen.Text = "Open";
    btnOpen.Location = new System.Drawing.Point(192, 56);
    btnOpen.Click += new System.EventHandler(btnOpen_Click);

    // Close button
    btnClose = new Button();
    btnClose.Text="Close";
    btnClose.Location = new System.Drawing.Point(275, 56);
    btnClose.Click += new System.EventHandler(btnClose_Click);

    // Add the controls to the form
    this.Controls.Add(label1);
    this.Controls.Add(txtRssURL);
    this.Controls.Add(btnOpen);
    this.Controls.Add(btnClose);

}

// Close button event
//
public void btnClose_Click(object sender, System.EventArgs e)
{
  ChoseOpen = false;
  using (sender as Form)
  {
    Close();
  }
}

// Open button event
//
public void btnOpen_Click(object sender, System.EventArgs e)
{
  ChoseOpen = true;
  this.Close();
}

}
```

```csharp
public class MyMenu : System.Windows.Forms.MainMenu
{
  // Member Variables
  public  System.Windows.Forms.MenuItem miFile;
  public  System.Windows.Forms.MenuItem miFileOpen;
  public  System.Windows.Forms.MenuItem miFileClose;
  public  System.Windows.Forms.MenuItem miFileExit;

  //
  // Default constructor
  //
  public MyMenu()
  {
    // Create your Main Menu item
    miFile = new MenuItem("&File");
    this.MenuItems.Add(miFile);

    // Create the File menu items
    miFileOpen = new MenuItem("&Open");
    miFileClose = new MenuItem("&Close");
    miFileExit = new MenuItem("E&xit");

    // ...and add them to the File menu item
    miFile.MenuItems.Add(miFileOpen);
    miFile.MenuItems.Add(miFileClose);
    miFile.MenuItems.Add(new MenuItem("-"));
    miFile.MenuItems.Add(miFileExit);

  }
}

class MyMainForm : Form
{

  public MyMenu mainMenu;

  public MyMainForm()
  {
    this.Text = "Main Form";
    mainMenu = new MyMenu();
    this.Menu = mainMenu;
    this.Height = 600;
    this.Width = 800;
```

```csharp
      // Assign your event handler
      mainMenu.miFileOpen.Click += new System.EventHandler(this.miFileOpen_Click);
      mainMenu.miFileClose.Click += new System.EventHandler(this.miFileClose_Click);
      mainMenu.miFileExit.Click += new System.EventHandler(this.miFileExit_Click);
    }

    public void miFileOpen_Click(object sender, System.EventArgs e)
    {
      // Implementation goes here
      MyDialog dlgFileOpen = new MyDialog("File Open");
      dlgFileOpen.ShowDialog();
      if (dlgFileOpen.ChoseOpen)
      {
        Console.Out.WriteLine(dlgFileOpen.txtRssURL.Text);
      }

    }

    public void miFileClose_Click(object sender, System.EventArgs e)
    {
      // Implementation goes here
    }

    public void miFileExit_Click(object sender, System.EventArgs e)
    {
      // Implementation goes here
      Console.Out.WriteLine("File Exit clicked");
      this.Close();
    }

}


class Test
{
  static public void Main(string[] args)
  {
    // Fixed Dialog
    Application.Run(new MyMainForm());
  }
}
```

Note The lines of code in bold represent the changes you need to make to detect and act upon the user's interaction with the dialog box.

Using Windows.Forms Controls

I've shown how to create application forms and dialog box forms, how to add and place controls, and how to interact with the user via event handlers. This has formed the start of your RSS aggregator's main window and the dialog boxes that are invoked from a user's interaction with the main window's menu. You'll now take a more detailed look at some of the controls available, some of which you used within your dialog box. Obviously, it's not possible to cover all the controls available; far too many exist. However, I'll cover some of the main controls and allow you to use the knowledge gained to further investigate the other controls available as part of the .NET Framework as well as the wealth of external controls you can buy off the shelf.

I'll cover the Panel, Label, TextBox, ListBox, and DataGrid controls from a high level. I'll cover how to use each control, introduce the relevant sections of code, and then present the complete listing and a view of what the application should look like. This will complete the Windows Forms–based implementation of your RSS aggregator's core user interface.

Panel

The Panel class defines the look and behavior for the Panel control, which is a container control that allows other controls to reside within it. For instance, if you add a control to an instance of your Panel class and set the AutoScroll property to true, you'll cause the Panel control to display scrollbars as necessary in order to give you access to the controls within it that may not be visible on the screen.

You'll use the Panel control to encapsulate the following three main areas of your application's main form:

- Subscription list

- List of threads

- Thread contents

The following code shows how you first declare three reference types of type System. Windows.Forms.Panel and place them as private members in the main form of your application:

```
private Panel pnlSubscriptions;
private Panel pnlThreads;
private Panel pnlContents;
```

In addition, you'll also declare member variables for the user controls you'll add to your user interface. This code will reference a DataTable class that will require you to import the System.Data namespace (remember the using command). This declaration is as follows:

```
private Label lblSubscriptions;
private TextBox txtContents;
private DataGrid dgThreads;
private ListBox lstSubscriptions;
private DataTable t;
```

In your main form constructor, you'll instantiate these Panel references, which are ready to contain the controls that you'll create later in this chapter. It is also at this point that you insert the code to instantiate any other dependent controls for your user interface, which allows all related code to be grouped early in the process. For example:

```
pnlSubscriptions = new System.Windows.Forms.Panel();
pnlThreads = new System.Windows.Forms.Panel();
pnlContents = new System.Windows.Forms.Panel();
```

Again, in a similar fashion, you can construct your user interface controls at this point, as shown in the following code:

```
lblSubscriptions = new System.Windows.Forms.Label();
lstSubscriptions = new System.Windows.Forms.ListBox();
dgThreads = new System.Windows.Forms.DataGrid();
t = new System.Data.DataTable();
txtContents = new System.Windows.Forms.TextBox();
```

After you have created your Panel instances, you can place and size them appropriately on your main form and initialize any other attributes such as assigning an arbitrary name or setting a table index, as shown in Listing 6-10.

Listing 6-10. *Panel Initialization Example*

```
// Initialize pnlSubscriptions
pnlSubscriptions.AutoScroll = true;
pnlSubscriptions.Controls.Add(lblSubscriptions);
pnlSubscriptions.Controls.Add(lstSubscriptions);
pnlSubscriptions.Location = new System.Drawing.Point(8, 8);
pnlSubscriptions.Name = "pnlSubscriptions";
pnlSubscriptions.Size = new System.Drawing.Size(208, 432);
pnlSubscriptions.TabIndex = 0;

// Initialize pnlThreads
pnlThreads.Controls.Add(this.dgThreads);
pnlThreads.Location = new System.Drawing.Point(224, 8);
pnlThreads.Name = "pnlThreads";
pnlThreads.Size = new System.Drawing.Size(472, 208);
pnlThreads.TabIndex = 1;

// Initialize pnlContents
pnlContents.Controls.Add(txtContents);
pnlContents.Location = new System.Drawing.Point(224, 224);
pnlContents.Name = "pnlContents";
pnlContents.Size = new System.Drawing.Size(472, 216);
pnlContents.TabIndex = 2;
```

You may notice that the Panel controls have had controls assigned to them; you do this at this point to ensure that any actions that may affect the size of the panels can take into account the controls that are associated with them and size these also.

Label

The Label class defines a fixed (usually noninteractive) piece of text that exists on a form. The Label control usually describes the function of another control that may be present; for example, in your dialog box, the Label control defined the purpose of the TextBox control. Another (less obvious but important) use for the Label control is the ability to assign it an *accelerator key*. This key is denoted by an underlined character; in your menu class, an ampersand (&) character precedes the key you want to act as the accelerator key.

For example, if you want the *R* in *RSS URL* to be the accelerator key, you use the ampersand symbol just before the letter *R* within the description, as shown in the following code:

```
label1.Text = "Enter &RSS URL:";
```

When the user selects the accelerator key (by holding down the Alt key first), the focus moves to the control that contains the text with the accelerator key assigned to it, in this case the Label control. And because the Label control cannot have focus, it is automatically transferred to the next control, the TextBox, for which the Label control was the description. Perfect!

Note The accelerator key is usually assigned to the first character of the word that describes the control's use, unless of course this happens to already be in use.

You'll now create another Label control that will indicate the purpose of your list box. In same way as you did with the Panel control, place a member variable for the form in the main form and then create an instance and initialize it within the constructor. The initialization of this control is as follows (I've already discussed its declaration and initialization):

```
// Initialize your subscriptions label
lblSubscriptions.Location = new System.Drawing.Point(8, 8);
lblSubscriptions.Name = "lblSubscriptions";
lblSubscriptions.Size = new System.Drawing.Size(192, 23);
lblSubscriptions.TabIndex = 1;
lblSubscriptions.Text = "Subscribed Feeds:";
```

TextBox

You've already used the TextBox class in your dialog box. It is primarily used to allow the user to enter basic text or some description. You can even disguise the text entered for passwords by using a special PasswordChar property. In addition, it can contain single or multiple lines and can be told whether to support embedded tab characters. It's a flexible control that is surpassed only by its older brother, the Rich TextBox control, which allows far more elaborate text input to occur.

In this case, you are interested in holding only a single line, so the Multiline property that controls this is set to false. However, if you wanted to use a textbox to hold an address, you would set the Multiline property to true and could also use the ScrollBars property to allow the user to scroll through the text contents. For this example, you will use a TextBox control to hold the contents of the RSS feed. The following code shows the initialization of this control:

```
// Initialize your context textbox
txtContents.AutoSize = false;
txtContents.Location = new System.Drawing.Point(8, 8);
txtContents.Name = "textBox1";
txtContents.ScrollBars = System.Windows.Forms.ScrollBars.Both;
txtContents.Size = new System.Drawing.Size(456, 200);
txtContents.TabIndex = 0;
txtContents.Text = "";
```

This will define your TextBox control with scrollbars for navigating your selected RSS feeds' contents. You previously added this control to the appropriate Panel control, which was achieved in the same way as controls are added to forms—using the Add method on the Controls property, as shown here:

```
pnlContents.Controls.Add(txtContents);
```

ListBox

The ListBox class encapsulates a ListBox control, which as its name suggests has some commonality with the TextBox control in that it represents text but in a list format. A ListBox control has several rows that represent rows of text that the box contains. The user may select an individual row. Or, if the control has been configured, the user may select more than one row. For this example, you will use the ListBox control to represent the RSS feeds that the user has subscribed to, and when a user selects a row, this indicates to the application that any further functional requests are based on the context of that feed. For example, if the user wanted to refresh the contents for the RSS feed window, the user would do this by selecting the RSS feed item within the list box. The way in which the ListBox control is defined, instantiated, and initialized is similar to other controls, so I'll focus this time on the initialization of the control and leave the definition and instantiation in your capable hands (you'll need to name the reference lstSubscriptions). The control is initialized as follows:

```
// Subscriptions ListBox
lstSubscriptions.Location = new System.Drawing.Point(8, 32);
lstSubscriptions.Name = "lstSubscriptions";
lstSubscriptions.Size = new System.Drawing.Size(192, 394);
lstSubscriptions.TabIndex = 0;
```

You now have the ListBox control in place to hold your RSS subscriptions and to act as the trigger for displaying the threads of discussion available for the selected feed. Finally, you need to display the threads of discussion and allow the user to select one, which calls for a more complex control—the DataGrid.

DataGrid

The DataGrid class encapsulates the functionality for one of the most advanced .NET standard controls; it allows you to display information using both rows and columns, and it allows the information to come from numerous sources, including a database connection. For this example, you'll use the DataGrid control primarily because of its ability to easily display multiple columns and to have a DataSource control provide the data. I'll focus on the initialization of the control, which at the moment is pretty simple. This is because the columns, and so on, are defined from the DataSource control that feeds the DataGrid control. Here's the initialization:

```
// Initialize the Threads DataGrid

dgThreads.DataMember = "";
dgThreads.Location = new System.Drawing.Point(8, 32);
dgThreads.Name = "dgThreads";
dgThreads.Size = new System.Drawing.Size(456, 168);
dgThreads.TabIndex = 0;
```

Phew, that's a lot to take in! I'll present the entire application, as written so far, which now includes the main window and its core user interface controls. It includes a menu from which you can either exit the application or open a new RSS feed. The File ➤ Open menu option allows you to either cancel the operation or enter a suitable URL for your RSS feed and confirm this operation with the Open button. However, currently this will simply output the URL string to the console window. Listing 6-11 shows the code so far with the omission of the Menu and Dialog classes for brevity.

Listing 6-11. *The RSS Aggregator's Core User Interface Class*

```
using System;
using System.Windows.Forms;
using System.Data;

class MyMainForm : Form
{
  // Member variable declaration
  public MyMenu mainMenu;

  private Panel pnlSubscriptions;
  private Panel pnlThreads;
  private Panel pnlContents;
```

```
private Label lblSubscriptions;
private TextBox txtContents;
private DataGrid dgThreads;
private ListBox lstSubscriptions;
private DataTable t;

public MyMainForm()
{

  mainMenu = new MyMenu();
  this.Menu = mainMenu;

  // Assign your event handler
  mainMenu.miFileOpen.Click += new System.EventHandler(this.miFileOpen_Click);
  mainMenu.miFileClose.Click += new System.EventHandler(this.miFileClose_Click);
  mainMenu.miFileExit.Click += new System.EventHandler(this.miFileExit_Click);

  // Construct your GUI controls
  lblSubscriptions = new System.Windows.Forms.Label();
  lstSubscriptions = new System.Windows.Forms.ListBox();
  dgThreads = new System.Windows.Forms.DataGrid();
  t = new System.Data.DataTable();
  txtContents = new System.Windows.Forms.TextBox();
  pnlSubscriptions = new System.Windows.Forms.Panel();
  pnlThreads = new System.Windows.Forms.Panel();
  pnlContents = new System.Windows.Forms.Panel();

  // Initialize pnlSubscriptions
  pnlSubscriptions.AutoScroll = true;
  pnlSubscriptions.Controls.Add(lblSubscriptions);
  pnlSubscriptions.Controls.Add(lstSubscriptions);
  pnlSubscriptions.Location = new System.Drawing.Point(8, 8);
  pnlSubscriptions.Name = "pnlSubscriptions";
  pnlSubscriptions.Size = new System.Drawing.Size(208, 432);
  pnlSubscriptions.TabIndex = 0;

  // Initialize lblSubscriptions
  lblSubscriptions.Location = new System.Drawing.Point(8, 8);
  lblSubscriptions.Name = "lblSubscriptions";
  lblSubscriptions.Size = new System.Drawing.Size(192, 23);
  lblSubscriptions.TabIndex = 1;
  lblSubscriptions.Text = "Subscribed Feeds:";
```

```csharp
// Subscriptions ListBox
lstSubscriptions.Location = new System.Drawing.Point(8, 32);
lstSubscriptions.Name = "lstSubscriptions";
lstSubscriptions.Size = new System.Drawing.Size(192, 394);
lstSubscriptions.TabIndex = 0;

// Initialize pnlThreads
pnlThreads.Controls.Add(this.dgThreads);
pnlThreads.Location = new System.Drawing.Point(224, 8);
pnlThreads.Name = "pnlThreads";
pnlThreads.Size = new System.Drawing.Size(472, 208);
pnlThreads.TabIndex = 1;

// Initialize dgThreads
dgThreads.DataMember = "";
dgThreads.HeaderForeColor = System.Drawing.SystemColors.ControlText;
dgThreads.Location = new System.Drawing.Point(8, 32);
dgThreads.Name = "dgThreads";
dgThreads.Size = new System.Drawing.Size(456, 168);
dgThreads.TabIndex = 0;

// Initialize pnlContents
pnlContents.Controls.Add(txtContents);
pnlContents.Location = new System.Drawing.Point(224, 224);
pnlContents.Name = "pnlContents";
pnlContents.Size = new System.Drawing.Size(472, 216);
pnlContents.TabIndex = 2;

// Contents TextBox
txtContents.AutoSize = false;
txtContents.Location = new System.Drawing.Point(8, 8);
txtContents.Name = "textBox1";
txtContents.ScrollBars = System.Windows.Forms.ScrollBars.Both;
txtContents.Size = new System.Drawing.Size(456, 200);
txtContents.TabIndex = 0;
txtContents.Text = "";

// Initialize the form
this.Text = "Main Form";
this.ClientSize = new System.Drawing.Size(704, 449);
this.Controls.Add(this.pnlContents);
this.Controls.Add(this.pnlThreads);
this.Controls.Add(this.pnlSubscriptions);

}
```

```
  public void miFileOpen_Click(object sender, System.EventArgs e)
  {
    // Implementation goes here
    MyDialog dlgFileOpen = new MyDialog("File Open");
    dlgFileOpen.ShowDialog();
    if (dlgFileOpen.ChoseOpen)
    {
      Console.Out.WriteLine(dlgFileOpen.txtRssURL.Text);
    }
  }

  public void miFileClose_Click(object sender, System.EventArgs e)
  {
    // Implementation goes here
  }

  public void miFileExit_Click(object sender, System.EventArgs e)
  {
    // Implementation goes here
    Console.Out.WriteLine("File Exit clicked");
    this.Close();
  }
}


class Test
{
  static public void Main(string[] args)
  {
    // Fixed Dialog
    Application.Run(new MyMainForm());
  }
}
```

Before you compile this, it's worth pointing out that the implementation in Listing 6-11 now uses the Panel control as a container for elements of the user interface, specifically for the feed subscriptions, the threads, and the thread contents. You add these to the main form's list of controls using the Controls property and its associated Add() method, as follows:

```
this.Controls.Add(this.pnlContents);
this.Controls.Add(this.pnlThreads);
this.Controls.Add(this.pnlSubscriptions);
```

If you now successfully compile and execute the application, you should see a screen similar to Figure 6-16.

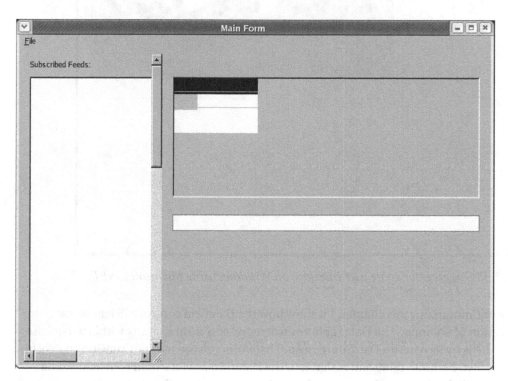

Figure 6-16. *RSS aggregator's core user interface on Linux using Mono*

It's worth pointing out that at the time of this writing, the same code running on Microsoft's .NET implementation yields a far more complete result. This is in part because of the resolution in which the application could be running but can also be attributed to the maturity of the Windows Forms implementation within Mono. You may notice that the TextBox control toward the bottom-right corner of Figure 6-16 is far bigger when running under Microsoft's .NET than under Mono's .NET, as shown in Figure 6-17. This is purely an implementation issue that will be resolved as the Mono implementation matures.

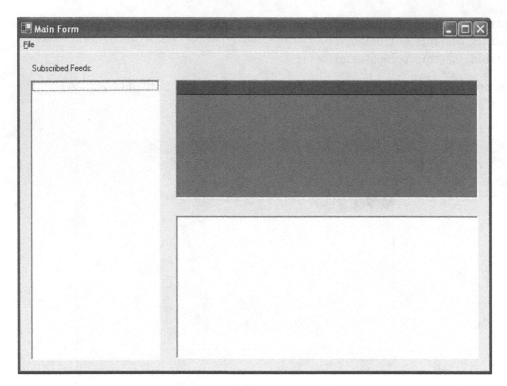

Figure 6-17. *RSS aggregator's core user interface on Windows using Microsoft's .NET*

Before summarizing this chapter, I'll show how the DataGrid control will handle the automatic creation of columns. The DataTable control represents a Table entity within a database and therefore is by its nature a DataSource also. Therefore, you can use the DataGrid control to create your own fictitious table and assign it to the DataGrid as you would your actual data source. This will display the columns you define; however, with no data in it, only a single, empty row will be displayed. For example, define your table instance, and assign it to the DataGrid control using the following code:

```
t.Columns.Add("Title");
t.Columns.Add("Date");
t.Columns.Add("Author");
t.Columns.Add("Subject");
dgThreads.DataSource = t;
```

The result, when executed, should consist of your form with the controls in place and an empty DataGrid, as shown in Figure 6-18.

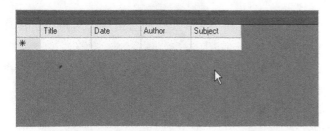

Figure 6-18. *The DataGrid using your mock table*

What's New in Version 2.0?

Creating rich user interfaces has never been so easy with the introduction of Windows Forms 2.0 and the collection of classes, and their methods and attributes, that are available within the System.Windows.Forms namespace. The number of classes has increased by about 67 percent, and the number of members and attributes associated with them has increased by about 127 percent. This indicates the importance placed on Windows Forms. It is obviously not possible to cover all these classes and their members, but Table 6-4 lists the key improvements.

Table 6-4. *New Windows Forms Features*

Feature	Description
UI controls	Improvements have been made to some of the core user interface controls such as the MainMenu control, which now supports graphical images against each menu item, a fully functional toolbar, and a Web browser control.
Layout	A number of new layout controls have been provided to enhance the visual management of controls through layout at both design time and runtime. Some examples include SplitContainer for splitting a window into different areas and TableLayout for providing a tabular format for laying out your user interface controls.
Data binding	A number of new user interface controls are provided that simplify the binding of data to a control for its visual representation. This includes data record management styles such as master-detail and VCR-type support.
Control management	The ControlArray component has been introduced (it existed in Visual Basic) that allows multiple controls to be collectively managed through an array and its associated capabilities.
Asynchronous calls	Components have been provided that encapsulate a worker thread to support asynchronous processing within your user interface, specifically related to the visual feedback of a task. For example, you could provide a visual progress bar for file loading, which would work in parallel with the file-loading operation using threads.
Other	Some generic improvements include the enhancement of controls such as the TextBox and ComboBox controls to now provide autocomplete functionality, providing a more intuitive and comprehensive data input experience.

Managing Layout in Your User Interface

Placing controls onto a form when designing and implementing your application's user interface can be time-consuming and problematic. For example, absolute positioning does not support windows being resized; in addition, adhering to user interface guidelines can be resource intensive to implement. Version 2.0 of the Windows Forms framework has introduced a number of controls whose functionality is specifically aimed at the layout of controls. A couple of examples are the FlowLayout control and the TableLayout control. These, as their names suggest, support the automatic layout of container controls in either a flow manner (usually from right to level) or a tabular manner (with rows and columns). Those of you with Java experience may find some similarities with layout functionality within user interface frameworks such as the Abstract Working Toolkit (AWT) and Swing.

Control Improvements

In addition to providing a set of new controls, improvements have been made to existing controls. A good example of this is the support for autocompletion.

Autocomplete Support

The automatic completion feature is becoming more common within user interfaces to help guide the user through data entry. Depending on the configuration, this feature allows the text being entered to be matched against a defined source and suggestions made. You implement this through two properties that have been associated with controls such as the TextBox control:

- AutoCompleteMode

- AutoCompleteSource

AutoCompleteMode defines the behavior of this feature and has the set of enumerated shown in Table 6-5.

Table 6-5. *AutoCompleteMode Enumerated Values*

Value	Description
None	Switches this feature off
AutoSuggest	Automatically suggests a matching value via a drop-down list
AutoAppend	Automatically appends a matching value to your text
AutoSuggestAppend	A combination of the previous values, automatically appending text while also suggesting completion options

AutoCompleteSource defines the source of data against which this feature will perform its matches; these sources are indicated by a set of enumerated values, as shown in Table 6-6.

Table 6-6. *AutoCompleteSource Enumerated Values*

Value	Description
FileSystem	Uses the file system
HistoryList	Uses the URL history list
RecentlyUsedList	Uses the recently used URL history list
AllURL	Uses all URL history (a combination of HistoryList and RecentlyUsedList)
AllSystemSources	Uses a combination of FileSystem and AllURL

Table 6-6. *AutoCompleteSource Enumerated Values*

Value	Description
CustomSource	Allows you to define your own source as a collection of items stored in the AutoCompleteCustomSource property
None	Indicates no source

The following code shows how you can use this to enhance your RSS aggregator application:

```
TextBox RSSUrl;
RSSUrl = new TextBox();
RSSUrl.AutoCompleteMode = AutoCompleteMode.AutoSuggestAppend;
RSSUrl.AutoCompleteSource = \AutoCompleteSource.AllURL;
```

This would provide the automatic completion support for the RSS aggregator's URL textbox. It means the textbox automatically suggests matches from both the historical and recently used URL lists that exist within your local browser. This would enable the user to select a URL that they may have found through their Web browser some time ago.

Data Binding

The support for data binding within .NET 1.*x* was admirable, with a number of controls supporting arbitrary data binding to a variety of data sources. These controls already supported the ability to see the results of data binding at both runtime and design time within an IDE, the later being particularly powerful when prototyping or designing your user interface. These controls have been enhanced, but more important, some additional controls have been introduced. The following sections show some of the key controls.

GridView

A new GridView control supports the tabular layout of information and features advanced functionality, including the following:

- Enhanced user interface customization such as the support for themes, formatting, and layout

- Enhanced view functionality such as the dynamic reordering of columns

- Rich support for different data sources including images

Data Container

The ability for controls to be data-bound is an important element when building user interfaces that support functionality such as data entry. Whilst simplifying the task of building such applications, this method still requires you to add fields to your form manually and possibly add the implementation of Create, Retrieve, Update, and Delete (CRUD) functionality. The DataContainer control, when bound to a DataSource control, can automatically add the fields from its associated data source for you and as such create a fully functional CRUD-compliant screen with little code.

Summary

In this chapter, I covered a massive topic with a focus on what you need to do to create a main form, complete with controls and a dialog box that links to the main menu. I discussed the differences between windows, both form and dialog box variations, and I also discussed how you can put event handlers to work to provide the implementation behind a user's actions. Finally, you looked at some of the controls available as part of the .NET Framework, and I showed how you can place and manipulate them to provide the foundation for this book's project, the RSS aggregator.

The `Windows.Forms` namespace is huge; to do it justice is simply not possible within one chapter. Therefore, I provided a good foundation for you to continue exploring at your own leisure. It's also worth mentioning that under .NET, Mono is not limited to Windows Forms as the only method for implementing your user interface. The GNOME toolkit (Gtk#) is another powerful user interface technology stack and, in some cases, far more mature. Therefore, you'll spend Chapter 7 comparing the two technologies and looking at how to make an informed decision about which one to use. I'll also provide a foundation in using Gtk# with Mono to implement your own user interfaces.

CHAPTER 7

■ ■ ■

Introducing Gtk+, Glade, and User Interfaces

In the previous chapter, you learned about the available technologies for designing and developing your GUI. The .NET Framework provides its own API called Windows Forms, which has been developed entirely using the .NET Framework and associated class libraries. This enables interoperability between any implementation of the CLI, so the same code will run the same on Microsoft's .NET implementation, on Mono's .NET implementation, and so on. The Windows Forms class libraries are still under development and are not as mature as the other open-source technologies; however, progress is being made quickly. You should always consider Windows Forms (in addition to other user interface technologies) when deciding which user interface class library to use. A good example of an additional user interface library to consider is the GIMP toolkit (Gtk+) and consequently Gtk#, the .NET wrapper for Gtk+.

In this chapter, I'll introduce the features provided by Gtk+, show you how to embrace these features using the Gtk# API, and finally cover some of the tools that support designing and developing your user interfaces using Gtk+ such as Glade.

What Is Gtk+?

Gtk+ is a toolkit that was explicitly designed for implementing user interfaces on a number of platforms. The brainchild of Peter Mattis, Spencer Kimball, and Josh MacDonald, the original Gtk started as a collection of widgets for the GNU Image Manipulation Program (GIMP) but has since grown in popularity and scale to be used by a significant number of applications, including the GNOME desktop. Its popularity has been encouraged through its language independence, which is achieved through language bindings (also called *wrappers*). These wrappers provide the API for accessing the Gtk+ toolkit from multiple languages such as C, C++, Java, Perl, Python, and of course C#. You can find a complete list of language bindings at http://www.gtk.org/bindings.html. In recent years, Gtk's development has been coordinated by Peter Mattis with input from a number of dedicated authors; the extended version is called Gtk+. The Gtk+ toolkit fundamentally consists of a number of libraries, including the following:

- *Glib*: A core library that provides important basic functionality required by not just Gtk+ but also by GNOME. This functionality includes support for threads, data structures, event handling, and so on.

- *Pango*: Provides support for layout management and text rendering, including the ability to provide support for internationalization.

- *Accessibility Toolkit (ATK) library*: Provides support for accessibility standards to be used in tools for people with special needs, such as the visually impaired. Some examples of accessibility tools include screen readers, magnifiers, and so on.

Getting Started with Gtk+

To use Gtk+ within the Mono environment, you'll need to ensure that you have the necessary files installed. You can find the .NET language bindings for Gtk+ (called Gtk#) and the required Gtk+ libraries at their respective home pages on the Internet:

- *Gtk# home page*: http://gtk-sharp.sourceforge.net/

- *Gtk+ home page*: http://www.gtk.org

However, the recommended location for downloading the Gtk# .NET bindings, assuming you already have Gtk+ installed, is the Mono project's home page at http://www.mono-project.com.

Installation is simple but again is platform specific. For Linux, several RPMs and source RPMs (SRPMs) are available on the Mono project's home page; you can download and install them using your favorite package manager, such as Yum or RPM. You can also use the appropriate package manager to confirm that the installation was successful. Although Gtk+ is almost native to the Linux platform, an installer is available for the Windows platform (along with some other packages, such as the Gtk+ runtime and documentation) on the Novell Forge Web site (see http://forge.novell.com/modules/xfcontent/downloads.php/gtk-sharp/GTK-Sharp%20Runtime). You can install it by simply executing the Win32 installer program. Figure 7-1 shows the final page of the installer.

Figure 7-1. *Gtk+ Win32 installer*

Once you've installed it, you can begin developing your Gtk+ applications using the Gtk# API provided and the Mono C# compiler, but you will come to realize that developing a user interface using code alone is not much fun. I recommend that when developing user interfaces, you utilize an IDE to take the hassle out of managing your user interfaces and laying out the controls. I've already discussed various IDEs, such as MonoDevelop and Eclipse, that include a user interface design element. In the case of Gtk+, you can use Glade, which provides a free user interface designer that integrates with the Gtk+ toolkit.

Using Glade for User Interface Design and Development

In the following sections, I'll cover how to use Glade as a user interface design tool; fortunately, it takes the effort out of designing the visual aspects of your application. Glade will be installed automatically as part of the Gtk# installation, so you should find that the utility is already present. If it isn't, then download and install it as appropriate from the Glade home page at http://glade.gnome.org.

What Is Glade?

Glade is an open-source tool that allows you to visually design your user interface using the Gtk+ toolkit and then save this visual representation as an XML file that can be dynamically loaded and utilized by an application that is using the appropriate library. Figure 7-2 shows the Glade interface.

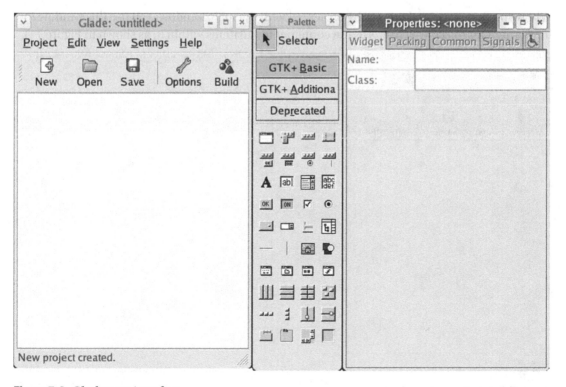

Figure 7-2. *Glade user interface*

Using Glade is not limited to open-source platforms such as Linux. You can find a "port" to the Windows platform at `http://gladewin32.sourceforge.net/`. The following are two benefits of using a graphical tool for designing user interfaces:

- First, the visual representation of your applications is best defined using visual techniques. In other words, it's difficult to visualize how a user interface will look without actually seeing the end results, and to that extent, being able to place controls on a canvas and move them to gauge the look and feel of your application is compelling (and in my opinion mandatory).

- Second, the round-trips (code, change, compile, run) required to perform the same tasks in code are significant, so it is highly recommended that you design all user interface elements using an appropriate tool, such as Glade or MonoDevelop.

In the following sections, I'll cover the Glade user interface and give you a feel for how to use the application.

Navigating the Glade User Interface

The Glade tool makes defining the user interface to your application simple. Not surprisingly, you interact with Glade through a GUI. It's presented as three windows that interact with one another, including the main window, the Pallet window, and the Properties window. In the following sections, I'll introduce each window in turn and summarize its purpose. Then I'll show how to use these windows to define your user interfaces.

Main Window

When you first start Glade, you'll be presented with the main window. You use this window to implement a *project*, which acts as the container for all items within it, as shown in Figure 7-3.

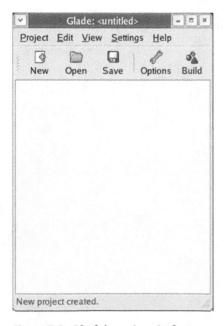

Figure 7-3. *Glade's main window*

Figure 7-3 depicts the main window with a new project created (as indicated in the status bar). You can access the options available to you at this stage either through the menu or through the toolbar. The menu options are available under five main menus, as listed in Table 7-1.

Table 7-1. *Glade Menus*

Menu	Menu Items
Project	Create, Open Save, Build, and Options
Edit	Cut, Copy, Paste, and Delete
View	Show Palette, Show Property Editor, Show Widget Tree, and Show Clipboard
Settings	Show Grid, Snap to Grid, Show Widget Tooltips, Set Grid Options, and Set Snap Options
Help	Contents, FAQ, and About

You can access a subset of this functionality through the toolbar buttons.

Note The menu items may vary depending on your version of Glade.

Palette Window

The Palette window provides a graphical view of the controls available for use within your user interface. You can display a list of the controls, or *widgets*, by selecting the button associated with the category of controls you want to view, as shown in Figure 7-4.

Figure 7-4. *Glade's Palette window*

The categories exposed via the buttons include the following:

- *Gtk+ Basic*: This holds the basic controls that form the foundation of most GUIs (for example, the Window control and the Button control).

- *Gtk+ Additional*: This holds controls that are useful but used less often (for example, the Font Selection Dialog control and the Calendar control).

- *Deprecated:* This holds controls that are no longer being developed and have since been replaced but are shown for backward compatibility.

■**Note** You can create your own Gtk+ controls and add them to Glade's Palette window for use in your applications, although this is a more advanced topic and beyond the scope of this chapter. If you want to try this, study the Gtk+ documentation (see `http://www.gtk.org/documentation.html`) and the Glade API documentation (see `http://developer.gnome.org/doc/API/2.0/glib/index.html`).

Properties Window

The Properties window allows you to view and modify a variety of properties associated with the control that currently has the focus. These properties are categorized via a series of tabs, as shown in Figure 7-5.

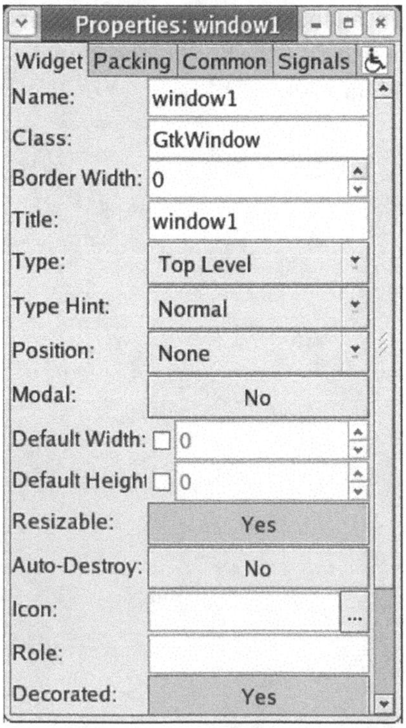

Figure 7-5. *Glade's Properties window*

You can access a tab by simply selecting it; the properties associated with that category then display for you to view or edit. These categories are as follows:

Widget: This set contains the core properties associated with the selected control and are typically focused on visual attributes such as DefaultWidth, DefaultHeight, and so on.

Packing: These properties are associated with those controls that have an array of elements and prescribed order. For example, the Tab control is an array of tabs with properties that can be modified through the Packing tab.

Common: As its name suggests, this set contains the common properties associated with a given control, both visual and programmatic. These properties are common to all controls and as such are contained on their own tab. For example, this includes Width, Height, Modal, and Event masks (indicators of which events you want to be raised).

Signals: These properties allow you to associate event handlers with events (that is, *signals*) that the control may encounter. These signals are hierarchical in nature and so include all the events that may be thrown by the control and all the descendants. In the example of a Window widget, these events could come from the object hierarchy; specifically, the parents of a Window control are GtkWindow, GtkContainer, GtkWidget, GtkObject, and GObject. Phew! Once you have selected your signal, you can then associate a method that would trap the event when fired.

Accessibility: These controls allow you to modify attributes to make your applications more accessible. For example, the ZoomText control provides a "zoom" window for the visually impaired that displays text in a large font; to use it, you associate a label with the control that the application looks for and then displays.

Other Windows

In addition to the three main windows discussed, two other windows are accessible by choosing the View menu option and selecting one from within the list. This menu selection will toggle between the window being open or closed. These windows are the Widget Tree window and the Clipboard window.

The Widget Tree window displays the container hierarchy for controls currently in the selected window. For example, a Window control may contain several controls, which in turn may be containers for yet more controls; you can find all these controls listed in the Widget Tree window, as shown in Figure 7-6.

The Clipboard window allows you to track the controls that you may have copied to the Clipboard (see Figure 7-7). You may copy more than one control to the Clipboard at a time, and these will be listed within the Clipboard window. You can then select the item you want to paste by simply selecting it within the Clipboard window.

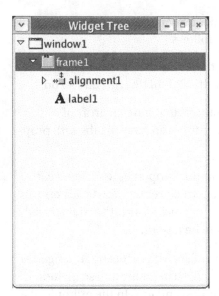

Figure 7-6. *Glade's Widget Tree window*

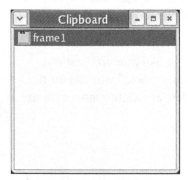

Figure 7-7. *Glade's Clipboard window*

Creating Your First Project

You should now have a good understanding of the user interface associated with Glade and how to navigate it to find your desired functionality. In this section, I'll focus on using Glade to create your application's user interface visually rather than programmatically (as you did in Chapter 5).

The first step when using Glade is to either open a preexisting project or create a new one. As this is your first project, you'll start by creating a new project; simply select Project ➤ New to create a new project. You'll then be asked to confirm this request; click OK. This will subtly change the main window by indicating in the status window that a project has been created, as shown in Figure 7-8.

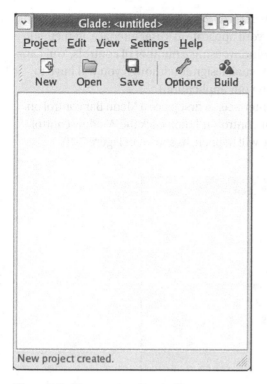

Figure 7-8. *New project created*

You may now start to create your user interface; to begin, you'll need to select the Window control from the Palette window, the starting point for a user interface. This control is easily identifiable in the top-left corner of the Gtk+ Basic palette. After selecting this you'll notice that a *window1* entry (its title) is displayed within Glade's main window, and the Window control itself will appear so you can work on it. At this point, you should give the main window a name by accessing its properties; name your main window frmMain. Figure 7-9 shows a blank window, complete with a grid onto which you can place controls.

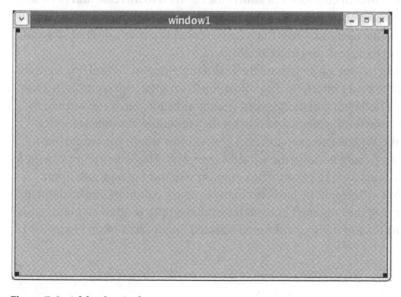

Figure 7-9. *A blank window*

Once you have the window as your core construct, you can start to use this canvas to add more controls to the form and visually begin to build your application's user interface. Remember, in Chapter 5 you created your application's main window using a number of controls. You can do the same thing here but instead use Glade as a visual designer (although you will have to work with the code later to use the user interface in your application).

For now, you'll concentrate on designing your interface, so first place a Menu Bar control on the form. However, if you simply select the Menu Bar control and then click the Window control, indicating that you want to add it, something strange will happen, as shown in Figure 7-10.

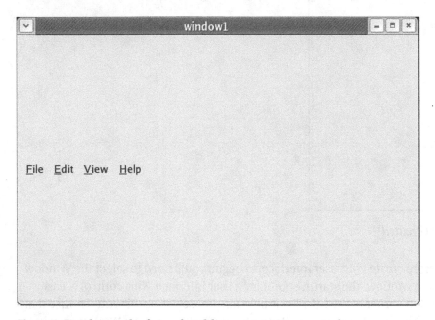

Figure 7-10. *The result of simply adding a Menu Bar control*

As I'm sure you'll agree, this isn't what you intended! This is because Glade uses a mechanism called *packing*. (Remember the Packing tab within the Properties window?) Packing is a method used to handle the layout of controls that allows the controls to increase and decrease in size along with the main window. At first you'll find this a little distracting, but in the long run it makes for far more usable user interfaces that can be scaled to a user's desired size and for the most part retain their look, feel, and functionality.

The keys to using packing to your advantage are the Horizontal Box and Vertical Box controls that are container controls for a user interface; they allow you to arrange your controls in a way that makes sense visually to both you and the users of your application. So, if you wanted to add two rows to your form, one for the menu and one for the content, you would select the Vertical Box control from the Widget category and click the window where you would like to place the box (in this case anywhere because the window is empty). This will prompt you for the number of rows (or columns for a Horizontal Box control) you want to add, and upon confirming this, the window will be split by however many rows (or columns) you've defined. Once confirmed, you'll see that the container control has added empty window elements with a separator based on the number of rows (or columns) selected. In the example in Figure 7-11, you can clearly see the two rows with a separator in the middle of the window, and each window *pane* has a grid onto which you can place controls.

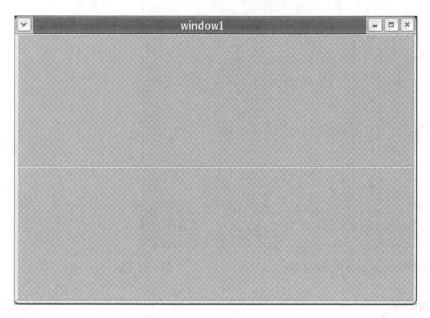

Figure 7-11. *The window with two rows*

Now that you have two row containers on your form, you can place controls within these; for example, you could place your menu in the top row, which would then leave the bottom row for other controls.

Creating Your RSS Aggregator's First Window Using Gtk#

I've explained the concepts behind using the Glade user interface designer tool to define your application's GUI, so I'll now walk you through defining the user interface for the RSS aggregator's main application window. I'll also discuss Glade's output and how you can use it for attaching functionality via event handlers. Although the source code for the RSS aggregator uses Windows Forms, you are free to choose Gtk# as your user interface technology if you prefer.

Adding Your Menu and Containers

Starting within an empty window, let's add two rows that will contain both the menu and the content for the rest of the application. You do this by first choosing the Vertical Box and placing it in the Window control to split the window into two rows. This will leave you with a window that looks like the earlier Figure 7-11. Then you select the Menu Bar control and place this in the top row of your window, which will cause the row to automatically size the menu, leaving the rest of the canvas free. You'll then use the Horizontal Box in the remaining canvas to add two more columns, splitting the rightmost column into two rows using the Vertical Box. Figure 7-12 shows the result.

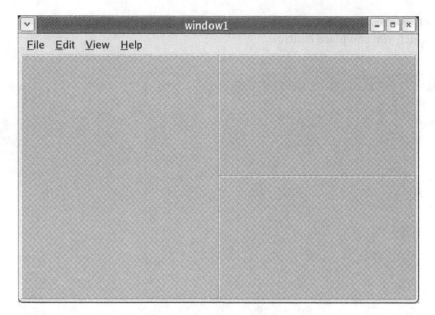

Figure 7-12. *Window with menu and placeholders*

Adding Your Main Controls

Next, add a List or Tree View control to the leftmost pane (for the RSS feed subscriptions) and to the right-top pane (for the threads). The bottom-right row holds the contents for each thread selected using a Text View control. Figure 7-13 shows the result.

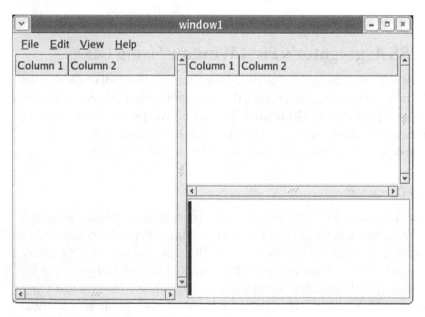

Figure 7-13. *The window with all controls in place*

Note If you want to see the packing feature in action, try resizing the window and watch how the controls within it scale respectively, keeping their aspect ratios.

The main application window is now starting to take shape; however, some of the controls have properties that need modifying. For example, your RSS subscription list has two columns when you need only one, and the main menu has options you do not need. To address this, I'll show how to complete the Glade user interface tutorial by discussing the options for modifying these properties.

You'll start with the main menu; far too many options are available at the moment, as these were added by default. You simply want a File menu with Open, Close, and Quit items. So, select the Menu Bar control, and view the Properties window, as shown in Figure 7-14. Alternatively, right-click the Menu Bar control, which will display a context-sensitive menu, as shown in Figure 7-15.

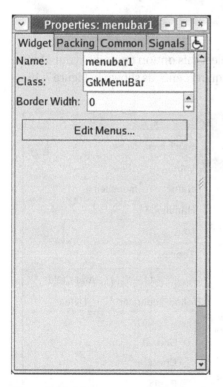

Figure 7-14. *Menu control's Properties window*

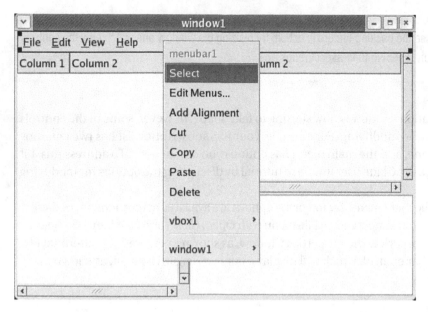

Figure 7-15. *Menu control's context-sensitive menu*

In either case, the Edit Menu option is available, so select this option to modify your Menu Bar control via the Menu Editor dialog box to match your requirements, as shown in Figure 7-16.

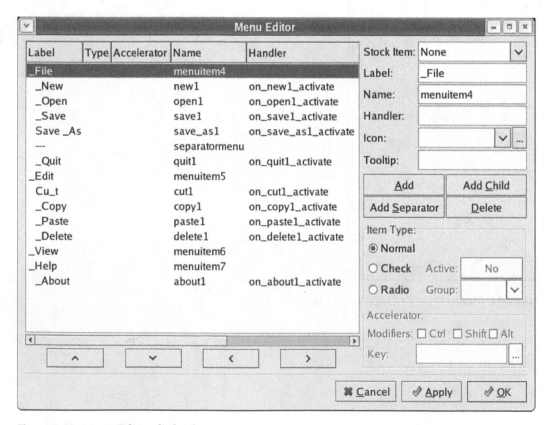

Figure 7-16. *Menu Editor dialog box*

Before I continue, I'll pass on some tips for working with the Menu Bar control used as an application's main menu:

- Menu items are parents and as such can have child items. You can add these by clicking the Add Child button. The child items appear only when the parent menu item has been selected.

- A menu item can be based on a stock item, which is a menu item that is standard within the GNOME desktop and can have associated accelerator keys, icons, and names. For speed, you can choose a stock item on which to base your menu item. This ensures consistency and saves you some typing.

The final product is a window with controls that have been tailored using the properties that are associated with them. Some will need programmatic modification (which you'll perform throughout later chapters in the book), but for now your application window is complete, as shown in Figure 7-17.

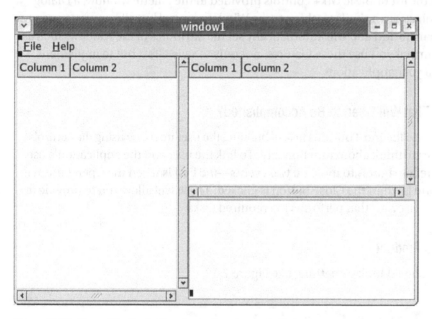

Figure 7-17. *Your Glade-defined application window*

The next step is to define your Open Feed dialog box, in a similar fashion to the File Open dialog box you created in Chapter 6 (although in this instance you're giving the dialog box a different title and using the Glade application).

Creating a Dialog Box

I'll approach the explanation of this process slightly differently to help cement the knowledge gained in the previous section. I'll start by listing the controls you'll be using in this chapter, including packing containers. I'll then discuss some of the tasks required to get the dialog box looking good, and finally I'll present the complete user interface.

What Controls Are Required?

If you cast your mind back to Chapter 6, the purpose of the dialog box (in this case Open Feed) that is linked to the File ➤ Open menu item is to allow users to enter URLs that point to the RSS feeds they want to subscribe to; therefore, the controls required to enable this are as follows:

- *Label*: This simply acts as the text associated with the textbox, advising users that they need to enter an RSS URL.

- *TextBox*: This control provides the user with a way to enter the RSS URL.

- *Button*: You'll use two Button controls. The Open button allows the user to confirm that the URL is correct and start the subscription process. The Close button allows the user to cancel the operation and return to the main application window.

At this point, you could build the user interface using a similar method to that described for your RSS aggregator's main window; however, you can do it in a far simpler way. You'll notice that as part of the list of Basic Gtk+ controls provided in the Palette window, a Dialog control exists. This behaves in a similar fashion to the Window control but allows you to specify which buttons you want to add and will automatically set the attributes of the window, such as Style. I highly recommend you use these features, not only to save effort but to implement consistency across all your applications.

What Are the Tasks That Will Need to Be Accomplished?

Once you have completed the most obvious task of building the user interface using the controls available, you can start to think about functionality. To link the user and the application's user interface, you must define signals to indicate two events—the first is when the Open button is clicked, and the second is when the Close button is clicked. These will allow you to provide an implementation for each event that performs the required tasks.

Viewing the Finished Product

The finished product should look something like Figure 7-18.

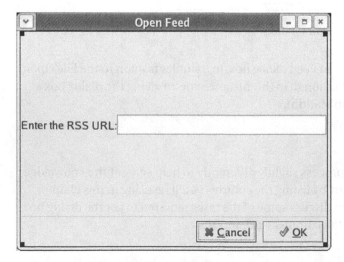

Figure 7-18. *An example Open Feed dialog box*

Examining Glade's Output

The Glade application stores the representation of each window, its controls, and the associated property values in XML. This is a platform-independent standard that was ratified by the W3C standards body, the same body that ratified other ubiquitous standards such as HTML. I'll discuss this in far more detail in Chapter 8, but for now I'll briefly cover the result from saving the Glade project.

If you examine the file system, you'll notice a file with a .glade extension. This is the file that is created by Glade; it is an XML representation of the windows and their controls. Listing 7-1 shows an example file; a detailed understanding is not required, but for background information I'll present its structure.

Listing 7-1. *An Example* .glade *File*

```
<widget class="GtkWindow" id="frmFileOpen">
  <property name="visible">True</property>
  <property name="title" translatable="yes">File Open</property>
  <property name="type">GTK_WINDOW_TOPLEVEL</property>
  <property name="window_position">GTK_WIN_POS_NONE</property>
  <property name="modal">False</property>
  <property name="resizable">True</property>
  <property name="destroy_with_parent">False</property>
  <property name="decorated">True</property>
  <property name="skip_taskbar_hint">False</property>
  <property name="skip_pager_hint">False</property>
  <property name="type_hint">GDK_WINDOW_TYPE_HINT_NORMAL</property>
  <property name="gravity">GDK_GRAVITY_NORTH_WEST</property>

  <child>
    <widget class="GtkVBox" id="vbox3">
      <property name="visible">True</property>
      <property name="homogeneous">False</property>
      <property name="spacing">0</property>

    <child>
      <widget class="GtkHBox" id="hbox3">
        <property name="visible">True</property>
        <property name="homogeneous">False</property>
        <property name="spacing">0</property>
```

Those of you familiar with XML should have little trouble following this snippet, and those of you who don't use XML regularly should still find the contents fairly self-explanatory. I'll now highlight some key elements of the file.

The following element is defining the start of a widget item that belongs to the GtkWindow class and has an id value of frmFileOpen. You should recognize this as the start of your File Open dialog box.

```
<widget class="GtkWindow" id="frmFileOpen">
```

The following element is a `property` element that will be contained within another element and that defines the value of a property named `visible`. In this instance, it has a value of True, and because this snippet came from your Window widget, you can surmise that this means the window will be visible by default.

```
<property name="visible">True</property>
```

Finally, this is the complete construct for a control on your user interface:

```
<widget class="GtkTreeView" id="tvSubscription">
    <property name="visible">True</property>
    <property name="can_focus">True</property>
    <property name="headers_visible">False</property>
    <property name="rules_hint">False</property>
    <property name="reorderable">False</property>
    <property name="enable_search">False</property>
</widget>
```

As you can probably deduce, this represents the Tree View control you will use for your subscription list, including its property values. You shouldn't find it too difficult to follow the rest of the XML file produced; Chapter 9 will provide you with the necessary information to fully understand the power and features of XML.

Using Glade's Programmatic Interface

You've seen how to use the Glade application to define the user interfaces for your application, and I've touched on how Glade holds this representation using XML. You'll now look at how you can use this file to invoke an instance of your user interface and hook into the signals (events) that may be associated with it.

Note I won't attempt to provide the complete implementation for the RSS aggregator in this chapter; I'll simply demonstrate how to take the user interface and provide functionality that is invoked by the user. All the source code and the full implementation of the RSS aggregator application is available for download from the Source Code section of the Apress Web site (`http://www.apress.com`).

What Do You Need?

To start using Glade, the user interface as defined by your XML file is not enough, although it is obviously a crucial component of the overall solution. In addition to the user interface file, you'll also need two supporting libraries related to the Glade API:

- Gtk# libraries (`http://gtk-sharp.sourceforge.net/`)

- Glade libraries (already downloaded with Glade)

The runtime assemblies contain the implementation for both Gtk+ (the individual user interface components) and Glade (the user interface building blocks), both of which are necessary to ensure that your code runs. In addition to this, you need the libraries against which you can implement your code and provide the necessary namespaces (both Gtk and Glade).

You can install the Gtk# package using packages (.rpm files) provided on the Mono home page (http://www.mono-project.com) using a command similar to this:

```
rpm -iv gtk-sharp*
```

■ **Note** On my system, this installed the packages using files that begin with gtk-sharp, as these were the only two in my directory. You could, of course, fully qualify the filenames if you wanted to do so. Installing the appropriate package on your Linux platform is a little less rewarding than on Windows, as you'll merely see the package manager's indication of success.

Also, not only is the Glade user interface designer available on the Windows platform, but the Gtk# packages are too. The installation here is slightly different, as it uses the Windows installer. If successful, you should see a screen similar to Figure 7-19.

Figure 7-19. *Successful Gtk# installation on Windows*

■ **Note** You'll need to include the glade-sharp and gtk-sharp assemblies when compiling your application by using the -pkg: command-line option, so -pkg:gtk-sharp -pkg:glade-sharp is necessary.

Creating an Instance of a User Interface

To start implementing the user interface that you defined with the Glade application, you'll need to use the API exposed by both Gtk# and Glade that is provided in the runtime assemblies installed in the previous steps. The first task is to declare your interest in these libraries through your code by importing the relevant namespaces; these are Gtk for Gtk# and Glade for Glade. The following code snippet is from the GtkMainWindow.cs file that is available for download from the Apress Web site:

```
using Gtk;
using Glade;
```

The next step is to define a class that acts as a wrapper for the user interfaces you have defined, so if you start by concentrating on the main application window, you can create a class that encapsulates this functionality and integrates with both Glade and Gtk# as necessary. Listing 7-2 shows this code.

Listing 7-2. *Creating a Gtk# Window Class*

```
public class MainWindow
{
  public MainWindow ()
  {
    Glade.XML gui = new Glade.XML ("./RSSAggregator.glade", "frmMain", "");
  }
}
```

I've highlighted the main line of code that loads and creates an instance of a user interface window using the declarative file created (referenced within the source code as RSSAggregator. glade) when the Glade project is saved and you reference the name of the resource you want to display. The Glade.XML class's constructor takes three parameters:

- The .glade user interface file.

- The name of the window to display within the file.

- Translation domain. You'll use blank (""), which is the default, for this example.

You'll use this method to load your XML file and reference the main window, in this case called frmMain. But please remember that the path to your .glade file must be correct; otherwise, the code will not execute correctly. My personal preference is to either store the files in the application's main directory or create a subdirectory to store them that is entitled ui (short for *user interface*). In either case, for the Mono compiler to successfully produce an executable, it must be able to resolve these locations when compilation occurs. You can now build the body of your main application to use this Window class and create an instance to display your main window (see Listing 7-3).

Listing 7-3. *Creating a Gtk+ Window Using Gtk#*

```
public class MainApp
{
  public static void Main(string[] args)
  {
    Gtk.Application.Init();
    MainWindow wndMain = new MainWindow();
    Gtk.Application.Run();
  }
}
```

> **Note** In some cases, the .glade file's contents may not be valid between different operating system and/or Gtk+ and Gtk# libraries. Always ensure that you test your code on all the platforms on which you want your application to run.

The first statement, Gtk.Application.Init(), initializes the Gtk+ ready for operation and is a mandatory call to use the Gtk+ toolkit. The second statement is pretty self-explanatory; it creates a reference to an instance of your wrapper class and instantiates it. If you recall, in Listing 7-2, this is the code that creates an instance of the Glade.XML class using your .glade file and the main application's window name. This may be OK for the main application window, but what if you wanted to be a little more specific about how you created and showed windows? You can rewrite the previous code to work as shown in Listing 7-4.

Listing 7-4. *Example of Controlled Window Creation*

```
public class MainWindow
{
  public Gtk.Window win;
  Glade.XML xml;

  public MainWindow ()
  {
    xml = new Glade.XML ("./RSSAggregator.glade", "frmMain", "");
    win = (xml.GetWidget("frmMain") as Gtk.Window);
  }
}
```

The new lines of code define both your Glade.XML class reference type called xml (at a class level) and a new class member of reference type Gtk.Window named win. These are important because the XML class is still loaded, but you are specifically retrieving the window as a Gtk.Window reference type by using the GetWidget() method, passing the name of the widget (in this case, Window) and then typecasting this as a GtkWindow object. The first point to note is that the cast is valid because, ultimately, Gtk.Window descends from Gtk.Widget. The hierarchy is as follows:

```
System.Object
  Glib.Object
    Gtk.Object
      Gtk.Widget
        Gtk.Container
          Gtk.Bin
            Gtk.Window
```

Additionally, you need this cast to access all the methods, attributes, and properties associated with the Gtk.Window class. Once you have an object of this reference type, you can access its methods, specifically the ShowAll() method that displays the widget (your window) and all of its child widgets (the controls). This will cause your window to become visible and allow the user to interact with it. Finally, you need to add an Application.Run() method to ensure that the application doesn't just terminate immediately. The revised Main() method is as follows:

```
public static void Main(string[] args)
{
  Gtk.Application.Init();
  MainWindow wndMain = new MainWindow();
  wndMain.win.ShowAll();
  Application.Run();
}
```

Attaching Signal Event Handlers in Code Using C#

The user interface has been encapsulated in a class, and you now know how to load this into your application and display it. But what about the event handlers? The signals, as defined against the controls on your user interface, need to be "glued" to the methods that will be called within your code when a signal is raised. I'll now show ways of connecting these to your application.

Connecting Using Autoconnect

You have several ways to implement signal methods and connect these to the user interface. One way is to use a simple method called Autoconnect(), which connects the signals defined in the XML Glade file with static handler methods provided by the application. The reference to the control that raises the event is then passed as a parameter to the event handler being called.

I'll now show to implement the Quit menu option, which will close the RSS aggregator's main window, by first defining your signal handlers. The following code shows the Quit menu option with a placeholder for its implementation that simply outputs some text to the console (you'll look at providing its correct implementation next):

```
public void on_quit1_activate(System.Object o, EventArgs args)
{
  // Output some simple text to the console window
  Console.Out.WriteLine("File QUIT signal");
}
```

The method signature is always the same. It has a publicly scoped method with a void return type (no return type) and two parameters, the sender object and event arguments. The important aspect to remember is that the name of the method must match the signal name defined within Glade. In this case, this maps to the Quit menu item line in Glade, as follows:

```
<signal name="activate" handler="on_quit1_activate"
last_modification_time="Sun, 05 Jun 2005 19:10:14 GMT"/>
```

Once all your signal handlers have been defined, you'll need to connect the application to your user interface using the Autoconnect() method mentioned. The following line achieves this by passing a pointer to the application using the reserved this keyword:

```
xml.Autoconnect(this);
```

This is required so that Glade can connect the signal handler methods to the user interface using .NET's reflection (more about this later in the book) to match the method names.

You've now completed one example of an event handler, so you can provide the event handler methods for the other menu items that are defined in the main window, as shown in Listing 7-5. To check easily that the events are being fired, you can provide a placeholder for the event handler's implementation in the form of a simple line that outputs some text to the console. I find this to be a useful technique for checking that the events are being fired by using the user interface and watching the terminal window from which the application was launched (you should see the event text being output when appropriate).

Listing 7-5. *Signal Methods with Placeholder Implementation*

```
// Open menu item signal
public void on_open1_activate(System.Object o, EventArgs args)
{
  Console.Out.WriteLine("File OPEN signal");
}

// Close menu item signal
public void on_close1_activate(System.Object o, EventArgs args)
{
  Console.Out.WriteLine("File CLOSE signal");
}

// Quit menu item signal
public void on_quit1_activate(System.Object o, EventArgs args)
{
  Console.Out.WriteLine("File QUIT signal");
}

// About item signal
public void on_about1_activate(System.Object o, EventArgs args)
{
  Console.Out.WriteLine("ABOUT signal");
}
```

Connecting Your Signals Directly

You can use another, slightly more involved method for providing signal implementation without using the Autoconnect() method, which is to directly assign the methods using delegates, in a similar fashion to Windows Forms. I'll now show how you can connect your Quit menu signal alone.

The following code obtains a pointer to the Gtk.MenuItem reference by using the GetWidget() method and casting it to the appropriate type:

```
Gtk.MenuItem mnuQuit = (xml.GetWidget("quit1") as Gtk.MenuItem);
mnuExit.Activated += new EventHandler(on_quit1_activate);
```

Thereafter, you can access the Activated event, which is a C# delegate, and use the + operator to add a new event handler. You construct this using the EventHandler reference type and passing the name of the method that will then provide its implementation. This is more complicated, as I'm sure you'll agree. The line within the XML Glade file that identifies the menu item and its class type is as follows:

```
<widget class="GtkImageMenuItem" id="exit1">
```

Displaying and Handling Your File Open Dialog Box

The method is the same for handling any other windows, including modal dialog boxes, except that you would set the modal property to yes if you needed a modal window. This would be detected by the Show methods automatically. In the following extract, you can see that the modal property for the File Open dialog box is set to false:

```
<property name="modal">False</property>
```

The method for connecting signals to your application's event handlers is the same as I discussed before: you use either the Autoconnect() method or the delegate assignment method. For example, if you wanted to provide an implementation for the Quit menu item to close the application, then the event handler would be as follows:

```
// Quit menu item signal
public void on_quit1_activate(System.Object o, EventArgs args)
{
  // Quit the application
  Application.Quit();
}
```

As you can see, there is a lot of commonality between the programming interface surrounding Windows Forms and Glade with Gtk+. The following section covers the advantages and disadvantages of each to help you decide which to use.

Comparing Glade and Windows Forms

I've now covered some of the concepts of the two main GUI technologies available within Mono today. These include the .NET Framework's own Windows Forms technologies and the open-source Glade and Gtk+. Both are extremely powerful, and both have advantages and disadvantages. But when starting a project that requires some kind of user interface, you'll be faced with the daunting decision of which technology stack to use. Indeed, you may even decide not to use either of the technologies discussed and instead use an alternative technology stack such as Open XUL (http://xul.sourceforge.net/).

Table 7-2 evaluates each technology; refer to the table to make an informed decision regarding the technology to use for your GUI requirements.

Table 7-2. *Feature Comparison*

Feature	Glade/Gtk+	Windows Forms
Supported platforms	Linux/Windows	
Supported languages	Various	.NET based
Stability	Stable	Stable but under development
Features	Extensive	Extensive
Extendibility	Very good	Good
Portability	Very good	Very good

As you can see, the technologies are pretty comparable, and the only really decisions relate to the relative immaturity of the Mono Windows Forms implementation (at the time of writing anyway). However, both technologies are stable enough to use and portable across various platforms, with the caveat that Glade requires libraries beyond those provided by the .NET Framework.

Summary

In this chapter, I discussed the features of Glade and the Gtk+ toolkit and how to use these two technology stacks collaboratively to build platform-independent GUIs. Gtk+ acts as a multi-platform toolkit for creating GUIs and includes a comprehensive set of controls (known as *widgets*) that can be used to build your application's user interface by implementing the Gtk# .NET wrapper to access the Gtk+ API from your Mono application. Glade provides a GUI designer that allows you to build your user interfaces using Gtk+ widgets and save them in a language-independent format called XML. To accompany the designer, Glade also provides libraries that you can use to harness your user interfaces and dynamically load and use them at runtime with a variety of languages, including those supported by Mono.

CHAPTER 8

■■■

Using ADO.NET

GUIs are indeed an important aspect of applications that interact with users. However, arguably of equal importance is the ability of an application to read or write data to some kind of persistent storage, and an obvious candidate for this is a database. Numerous database types are available, with numerous database vendors providing them. You might be using an object-oriented database or, more likely, a relational database (often shortened from *relational database management* system (RDBMS)); your database might be an open-source database such as MySQL or a commercial database such as Microsoft SQL Server or Oracle 10g. In either case, you'll need to connect to this database and interact with it by either reading data or storing application-specific data that can be retrieved later. This interaction will usually take place through some kind of API, and this is the problem. All vendors typically have their own API—the objects, methods, attributes, properties, and events that allow your application to harness the functionality provided by their database. Typically, these APIs change from database to database.

In this chapter, I'll provide an overview of ADO.NET, .NET's primary data access model for database interaction. In addition, I'll discuss how you can use ADO.NET within your application and explain how this relates to other database standards such as ODBC.

Overview of ADO.NET

In 1996, Microsoft released a database access model called ActiveX Data Objects (ADO), which had roots in other technologies such as Data Access Objects (DAO). The aim of both ADO and DAO was the same: to provide a common set of classes that exposed an object model and interface for accessing your persistent storage, usually a database. Microsoft completely rebuilt the ADO technology stack after version 2.6, and thus ADO.NET was born, containing significantly more features and using XML as its underlying data storage model for interoperability.

Generally speaking, the new features of ADO.NET embody the following characteristics:

- *Interoperability*: ADO.NET works with technologies other than .NET and exchanges information between operating systems via XML.

- *Performance*: Your application can offer good performance using features such as connection pooling where a pool of connections is retained, avoiding the overhead of creating a connection each time.

- *Scalability*: Your application can cope with an increase in capacity with regard to users or database transactions.

- *Ease of use*: Although ADO.NET is powerful and feature rich, its structure ensures that it is still easy to use through a rich type-safe programming model.

As you can see from this list, ADO.NET is a comprehensive and powerful technology that is accessible through a rich set of classes, members, and types. Figure 8-1 shows an architectural view of the main components of ADO.NET.

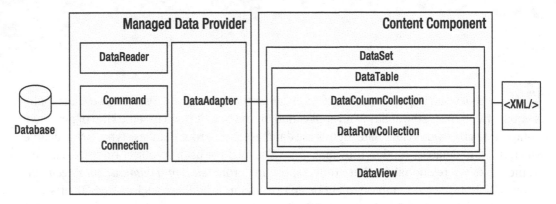

Figure 8-1. *ADO.NET architecture*

The ADO.NET programming model focuses on two groups of classes that provide suites of functionality for content and for data providers. The *data providers* provide an interface to the data and are used by content providers or your own code as a standard means of access. The *content components* store data and provide functionality to allow you to manipulate the data. These concepts are exposed by a number of namespaces, as shown in Table 8-1, and are discussed in more detail shortly.

Table 8-1. *.NET Data Namespaces*

Namespace	Description
System.Data	ADO.NET core namespace (mandatory for all ADO.NET interactions)
System.Xml	XML-based functionality (core to the System.Data functionality)
System.Data.Common	Classes shared by the .NET data providers
System.Data.OleDb	Classes for the OLE DB data provider functionality
System.Data.SqlClient	Classes for the SQL Server data provider functionality
System.Data.SqlTypes	Data types to support the System.Data.SqlClient classes

Introducing Database Terms

In the course of focusing on ADO.NET, this chapter uses certain database concepts and terms that you may not be familiar with; Table 8-2 introduces these terms for those readers who are new to using databases. If you are conversant in database terms, you can skip to the "Introducing Data Providers" section.

Table 8-2. *Database Terms*

Term	Description
Database	A database stores information in an organized way and is implemented by an RDBMS such as MySQL, Oracle, or SQL Server.
Connection	A client or user of the database must connect to the database using a connection. A database may have a connection pool where a number of connections are prepared for use, which results in an increase in speed.
Structured Query Language (SQL)	The method in which a user interacts with the database is most often through SQL, a standard language through which database commands and tasks can be accomplished. It consists of the Data Definition Language (DDL) and the Data Manipulation Language (DML).
Data Definition Language (DDL)	This language allows you to define the database schema, which consists of objects such as tables, indexes, columns, and so on.
Data Manipulation Language (DML)	This language allows you to manipulate data within the database, including adding, removing, or updating rows.
Schema	A database consists of a structure, or schema, that contains objects such as tables and columns. This structure is a formal representation of using a language such as SQL that is supported by the database management system.
Table	An object that holds data within a database. Associated concepts are columns, rows, and indexes. An example is an `Employee` table.
Row	A row is an instance of data is held in a table; for example, an `Employee` table may hold one row per employee.
Column	A table contains individual data elements, or columns, for holding information. For example, the `Employee` table may have an `Employee Name` column.
Transaction	When a command is issued against a database, it can be part of a transaction. This allows one or more commands to be collected and either committed (written to the database) or rolled back (reversed out of the database).

Introducing Data Providers

A *data provider* provides a layer of abstraction above the database access and allows you to connect to a database, performing commands that may or may not return any results. DDL commands such as UPDATE and INSERT return no results and are executed directly against the database. Conversely, DML commands such as SELECT do return results, and these are usually stored within a content component such as a DataSet for ad hoc manipulation.

The data provider's implementation takes place through the following core set of components:

- Connection

- Command

- DataReader

- DataAdapter

I'll provide a more detailed description of these components and their responsibilities in the following sections, but generally two sets of data providers exist. The first type of data provider is a generic implementation provided in the `System.Data.OleDb` namespace. The second type of data provider offers higher performance but is a specialized implementation that is fine-tuned for a specific database such as MySQL, Oracle, or Microsoft SQL Server. Therefore, if you want your application to target a specific database provider such as Oracle, you can use a specialized data provider and gain an increase in performance and features. However, this will mean your application is hardwired to Oracle. If, on the other hand, you want to ensure that your application is more database agnostic, you can either choose one of the generic data providers or implement the ability to customize which data provider you choose in code.

Connection

A *Connection* class encapsulates the properties and methods necessary to establish a connection with an underlying database. An example of the properties available includes a *connection string*, which establishes a database connection. In turn, the connection string is used by some of the ADO.NET class methods such as `Open()` and `Close()`, which open and close a connection to a database, respectively.

Command

The *Command* class encapsulates a database command that can be performed against a database connection. This command may be a simple textual string representing the SQL command to execute, or it could include parameters that are used by the SQL code as dynamic mechanisms. In addition, the command may execute within the scope of a transaction should you require it, providing you with the ability to roll back, or undo, the command in case of an error or some such failure.

DataReader

The *DataReader* component provides access to a stream of data that may be read from the database using a Command object. This class offers fast execution speeds because of its sequential nature, running from start to end in a forward-only manner; you can also refer to this as a *forward-only cursor* (with the cursor being a database concept representing the current row).

DataAdapter

The *DataAdapter* component acts as the manager for your database access. It coordinates the database connection required, retrieving data through specific commands and storing the data within a DataSet for you to then manipulate. This manipulated (changed) data will then be fed back into the DataAdapter for updating the database.

Introducing Content Components

The data providers provide the underlying connectivity to the database, and the *content components* fulfill a complementary role by using the data providers to act as a storage mechanism and controlling access to the underlying data. This allows the user to interact with the data in a far more user-friendly manner and supports advanced features such as disconnected DataSets, where the data can be retrieved and then manipulated offline for later synchronization.

The two main content providers within the core .NET Framework are the DataReader (which acts as both a data provider and a content provider) and the DataSet, both of which provide access to the underlying data using data providers. Each has its own advantages and disadvantages, which you should consider carefully before deciding on your implementation.

I'll now provide a brief overview of the two components, together with their strengths and weaknesses, and then introduce two other content provider components that you may find useful.

DataReader

The *DataReader* provides read-only, forward-only access to the data from your database, which is provided to your application as a stream of data buffered into memory using a configurable number of rows at a time (the default is one row). It is the responsibility of your application to retrieve data from the cache (in-memory buffer) and process this as required. Because data is provided and stored in-memory and because it is read-only and forward-only, a DataReader offers extremely high performance. This component is an excellent choice when you are required to retrieve large amounts of data from your database or you require only a sequential pass of data with read-only privileges. If you want to retrieve information in a read-only, high-performing manner, as you may do when listing the items in an audit log (a textual file that is often used to store interactions with a system or application), then you should use a DataReader.

DataSet

In contrast to the DataReader, the *DataSet* component is a far more feature-rich component whose emphasis is on the two-way, read-write provision of data with a high level of interaction. For example, the DataSet caches data locally, allowing you to interact with the data offline, and it can be connected (also called *bound*) to controls for presenting data. The DataSet also provides an XML view of the data that can be exchanged with other remote applications using industry-standard protocols, such as HTTP, allowing two applications connected to the Internet to exchange data, for example.

This functionality doesn't come for free, however; it's provided at the cost of performance, and if you don't require this advanced functionality, then you should consider other components such as the DataReader. For example, if you want to retrieve data from multiple tables and not only view this information but also update it or add data to it, then you should use a DataSet component. If, for example, you wanted to bring together the data from an Employee table and a Salary Review table, you would be able to view and manipulate this within a single DataSet, even though the information resides in two discrete tables.

DataTable

You may have noticed that when describing the DataSet component, I made no reference to specific tables or any database-type semantics, including relationships. This is because the DataSet component's only concern is data, and therefore you can retrieve data from multiple databases with multiple constraints. In contrast, the *DataTable* has a one-to-one relationship with a table in a database, and multiple tables represent data internally within a DataSet.

The DataTable has a schema, defined by its columns and constraints. It also has rows, which hold actual data and are therefore synonymous with a row in a database table. For example, you might use a DataTable when you want to access advanced functionality such as the constraints or indexes that are defined against a table but you need to access only one database table at a time.

Note As you go from a DataReader to a DataTable to a DataSet, you'll notice an incremental increase in the amount of processing power they require. Therefore, using them inappropriately will slow down your application. Always use the component that best meets your functional requirements.

DataView

A *DataView* component is synonymous with a view in a database and, as its name suggests, describes a view of the data that may reside in a DataTable. You may have more than one view of the same data; for example, in one view you may expose more columns than in another. For example, you might provide a view of employee data where one view includes personal information, such as salary, and another doesn't.

A DataView may also have dynamic constraints, such as a filter, that shape the data on a particular column; you can then change this filter's value to provide a dynamic view of the data. For example, you might use the DataView when you require a view on existing data in a database table where an index does not exist. If you want to analyze the data that already exists within a table but you require only read-only access, you can use a DataView control, which is synonymous with a database view. You could use it to provide a view of employees whose roles are of a specific type.

Installing a Data Provider

Data providers in .NET are powerful, allowing you to write components at a higher level of abstraction that is unconcerned with the underlying data provider. You still need to decide which data provider you are going to use to store your persistent information, and in the next sections of the chapter, I'll introduce you to the data provider you'll be using for this book's project.

Numerous data providers are on the market—some are commercial providers, and some are open-source providers. The market leaders in the commercial space are the Microsoft SQL Server and Oracle 10g relational databases. In the open-source world, MySQL (http://www.mysql.com/) and SQLite (http://www.sqlite.org/) are good examples of powerful databases. I'll show how to use the MySQL data provider in the RSS aggregator project for a number of reasons.

Why MySQL?

According to the official Web site, MySQL is the world's most popular open-source database. It's difficult to challenge such a bold assertion given its estimated six million users and growing use within large and mission-critical applications. Also, it's apparent such trends will continue given its aggressive development schedule; it has flourished into a powerful database provider with features usually available only in large, commercial database providers. Its wide platform support is another advantage, with versions available for Linux (numerous distributions), Windows, Mac OS X, and Unix (including Solaris, AIX, HP-UX, and so on).

The MySQL distributions all provide the same set of utility programs as standard, except for those programs that are platform specific. For example, server startup scripts are platform specific and are not used on the Windows platform. If you appear to be missing one or more of the programs discussed as you progress through this chapter, this may be because one of the Linux RPM distributions has not been installed (RPMs are more specialized), so you may need to revisit the MySQL home page to download and install the missing applications. In fact, you should install the latest stable set of binaries from the MySQL home page to ensure you are working with a current, stable version. I'll now provide a simple overview of how to install MySQL 4.1 on the two platforms covered in this book, Microsoft Windows and Linux.

Installing MySQL on Linux

Installing MySQL on Linux is fairly straightforward, although the likelihood is that this won't even be necessary, as most distributions, including Fedora, include a version of MySQL by default. Fedora Core 3, for example, includes MySQL version 3.23, so it's simply a case of ensuring you select this option when installing your distribution. You should note that this is an older version of MySQL, as is often the case with versions that ship with various Linux distributions. Therefore, I recommend checking that you are using the most current stable version; if you are not, then download and install it as appropriate for the version of the operating system you are running. If your Linux distribution does not include MySQL, then you can use the MySQL Web site to download either prebuilt binaries or the source code, and this will enable you to get started. Whilst using a preinstalled version of MySQL is the simplest method, I always recommend using the latest stable version for the operating system you are using. See the MySQL home page for more details (http://www.mysql.com/).

The first step is to download the required files from http://dev.mysql.com/downloads/. I recommend downloading both the server and client RPMs. Once you have downloaded them, you can install them with a command similar to the following one (replacing VERSION with the appropriate version you've downloaded):

```
rpm -i MySQL-server-VERSION.i386.rpm
rpm -i MySQL-client-VERSION.i386.rpm
```

Once you've successfully installed MySQL, you can refer to the MySQL home page for further instructions on how to correctly configure and verify that the installation worked. You can find these instructions at http://dev.mysql.com/doc/mysql/en/linux-rpm.html.

Installing MySQL on Windows

The first step when installing MySQL on the Microsoft Windows platform is to obtain the media (from http://dev.mysql.com/downloads/) as both source code and installable binaries. The

Windows version of MySQL, from version 4.1.5 and later, comes with an installer that provides a extremely simple mechanism for installing and performing the core configuration of your database. Table 8-3 lists the types of downloads available for Windows.

Table 8-3. *MySQL for Windows Types*

Type	Description
Windows Essentials	Optimized MySQL components, without debug files
Windows	Complete MySQL for Windows package, including debug files and wizards
Windows Installer	MySQL binary files only (requires manual configuration)

My recommendation is that you install the Windows Essentials version, as this provides all the core components necessary and provides a configuration wizard for ease of use. Once you've downloaded it into your preferred directory, you can start the installation simply by double-clicking the binary file. The installation will start with the first page of the wizard, as shown in Figure 8-2.

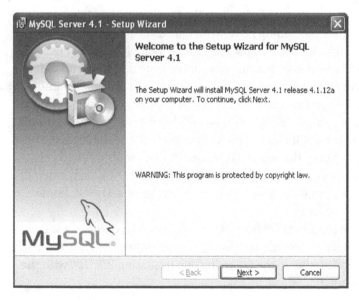

Figure 8-2. *First page of the Setup Wizard*

As you progress through this wizard, you'll be prompted for the type of installation, which affects the components installed. At this point, I recommend a complete installation. This may install some components that are not required, but disk space is relatively cheap, and this will avoid potential problems later. The next prompt will be for you to create a logon account, and at this point you can use a free account, use an existing account, or skip the process altogether. The choice is yours, but a free account will allow you to receive updates on MySQL, so it's pretty useful. Also, the wizard allows you to configure the MySQL subscriptions information slightly.

Once the installation is complete, you'll see a screen that not only informs you of this but also offers you the option to start the MySQL Server Instance Configuration Wizard, as shown in Figure 8-3. This useful configuration wizard allows you to configure the MySQL server instance that you just installed.

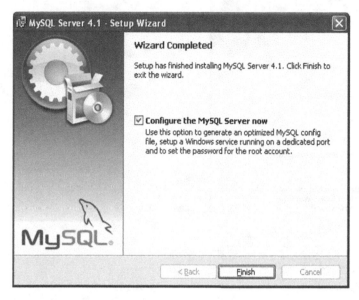

Figure 8-3. *Windows MySQL installation complete*

I recommend you select the Configure the MySQL Server Now option (it's chosen by default) and continue with the configuration wizard. This will allow you to configure MySQL for optimum performance on your machine. The configuration wizard provides two options, as shown in Figure 8-4. One is for a detailed configuration that gives you access to the nuts and bolts of MySQL for a finely tuned installation. The other option is to use a standard configuration, which is aimed at machines that do not already have MySQL on them. This option applies a simple standard configuration that can be further refined manually later.

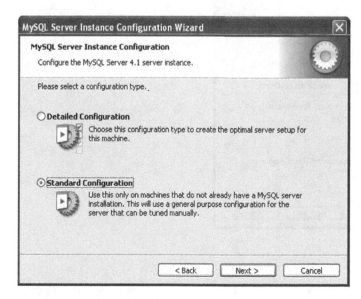

Figure 8-4. *Selecting a configuration type*

After selecting the appropriate option, you'll be asked to decide how to run your MySQL server instance and will be offered the option of adding the binary directory to your search path for convenience. I recommend you select both of these options, as shown in Figure 8-5.

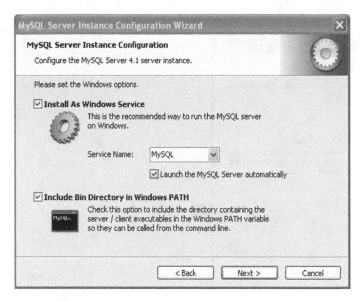

Figure 8-5. *Adding the binary directory*

Finally, you'll be asked to provide some configuration details about the logon security required, as shown in Figure 8-6. I recommend you leave the default option of modifying the security settings and enter a password that you will be able to remember but, like all passwords, is difficult to guess.

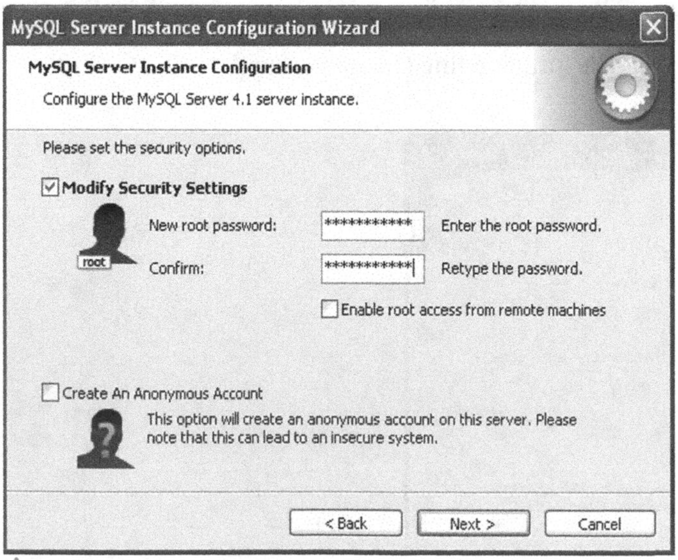

Figure 8-6. *Picking a password*

The last screen allows you to execute the configuration script that will apply the changes selected to the MySQL server instance, configuring it in the process. This screen will show you its progress as the configuration takes place and will finally prompt you to click the Finish button to close the wizard, as shown in Figure 8-7. You can find the configuration details for MySQL in the root of your installation directory, within a file called my.ini.

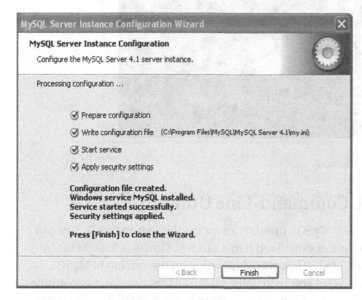

Figure 8-7. *Completing the installation*

This will complete the installation of MySQL and should automatically start the Windows service that runs the MySQL instance. You can check that MySQL is running correctly by using the MySQL command-line client, which is installed as part of the MySQL installation and should be available within your Start menu. (Be warned, though, that this logs you on as the root user.) Alternatively, you can start the program at the command line by connecting as the root user, as follows:

```
mysql --user=root -p
```

This command will prompt you for the password. You can append the password to the -p flag, but be aware that this will store the password in log files as plain text and could be used maliciously. If either command is successful, this should connect you to your running MySQL server instance, and you can issue commands against the database. The --help option provides a list of commands, but for now just check that the MySQL instance is running by using the status command. This should display a screen similar to Figure 8-8.

You should now have a working MySQL installation, which you can use to follow along with the discussion of ADO.NET.

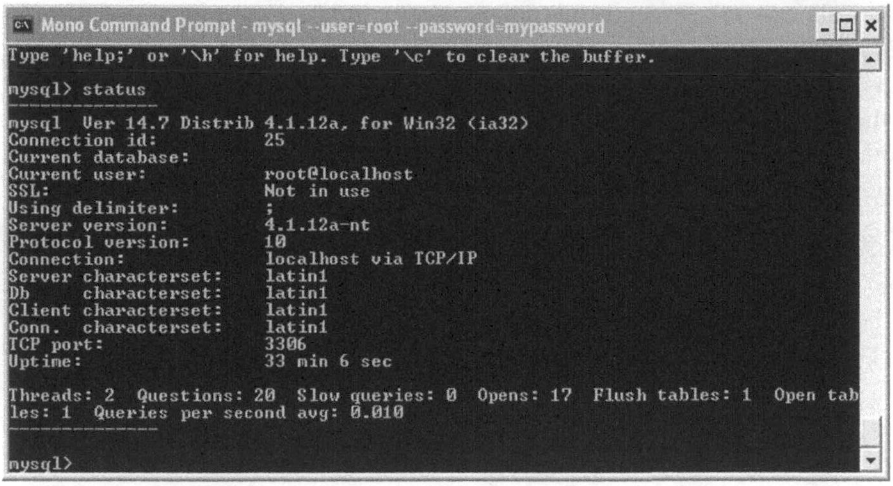

Figure 8-8. *Verifying successful installation*

Using Common MySQL Command-Line Utilities

Table 8-4 summarizes some of the key MySQL utilities. To access the user manuals, you can find the MySQL documentation online or download it in a variety of formats from http://dev.mysql.com/doc/mysql/en/index.html. (However, depending on the version of MySQL you're installing and the operating system you're installing it on, all the command-line utilities may not be available.) You can learn more about these utilities in the MySQL documentation at http://dev.mysql.com/doc/.

Table 8-4. *MySQL Utilities*

Name	Description
mysql	Command-line client for MySQL
mysqlcc	MySQL Control Center
MySQLAdministrator	MySQL Administrator
MySQLQueryBrowser	MySQL Query Browser
mysqlcheck	Table maintenance client
mysqldump	Make database backups
mysqlimport	Imports data files
mysqlshow	Displays information about databases and tables

Creating a Database

To store your data related to the RSS aggregator, including the subscription list, you need to define a database schema that your database will use to represent the data. This will allow the RSS aggregator to download information to the database and support offline storage, something that could be configurable. The first requirement for implementing a database from a database schema is its design, as shown in Figure 8-9.

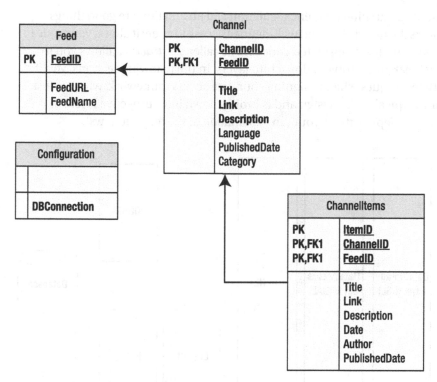

Figure 8-9. *RSS aggregator's database schema*

You can find the database schema design documentation and the implementation that uses SQL in a script file on the Apress Web site. For the discussions from this point forward, I'll assume you have created your database within MySQL and have called it RSSAggregator.

Note It's at this point that you should have a good understanding of both RDBMSs and ADO.NET. The ADO.NET suites of classes are provided as part of the .NET Framework, and Mono has also provided an implementation of the same classes as part of its implementation of the framework. Therefore, the code you write using Microsoft's implementation of .NET will run under Mono's implementation of .NET, assuming of course that all class functionality has been implemented.

I'll now provide some recommendations on good practices for architecting your database applications and then introduce how to use ADO.NET to interact with your database as part of the RSS aggregator project.

Understanding Data Encapsulation Design

I've now covered the basic principles of database access using ADO.NET and Mono, so you can start to put this into practice within the RSS aggregator project. Before I show how to do this, though, I'll explain some general principles surrounding data encapsulation within your application and how you'll be designing your framework of classes to achieve this.

In the world of software architecture, encapsulation and abstraction are good things. *Encapsulation* promotes the use of clear and well-defined access to code; it allows your code to support a contract between the encapsulated code and its caller. *Abstraction* allows you to reduce complexity by breaking a problem down into layers. In the following sections, you'll learn how to use both techniques when designing your data access framework, which is just one of the tiers within a typical *n*-tier design and is broken down into respective layers of responsibility. Figure 8-10 depicts this layout (an explanation of the terms follows).

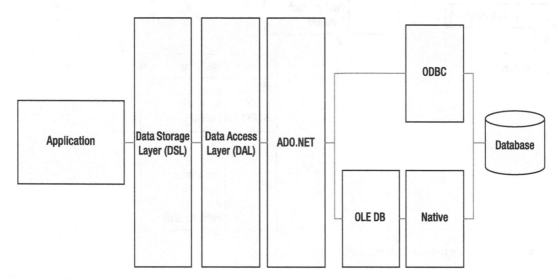

Figure 8-10. *The data tiers and their layers*

Data Access Layer

The first requirement of the framework is to establish a connection with the database and subsequently communicate with it. This layer is typically known as a *data access layer* (DAL). In a way, ADO.NET is already providing you with a certain level of abstraction, but if you wanted to change your database provider, you would need to recompile your application. The example in this section uses ODBC, which provides this level of abstraction by allowing you to connect using metadata held in a *data source name* (DSN). The DSN sits outside your application within the ODBC Manager and allows you to modify the database provider at runtime. However, if you wanted to benefit from the fastest possible access to your database, you would more likely use an OLE DB database provider, which doesn't provide the same level of abstraction as ODBC. Therefore, you'd need to implement this in the code, and the DAL is the most appropriate place for it. You would expose the connection attributes required through an external configuration file, and the DAL would read this to resolve its connection parameters.

For this example, you will implement the DAL as a class, which is then consumed within the application, typically by data storage layer (DSL) entities, to allow access to the database. Therefore, you need a number of core methods, as listed in Table 8-5.

Table 8-5. *DAL Operations*

Method Name	Description
Open()	Establishes a connection with the database
Close()	Releases an open connection with the database
Create()	Creates a new record within the database
Read()	Reads data from the database
Update()	Updates data within the database
Delete()	Deletes data within the database

Using the methods listed in Table 8-5, you are now in a position to create your class framework, and for the first time you'll start to build your application namespace. Listing 8-1 shows the skeleton for the class with placeholders for all methods except the constructor that receives and sets the internal connection string for the database. Throughout the rest of the chapter, you'll learn how to provide an implementation for each method, and I'll describe the appropriate ADO.NET implementations throughout the chapter.

Listing 8-1. *Base DAL Class*

```
namespace RSSAggregatorData
{
  public class DataAccessLayer
  {
    // Members
    //
    private string connectionString;

    // Constructor
    //
    public DataAccessLayer(string connectionString)
    {
      this.connectionString = connectionString;
    }
```

```csharp
// Open - Establish a database connection
//
public void Open()
{
  // TODO - Implementation
}


// Close - Close a database connection
//
public void Close()
{
   // TODO - Implementation
}


// Create - Create a database record
//
public void Create()
{
  // TODO - Implementation
}

// Read - Read one or more database records
//
public void Read()
{
 // TODO - Implementation
}

// Update - Update an existing database record
//
public void Update()
{
  // TODO - Implementation
}

// Delete - Delete an existing database record
//
public void Delete()
{
  // TODO - Implementation
 }
 }
}
```

In summary, a DAL is an essential layer for encapsulating database access, and you'll build an example DAL throughout this chapter. You can then modify this to support OLE DB database access if required, thus allowing your application to be completely configurable. The design in Listing 8-1 is obviously the start of a framework, so you may have different polymorphic variants of a given method. (For example, each method may provide a different implementation; see Chapter 4 for more about polymorphism.) In addition, you may decide to add some supporting methods, but at its core, the class design in Listing 8-1 represents the mandatory components of a DAL.

Caution As in most of this book, to ensure the code is concise and focused, the listing does not include exception handling. You should always include appropriate error handling, which you can find in the code download for the RSS aggregator.

Data Storage Layer and Entities

In addition to accessing the database provider, you'll need a method for storing and manipulating data within the RSS application. This again should typically use encapsulation and provide a home for your data and the data manipulation methods provided. Several data content providers are available for storing data, some of which I've discussed in this chapter. For example, you could use a DataTable component in your code to encapsulate a database table; alternatively, a DataSet component could encapsulate a database result from a SQL command. Which is most appropriate depends on the data you are storing, but in essence, you'll be creating a class that stores the data. This will occur either through one of the predefined content providers or through your own mechanism using intrinsic .NET data types such as structures or arrays.

The design mechanism I'll be using for the DSL entities involves using an ADO.NET DataSet as the container for the entity data, which will be contained within the data storage class, herein referred to as a *data entity* class, as shown in Listing 8-2.

Listing 8-2. *Base Data Storage Layer Class*

```
using System.Data;
using System.Data.Odbc;
using RSSAggregatorData.DataAccessLayer;

namespace RSSAggregatorData.DataStorageLayer
{
  public abstract class DataEntity
  {
    // Members
    //
    protected DataSet data;
    protected DataAccessLayer dal;
```

```
    // Constructor
    //
    public DataEntity()
    {
      // Read the connection string from the application's central config file
      // but for the moment we'll hard-code it
      string conn = "DSN=rssaggregator;UID=root;PWD=mypassword";
      dal = new DataAccessLayer(conn);
    }
  }
}
```

■**Note** In this listing, I've hard-coded the connection string within the DSL; however, this will be sourced from a configuration file, which will be covered in Chapter 9.

Once you have the construct for the core data entity class, you can begin to implement this abstract class in specialized data entity classes that map to the data entities that are required by your application and stored within your database. This implementation takes the form of these two classes:

- A data container structure

- A data entity class

The *data container structure* contains only the data and is implemented using C# types to hold the actual data. For example, you may have a structure that holds your configuration data with the connection string being defined as a string. You may have multiple instances of data containers, stored in C# arrays, that hold the data for multiple rows as required by the RSS feed's list data. The *data entity class* then uses the data container within this structure when performing its CRUD actions. For example, if you wanted to create a record, you'd pass the data values in a data container structure for the data entity class to insert into the database using its appropriate method.

As you progress through the chapter, you'll focus on two instances of these data components, one for the RSS aggregator's configuration and one for the list of RSS feeds to which users have subscribed. The actual implementation, and how the structure holds the data and a class to provide the implementation, will become clear as you implement the RSS aggregator's data access and data storage classes.

Using the MySQL Data Provider

The next sections of this chapter will concentrate on providing an implementation of the DAL and DSL, utilizing the ADO.NET framework and associated classes for database interaction. A prerequisite for this is the installation of an appropriate ADO.NET-based driver, so I'll start by introducing the options available to you and then discuss which option I have chosen to use in the examples and why.

Installing a Database Connector

You must have connectivity from the machine attempting to access the database (known as the *client*) to the machine hosting the database (known as the *server*). This connectivity is provided through a *connector* (also known as a *driver*), and MySQL provides several types of connectors on its Web site (`http://dev.mysql.com/downloads/connector/`). These include the following:

- Generic connector implemented as an ODBC driver

- Java connector implemented as a JDBC driver

- .NET connector using ADO.NET

- MBean implemented as a Java Management Extensions (JMX) driver

Given the topic of this book, I'll focus on the ADO.NET driver, although you could use the ODBC-compliant driver if required. This will, however, mean that the .NET connector must be installed on the machine where the code is being executed. In a traditional client-server application, this means you would need to install the connector along with the client application. However, when implementing a browser-based application, the application could use an ASP.NET code base, so it would be the server-side ASP.NET code that would use the database code. In such an example, the .NET connector would be required only on the server, alongside the ASP.NET code. The other driver types I'll leave for the inquisitive, as they are beyond the scope of this book.

Once you have downloaded the appropriate connector and installed it as directed within the connector's installation instructions, you should be ready to start using the connector within your applications. In the case of the .NET connector, this by default installs the connector and related files in a subdirectory within the MySQL directory called `MySQL Connector Net 1.0.4` and provides the .NET Framework 1.0 and 1.1 versions of the connector.

Connecting to a Database

Once you have installed the appropriate driver, you are ready to start the first task, which is connecting to your database. In this chapter, I'll be focusing on the ADO.NET driver, although the code will require little modification to work with the different types of .NET drivers available, such as the MySQL-specific ADO.NET connector called Connector/Net. The first step is to ensure that you include the relevant namespace; in this case, you'll import the namespace (and dependent namespaces) using the following lines of code:

```
using System.Data;
using System.Data.Odbc;
```

Note When compiling the code, don't forget that you'll need to reference the appropriate assembly. In the case of MySQL, you should reference the `MySql.Data.dll` assembly. For convenience, I suggest you install this into the GAC so that your executing application can find it.

When using ODBC, you can connect to a database in one of two ways. The first is to use a DSN as defined within the ODBC Administration tool, and the second is to specify the details held in the DSN within the connection string. I'll discuss both of these methods as you progress through this chapter.

A connection is represented by the OdbcConnection class, which encapsulates a database connection through an ODBC driver. Therefore, using the ODBC configuration (the DSN), the OdbcConnection class represents an open connection to a MySQL database. It has two constructor implementations—one that takes a connection string and one that doesn't. For simplicity, I'll show how to use the one that does take a connection string, although you could access the ConnectionString property instead. The connection string takes a format based on a set of key/value pairs, separated by semicolons. The connection has numerous settings for various aspects; these are defined within the documentation that accompanies the driver. Table 8-6 provides a list of the essentials to establish a connection.

Table 8-6. *ConnectionString Key/Value Pairs*

Key	Value Description
Using DSN	
dsn	DSN as defined within the ODBC Administration tool
uid	User ID for the MySQL account being used
pwd	Password for the MySQL account being used
Not Using DSN	
driver	Name of the ODBC driver to use
server	Name or network address of the instance of MySQL to connect to
database	Name of the database to connect to
uid	User ID for the MySQL account being used
password	Password for the MySQL account being used
option	Options to pass to the ODBC driver

In this case, you can reference the server by the localhost name. The database name will be rssaggregator, and you'll use the username/password combination of root/mypassword as before. Therefore, the connection string should look like so:

```
"driver={MySQL ODBC 3.51 Driver};server=localhost;uid=root;password=mypassword;
database=rssaggregator"
```

■**Caution** Don't forget that within your DAL, the connection string is received from the calling entity that belongs to an application that owns the location. You could have included the connection string within the DAL itself, but this would reduce flexibility.

The first task is to provide an implementation for the Open() method within the DAL; this involves creating an instance of a connection class, which in this case is of type OdbcConnection. Next, call the Open() method exposed. The code looks like this:

```
// Open - Establish a database connection
//
public bool Open()
{
  connection = new OdbcConnection(this.connectionString);
  connection.Open();
  return false;
}
```

If you examine the code, you can see it is pretty straightforward. The example uses a local member variable within the DataAccessLayer class called connection, which is of type OdbcConnection. This represents a connection for the DAL instance to use, which should be kept open only for as long as is needed. Once you have instantiated it using the connection string, you can then call the Open() method to establish a connection. Please note that at this point you haven't capture any exceptions; these will simply be passed back to the calling program.

Note Please note that these data tier–based classes are compiled into a library assembly that represents the data tier and therefore will need to be referenced in any test-bed applications.

The following simple test-bed application instantiates an instance of the DAL, in the same way as the data entity class does, and tests the methods as required:

```
using System;
using RSSAggregatorData;

class Test
{
  public static void Main(string[] args)
  {
    DataAccessLayer dal =
      new DataAccessLayer("DSN=rssaggregator;UID=root;PWD=mypassword");
    dal.Open();
  }
}
```

Note To prove that the example was working (given that silence indicates success), I deliberately provided an incorrect password, and this threw an exception, as expected.

Disconnecting from a Database

Disconnecting from the database is rudimentary, as you simply need to call the `Close()` method of the database connection as represented by the connection member variable. The implementation for this method is as follows:

```
// Close - Close a database connection
//
public void Close()
{
  if ((connection != null)
  && (connection.State != ConnectionState.Closed))
    connection.Close();
}
```

This example demonstrates a technique known as *defensive programming*, which is something I highly recommend. Rather than simply calling the `Close()` method, the code first checks that the `connection` object is not `null`; if it is, the call would simply throw an exception. In addition, it also uses the `State` property of `OdbcConnection` to determine whether it's worth closing the database connection. If this state is anything other than `ConnectionState.Closed`, then the `Close()` method is executed.

Reading Data from Your Database

The next most useful task the DAL can perform is to retrieve data from the database in a data entity object. At this level, the DAL is concerned only with issuing a SQL command against the database to retrieve the data. If the DAL is not specific to database storage mechanisms, then this method may change. However, such a wide breadth is beyond the scope of this book. The data entity has the knowledge regarding the semantics of the data table(s) you are querying. For example, it knows the columns that need to be retrieved and the indexes available, so it makes sense for the data entity to build the most appropriate SQL string. As a result, in this section, you'll start to provide the implementation for one of the data entity objects used by the RSS aggregator, and the RSS feed is a good starting point.

The first step is to define the data container struct that maps to the database table containing the data. For each column defined within the database that you may want to access, you have a corresponding member in the structure. You will ultimately use this to either retrieve data from or write data to the database. The RSS feed's data container would look like the following code, taking into account the database schema defined:

```
public struct RSSFeed
{
  public int ID;  // Holds the feed ID
  public string feedName;  // Holds the feed name
  public string feedURL;  // Holds the feed URL
}
```

This structure has a one-to-one mapping with the database table, although in theory you could choose to arrange the data differently within the data container. The data entity then uses this data as a transport mechanism for the actual data, both coming from and going to the database. The following code shows how to start implementing the RSS feed's data entity class, remembering to inherit the functionality from the abstract base data entity class:

```
public class RSSFeedDataEntity : DataEntity
{
  // Any implementation goes here
}
```

You'll notice that the previous code does not yet provide any methods, other than those inherited. It is merely the skeleton class for which you will expand and provide an implementation. You'll need to extend this class to retrieve data from the database, and in the first instance you'll look at returning a single row identified by its unique key, in this case the ID column. The implementation is as follows:

```
public RSSFeed ReadSingle(int ID)
{
  RSSFeed feed;
  string sql = "SELECT FeedID, FeedName, FeedURL FROM feed WHERE ID=";
  OdbcDataReader dr = dal.ReadAsDataReader(sql + ID.ToString());
  feed.ID = dr.GetInt32(0);
  feed.feedName = dr.GetString(1);
  feed.feedURL = dr.GetString(2);
  return feed;
}
```

■**Note** If you use the asterisk (*) wildcard within SQL, this will return all columns, the order of which is determined by the database server. Therefore, when accessing columns using a positional index, it is always recommended you explicitly define the column names in an order that matches your code.

You'll notice a dependency on the DAL providing a ReadAsDataReader() method. Therefore, you replace the generic Read() method stub with two implementations, one that reads the data back into an OdbcDataReader object (for fast read performance) and one that returns the data into a DataSet so that it can be updated. The ReadAsDataReader() method implementation is follows:

```
public OdbcDataReader ReadAsDataReader(string sql)
{
  OdbcDataReader rdr = null;
  // Establish a connection
  //
  Open();
  // Read the data
  //
  OdbcCommand cmd = new OdbcCommand(sql, this.connection);
  rdr = cmd.ExecuteReader();
  rdr.Read();    // Move to the first row
```

```
// Return the data
//
return rdr;
}
```

In the previous example, you establish a connection with the database (using the Open() method) and then create a new OdbcCommand, passing both the SQL you want to execute and the database connection. You are then able to execute the SQL against the database connection (using ExecuteReader()) and return the OdbcDataReader object, which (following the Read() method being called) will be located at the identifying row (assuming a row was returned). You can then return this OdbcDataReader object for processing.

But what if you wanted to retrieve more than one row, or even all the rows available within the table? You could easily achieve this by modifying the SQL that is passed to not filter on a given ID; therefore, the ReadAll() method's implementation would be as follows:

```
public ArrayList ReadAll()
{
  ArrayList list = new ArrayList();
  string sql = "SELECT * FROM feed";
  OdbcDataReader dr = dal.ReadAsDataReader(sql);
  do
  {
    RSSFeed feed;
    feed.ID = dr.GetInt32 (dr.GetOrdinal("FeedID"));
    feed.feedURL = dr.GetString(dr.GetOrdinal("FeedURL"));
    feed.feedName = dr.GetString(dr.GetOrdinal("FeedName"));
    list.Add(feed);
  } while (dr.Read());
  return list;
}
```

Notice that you use the same DAL method. Although the SQL has changed to remove any constraint, you simply return all the rows available from the table. You'll notice two other differences: one is that you are using a different method for accessing the data returned, and the other is that within the method you can no longer simply return a single RSSFeed structure, because more than one row may exist.

Let's first examine the method used for accessing the data returned, which was changed to select *all* columns (using the asterisk wildcard) from the database, which is generally not good practice but has been handled in code. Each of the column values returned is accessed using its column name and a combination of the GetString() and GetOrdinal() methods. Consider the following code snippet:

```
feed.ID = dr.GetInt32 (dr.GetOrdinal("FeedID"));
```

■ **Note** GetOrdinal() is case-sensitive, so be careful when declaring the name of the database column.

You can break this down into a number of discrete parts; the first element processed is the dr.GetOrdinal("FeedID") section, which returns the index number of the FeedID column, as found in the DataReader component. This allows you to refer to a column's value by name and not position, despite the SQL returning all columns in an order that it chooses. The next section is the dr.GetString() method, which returns the string value for the column at a given position, which you can ascertain by using the GetOrdinal() method. The next main difference is that because more than one row may be returned, you have a couple of options. You could create and manage an array of RSSFeed structures, but why bother? The .NET Framework provides a number of Collection classes all within the System.Collections namespace, and you'll be using the ArrayList collection that behaves exactly as it sounds—allowing you to dynamically manipulate a list of Object classes (from which all objects are derived within .NET). Just for clarity, I've highlighted in bold the code associated with the class initialization, and where you are adding objects to the list, as you can see, it's pretty self-explanatory.

You can modify the simple test-bed application to interpret this collection, as shown in the following example:

```
using System;
using System.Collections;
using RSSAggregatorData;

class Test
{
  public static void Main(string[] args)
  {
    RSSFeedDataEntity feedEntity = new RSSFeedDataEntity();
    ArrayList list = feedEntity.ReadAll();
    RSSFeed feed;
    for (int i=0; i<list.Count; i++)
    {
      feed = (RSSFeed)list[i];    // Typecast the object to our type
      Console.Out.WriteLine(" Row "+i+" ID="+feed.ID.ToString()+",
        Name="+feed.feedName+", Url="+feed.feedURL);
      }
    }
}
```

This code simply runs through the ArrayList and outputs the data contained within, casting the Object type as held within the collection to the RSSFeed type. You know this a cast is safe because you are in control of the Object type being added in the first place. Here is an example of some output from the test-bed application:

```
Row 0 ID=1, Url=www.mamone.org, Name=mamone.org
Row 1 ID=2, Url=www.bbc.co.uk, Name=bbc news
```

Writing Data to Your Database

I've covered the basics for reading data from your database; I'll now show how to update the data within your database using a couple of techniques. These are the two techniques available:

- Direct SQL execution

- DataSet functionality

For both of these techniques, you may use either the direct SQL approach or the .NET Framework's DataSet object. The updates are all based on one of three possible scenarios:

- Deleting an existing record from the database

- Inserting a new record into the database

- Updating an existing record in the database

Deleting a Row

The scenario I'll demonstrate is straightforward and similar to the techniques you used to read data from the database earlier. You'll start by looking at how to delete data from the database using the direct SQL approach. All the previous scenarios, when dealing with direct SQL manipulation, require that the SQL to be executed is passed to OdbcCommand and then executed against the database. You can implement the Delete() method using this technique and passing the unique ID to the method for locating the record to delete. The first step is to provide the implementation within the DAL, as follows:

```
// DeleteDirectly - Delete an existing database record
//
public int DeleteDirectly(string sql)
{
  Open();
  OdbcCommand cmd = new OdbcCommand(sql, this.connection);
  return cmd.ExecuteNonQuery();
}
```

The ExecuteNonQuery() method will apply a SQL statement directly against a database, as pointed to by the connection that is passed with the SQL when OdbcCommand is instantiated. This method will return the number of rows affected for all update-type SQL functions (that is, UPDATE, INSERT, and DELETE), and it will return -1 for all other SQL commands such as SELECT. In this instance, you simply pass back the number of rows deleted, and the DataEntity class can then interpret this as required.

After you've implemented the DAL method, you can provide the delete functionality to your DataEntity class. This will take the primary key of the table that identifies the row to delete (in this case the Feed table) and subsequently deletes it. The implementation is as follows:

```
public bool DeleteDirectly(int ID)
{
  // Execute the command and return true if more than row was deleted
  return (dal.DeleteDirectly("DELETE FROM feed WHERE ID="+ID.ToString()) == 1);
}
```

As you can see, the implementation is simple—you pass the SQL statement to the DAL's `DeleteDirectly()` method and return `true` for success if a single row was deleted or return `false` to indicate a failure.

Inserting or Updating a Row Directly

Adding a new record to a database is similar to reading and deleting methods. This involves using the `INSERT` SQL statement, which is again executed directly against the database through the DAL after being called by the data entity object. The mechanism for building the SQL within the data entity object is the same for both the `CreateDirectly()` and `UpdateDirectly()` methods with the difference being the SQL passed. The following are the implementations for these methods, starting with the DAL:

```
// CreateDirectly - Create a database record
//
public int CreateDirectly(string sql)
{
  Open();
  OdbcCommand cmd = new OdbcCommand(sql, this.connection);
  return cmd.ExecuteNonQuery();
}


// UpdateDirectly - Update an existing database record
//
public int UpdateDirectly(string sql)
{
  Open();
  OdbcCommand cmd = new OdbcCommand(sql, this.connection);
  return cmd.ExecuteNonQuery();
}
```

You then need to call the data entity methods, calling their respective DAL methods as described previously. I'll introduce each method next, with a short explanation following each code block. The first method is the `CreateDirectly()` method, used to insert a new record:

```
// CreateDirectly() - Creates a database row using the Direct SQL method
//
public bool CreateDirectly(int ID, string name, string url)
{
  string sqlINSERT = "INSERT INTO Feed(ID, NAME, URL) VALUES({0},'{1}','{2}')";
  sqlINSERT = String.Format(sqlINSERT,ID,name,url);

  // Execute the command and return true if a row was inserted
  return (dal.CreateDirectly(sqlINSERT) == 1);
}
```

You'll notice that the signature of this method expects the values to be passed directly to it, which is unnecessary because the values may already exist within the data entity object to which the method belongs. I'll leave you with the task of using polymorphism to provide a different method signature for the CreateDirectly() method that uses the member variables available. A hint is that your CreateDirectly() method will not take any parameters and instead will use an instance of a data container structure held within the class. Let's now consider the UpdateDirectly() method:

```
// UpdateDirectly() - Updates a database row using the direct SQL method
//
public bool UpdateDirectly(int ID, string name, string url)
{
  string sqlUPDATE = "UPDATE Feed SET NAME='{0}', URL='{1}' WHERE ID={2}";
  sqlUPDATE = String.Format(sqlUPDATE,name,url,ID);

  // Execute the command, and return true if a row was updated
  return (dal.UpdateDirectly(sqlUPDATE) == 1);
}
```

The signature for the UpdateDirectly() method is similar to the InsertDirectly() method in that to takes the same three parameters; however, the SQL statement is slightly different because you must apply a filter to find the correct row. You could use the data entity's own member variables if they are initialized, but you are assuming in this instance that they are not and therefore are using an explicit method signature instead.

Using the DataSet Class

You've looked at how to read data from your database to insert, modify, and delete records using direct SQL applications, but what about the .NET Framework's DataSet? In the following sections, you'll learn how to achieve the same functionality by using the DataSet framework class to act in the same way but in a locally cached environment. This has the advantage of being able to work when a database connection is not available and as such allows users to continue using the application as if they were connected to a database. (Certain scenarios do require a database connection, such as reading the latest information from a database.) I'll provide an overview of how the DataSet is structured.

The Tables array property lists all DataTable class instances that are represented by the DataReader, which in this case is always singular because you have one data entity per physical table. The DataTable class then contains Rows, a property that exposes a collection of DataRow class instances that represent a single row within the DataSet. Finally, within the DataRow class type is an array of DataColumns, one for each column that exists within the table schema.

Reading Data

Whilst the DataSet can work in a connectionless environment, the DataReader cannot. I'll start by discussing how data can be read from a database and used to populate your DataSet class instance. As usual, the first implementation you'll look at is within the DAL. For this example, call your method ReadAsDataSet(), which will return the resulting DataSet to its caller, in this case the data entity class. Consider the following implementation:

```
// Read - Read one or more database records, and return the resulting DataSet
//
public DataSet ReadAsDataSet(string sql)
{
  // Establish a connection
  //
  Open();
  // Read the data
  //
  DataSet dataset = new DataSet();
  OdbcDataAdapter adapter = new OdbcDataAdapter();
  adapter.SelectCommand = new OdbcCommand(sql, this.connection);
  adapter.Fill(dataset);
  // Close database connection
  //
  Close();
  return dataset;
}
```

The method follows a similar pattern by ensuring that a database connection is established first using the Open() method. After this, a new DataSet instance is created, as is an OdbcDataAdapter class instance. OdbcDataAdapter serves as a bridge between a DataSet and the database for retrieving and saving data. OdbcDataAdapter implements this bridge by providing a Fill() method to load data from the data source into the DataSet and using the Update() method to send changes made in the DataSet back to the data source. You'll execute the Fill() method after assigning the SelectCommand to use, which is a vanilla OdbcCommand class as you have used before and for which I've highlighted as important lines of code. This will read the data and populate the DataSet with the results returned. Finally, you can close the database connection, which allows the connection to be returned to a possible pool of connections and be reused. This is something that was not possible with the direct SQL methods because they depend on a database connection to work.

Once the DAL method is complete, you are able to implement the data entity classes methods to utilize the DAL, enabling you to read data directly into your data entity's DataSet member. The following implementations demonstrate methods within the data entity class that read both a single row (ReadSingleToDataSet()) and all rows (ReadAllToDataSet()):

```
// ReadSingleToDataSet() - Read a single record from the database
//                                         into the embedded DataSet
//
public bool ReadSingleToDataSet(int ID)
{
  data = dal.ReadAsDataSet("SELECT * FROM feed WHERE ID="+ID.ToString());
  return (data != null);
}
```

```
// ReadAllToDataSet() - Read all  records from the database into
the embedded DataSet
//
public bool ReadAllToDataSet()
{
  data = dal.ReadAsDataSet("SELECT * FROM feed");
  return (data != null);
}
```

You can now write a simple test-bed application to check that these methods work as expected, as follows:

```
// Read a single row with an ID of 1
//
RSSFeedDataEntity feedEntitySingle = new RSSFeedDataEntity();
feedEntitySingle.ReadSingleToDataSet(1);
// Manipulate the feedEntity.data property here


// Read ALL rows
//
RSSFeedDataEntity feedEntityAlll = new RSSFeedDataEntity();
feedEntityAll.ReadAllToDataSet();
// Manipulate our feedEntity.data property here
```

Updating Data Within a DataSet

Once you have read the data, you can use the DataSet's methods to create new rows, update existing rows, and delete an existing row from the database. In this section, you'll start by updating an existing row. You can navigate to a single row using its primary key by using the Table property (index 0, as it's the only one) and its subsequent Rows property, which has a Find() method. This method takes an array (one element in this case) of primary key values to sort the rows on and returns a matching DataRow class instance, as shown here:

```
// DeleteFromDataSet() - Deletes a row from the
//                                   internal DataSet using the ID primary key
public voidl DeleteFromDataSet(int ID)
{
  DataRow row = data.Tables[0].Rows.Find(ID);
  if (row != null)
  {
    row.Delete();
  }
}
```

Once you have found a DataRow instance, you can use the Delete() method to remove the individual row, as shown previously. Once you have deleted the row from the DataSet, you must call the Update() method to synchronize this with the database. You can add an UpdateDatabase() method to the data entity class, as follows:

```
// UpdateDatabase - Synchronizes the DataSet with the database
public void UpdateDatabase()
{
  dal.adapter.Update(this.data);
}
```

This will invoke the Update() method on OdbcDataAdapter, which must also be exposed within the DAL. You do this by ensuring that the OdbcDataAdapter instance (called adapter) is a member variable and initialized within the constructor, as follows:

```
public OdbcDataAdapter adapter;

// Constructor
//
public DataAccessLayer(string connectionString)
{
  this.connectionString = connectionString;
  adapter = new OdbcDataAdapter();
}
```

■**Note** The Update() method requires a valid DeleteCommand when passed a DataRow collection with deleted rows.

When first executed, this may throw an InvalidOperation error. This is because the DataSet has noticed that a row has been removed but doesn't have a corresponding DeleteCommand associated with it to make the necessary changes to the database. The same would be true of any insert or update commands (InsertCommand and UpdateCommand, respectively).

These commands can be parameterized SQL, can be created within the .NET environment, or can be database stored procedures (a precompiled database equivalent). In this example, you'll use .NET parameter SQL statements that are associated with the adapter before the Update() method is called, as follows:

```
// Set up DeleteCommand
OdbcCommand cmd = new OdbcCommand("DELETE FROM Feed WHERE ID = ?",
dal.adapter.SelectCommand.Connection);

cmd.Parameters.Add("@ID", OdbcType.Int, 0, "ID");
al.adapter.DeleteCommand = cmd;
```

You would need to add a similar OdbcCommand for both InsertCommand and UpdateCommand, but I'll leave you to implement these, allowing you to flex your newfound knowledge.

Supporting Transactions

The database examples you've seen so far have involved only a single transaction, which is a single action required of the database and a binary result—either it works or it doesn't. But what if you wanted to update the database using more than one action? For example, what if you updated one record in a database table, which in turn required other dependent records to be updated in a single atomic operation? You can do this using transactions.

The following are the locking mechanisms used within transactions to avoid conflicts:

- Pessimistic locking

- Optimistic locking

The *pessimistic* mechanism involves locking rows of data until the user explicitly releases the lock. This, as its name suggests, plays it safe by locking required data. Alternatively, the *optimistic* mechanism involves attempting to lock data at the last minute. In other words, it assumes that data isn't being used.

The DataSet implements the optimistic database concurrency model through the OdbcDataAdapter class, but you can still create transaction objects that are associated with its database connection. For example, consider the following new UpdateDatabase() method code defined in the RSSFeedDataEntity class:

```
// UpdateDatabase - Synchronizes the DataSet with the database
public void UpdateDatabase()
{
  // Create the transaction
  OdbcTransaction tran;
  tran = dal.adapter.UpdateCommand.Connection.BeginTransaction();

  try
  {
    // Perform the update
    dal.adapter.Update(this.data);

    // Commit the transaction; this MAY throw an error
    tran.Commit();
  }
  catch
  {
    // Roll back the failed transactions
    tran.Rollback();
  }
}
```

This example starts a transaction on the database connection associated with the UpdateCommand property and then uses the Commit() method to commit any database changes made after synchronizing with the database using the Update() method. If the commit fails, an exception is thrown. This is caught and processed by calling the transaction's Rollback() method, which reverses any changes made to the database.

An alternative to the previous method is to directly create your transaction and issue SQL commands against it. You can do this in the DAL by creating a method called CreateTransaction(), as shown here:

```
// CreateTransaction - Creates the database transaction on
the connection within the DAL
//
public void CreateTransaction()
{
  tran = connection.BeginTransaction():
}
```

You must therefore have an OdbcTransaction member called tran within the DAL class. The definition for this is as follows:

```
OdbcTransaction tran;
```

You can then use the data entity methods to directly update the database, and when ready, you can use the transaction created previously to either commit or roll back the transaction. This provides a fine level of control over your data whilst retaining the flexibility and abstraction of the classes you have defined.

Connecting Your Database to the User Interface

In Chapters 6 and 7, you discovered some of the user interface technologies available, namely, Windows Forms and Gtk#. In this chapter, you looked at how you can access your database in a structured manner by utilizing the ADO.NET suite of classes in your own code. The next step is to hook the reading or writing of your data to your RSS aggregator's user interface.

I'll refresh your memory regarding the most appropriate place to load data into your user interface. You may remember that a GUI exposes several events that are fired under certain circumstances. For example, when a Windows Forms application is loaded (when the application starts, for example), a Load event is fired, and this occurs before a form is displayed for the first time. This is an ideal opportunity to display some default information such as the feeds already subscribed to by users. For this example, you'll use this event to populate the RSS aggregator's main form with some default information. Of course, numerous other events could be trapped and used as an opportunity for displaying form data. For example, you may want to display the information associated with an RSS feed when the user chooses an Open Feed menu option and confirms with the OK button. The principles are the same, but the events are pertinent to your application.

So, the first step in the main application window is to provide a method that matches the Load event of the Form class and that can be hooked into the main form of your RSS aggregator application. The method signature for the form's Load event is follows:

```
public void MyForm_Load(object sender, System.EventArgs e)
{
  // Data initialization goes here
}
```

In addition to the method declaration, you now need to attach this to the form's Load event. You do this by creating a new EventHandler that points to the required method and is assigned to the event being trapped, in this case the Load event. The code for this is placed within the form constructor, like so:

```
MyForm.Load += new System.EventHandler(MyForm_Load);
```

Now you're in a position to provide an implementation for the Load event, and it's here that you'll read the feeds that have been subscribed to and populate the ListBox control on the user interface that holds them.

As you may remember from the "Reading Data from the Database" section, you provided the definition and implementation for a ReadAll() method as part of the RSSFeedDataEntity class that reads all the feeds within the database. You'll use this to return the data, and then you can iterate through the data, populating your user interface control. So, the first step is to call the method and check whether any data is returned by looking at the Count property and seeing whether its value is zero. You do this like so:

```
ArrayList feeds = ReadAll();
if (feeds.Count > 0)
{
  // Not empty
}
```

If data is returned, you are now in a position to interpret it, which in this case means cycling through all the values and adding the feed information to the user interface component that represents the list of subscribed feeds. You do this using the foreach command, assigning each item in the array to an RSSFeed structure, which is the type previously added as part of the ReadAll() method. This is as follows:

```
foreach (RSSFeed feed in feeds)
{
  // Add the data to the user interface component
}
```

You can then access the attributes associated with this structure to gain access to the feed information. You may remember that you created a ListBox control as a member of your form to hold the feed subscription information and called this lstSubscriptions. You can enclose this code in calls to BeginUpdate() and EndUpdate(), which stop and start the control being repainted accordingly. This allows the form to be populated efficiently without .NET attempting to repaint the control in between, and the end result is not flickering whilst the population occurs. The revised code with these method calls is as follows:

```
lstSubscriptions.BeginUpdate();
foreach (RSSFeed feed in feeds)
{
  // Add the data to the user interface component
}
lstSubscriptions.EndUpdate();
```

So, finally you're in a position to add the data. You do this simply by using the Items property of the ListBox that points to the items in the list, calling the Add() method to add an item, and passing the string representing the item accordingly. The following code shows how to do this:

```
lstSubscriptions.BeginUpdate();
foreach (RSSFeed feed in feeds)
{
    // Simply add the name of the feed to the list
    lstSubscrptions.Items.Add(feed.FeedName);
}
lstSubscriptions.EndUpdate();
```

Depending on the sample data you have added to the Feed table within your database, if you start your application including the new code, the user interface control representing the feeds subscribed to should now be populated. If not, check that your database method is returning data and the event is being fired correctly.

Summary

As you can see, the ADO.NET namespace and its associated classes are extremely versatile and feature rich. As a result, numerous classes and features exist that I did not have the space to cover in this chapter alone. This chapter merely provided the foundation. I discussed the requirements for database interaction and used a well-known open-source database provider, MySQL, in the examples. I also discussed the design for the data abstraction layer in the form of the DAL and DSL, through which I have demonstrated how to implement these techniques:

- Establishing a database connection

- Closing a database connection

- Reading data from the database

- Writing data to the database

I also touched on the concept of transactions, which allow numerous database changes to be written to the database as a single atomic operation, with changes being rolled back if an error occurs. I finished the chapter by showing how to join user interface code and database code to provide a user interface that is populated from the database.

For a more detailed understanding, I recommend you spend some time exploring and practicing your ADO.NET implementations by referring to the RSS aggregator's source code, which uses the two distinct layers demonstrated in this chapter for all its database handling. I also recommend the book *ADO Programmer's Reference* by David Sussman (Apress, 2004).

CHAPTER 9

■■■

Using XML

Assign ten developers to a task, and they'll devise ten different ways to implement it. Indeed, the IT community has long struggled with coming to grips with standardized implementation methodologies. Data is no different; it too has numerous ways it which it can be represented. For example, it's commonplace to store data using fixed files when the data's length and content is fixed and variable-length formats when the contents can vary. However, while these types of formats offer convenient means for representing and parsing data, neither a fixed file nor a variable-length format is self-describing, meaning you need to understand the file format before you can decipher the information within it.

This problem manifests itself in corporate organizations through the inability of a company's applications to exchange data. If this is such a problem within one organization, imagine how hard it is for different organizations to exchange data, which is a necessity in order for organizations to work together. Also, just including data in the storage media may not be sufficient; you might not only want to represent content but also want to represent metadata about the content. In other words, you may want to provide the receiving application or user with a definition of the data itself. For example, when you exchange date values as a string, you can include metadata that describes the format and the day, month, and year components.

This is where markup languages can help; they represent data as well as information describing the data's context. You've probably used HTML, one of the most famous markup languages. HTML allows the contents of a Web page to be represented, as well as its structure. For example, HTML allows you to represent data such as tables or paragraphs and denote whether text is displayed in bold or italic. HTML, like a number of other markup languages, has been influenced by XML and its ancestors such as Standard Generalized Markup Language (SGML). The .NET Framework too has been influenced by XML; it uses XML extensively for both its configuration files and as a means for representing data.

Some examples of where the .NET Framework uses XML are as follows:

- Web Services

- Configuration files

- Data representation in ADO.NET

Several XML-based industry-standard specifications support Web Services; for example, the description and capability of a Web Service is performed by the Web Services Description Language (WSDL). Another good example is that the XML Schemas technology enforces an XML document's structure and contents through schemas. In all these cases, the protocols used to implement such functionality are defined using XML.

In addition, the .NET Framework and its associated classes (and the IT industry) support these standard specifications. For example, ADO.NET uses XML to store representations of its data, and the DataSet component (discussed in Chapter 8) is able to work in a disconnected manner through its ability to use XML to store and manipulate the data it contains.

This chapter examines the history of XML, describes its features, and shows you how to incorporate the XML functionality that is built into the .NET Framework within your Mono applications.

Exploring the History of XML

In the following sections, I'll describe XML's roots, explore its fundamental principles, and give you some insight into why it was created.

What Is a Markup Language?

As mentioned, a *markup language* offers a means of representing not only data but also additional information about that data. The term has its foundations in the publishing industry, where instructions to the printer would be included in an annotated manuscript. Several individuals were involved in defining early markup languages; IBM researcher Charles Goldfarb is considered the father of modern-day markup languages through his work on IBM's Generalized Markup Language (GML). GML later evolved to the SGML, which served as the foundation from which XML was created.

You can find early examples of markup languages within Unix-based typesetting tools such as Scribe, one of the first markup languages to separate structure from presentation. Scribe went on to influence SGML and is considered a direct ancestor of HTML, which was created by Sir Tim Berners-Lee (see `http://en.wikipedia.org/wiki/Tim_Berners-Lee`), who is also attributed as the co-inventor of the World Wide Web.

What Are the Origins of XML?

After its creation, HTML soon became widely used around the world to build Web sites. HTML was great for defining Web pages and their content, but defining business data was a struggle. This was mainly because of HTML's lack of extensibility. (It recognized only a standard set of tags.) Although HTML originally promoted one its key features as its support for interoperability, it failed to provide a sufficient platform for representing data in an extensible but easily understood manner.

The World Wide Web Consortium (W3C) therefore looked to combine the power offered by SGML with the simplicity of HTML. The result was XML; the W3C released the specification for XML 1.0 in 1998 and released a second version in 2000.

Why Do You Need XML?

The benefits of XML are numerous:

- Extensible through the ability to define your own tags

- Standard through its W3C ratification and through industry support

- Platform independent through its support on a number of operating systems

- Simple to implement and is in a human-readable form

In the following sections, I'll elaborate on these features in more detail, justifying why these issues are important. To begin, consider the following XML document, which embodies several of the benefits I'll discuss in this section:

```
<?xml version="1.0" encoding="UTF-8"?>
<Author>
  <FirstName>Mark</FirstName>
  <LastName>Mamone</LastName>
</Author>
```

Extensible

Extensible means that an XML document's structure is not fixed. It is you who defines the structure of the XML document, thereby making your document *self-describing*. This ability to define your own structure, coupled with the way in which an XML document is interpreted, means you are free to extend the document to describe the data you want represented by it. You can create your own XML structure based on the content you want to permit. This will often mean that the code you have written to interpret the document remains unchanged. I'll cover some examples of this in the "Representing Data Using XML" section later in this chapter.

Standard

Another key feature is that the W3C has ratified the XML standard and has issued a public specification. This means any XML document that is said to *conform* to the 1.0 specification can be interpreted on any platform with the same result. Standards are important in order to ensure interoperability!

Platform Independent

The ratification of the XML specification as a standard, as I've mentioned, is important to ensure interoperability. Provided that your XML document conforms to the specification, the XML interpreter you are using—whatever its platform (Microsoft Windows, Linux, Unix, Mac OS X, and so forth)—will be able to interpret and process the document. This is important because the boundaries of both corporate and Internet-enabled applications often involve numerous platforms; therefore, the ability for your application to talk and interact with another application without knowledge of its platform is paramount.

Simple

Perhaps one of the most important aspects of XML is that it is simple! This was one of the key aims when basing XML on the complex language of SGML. This would help ensure its widespread adoption.

Exploring the Structure of an XML Document

I'll now cover the language itself, its features, and how the .NET Framework, including Mono, embraces the technology. Listing 9-1 shows a well-formed (more on this in the "Valid vs. Well-Formed Documents" section) XML document that holds the configuration for the RSS aggregator project.

Listing 9-1. *A Well-Formed XML Document*

```
<?xml version="1.0" encoding="UTF-8" standalone="yes"?>
<configuration>
  <general>
    <MaxFeeds>10</MaxFeeds>
  </general>
</configuration>
```

Introducing an XML Document's Elements

The XML specification defines that a well-formed XML document starts with a *prolog* and contains exactly one *root* element.

Prolog

The first line of an XML document is known as the *prolog*, which indicates that it is an XML document (or not) and denotes specific attributes about the XML document. In Listing 9-1, the prolog looks like this:

```
<?xml version="1.0" encoding="UTF-8" standalone="yes"?>
```

The first item to note is that markup items are enclosed within angled brackets, indicating that the text has special meaning and doesn't refer to content. These items are also referred to as *elements* or *tags*, which I'll cover in more detail in the "Introducing Elements, Attributes, and Content" section. The prolog markup begins with <?xml, indicating that what follows is an XML document. Following this are three name/value combinations, also called *attributes*, associated with the element. These attributes relate to the element in which they appear; therefore, in this example, the attribute values defined in this prolog affect the whole document because the element applies to the whole document. Table 9-1 shows a prolog's supported attributes.

Table 9-1. *XML Prolog Attributes*

Attribute	Description
version	The specification version to which the XML document conforms.
encoding	The encoding format used, in this case Unicode Transformation Format 8-bit (UTF-8). This is optional.
standalone	Whether the document is accompanied by a Document Type Definition (DTD). This is optional.
xmlns	Defines the namespace(s) used, qualifying the element and attribute names. This is optional.

In Listing 9-1, the document conforms to version 1.0 of the XML specification, uses UTF-8 encoding, and does not contain a DTD. (I'll cover DTDs in the "What About DTDs?" sidebar.) This is a typical XML prolog like the one you'll be using within the XML documents in this chapter.

Root Element

Other than the prolog, an XML document must have a *root* element, which is the first element defined after the prolog. All the elements following the root element must be children of it. In Listing 9-1, the root element of the document is the `<configuration>` element, which, as expected, has both an opening and closing element tag.

Introducing Elements, Attributes, and Content

In the following sections, I will further explain the structure of an XML document in terms of its elements, attributes, and content. You'll also learn how to interpret and define your own XML documents, a requisite skill prior to integrating the .NET Framework's support of XML into your applications.

Elements

An element must conform to certain rules. First, its opening element must have a corresponding closing element. The syntax for this is as follows:

```
<element_name></element_name>
```

Second, the content of an element may contain one or a combination of the following elements:

- *Parsed character data*: An element can contain raw data that can be parsed, such as a string. This is instead of containing child elements.

- *Child elements*: An element can contain *child* elements, which in turn may contain parsed character data or more child elements.

- *Nothing (empty)*: This refers to an empty element with no parsed character data or child elements.

Consider the following snippet:

```
<ElementName>
  <NestedElementName>content here</NestedElementName>
  <NestedElementName attribute1="value1">content here</NestedElementName>
  <NestedElementName></NestedElementName>
</ElementName>
```

The root element in this example is defined as `<ElementName></ElementName>`, with numerous nested elements within it, all named `<NestedElementName></NestedElementName>`. The first of these elements holds content in the form of `content here`. The second of these elements holds the same content but has an associated `attribute1` attribute with a corresponding value of `value1`. (You'll learn more about attributes in the next section.) The final element holds no content and has no associated attributes; it's considered to be an *empty element*. Note that for empty elements, instead of using an opening and closing element, you can use shorthand, as follows:

```
<EmptyNestedElement/>
```

Attributes

In addition to using elements, you can also assign *attributes* to an element. These attributes are associated with the element against which they are defined. The name of an attribute is pretty much open, although attributes beginning with XML are reserved. The syntax for attributes is as follows:

```
<tag attributename1="value1" attributename2="value2">…</tag>
```

Note You *must* enclose the value of an attribute in quotes, either single or double, even if the text is a continuous stream over more than one line. If your content itself contains quotes, you can use escape characters to represent these special characters. For a single quote, you use &#39, and for a double quote, you use &#34, with the &# sequence denoting an escape character.

You can use an attribute to embellish the content and meaning of an element. For example, you could have an attribute called font that defines the font face to be used when rendering the content within the element.

Note You should limit your use of attributes, because they are less extensible than elements and therefore implicitly limit the ability of your application to cope with change.

Valid vs. Well-Formed Documents

For an XML document to be considered *well-formed*, it must adhere to a number of rules:

- It has a prolog.

- It contains one root element.

- All elements are correctly paired, and the element name is the same in both the starting tag and the closing tag.

- All attributes must be uniquely named within each element.

If your XML document observes these rules, it is considered to be well-formed; this does not, however, mean that the document is *valid*. A document is considered valid when its content matches a formal description that is associated with it.

So, how do you know if the structure is as expected? How do you associate the rules governing its structure with an XML document? You do this using an XML *schema*.

An XML schema allows you to define what is considered a valid structure, which includes, amongst other things, the XML elements that are permitted within the structure of the document. You can reuse schemas because they're defined in XML and held in an XML document, which can then be referenced from other XML documents. More important, however, schemas enforce business rules, allowing your document to pass validity tests when matching the formal description held in the schema associated with it.

I'll discuss XML schemas in more detail later in the "Enforcing Data Integrity Using XML Schemas" section of this chapter.

Using XML Namespaces

An XML *namespace* has the same functionality as in C# and other object-oriented languages that support namespaces. A namespace provides a means of qualifying element and attributes names, ensuring that no ambiguity exists. This is an important concept for schemas because you can then import elements from other schemas and mix and match elements with your XML document, qualifying which schema they belong to using namespaces. For instance, consider the following example:

```
<title>Name of Book</title>
<title>Name of Web Page</title>
```

Both of these elements are identically named; however, they have different semantic meanings. The first describes a book, and the second describes the title of a Web page, as defined within HTML. You would want to apply these two semantic meanings but may want the data for both to be contained within the same XML document. In this instance, using a namespace would be mandatory to avoid conflict; you would just define two namespaces to give the different elements (with the same name) their own, unique meanings.

Referencing an XML Namespace

You can reference a namespace within your XML document's prolog using the xmlns attribute. The syntax is as follows:

```
xmlns:namespace-prefix="namespaceURI"
```

The name of the namespace is used only to uniquely identify the namespace; in other words, it's not physically referenced, but the name should be unique. Once you have named your namespace (and optionally aliased it), you can then use this alias within your XML document to qualify an element or attributes as belonging to that namespace. You do this by prefixing the element or attribute with the namespace alias defined. For example:

```
< NamespaceAlias: ElementName>…</ NamespaceAlias: ElementName>
```

Note Some companies place a Web page's address in the namespace to provide information about the namespace; see http://www.w3.org/TR/html4/ for an example.

What Effect Do Namespaces Have?

As I have shown, using a namespace reference allows you to qualify an element or attribute by including the namespace alias. This qualification (shown in bold in the following code) means that the two elements may have a different semantic meaning depending on the semantics of the namespace being included:

```
<rss:dbconnection >...</ rss:dbconnection >
<dbconnection>...</dbconnection>
```

The two elements named `<dbconnection>` may have different semantic meanings because one is associated with the `rss` namespace and the other isn't. However, you must be aware that you can also define a default namespace, so even if the second element doesn't explicitly reference a namespace, it may inherit one by default; this is something you'll need to check. For instance, you can define a default namespace by simply not giving it a prefix, as follows:

```
<configuration xmlns="http://www.mamone.org/mynamespace" >
```

In this document, an element will automatically belong to this namespace. But what if you wanted to include more than one namespace? How would you define an XML document that included more than one namespace and allowed you to associate elements with the different namespaces? You do this by simply listing the namespaces and then associating an alias, as shown here:

```
<configuration "xmlns:rss=http://www.mamone.org/myrssnamespace"
xmlns:non='http://www.mamone.org/mynonrssnamespace'>
```

This example defines two namespaces, one with an alias of `rss` and the other with an alias of `non`. You can then use these namespaces to qualify the XML elements and tags, as shown here:

```
<rss:dbconnection >...</ rss:dbconnection>
<non:dbconnection >...</non:dbconnection>
```

You could have set one of these as the default namespace and avoided using this qualification within any relevant element and attribute references, but my preference when using more than one namespace is to prefix all elements for clarity. This is of course optional.

Representing Data Using XML

This is a good point to return to the configuration document that will hold the configuration data associated with the book's RSS aggregator project and examine how you can create a simple XML schema to ensure the document is not only well-formed but also valid. I'll also explain namespaces in a little more detail, something that is intrinsically linked to XML schemas.

The RSS aggregator has a number of customizable features that you can store in an XML document and load at runtime. This document is validated against a simple XML schema to ensure its structure is as you expect. An example configuration file is as follows:

```
<configuration>
  <defaultfeed>name</defaultfeed>
  <dbconnection>DSN=rssaggregator</dbconnection>
  <maxchannelitems>30</maxchannelitems>
</configuration>
```

You may notice that the database connection string is stored within this configuration file in the <dbconnection> element. In addition, the default feed to be opened is also stored within an element called <defaultfeed>. Finally, configuration information relating to the maximum number of channel items held is defined within the <maxchannelitems> element.

You can now look at how to use an XML schema to enforce this structure.

Enforcing Data Integrity Using XML Schemas

The topic of XML schemas is immense and warrants a book in its own right. Given this scope, I'll define a simple XML schema to apply against the XML configuration document, and I'll highlight some of the key topics, providing you with enough information to make further forays into the subject of using schemas. XML schemas are important not just within the .NET Framework but also within the IT industry as a whole.

Numerous XML schemas are being produced for use in various fields in the IT industry. For example, XML schemas exist for representing mathematical formulae (MathML), for representing biometric information, for representing voice information (VoiceXML), and for representing numerous Web Service elements through SOAP and the WS-* series of specifications (WS-Security, WS-Addressing, WS-Management, and more).

The XML document shown in Listing 9-2 is the XML schema for the RSS aggregator's XML configuration file. It's written in XML so should be fairly easy to follow, even if you don't fully understand its meaning.

Listing 9-2. *XML Schema for the RSS Aggregator's XML Configuration File*

```
<?xml version="1.0"?>
<xs:schema xmlns:xs="http://www.w3.org/2001/XMLSchema"
targetNamespace="http://www.mamone.org/rssconfiguration"
xmlns="http://www.mamone.org/rssconfiguration"
elementFormDefault="qualified">

<xs:element name="configuration">
    <xs:complexType>
      <xs:sequence>
        <xs:element name="defaultfeed" type="xs:string"/>
        <xs:element name="dbconnection" type="xs:string"/>
        <xs:element name="maxchannelitems" type="xs:string"/>
      </xs:sequence>
    </xs:complexType>
</xs:element>

</xs:schema>
```

WHAT ABOUT DTDs?

I should probably mention DTDs, which were the precursor to XML schemas. The purpose of a DTD is to define the permitted building blocks of an XML document; in other words, a DTD describes an XML document's structure with a list of legal elements. The equivalent DTD for the XML schema shown previously is as follows:

```
<?xml version="1.0"?>
<!DOCTYPE note [
  <!ELEMENT configuration (defaultfeed,dbconnection,maxchannelitems)>
  <!ELEMENT defaultfeed (#PCDATA)>
  <!ELEMENT dbconnection (#PCDATA)>
  <!ELEMENT maxchannelitems (#PCDATA)>
]>
```

As you can see, it's not represented in XML and is pretty hard to understand. This is one of the reasons that DTDs have been dropped in favor of schemas. Other reasons include readability and standardization, so I recommend you use XML schemas in all instances.

Schema Declarations

I'll take you through creating a schema one step at a time, but I'd like to reiterate that XML schemas are a complex topic. If you want to use XML schemas and understand them in more detail, I recommend further research of your own. That said; I'll now cover the aggregator's schema.

Skipping the XML prolog, the first element looks like this:

```
<xs:schema xmlns:xs="http://www.w3.org/2001/XMLSchema"
targetNamespace="http://www.mamone.org/rssconfiguration"
xmlns="http://www.mamone.org/rssconfiguration"
elementFormDefault="qualified">
```

This starts by defining the root element called schema and associating it with a namespace prefix of xs and a namespace uniform resource indicator (URI) of http://www.w3.org/2001/XMLSchema, which is the uniform resource locator (URL) from which the elements and data types will come. (Navigate to this Web site for more information.)

The next lines define the elements and tags that can be defined within an XML document that conforms to the schema; the URI for this schema is http://www.mamone.org/rssconfiguration (which is also used as the default namespace to avoid convoluting the code with namespace alias prefixes). This takes place in the following snippet of XML:

```
targetNamespace="http://www.mamone.org/rssconfiguration"
xmlns="http://www.mamone.org/rssconfiguration"
```

The last line, shown next, indicates that XML documents using this schema must have all their elements and attributes qualified with a namespace (that is, they must belong to a namespace), either by directly referring to the namespace alias or via the declaration of a default namespace:

```
elementFormDefault="qualified">
```

Looking at Complex and Simple Types

This covers the XML schema declaration. Now let's look at the language that actually defines the specification for any XML document that uses this XML schema (so that using the schema defines what structure is permitted). This is where the topic of XML schemas can become extremely complicated; they are powerful and as such are represented by a comprehensive language of their own. I will cover a fairly simple definition, qualifying the elements that can be included in the RSS aggregator's XML configuration file.

If you refer to the XML document in Listing 9-1, you'll see that it contains a single element called <configuration>, which in turn may contain several elements that all hold values used by the RSS aggregator.

In the example schema shown in Listing 9-3, an element is defined called <configuration>, which in turn may contain a sequence of elements, all of which are qualified by a specified element name and value type.

Listing 9-3. *An Example XML Schema*

```
<xs:element name="configuration">
    <xs:complexType>
      <xs:sequence>
        <xs:element name="defaultfeed" type="xs:string"/>
        <xs:element name="dbconnection" type="xs:string"/>
        <xs:element name="maxchannelitems" type="xs:integer"/>
      </xs:sequence>
    </xs:complexType>
</xs:element>
```

What Is a Simple Type?

The root element is given a name of configuration and can contain text or simple types. A *simple type* is a child-only element that has an associated value; a good example of a simple type is the child element defined within the complex type named configuration. For example:

```
<xs:element name="defaultfeed" type="xs:string"/>
```

In this case, the simple types map to the built-in data types listed in Table 9-2.

Table 9-2. *Built-in Data Types*

Type	Description
xs:string	String content
xs:decimal	Decimal content
xs:integer	Integer content
xs:boolean	Boolean content, true or false
xs:date	Date content
xs:time	Time content

■Note You can also define constants using the fixed attribute on a simple type definition, for example, fixed="mydefaultfeed".

What Is a Complex Type?

By comparison, a *complex type* contains more than just content based around one of the built-in types. Specifically, the <configuration> item is a complex type because it contains numerous simple types that are defined within a sequence (indicated by the <sequence> element). This specifies that only elements with these names may be included within the <configuration> element.

Using an XML Schema

You have defined the XML schema and created your XML document, but how do you tie the two together, ensuring that your XML document conforms to the XML schema? As you can probably imagine, the next step is to define the namespace that the XML document uses and reference the schema you have declared, also including the location of the actual XML schema file so that it can be loaded for verification. You do this by referencing the namespace and XML schema, as shown here:

```
<configuration xmlns="http://www.mamone.org/rssaggregator"
xmlns:xsi="http://www.w3.org/2001/XMLSchema-instance"
xsi:schemaLocation="http://www.mamone.org/rssaggregator.xsd">
```

This would immediately follow the XML document's prolog. The default namespace declaration should be familiar to you now; however, notice that you also reference the actual XML schema document using the elements shown in bold. These define the XML schema namespace, and then you use a special attribute called schemaLocation to point to the actual XML schema file, which usually has an .xsd extension. The complex XML document is as follows:

```
<?xml version="1.0"?>
<configuration xmlns="http://www.mamone.org/rssaggregator"
xmlns:xsi="http://www.w3.org/2001/XMLSchema-instance"
xsi:schemaLocation="http://www.mamone.org/rssaggregator.xsd">

<configuration>
  <defaultfeed>name</defaultfeed>
  <dbconnection>DSN=rssaggregator</dbconnection>
  <maxchannelitems>30</maxchannelitems>
</configuration>
```

Why Use an XML Schema?

An XML schema is the specification for your XML document; it defines what is expected and so identifies what is an exception. In the IT world today, the transmission of data between systems is extremely common, and to support heterogeneous platforms, the use of XML is almost ubiquitous. Therefore, to ensure that the data sent conforms to what is expected, XML schemas represent an excellent way of enforcing that contract. In addition, XML schemas have a number of other advantages:

- They are written in XML and so are extensible and based on standards; using an XML schema means that it can be read and understood by humans and computers alike.

- You can reuse your XML schemas across your XML documents and applications. For example, your organization may create an XML schema to validate some business data. You can use this business data in numerous areas within the same business, and you can share the XML schema and thus achieve reuse.

- You can reduce errors through the ability to validate the data being added to an XML document for which an XML schema exists.

- You can reference multiple XML schemas in a single document, which means you are not limited to a single schema for a single XML document. An organization may have a complex document with different elements within it, and the ability to use one or more XML schemas means that this sort of complex document may still be validated.

Table 9-3. *XML-Related Resources*

Description	Link
XML tutorial	http://www.w3schools.com/xml/default.asp
XML schema tutorial	http://www.w3schools.com/schema/default.asp
XML namespace tutorial	http://www.w3schools.com/xml/xml_namespaces.asp
XML specification	http://www.w3.org/TR/REC-xml/

Introducing XML-Related Technologies

The invention of XML has spawned several related technologies/languages that are defined in XML with the appropriate support within XML parsers. These technologies are as follows (although this list is not exhaustive):

- Extensible Stylesheet Language (XSL)

- XSL Transformations (XSLT)

- XML Path (XPath)

- XML Schemas

■**Note** XPath is not actually represented in XML. XPath uses a compact, string-based syntax rather than a structural syntax like XML's element-based syntax. This allows XPath expressions to be used in XML attributes and within URIs.

I'll now provide a brief description of XSL, XSLT, and XPath so that you can choose to investigate these further and perhaps incorporate their features in your application. Later in the "Traversing XML Documents" section, you'll gain considerable insight into one in particular, XPath, because you'll use it in the RSS aggregator project.

XSL: XSL allows you to create style sheets for XML documents and use this representation for marking up content and for rendering the output graphically.

XSLT: XSLT allows you to represent how an XML document is transformed and uses XSL as the syntax for formatting individual elements. For example, if you have the raw contents of a Web page returned as an XML document, you can use an associated XSLT document to describe how this is rendered into HTML for viewing as a Web page.

XPath: As you can imagine, XML documents can become large and complicated, with numerous nested elements. The XPath language was created to make navigating XML documents far easier. For example, you may choose to cycle through all the child elements of a given element and apply some processing against them.

Using XPath and XSLT together against raw XML documents is a powerful combination and the foundation for numerous Web sites and their rendering technology.

Using the .NET Framework and XML Together

The .NET Framework, as I've mentioned, uses XML as its core technology in a number of areas. I'll start by introducing the class libraries, and their associated namespaces, that are available within the .NET Framework. The namespaces available are as follows:

- `System.Xml`: This namespace provides support for XML, including support for DTDs, even though it has been replaced by XML schemas.

- `System.Xml.Schema`: This namespace provides a suite of classes to support the definition and use of XML schemas within your XML documents. It supports W3C XML Schema Definition (XSD) documents.

- `System.Xml.Xsl`: This namespace provides a suite of classes to encapsulate XSLT functionality and supports the version 1.0 recommendation.

- `System.Xml.XPath`: This namespace provides a suite of classes to encapsulate the XPath parser and its evaluation engine; it also provides an implementation of the XPath 1.0 recommendation.

- `System.Xml.Serialization`: This namespace provides a suite of classes to serialize objects into XML-based documents or streams. The key class in this namespace is `XmlSerializer`.

As you can imagine, the scope of these namespaces, their classes, their methods, and their properties is considerable, so I'll focus on the `System.Xml` namespace initially, which provides the core functionality for reading, writing, and interpreting XML documents.

Caution From this point forward, I'll focus on XML documents that do *not* have an associated XML schema. This is for simplicity and to help you when debugging your application.

The example XML file you'll be using is based on typical output returned by an RSS feed. It's a little more complicated than the configuration file I discussed previously, but given this is a critical part of the RSS aggregator project, it's the most obvious example to use. Take some time to review the RSS feed example shown in Listing 9-4.

Listing 9-4. *RSS Feed Example*

```
<?xml version="1.0" encoding="ISO-8859-1" ?>
<rss version="2.0">
  <channel>
    <title>Recent News | Technology | UK Edition</title>
    <link>http://mamone.org/ rss/technology/default.stm</link>
    <description>Updated often</description>
    <language>en-gb</language>
    <lastBuildDate>Tue, 05 Jul 05 15:02:50 GMT</lastBuildDate>
    <copyright>Copyright: (C) Mark Mamone</copyright>
    <docs>http://www.mamone.org/syndication/</docs>
    <ttl>15</ttl>
```

```
<image>
  <title>Mark's News</title>
  <url>http://mamone.org/img/marks_news_120x60.gif</url>
  <link>http://www.mamone.org</link>
</image>

<item>
  <title>Mark Mamone publishes book</title>
  <description>Apress has recently published the
  Practical Mono book</description>
  <link>http://mamone.org/rss/technology/4649361.stm</link>
  <guid isPermaLink="false">http://mamone.org/rss/technology/4649361.stm</guid>
  <pubDate>Tue, 05 Jul 05 13:44:52 GMT</pubDate>
</item>

</channel>
</rss>
```

Creating the RSS Feed Class Library

An RSS aggregator needs to have, at its core, the ability to read and interpret XML documents in the form of RSS feeds. An RSS feed, as you can see from the previous example, is an XML document that conforms to the RSS specification. In this section, you'll create several classes that, when combined, provide the ability to read and interpret RSS feeds. You'll create a class that, when given an RSS feed document, can interpret and provide you with access to the data for displaying within a user interface and persisting to storage if required.

Figure 9-1 demonstrates the classes associated with the RSS feed's capability and articulates the design.

■**Note** Please note that for brevity, I've created the properties as public member variables rather than defining private member variables and using the properties feature of C#. This would have been preferable and is something I strongly encourage.

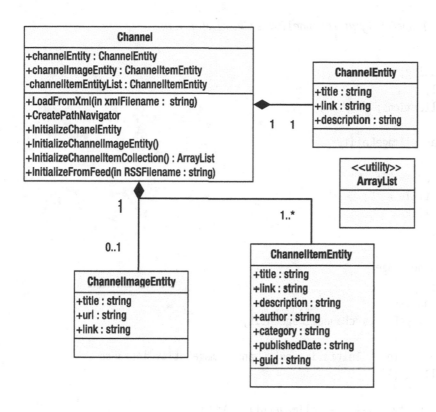

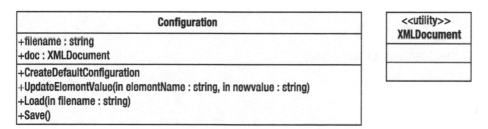

Figure 9-1. *Class diagram for XML-related classes*

I'll explain the implementation for these classes in the sections that follow.

The first class you'll look at is ChannelImage and its associated ChannelImageEntity class, both of which combine to define the properties and methods associated with the graphical image that can accompany an RSS channel. If an <image> element is present (it's an optional element), you will initialize its attributes and allow this class to provide an implementation for retrieving and displaying this image via a GUI through a consumer of this class. Listing 9-5 shows the class definitions.

Listing 9-5. *ChannelImageEntity and ChannelImage Class Definitions*

```
using System;
using System.Drawing;
using System.Xml;
using System.Collections;

public class ChannelImageEntity
{
  public string url = "";
  public string title = "";
  public string link = "";
}


public class ChannelImage
{
  // Member variables
  public ChannelImageEntity channelImageEntity;

  // Default constructor - Initialize out ChannelImageEntity instance
  public ChannelImage()
  {
    channelImageEntity = new ChannelImageEntity();
  }

  // Member methods
  public bool DownloadImage(string url)
  {
    // Todo
    return true;
  }

  public Image GetImage()
  {
    // Todo
    return null;
  }

}
```

I have provided the implementation for most of this class as part of the finished RSS project's source code (available in the Source Code section of the Apress Web site), so in this section I'll provide an overview for clarity. I'll concentrate on the key classes and its associated implementation, which consist of the Channel class and its associated entity classes. Let's start with the implementation of the Channel class whose basic structure is as follows:

```
public class Channel
{
  // Member variables
  public ChannelImage channelImage = null;
  public ChannelEntity channelEntity;
  public ChannelImageEntity channelImageEntity;
  public ArrayList channelItemEntityList;

  // Methods
}
```

This class will provide storage for the properties associated with a channel (via the ChannelEntity class) and also a collection of RSS items that are associated with the channel. This list will actually hold several ChannelItemEntity class instances that are contained within a .NET collection class, although I recommend you create your own enumerable class that can hold a list of such instances and return native objects of that type, rather than rely on typecasting. This is left to you as a future project, because its discussion here is not relevant to the topic of XML. In addition to the channel properties and item list, this class also provides methods for initializing the class from an XML document, which is the RSS feed.

Therefore, the Channel class represents the main class instance with properties (via associated entity classes) and methods. The entity classes are ChannelItemEntity and ChannelEntity, as shown in Listing 9-6.

Listing 9-6. *ChannelEntity and ChannelItemEntity Class Definitions*

```
public class ChannelEntity
{
  public string title = "";
  public string link - "";
  public string description = "";
}

public class ChannelItemEntity
{
  public string title = "";
  public string link = "";
  public string description = "";
  public string author = "";
  public string category = "";
  public string publishedDate = "";
  public string guid = "";
}
```

At this point, I've merely created the skeleton classes and described their intended usage. You'll now start to look at their implementations, and the end result will be RSS classes that provide all the functionality you need for the RSS aggregator application.

Reading XML Documents

I'll start by going through the classes that deal with reading an existing XML document that may have been created in a number of ways, either by writing code or by using your favorite editor, for example. The XmlReader class is an abstract class that all the previous classes inherit from and implement. The .NET Framework classes I'll cover are as follows:

- XmlTextReader: This abstract class provides an interface for reading and navigating an XML document, with the ability to read XML documents as node data.

- XmlNodeReader: This abstract class provides an interface for reading and navigating an XML document, with the ability to read XML documents as node data.

- XmlValidatingReader: This class provides XML data-reading capability but with full support for XML schemas.

- XmlDocument: This class represents a complete XML document, complete with XML schema support and traversal functionality.

I'll focus on the XMLTextReader class because it provides fast, forward-only access to an XML character stream but does not perform any data validation using any schemas that may be referenced. The flexibility it provides when traversing XML documents is limited; however, if you want to simply run through the XML document in a forward-only manner, this is an ideal class. Consider the following snippet of code, which simply opens an XML document using this class and scrolls through the file, outputting some pertinent information:

```
string xmlFilename = "rss.xml"
XmlTextTeader xmlrdr;
xmlrdr = new XmlTextReader(xmlFilename);
while (xmlrdr.Read())
{
  Console.Out.WriteLine("Type:"+xmlrdr.NodeType.ToString()+
" NAME:"+xmlrdr.Name+" VALUE:"+xmlrdr.Value.Trim());
}
```

A snippet of the output from this looks like this:

```
C:\Documents and Settings\Mark\My Documents>mono channel.exe
Type:XmlDeclaration NAME:xml VALUE:version="1.0" encoding
Type:Whitespace NAME: VALUE:
Type:Element NAME:title VALUE:
Type:Text NAME: VALUE: Mark Mamone publishes book
Type:EndElement NAME:title VALUE:
Type:Element NAME:description VALUE:
Type:Text NAME: VALUE: Apress has recently published the Practical Mono book
Type:EndElement NAME:description VALUE:
```

As you can see, this method requires that you track programmatically the node type, whether it's the start or end element. The other classes, XmlNodeReader and XmlValidatingReader, provide similar functionality but are still limited to forward-only XML reading. The requirements for the class are for more flexibility when it comes to querying the resulting XML file, with the ability to select individual nodes and their respective contents. For this, the .NET Framework provides the XmlDocument class, which is far more powerful, but this does come at a cost. It holds the XML document in memory, but for illustration purposes you can assume that the client machine has sufficient memory.

■**Note** Several XML processing constructs exist, including the DOM, which is fast and flexible but memory based. Alternatively, the Simple API for XML (SAX) model is a fast and memory-efficient stream of data but is limited in terms of power because it relies on your programmatic flexibility.

The XmlDocument class provides a similar method called Load, which takes the name of an XML file on a file system and loads this into memory. You are then able to use some of the more powerful features available within this class to traverse and read the elements of the RSS XML document and use this to initialize the RSS feed class instances. The two methods provided as part of the XML document class for querying an XML document are as follows:

- SelectNodes

- SelectSingleNode

As their names suggest, these are related, with the SelectNodes method returning more than one node and the singular method, SelectSingleNode, expecting and returning only a single node. In either case, these methods allow you to perform an XPath query against the XML document loaded into memory. This shows how you can use this within the Channel class to extract the node (the instance of an element) that contains the channel information:

```
// ReadChannelElement() - returns the XMLNode relating to the <channel> element
//
public XmlNode ReadChannelElement()
{
  XmlNode channelNode = doc.SelectSingleNode("//channel");
  return channelNode;
}
```

This simple method reads the single element called <channel> present within the RSS XML document (the specification states there can only be one) and returns this as an XmlNode object. The XmlDocument class in fact inherits from the XmlNode class, so it's this class that contains most of the core functionality required to manipulate and work with XML documents using the DOM parser. The XPath expression you are using, //channel, simply says, "Return the element with a name of channel from the root of the XML document."

Traversing XML Documents

You now have the XML document in memory, and you've written a simple method that returns the <channel> element node as XmlNode, although this isn't strictly necessary because XPath expressions are able to navigate through multiple nodes at multiple depths. The .NET Framework provides a namespace called System.Xml.XPath, which provides numerous classes that implement the XPath language and allow you to work with XML documents using the power of XPath and associated technologies such as XSLT. You will be using the XPathNavigator class that allows you to navigate an XmlDocument using XPath queries, which is exactly the functionality you require in order to extract the element values.

You have a few options for creating XPathNavigator. The XMLDocument class provides a CreateNavigator() method, which takes an XMLNode parameter and creates the XPathNavigator instance from this. However, you can replace the XMLDocument class type with the XPathDocument class type; this provides an in-memory XML document that is fine-tuned for fast, read-only performance, which is exactly what you need. This class also provides a CreateNavigator() method that returns an XPathNavigator instance you can use to traverse the XML document. Let's look at some code to achieve this.

First, modify the Channel class attributes to reflect that you need an XPathDocument and an XPathNavigator. You do this by declaring some member variables of this type, as shown here:

```
XmlDocument doc = null;
XPathNavigator nav = null;
```

Then you'll provide a method that initializes your XPathNavigator attributes if required; this is shown in the following method:

```
// CreateXPathNavigator - Creates an XPathNavigator from the XPathDocument
//
public void CreateXPathNavigator()
{
  if (nav == null)
    nav = doc.CreateNavigator();
}
```

Initializing the Channel Attributes

You are now able to use this XPathNavigator instance in the methods that initialize your class attributes; start by implementing a method that initializes the mandatory elements of ChannelEntity (refer to Chapter 9 for the discussion of entities) from the <channel> element, as defined in the RSS specification. Define the ChannelEntity with only those attributes that are mandatory within the RSS specification; the finished RSS aggregator will include more attributes than the following:

```
public class ChannelEntity
{
  public string title = "";
  public string link = "";
  public string description = "";
}
```

This class holds the data to represent a specific channel; therefore, you initialize these values to blank values initially. You can then pass this to a method within the Channel class for initialization from the RSS XML feed; the implementation for this initialization method is as follows:

```
// InitializeChannelEntity - Initialize the ChannelEntity passed from the RSS feed
//
public void InitializeChannelEntity(ChannelEntity channelEntity)
  {
    // Create the navigator from the channel element
    CreateXPathNavigator();
    if (nav != null)
    {
      if (channelEntity == null)
        channelEntity = new ChannelEntity();
      channelEntity.title = nav.Evaluate("string(//channel/title)").ToString();
      channelEntity.link = nav.Evaluate("string(//channel/link)").ToString();
      channelEntity.description = nav.Evaluate
      ("string(//channel/description)").ToString();
    }
  }
```

You'll notice that you are calling the CreateXPathNavigator() method that will, if necessary, create an XPathNavigator class instance to use called nav. You can then reference this instance to perform XPath-based expressions and traverse the XML data, using the Evaluate() method to return an individual element's contents and casting this (within XPath) as a string. This result is then used to initialize the ChannelEntity reference passed and its attributes.

Initializing the Optional ChannelImage Class

You have initialized the mandatory attributes of the Channel entity, but you may have noticed from the RSS specification that an <image> element may exist (it's optional). So, in the following code, you'll add a method that will look to see whether the image element is present and, if it is, create and initialize the ChannelImage entity class:

```
// InitializeChannelImage - Initialize the ChannelImage from RSS feed if possible
//
public void InitializeChannelImage()
{
  CreateXPathNavigator();
  if (nav != null)
  {
    XPathNodeIterator nodeItr = nav.Select("//channel/image");
    if (nodeItr.MoveNext())
    {
      if (channelImage==null)
        channelImage = new ChannelImage ();
        channelImage.channelImageEntity.url =
```

```
        nav.Evaluate("string(//channel/image/url)").ToString();
        channelImage.channelImage Entity.title =
        nav.Evaluate("string(//channel/image/title)").ToString();
        channelImage.channelImage Entity.link =
        nav.Evaluate("string(//channel/image/link)").ToString();
      }
    }
}
```

For the most part, you should now be familiar with the start of this method's implementation, as it's pretty similar to the previous example; however, I'd like to concentrate on a new feature used, and that's the XPathNodeIterator class. This class is the result of calling the Select() method on the XPathNavigator object, and it has the ability to support navigation through a node based on a given position (determined through an XPath expression). You can then perform the usual enumeration activities such as MoveNext(), and so on. This is what is used in this example; you selected the position of the <image> node (if it exists) and moved to the first element that matches it using the MoveNext() method. If no element exists, the enumeration returns false, and you don't initialize the ChannelImage entity.

Reading the Channel Items

Finally, traversing the RSS feed requires you to return the <item> elements that may exist for a given channel. You may find more than one channel item, and in most scenarios, this will be the case. As a result, you need to be able to traverse *all* the <item> elements and create ChannelItemEntity instances, adding them to a collection of items that you can use to display in the RSS aggregator's user interface. The first thing you need to do is define the method signature for initializing this list of channel items, as follows:

```
// InitializeChannelItemCollection - Return a collection of
// ChannelItemEntities as read from the RSS feed.
//
public ArrayList  InitializeChannelItemCollection()
{
}
```

You'll also need a member variable added to the Channel class to hold this list of items (you'll use the .NET ArrayList collection); this simple declaration is as follows:

```
ArrayList channelItems;
```

In addition, you'll need to use a ChannelItemEntity class definition, which has already been defined in the "Creating the RSS Feed Class Library" section. Now you are in a position to concentrate on the implementation of the InitializeChannelItemCollection() method, as shown in Listing 9-7. You'll be looking for *all* the <item> elements within the parent <channel> element and enumerate through these nodes (assuming some are found), creating individual ChannelItemEntity class instances and adding them to the overall collection, which you'll eventually return once the complete list has been enumerated.

Listing 9-7. *InitializeChannelItemCollection Method Implementation*

```
// InitializeChannelItemCollection - Return a collection of
ChannelItemEntities as read from
// the RSS feed.
//
public ArrayList  InitializeChannelItemCollection()
{
  ArrayList list = null;
  CreateXPathNavigator();
  if (nav != null)
  {
    XPathNodeIterator nodeItr = nav.Select("//channel/item");
    while (nodeItr.MoveNext())
    {
      // If an item has been found, initialize the ArrayList class type if necessary
      if (list == null)
        list = new ArrayList();

      // Create the ChannelItemEntity instance and initialize it
      ChannelItemEntity item = new ChannelItemEntity();
      item.title = nodeItr.Current.Evaluate("string(./title)").ToString();
      item.link = nodeItr.Current.Evaluate("string(./link)").ToString();
      item.description = nodeItr.Current.Evaluate("string(./description)").
      ToString();
      item.author = nodeItr.Current.Evaluate("string(./author)").ToString();
      item.category = nodeItr.Current.Evaluate("string(./category)").ToString();
      item.publishedDate = nodeItr.Current.Evaluate("string(./pubDate)").ToString();
      item.guid = nodeItr.Current.Evaluate("string(./guid)").ToString();

      // Add it to the collection
      list.Add(item);
    }
  }
  return list;
}
```

■**Note** You should ensure that you correctly define your textual strings for those methods that are case-sensitive, such as the Evaluate() method.

Again, the start of this method's implementation should be familiar because it uses an XPath expression of //channel/item to select all <item> elements within the parent <channel> element. You are then in a position to enumerate through this collection using a while{} loop and the MoveNext() method, which will return false and so will break the loop when all elements have been traversed.

The loop's implementation then creates an instance of the ChannelItemEntity class and initializes it with values from the current node; you do this using the same Evaluate() method on the current node, pointed to by the XPathNavigators Current property. The XPath syntax in this instance is to look for an element of a given name based on the current node's position; the ./ part of the XPath expression indicates the current node, and the rest is the element name.

Finally, you can plug all three methods into a single Channel class method that initializes the object with values from the RSS feed for the base <channel> element, its optional <image> element, and the multiple <item> elements that may exist. The implementation for this is as follows:

```
// InitializeFromFeed( filename ) - Initializes the Channel class and entities
 from the RSS feed
//                                  which is passed as an XML file
//
public void InitializeFromFeed(string RSSFilename)
{
  Load(RSSFilename);
  InitializeChannelEntity();
  InitializeChannelImage();
  channelItemEntityList = InitializeChannelItemCollection();
}
```

In this instance, provide the implementation for a method signature that takes the RSS feed in the form of an XML document that exists on the file system using the Load() method, which is provided as part of the code's XmlDocument class. In the next chapter, you'll look at networking and obtain this feed directly from the Internet using the RSS feed's URL. The following example shows how you use this method to return the <title> element's value of the current node as a string value, which can then be associated with the desired attributes:

```
nodeItr.Current.Evaluate("string(./title)").ToString();
```

To test the code, I wrote a simple piece of code that sent the values of each of the ChannelItemEntities attributes to the console, remembering to typecast the Object class type used in the ArrayList class to the ChannelItemEntity class, as shown in Listing 9-8.

Listing 9-8. *ChannelItem Test Application*

```
//
// Channel demo
//
Channel ch =  new Channel();
ch.InitializeFromFeed("rss.xml");

ArrayList l = ch.InitializeChannelItemCollection();
foreach (Object o in l)
{
  ChannelItemEntity e = (ChannelItemEntity)o;
  Console.Out.WriteLine("*******************************");
  Console.Out.WriteLine("<title> = " +e.title);
```

```
Console.Out.WriteLine("<link> = " +e.link);
Console.Out.WriteLine("<description> = " +e.description);
Console.Out.WriteLine("<author> = " +e.author);
Console.Out.WriteLine("<category> = " +e.category);
Console.Out.WriteLine("<publishedDate> = " +e.publishedDate);
Console.Out.WriteLine("<guid> = " +e.guid);
Console.Out.WriteLine("*********************************");
}
```

■**Note** You may notice that in the example shown in Listing 9-8, you are outputting two elements that, although they are members of the ChannelItemEntity class, they are optional within the feed and so have been omitted from the feed. This is normal; it just means that the values displayed will be blank.

As you may expect, this merely touches on the capabilities of XML manipulation and the querying features available within the .NET Framework, but it should give you a good foundation for some of the methods available for the fast querying of XML data.

Writing XML Documents

To complete the discussion of XML and the .NET Framework's support for it, I'll cover the ways in which you can programmatically create XML documents and modify them. This is obviously something that's not directly required when dealing with the RSS feed, as this is a read-only view of data that you have no control over. You will, however, need to use this functionality when offering the user the ability to customize certain elements of the RSS aggregator application for which the values are held in the XML configuration file.

Writing an XML Document

As you'd expect, the .NET Framework provides a few ways in which you can create an XML document, the simplest of which is to use the XmlTextWriter class. This class is similar to the XmlTextReader class you've already looked at in that it provides a fast method for creating an XML document using a forward-only textual stream. The configuration file's XML document format is as follows:

```
<configuration>
  <defaultfeed>name</defaultfeed>
  <dbconnection>DSN=rssaggregator</dbconnection>
  <maxchannelitems>30</ maxchannelitems >
</configuration>
```

Let's assume that this doesn't exist on your file system because the RSS aggregator has just been installed; you can use the XmlTextWriter class to create a default XML document that has the same structure as that shown previously. This functionality will be wrapped into a custom class called RSSConfiguration and will represent the configuration for the RSS aggregator application, held on the file system in XML. Listing 9-9 shows its definition (including empty methods for functionality that I'll provide an implementation for shortly).

Listing 9-9. *RSSConfiguration Class Definition*

```
public class RSSConfiguration
{
  // Member variables
  public string filename = "";
  public XmlDocument doc = null;

  // Creates a default XML document with default values
  public void CreateDefaultConfiguration()
  {
    // To be implemented
  }


  // UpdateElementValue
  // Updates the value of the specified element to a new value
  public void UpdateElementValue(string elementName, string newValue)
  {
    // To be implemented
  }

  // Save
  // Saves the XML document to disk using the same filename as that used to open it
  public void Save()
  {
    // To be implemented
  }
}
```

If you examine the previous code, you'll notice that I've provided two member variables. One is called filename and holds the name of the file on disk from which to load or write the configuration data. I've also defined a member variable called doc, which is of type XmlDocument, to hold the XML document and configuration data. I've declared several empty methods to represent the class's core functionality; I'll walk you through the implementation of these next, but you also need to provide a method for loading a configuration file from disk. Let's add this before you continue:

```
// Load - Loads the XML document from disk into memory
//
public void Load(string filename)
{
  this.filename = filename;
  doc = new XmlDocument();
  doc.Load(filename);
}
```

This implementation is pretty straightforward; you receive the filename to load as a parameter and set the `filename` member variable to equal this value. This is because this then references the same filename should any changes be made and saved to disk. You then initialize an instance of the `XmlDocument` class to hold the XML data and assign this to the `doc` member variable. Finally, you call the `XmlDocument`'s `Load()` method to load the named file from disk into the XML document. You're now in a position to start to provide the implementation for the first method, creating a default configuration file with default values. This method, called `CreateDefaultConfiguration()`, is as follows and will be part of a class that represents the RSS aggregator's configuration called `RSSConfiguration`:

```
// Creates a default XML document with default values
public void CreateDefaultConfiguration()
{
  XmlTextWriter xml = new XmlTextWriter("configuration.xml",null);
  xml.WriteStartElement("configuration");  // Start the <configuration> element
  xml.WriteElementString("defaultfeed", "");
  xml.WriteElementString("dbconnection", "");
  xml.WriteElementString("maxchannelitems", "30");
  xml.WriteEndElement();
  xml.Close();
}
```

The class is fairly simple to follow; you start by using a suitable constructor to create an instance of the `XmlTextWriter` class—one that takes the filename in the form of a textual string (in the case `configuration.xml`) and a second parameter that represents the encoding type. You pass `null`, which indicates UTF-8 as standard.

Once created, you can start the `<configuration>` element using the `WriteStartElement()` method that must eventually be followed by a `WriteEndElement()` method that simply closes the last element created, in this case outputting the `</configuration>` tag. You can nest the calls to `WriteStartElement()` as many times as is required for the correct XML representation, although in this case once is enough.

Now that the configuration element has been started, you are able to write the individual configuration elements in sequence; these are the `<defaultfeed>`, `<dbconnection>`, and `<maxchannelitems>` elements, all of which are empty except the last element, which has a default value of 30.

An alternative to this technique is to use the `XMLDocument` class to create an in-memory DOM and use methods such as `CreateElement()` or `CreateAttribute()` to manipulate this XML document in memory. You would then use the `Save()` method to serialize this to a persistent store such as a file.

Updating an XML Document

The previous example is fine for creating new XML documents, whether you use the forward-only stream method provided by `XmlTextWriter` or the in-memory method using `XmlDocument`, but what if you wanted to update the value of an existing element that you had previously read? In this instance, you must use the `XmlDocument` class type to hold the XML document in memory and manipulate it directly, saving the changes to disk when required.

In this example, you'll continue to use the configuration file, and you'll add a method for updating the value of a given element. Start by providing the implementation for such a method:

```
// UpdateElementValue - Updates the value of the specified element to a new value
//

public void UpdateElementValue(string elementName, string newValue)
{
  if (doc != null)
  {
    XmlNode node = doc.SelectSingleNode("//configuration/"+elementName);
    if (node != null)
    {
      node.InnerText=newValue;
    }
  }
}
```

If you ignore the defensive coding techniques of checking for null values, you'll notice that you are using the SelectSingleNode() method and passing a dynamically generated XPath expression. This will return a single XmlNode object (if found), and it's through this that you can access the node's content through the InnerText property, reading or setting it as required.

Please note that this method must be supported by first instantiating the XMLDocument object and then loading the XML from a source. In the RSS aggregator project, I've also provided a Save() method that in turn calls the XMLDocument class's Save() method, sending the contents to a filename of your choice. Listing 9-10 shows the full class implementation.

Listing 9-10. *RSSConfiguration Complete Implementation*

```
public class RSSConfiguration
{

  // Member variables
  public string filename = "";
  public XmlDocument doc = null;

  // CreateDefaultConfiguration
  // Create the configuration xml file with default values
  //
  public void CreateDefaultConfiguration()
  {
    XmlTextWriter xml = new XmlTextWriter("configuration.xml",null);
    xml.WriteStartElement("configuration");

    xml.WriteElementString("defaultfeed", "");
    xml.WriteElementString("dbconnection", "");
    xml.WriteElementString("maxchannelitems", "30");
```

```
    xml.WriteEndElement();
    xml.Close();
}

// UpdateElementValue
// Updates the value of the specified element to a new value
//
public void UpdateElementValue(string elementName, string newValue)
{
    if (doc != null)
    {
        XmlNode node = doc.SelectSingleNode(@"//configuration/"+elementName);
        if (node != null)
        {
            node.InnerText=newValue;
        }
    }
}

// Load - Loads the XML document from disk into memory
//
public void Load(string filename)
{
    this.filename = filename;
    doc = new XmlDocument();
    doc.Load(filename);
}

// Save - Saves the XML document to disk using
// the same filename as that used to open it.
//
public void Save()
{
    if (doc != null)
        doc.Save(this.filename);
}
```

Let's assume that this configuration file doesn't exist on your file system because the RSS aggregator has just been installed. The following code exercises the RSSConfiguration class methods as discussed, loading the XML file into memory and updating an individual element's value before then saving this file to disk:

```
RSSConfiguration cfg = new RSSConfiguration();
cfg.CreateDefaultConfiguration();
cfg.Load("configuration.xml");
cfg.UpdateElementValue("defaultfeed", "http://www.mamone.org");
cfg.Save();
```

Summary

This chapter first provided an overview of the history of XML, including its influences. I explained the benefits of using XML as a means for representing data, both from an extensibility point of view and also to support transferring data in a heterogeneous environment. I also covered some XML-related technologies in the form of namespaces and schemas, which provide qualification and validity surrounding the data that the XML represents.

I then covered the .NET Framework's support for XML and how you can implement the classes required for the RSS aggregator application. I introduced the namespaces available within the .NET Framework and the classes they provide, specifically those that provide basic reading and writing functionality. In addition to these basic features, I also discussed how you can traverse an XML document, extracting and interpreting the data required and using this within a C# class to represent your data internally and perform additional functionality such as supporting your persistent storage.

This chapter provided an implementation of the RSS feed classes that, when combined with Chapter 10's discussion of how to represent data entity classes, will allow you to persist this data to a database of your choice. You'll find the complete implementation for this code within the book's RSS aggregator project. The next chapter will focus on the network features available to you within the .NET Framework; you'll use these features to establish a connection to your RSS feed over the Internet and download the contents directly.

CHAPTER 10

■ ■ ■

Introducing Networking and Remoting

Most likely, you find computers to be fun! (If not, I doubt you'd be reading this book.) Your computer may not just be for fun, though—it's likely that your computer is a serious business tool, or maybe it's both. By day you might be using your computer for serious duties such as writing documents and designing business solutions, and by night you might be using it for fun such as playing computer games or writing code. In both cases, I guarantee that although your computer may be useful, it's far more useful (and the experiences you have on it are far more rewarding) if your computer is connected to a network. Consider the following examples:

- *Networked games*: Your personal computer or games console opens up a whole new world when you're playing other people from countries across the entire globe. Artificial intelligence (AI) has come along way, but it's not a replacement for a real person.

- *Internet*: The vast amount of information on the Internet is seemingly endless—surfing Web sites has replaced the newspaper for some people!

- *Exchanging information*: Whether this is in the form of e-mails, instant messages, or business transactions for corporate applications, the exchange of information is critical to the economy today, and this wouldn't be possible without a network.

All of these examples are possible only with a network. This may be a network that spans the globe (as is the case with the Internet), or it may be a network that is limited to your company, which may cover only certain regional areas. This book's RSS aggregator depends on the publication of information in the form of RSS feeds, which requires a network connection in order to work. Sure, you could configure your RSS aggregator to look at feeds that are created and local to your own machine, but where's the fun in that?

In this chapter, you'll learn what a network actually is, how the .NET Framework embraces it, and how you can use both .NET Framework features and an available network such as the Internet to enhance your applications and ultimately further enhance the RSS aggregator project.

Overview of Networking Concepts

In the following sections, I'll offer an overview of some key networking concepts. Specifically, I'll provide a foundation for the subsequent discussions about how these concepts are abstracted within the .NET Framework through various classes and how you can use these classes to interact with the Internet to obtain the RSS feed information.

What Is a Network?

As its name suggests, a *network* consists of two or more devices connected for the purpose of sharing information. Until fairly recently, devices were connected via a physical connection, usually a network cable. However, more recently, wireless network technologies, such as wireless fidelity (WiFi), Bluetooth, and infrared, are being used as alternatives to physically connected devices. Wireless technologies typically have limits in terms of distance and bandwidth (the amount of information that can be sent and the speed at which it can be sent); conversely, wired networks work at a far greater speeds but require the physical laying and connecting of cable.

What Types of Networks Are There?

You can group a network into one of three main types:

- Local area networks (LANs)

- Metropolitan area networks (MANs)

- Wide area networks (WANs)

Local Area Networks (LANs)

A LAN is usually a collection of independent computers situated in fairly close proximity to each other, such as within the same building. Their size can vary; for example, you may have a LAN that you've created at home that consists of only a few computers. Alternatively, a corporate LAN may link hundreds, even thousands, of computers within a building or campus.

Metropolitan Area Networks (MANs)

A MAN is a fairly new term for networking; it is used to represent mostly corporate customers with a large number of LANs with a typical geographical limit of about 50 kilometers (about 31 miles). It is ideally suited for sharing resources within a given region; for example, you may have a MAN representing joined LANs throughout a city.

Wide Area Networks (WANs)

If you're assuming that a LAN is local and that a MAN has a limited geographical limit, it stands to reason that a WAN extends the reach of a network over significant distances. The Internet, for example, could be considered a global WAN! A corporate customer will typically have a WAN that extends throughout a whole organization and supports sending e-mails or files between corporate users, regardless of their location. Figure 10-1 shows what a corporate network may look like.

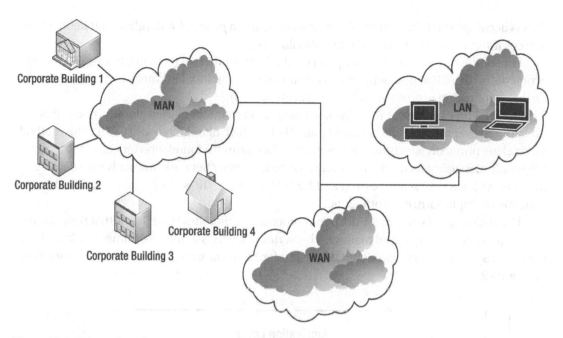

Figure 10-1. *Examples of a LAN, MAN, and WAN*

How Do All These Networks Connect?

If you consider a typical organization with a combination of LANs, MANs, and ultimately a WAN, you may be wondering how these network segments connect. How does a LAN in Building 1 connect to the LAN in Building 2? How does the London office connect to the New York City office? At an abstract level, it's pretty simple; they use different types of wires and languages! Let me explain.

A network, in its simplest form, is the physical connection (ignoring wireless for the moment) of machines using a cable. Many types of cables exist with different properties. CAT 5, a common cable standard for LAN cabling, can transfer data at the sorts of speed expected from a LAN. These segments of cabling are linked through several pieces of hardware (routers, switches, repeaters, hubs, and so on), and all of these have different properties. So, LANs are typically connected using wired cabling such as CAT 5 but have limits in terms of capacity (also known as *bandwidth*) and distance. What happens when you want more capacity? Then you can use *fiber-optic* cabling, which has much greater bandwidth but is expensive and fragile.

What about connecting WANs? You can't possibly stretch some CAT 5 cable across an ocean like the Atlantic (not easily at least), which is why alternatives exist such as using telephone lines or satellite technology for connecting LAN/MAN networks to form a WAN. This has an obvious cost implication, so careful planning is required; however, the business benefits often dictate that a WAN is necessary, so purchasing *leased lines*, a permanent connection between two points from a telephone provider, is often a common solution.

How Do Applications Communicate over the Network?

The mere existence of connected devices alone is not enough to enable the devices to communicate. Once a connection has been established, physical or otherwise, the device must be able to transfer data and agree on a format and method for doing so—a kind of network language.

This is accomplished through the definition and use of a *protocol*, a standard that defines how devices interact and the form their data should take.

One of the most common examples is TCP/IP. This protocol (actually, it's a collection of protocols, with TCP and IP being the two main ones) is the standard mechanism on which further application protocols, such as HTTP, are written.

In fact, you can think of the RSS specification as yet another application protocol; it is transmitted over the wire (the network) using HTTP, which ultimately uses TCP/IP. This method for stacking protocols is common practice and in fact forms the foundation for one of the future Microsoft messaging technologies, Indigo! Of course, other network protocols exist such as Internetwork Packet Exchange (IPX) and NetBIOS, but TCP/IP is ubiquitous in today's heterogeneous multiplatform environments.

Underpinning the network transport protocols are communication levels that pass control to one another in a sequential manner. This series of layers is a network framework known as the Open System Interconnection (OSI), a standard that consists of the seven layers shown in Figure 10-2.

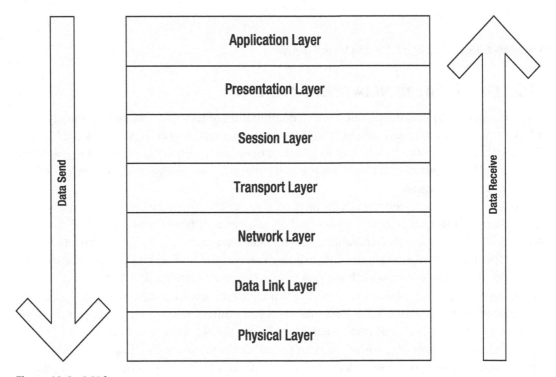

Figure 10-2. *OSI layers*

Application Layer

This layer provides application services for file transfers, e-mail, and other network software services. Telnet and FTP are applications that exist entirely in the application level.

Presentation Layer

The presentation layer transforms data into the form that the application layer can accept. This layer formats and may encode and/or encrypt data to be sent across a network, providing freedom from compatibility problems.

Session Layer

The session layer sets up, coordinates, and terminates conversations and exchanges between the applications at each end. It deals with session and connection coordination.

Transport Layer

This layer provides the transparent transfer of data between end systems, or *hosts*, and is responsible for end-to-end error recovery and flow control. It ensures complete data transfer.

Network Layer

This layer provides network direction using switching and routing technologies and creates logical paths, known as *virtual circuits*, for transmitting data from node to node.

Data Link Layer

At this layer, data packets are encoded and decoded into bits. The layer furnishes transmission protocol knowledge and management and handles errors in the physical layer, flow control, and frame synchronization. A *frame* is a unit of variable-sized data that the network encapsulates for transmission.

Physical Layer

This layer conveys the bit stream—electrical impulse, light, or radio signal—through the network at the electrical and mechanical levels.

How Do Machines Identify Themselves?

Once a machine is connected and you have a means of communicating through a protocol, a machine must be able to identify itself on a given network. This is required so that one device can start a conversation with other devices without broadcasting to the world! This takes place through a media access control (MAC) address that uniquely identifies a node of a network through its network interface card (NIC).

What Are the Internet, Intranet, and Extranet?

These topics probably need little introduction, but for completeness I'll provide an explanation. The *Internet* is a global network of devices consisting of millions of computers; it is therefore, by definition, the largest WAN in the world! It should be noted that the Internet is not the same as the World Wide Web; the former is the network of physical computers, and the latter consists of many servers which serve to provide Web-based services.

An *intranet* is a network of devices belonging to a specific organization; an intranet can therefore be thought of as a worldwide web whose boundary extends to that of the organization and is limited to the people within the organization or those who are given access by the organization. In the business world today, most organizations have an intranet to share information amongst employees.

Given these two concepts, there is a middle ground. What if your organization wanted to grant access to certain sections of its intranet to certain external suppliers? This controlled (and secured) extension of an intranet is referred to as an *extranet* and allows people outside the organization to have controlled access to the intranet in order to benefit both parties.

What Does a Typical Home Network Look Like?

You may not know it, but it's likely that your home computer is part of a LAN. Your computer is likely to have a built-in LAN connection; most modern computers have these installed on the motherboard by default. This will most likely take an RJ45 connection (the name given to the connector for typical CAT 5 cabling). It's also likely that you're connected to the Internet via broadband (also known as asynchronous digital subscriber line [ADSL]); this is probably achieved using a broadband modem or using a broadband modem/router combination. Alternatively, your computer may connect to your broadband modem/router either through a universal serial bus (USB) connection or through the LAN connection. Therefore, you have the makings of a small LAN to which you could attach more devices, as I do, for other members of the family. Figure 10-3 describes such a scenario; it's based on my own LAN.

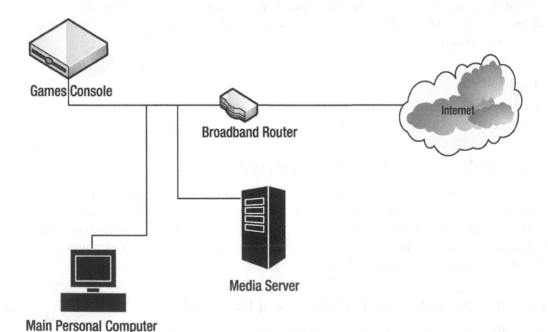

Figure 10-3. *Example of a home network*

As you can see, this small LAN has two permanent machines connected to it and a gaming console. Another machine often attaches to the network using a wireless LAN, which is provided by a suitable router. I'll now cover how you can embrace a network programmatically using the .NET Framework and Mono.

Network Programming Using .NET

The .NET Framework provides a feature-rich environment in which you can write network-enabled applications in a relatively short time. You can do this through classes that predominately sit within the System.Net namespace.

What Is System.Net?

The System.Net namespace provides several classes that, when combined, expose a powerful but simple API for many of the network protocols that exist today. You can split the namespace into the following key classes:

- System.Net.Dns

- System.Net.WebRequest and System.Net.WebResponse

- System.Net.Cookies

- System.Net.Sockets

System.Net.Dns

This .NET class provides access to functionality for DNS, which is an Internet (or intranet) service that translates a domain name (DN) into an IP address. This class includes methods such as GetHostByName and GetHostByAddress, which return the machine's DN from an IP address, and vice versa, given one of the items of information. A domain name is an English-type name that can be associated with an IP address; for example, www.mono-project.com is a domain name, and 10.0.0.1 is an IP address.

System.Net.WebRequest and System.Net.WebResponse

These .NET classes provide an abstract model for the .NET Framework's request-response model for accessing data from the Internet or an intranet. Applications can make requests through these classes using a URI and an address that refers to an object (that is, a device) on the Internet. The URI determines the correct descendant classes to use that have registered for the application. Table 10-1 lists the key mappings.

Table 10-1. *Request-Response URI Mappings*

URI	Class
ftp://	FtpWebRequest/FtpWebResponse
http://	HttpWebRequest/HttpWebResponse

System.Net.Cookies

This .NET class provides support for retrieving and manipulating information regarding cookies that may be held within an HTTP response. A *cookie* allows information to be passed between a Web server and a Web browser in the form of a text file that is embedded within the protocol, in this instance the header of HTTP. For example, when a Web site offers to record your username and any specific details for your next visit; this information is often (but not always) stored in a cookie.

System.Net.Sockets

This set of classes is arguably the most important in the System.NET namespace and is used by nearly all the classes discussed so far. These classes provide programmatic access to the network using *sockets*. This is a means of connecting your application to a specific network protocol in a software layer that has a standard implementation on most operating systems, including Windows, Unix, and Linux.

Whilst this is an important set of classes and ultimately allows you to develop your own custom protocols and implement code that talks directly to the network connection, a more likely scenario is that you will use classes that provide a higher level of abstraction such as the HttpWebRequest/Response classes.

Reading Pages from a Web Server

I'll now cover how to use the .NET Framework to simply download a Web page (ignoring any graphics associated with it at the moment) as a text string that you can then display or manipulate. The first task is to issue the request for the Web page, which involves creating the URL and using this when creating the Web request instance, as shown in the following code:

```
Uri uri = new Uri("http://www.example.com");
HttpWebRequest req = (HttpWebRequest)WebRequest.Create (uri);
```

The Create() method returns an instance of a descendant of the WebRequest class, which depends on the URI passed; therefore, because you passed an HTTP-based URI, the object instance created is actually of type HttpWebResponse, despite being an HttpWebRequest object. To utilize the full functionality that the HttpWebRequest type offers, assign it to a reference object of this type using a typecast operation, as shown in the following code snippet:

```
HttpWebResponse resp = (HttpWebResponse)req.GetResponse();
```

At this point, you're now in a position to interpret the response returned from the server and in this case output the textual content of the Web page. In this instance, create a text-encoding object based on UTF-8 (the default for Web pages in the West) and a StreamReader class for reading the response stream as text and outputting the result.

```
Encoding enc = System.Text.Encoding.GetEncoding("utf-8");
StreamReader sr = new StreamReader(resp.GetResponseStream(),enc);
string response = sr.ReadToEnd();
Console.Out.WriteLine(response;
```

And finally, it's good programming practice to close any open connections, so make sure to close the response stream and associated stream reader like so:

```
sr.Close();
webresponse.Close();
```

If your program runs successfully, the output should look something like Figure 10-4.

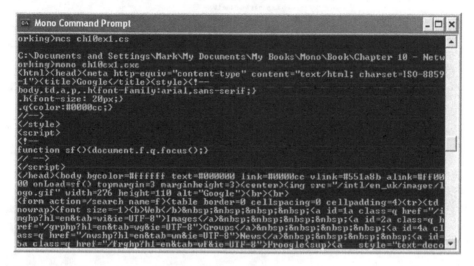

Figure 10-4. *Output of reading the Web page*

Send this output to a file using the following code:

```
FileStream file = new FileStream("ch10ex1.html", FileMode.CreateNew);
StreamWriter sw = new StreamWriter(file);
sw.Write(response;
sw.Close();
```

Then view this in the browser of your choice; the Web page will look like Figure 10-5.

With the exception of the missing graphics, which you would need to download and then resolve the links to display them, the Web page is complete. This example clearly demonstrates that the .NET Framework is hiding some of the implementation normally required and therefore providing you with the ability to write feature-rich applications using a minimum of code.

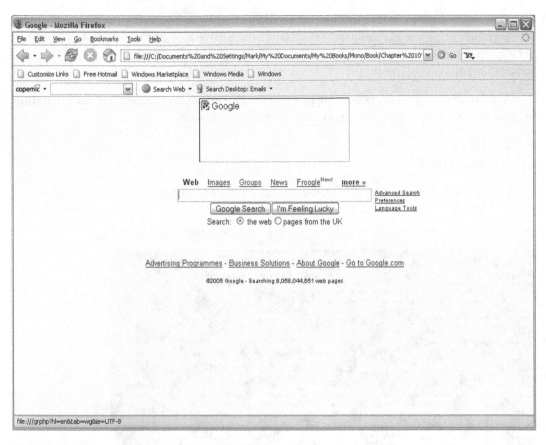

Figure 10-5. *Browser view of reading the Web page*

Writing the RSS Feed Handler

You can take this example and the principles demonstrated one step further to write the RSS aggregator's class, allowing it to download the provided RSS feed. This example is especially relevant to the previous example because the HTML page is nothing more than a markup language, and the protocol is HTTP, which was the same scenario for the RSS feed.

■**Note** To recap the requirements for the class, the XML document is provided on the Internet as an RSS feed, and the class's implementation needs to be able to read this file from a given URL and make this data available as an XML document. The RSS aggregator application can then manipulate this XML data as required.

Establishing the Extensions to the Channel API

To invoke the additional functionality you'll need for reading the XML RSS feed directly from the Internet, you need to extend the Channel class to provide suitable methods that represent the new API. Therefore, add a method that initializes the feed from a given URL, as opposed to from a file as in the previous chapter's implementation. This new method is as follows:

```
// InitializeFromURL( url ) - Initializes the Channel class
// and entities from the RSS feed which is passed as a URL
//
public void InitializeFromURL(string url)
{
  LoadFromURL(url);
  InitializeChannelEntity();
  InitializeChannelImage();
  channelItemEntityList = InitializeChannelItemCollection();
}
```

You may notice from this implementation (if not, I've highlighted it in bold) that a new method is required called LoadFromURL(), which takes a string url parameter and initializes the XML document from an available Internet connection. The signature for this method is as follows:

```
// LoadFromURL(uri) - Load
//
public void LoadFromURL(string url)
{
}
```

Now let's look at its implementation.

Establishing a Connection with an RSS Feed

The first step is to establish a connection with the RSS feed, and for this you can borrow some of the code you used for downloading the Web page in the previous example. Therefore, take the Channel class from the previous chapter, and extend this to obtain the XML directly from the Internet, rather than from a file. Also, take this opportunity to streamline some of the code using the C# features introduced in earlier chapters.

```
string url = http://www.example.com;
Uri uri = new Uri(url);
System.Net.WebRequest reqt = System.Net.HttpWebRequest.Create(uri);
```

Reading an RSS Feed

Once a connection has been established and the request sent, you can now interpret the response and store this in memory as an XML document, ready for manipulation.

```
using (System.Net.WebResponse resp = reqt.GetResponse())
{
  using (System.IO.Stream stream = resp.GetResponseStream())
  {
    // Interpret the XML data (currently as a stream here)
    stream.Close();
  }
}
```

You'll notice that this streamlines the code by using the `using` keyword, which sets the current scope for object interaction and behaves the same as if you had fully qualified all method accesses. Let's now consider how you can extend the implementation to take the XML data, currently within a `Stream` object, and load this into memory as an XML document.

You'll remember from the previous chapter that the `Channel` class uses an `XPathDocument` object to provide a fast, read-only view of the XML data and support XPath expressions, something you used to traverse your XML document previously. An `XPathDocument` constructor is present that takes an instance of a `Stream` object as a parameter and converts this data into an internal XML document representation. This is the construct you'll use to build the XML document:

```
XmlTextReader tr = new XmlTextReader(stream);
if (doc==null)
  doc = new XmlDocument();
doc.Load(tr);
```

Now that you have the instantiated XML document, the existing channel code will work unchanged, allowing you to traverse the XML document, extract items, and use this within the RSS aggregator application. Chapter 9 shows an example of how to manipulate this; however, you'll look at interpreting this data by rendering the output into the appropriate control of the RSS aggregator's application. You'll learn more about this in the "Integrating Network Capabilities into the Aggregator" section later in the chapter.

Using Proxy Servers

The network design of a system, especially within organizations, will often have a proxy server installed that acts as a *gateway* to another network, such as the Internet.

What Is a Proxy Server?

A *proxy server* is typically positioned between an application, such as a Web browser, and the final destination, a server. It's placed there for two reasons typically:

- Performance

- Filtering

A proxy server improves the performance of an application's request for data because typically a proxy server will have a cache store reserved for keeping information that has been requested. This is obviously overwritten over time, but in the scenario where a Web page has been returned and a subsequent request (either from the same device or from a different device) for the same Web page is made, it can then selectively be returned from the cache, which boosts performance considerably.

Filtering is another common requirement in organizations, especially when you need the ability to restrict access to Web pages that are considered inappropriate for business use. Figure 10-6 shows this process flow.

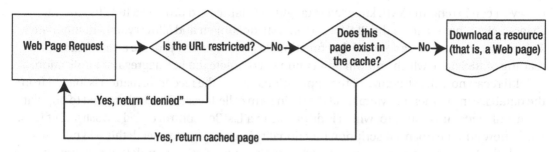

Figure 10-6. *Proxy process flow*

How Can You Use a Proxy Server?

The .NET Framework provides two methods for declaring the use of a proxy server for HTTP requests; these two methods are either at a *global* level or at a *per-request* level. The global level allows you to set a proxy at the System.Net namespace level, and all subsequent HTTP client classes such as WebClient and WebRequest will use this proxy. You do this by assigning an instance of a WebProxy class to the GlobalProxySelection class, as shown here:

```
System.Net.Uri proxyUri = new System.Net.Uri("http://127.0.0.1:3128");
System.Net.GlobalProxySelection.Select = new System.Net.WebProxy(proxyUri);
```

■ **Note** The proxy's IP address and port will almost certainly be different in your instance. Ensure you have the correct proxy details for your code to work. If you want to install and test your own proxy server, then you have many options. A good example is Squid, which you can find at http://www.squid-cache.org/.

As mentioned, an alternative is to create the WebProxy class in the same way but assign the Proxy property of your Web request to an instance of the WebProxy class created previously, as shown here:

```
System.Net.WebRequest req = System.Net.HttpWebRequest.Create(uri);
req.Proxy = new System.Net.WebProxy(proxyUri);
```

■ **Note** In the previous example, the proxy does not need the user to be authenticated; that is, it doesn't need a username and password. This may not be the case for all proxy servers, in which case you will need to provide the appropriate username and password.

Integrating Network Capabilities into the Aggregator

In Chapters 6 and 7, you developed the user interface framework defined default behavior. You then looked at retrieving some persistent data from a database in Chapter 8 and have now seen how you can extend the XML knowledge taught in Chapter 9 to provide a fully functional Channel class that retrieves the RSS feed as an XML document and allows you to manipulate it. This is a good point to tie some of that functionality together and provide a core feature, the reading of RSS data, which you will build upon to complete the RSS aggregator application.

I'll recap how the structure of the applications works: the feed information is loaded from the database into a member variable of the main form called feeds. This is then used to populate the list of feeds subscribed to, which is displayed in a ListBox control called lstSubscriptions. You'll now add the open subscription functionality in order to add a feed; this will need to refresh the list of subscriptions, so you will wrap this subscription population code into a method, as shown here:

```
// Refresh the subscriptions control from the list
//
public void RefreshSubscriptions()
{
  lstSubscriptions.BeginUpdate();
  lstSubscriptions.Items.Clear();
  foreach (RSSFeed feed in feeds)
  {
    // Simply add the name of the feed to the list
    lstSubscriptions.Items.Add(feed.feedName);
  }
  lstSubscriptions.EndUpdate();
}
```

You can now upload the code to initialize the subscription list to use this method, as shown in the following code, which can then be added to the form's Load event, which is more appropriate than the form constructor for initializing the contents of a graphical control. You can see this within the RSS aggregator's code available from the Source Code section of the Apress Web site.

```
// Initialize data
feeds = feedEntity.ReadAll();
if (feeds.Count > 0)
{
  // Initialize user interface control (lstSubscriptions) with feeds
  RefreshSubscriptions();
}
```

This has now provided you with the foundation to bring in the functionality offered by the new Channel class, specifically retrieving RSS data from the Internet. Let's first create an instance of this class at a form level to act as a reference to the current channel; this will be set to whichever feed the user has either selected from the list or just added through the File ➤ Open menu option (you'll add this feature shortly). You can declare this variable using the following declaration code:

```
// Define a reference to the current channel aka feed
Channel currentChannel = null;
```

You then further enhance the functionality provided so that when the user clicks the OK button from the File Open dialog box, the RSS feed is added to the list of subscriptions, and the list of subscriptions is refreshed (using the new method). Given that the user has asked to open the feed, you then display the list of available threads associated with that feed.

So, let's first enhance the event handler implementation associated with the user selecting the File ➤ Open menu item. This interaction takes place through the event handler called miFileOpen_Click. This is shown next, with its new functionality highlighted in bold:

```
public void miFileOpen_Click(object sender, System.EventArgs e)
{
  // Implementation goes here
  MyDialog dlgFileOpen = new MyDialog("File Open");
  dlgFileOpen.ShowDialog();
  if (dlgFileOpen.ChoseOpen)
  {
    // If the user has asked to open a feed, add this to the list
    // Create RSSFeed container
    RSSFeed feed = new RSSFeed();
    feed.feedName = dlgFileOpen.txtRssURL.Text;
    feed.feedURL = dlgFileOpen.txtRssURL.Text;
    // Add it to the list
    feeds.Add(feed);
    Console.WriteLine("->Added 'feed' to 'feeds' list");
    // Refresh the subscription control
    RefreshSubscriptions();
    // Set the current channel
    if (currentChannel == null)
      currentChannel = new Channel();
    currentChannel.InitializeFromURL(feed.feedURL);
    // Read the threads associated with the current channel
    RefreshThreads(currentChannel);
  }
}
```

The first task is to add the feed to the list of subscriptions. At this point, you're not checking that you've already added the feed. The main reason for adding the feed to the list is twofold; this first allows the user to select and view the threads associated with it. It also means that when the user closes the application, the list could be saved to disk, and the subscription will therefore be kept for the next time the application is loaded. Because the list of feeds is simply several RSSFeed items that are then displayed in the lstSubscriptions control using the new RefreshSubscriptions() method, you can simply create a feed and add it to the list, calling the refresh method manually to update the display. First you create a new RSSFeed item, and then you assign the feedName and feedURL attributes, which in this case is the URL:

```
// If the user has asked to open a feed, add this to the list
// Create RSSFeed container
RSSFeed feed = new RSSFeed();
feed.feedName = dlgFileOpen.txtRssURL.Text;
feed.feedURL = dlgFileOpen.txtRssURL.Text;
```

You then add this to the feed collection using the Add() method, as follows:

```
// Add it to the list
feeds.Add(feed);
```

And finally, refresh the display using the RefreshSubscriptions() method to show the newly added subscription:

```
// Refresh the subscription control
RefreshSubscriptions();
```

You can now set the current Channel class reference to an instance of the class that represents the RSS feed just opened. You may remember that you implemented a method called InitializeFromURL(). You'll use this with the URL of the RSS feed being opened, as follows:

```
// Set the current channel
if (currentChannel == null)
  currentChannel = new Channel();
currentChannel.InitializeFromURL(feed.feedURL);
```

This creates a new instance of the Channel class if the reference is null, and then once a known instance of the object exists, the InitializeFromURL() method is called, passing in the URL of the RSS feed. This will then create a connection to the feed and initialize its member values, including a collection of the threads associated with that feed. It is this collection that you will then display in the thread's DataGrid, as pointed to by the dgThreads control. The code that populates the dgThreads control is wrapped into a method in a similar manner to the RefreshSubscriptions() method, although this time you'll call the method RefreshThreads() and pass it a reference to the Channel class instance that contains the data, in this case currentChannel. This call is placed immediately after the Channel class initialization and is as follows:

```
// Read the threads associated with the current channel
RefreshThreads(currentChannel);
```

This nearly completes the implementation; you just have to implement the RefreshThreads() method that will tie the data being read from the RSS feed to the user interface and the user actually seeing the data. The implementation for this method is pretty straightforward; this is because the DataGrid control has a property called DataSource that supports the concept of *data binding*, allowing it to get its information directly from a component that supports the ability to present data to the control for viewing. This was described in Chapter 6, but the key concept here is that the DataGrid supports an ArrayList as a DataSource property, provided you set the MappingName property to ArrayList and create a DataGridTableStyle component that maps the data between the ArrayList and the DataGrid. So, provide the implementation for the RefreshThreads() method as follows:

```
// Refresh the threads control from the list
//
public void RefreshThreads(Channel channel)
{
  // Check the channel references
  if (channel != null)
```

```
  {
    if (channel.channelItemEntityList != null)
    {
      dgThreads.DataSource = channel.channelItemEntityList;
    }
  }
}
```

The key part of this method is in bold. This sets the DataSource property for the DataGrid to the ArrayList, called channelItemEntityList, provided by the Channel class. This member variable is initialized with a list of threads when the Channel class is initialized, so you can simply utilize this method to provide the data for the grid. The data binding feature of the Data-Grid control will automatically map the data from the ArrayList to the grid and display it; the final step you need to do is provide this mapping. Otherwise, an empty grid will be displayed, even though data exists. The code to provide this mapping is located in the form constructor because it needs to be done only once on initialization; the code is as follows:

```
// Create the DataGridTableStyle component
DataGridTableStyle tableStyle = new DataGridTableStyle();
tableStyle.MappingName = "ArrayList";

// Column 1 - Date
DataGridTextBoxColumn pd = new DataGridTextBoxColumn();
pd.MappingName = "PublishedDate";
pd.HeaderText = "Date";
pd.ReadOnly = true;
pd.Width = 150;
tableStyle.GridColumnStyles.Add(pd);

// Column 2 - Title
DataGridTextBoxColumn hd = new DataGridTextBoxColumn();
hd.MappingName = "Title";
hd.HeaderText = "Headline";
hd.ReadOnly = true;
hd.Width = 300;
tableStyle.GridColumnStyles.Add(hd);

// Add the style to the DataGrid
dgThreads.TableStyles.Clear();
dgThreads.TableStyles.Add(tableStyle);
```

The first step is to create the component and set the mapping name to ArrayList. This allows the only DataGrid to apply the mapping necessary between the items in the ArrayList and the columns in the grid. You can achieve this mapping by looking for properties within the items that have names that map the property of each column processed. This is important and is something I'll elaborate on shortly, but for now the following is the code to create this control, with the MappingName also being set appropriately:

```
// Create the DataGridTableStyle component
DataGridTableStyle tableStyle = new DataGridTableStyle();
tableStyle.MappingName = "ArrayList";
```

The next step is to create a `DataGridTextBoxColumn` component for each column that you want to display in your grid. In this case, the columns are `Date` and `Headline`. This component provides the mapping to the property name in the `ArrayList` through the `MappingName` attribute, as well as a custom column title using the `HeaderText` attribute. You also set `Width` and its `ReadOnly` property to true, as these are noneditable fields. The following code initializes both the `Date` and `Headline` columns:

```
// Column 1 - Date
DataGridTextBoxColumn pd = new DataGridTextBoxColumn();
pd.MappingName = "PublishedDate";
pd.HeaderText = "Date";
pd.ReadOnly = true;
pd.Width = 150;
tableStyle.GridColumnStyles.Add(pd);
// Column 2 - Headline
DataGridTextBoxColumn hd = new DataGridTextBoxColumn();
hd.MappingName = "Title";
hd.HeaderText = "Headline";
hd.ReadOnly = true;
hd.Width = 300;
tableStyle.GridColumnStyles.Add(hd);
```

In the previous example, each column is added to `DataGridTableStyle`, and their style attributes are set using the `Add()` method. It's important to note that the order in which the columns are added is the order in which they are displayed. Also, you can choose which columns to display and with which headings; in this case, you're displaying two of seven possible columns, and you're changing the column titles to be more meaningful (from `PublishedDate` to `Date` and from `Title` to `Headline`). Finally, add the style to the grid using the following code:

```
// Add the style to the DataGrid
dgThreads.TableStyles.Clear();
dgThreads.TableStyles.Add(tableStyle);
```

This will activate the style against the grid and cause the `ArrayList`-based data source to be interpreted correctly. The only thing left is to ensure that you have public properties for each of the items you want to display in the grid. My recommendation is to always make your member variables private and control their exposure through properties, setting their value using the set property and retrieving their value using the get property. I won't show the complete list of properties (which is available within the source code), but in order for the code to work, you need to ensure that the two previous values are exposed as follows within the `ChannelItemEntity` class:

```
public string Title
{
  get { return this.title; }
}
public string PublishedDate
{
  get { return this.publishedDate; }
}
```

Note The property `Title` maps to `MappingName` of `Title` in Column 2, and the property `PublishedDate` maps to `MappingName` of `PublishedDate` in Column 1. This mapping must be correct for data to be shown.

If you now recompile the code with the additions and open an RSS feed of your choice, then you should see a screen similar to Figure 10-7, with the exception that the thread information will obviously be different.

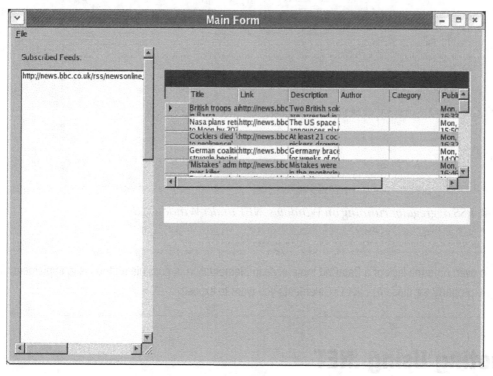

Figure 10-7. *RSS aggregator running on Mono under Linux*

Note The version of Mono under Linux displays all columns, even if a column was not added programmatically, as shown earlier. If you compare this to the Windows version in Figure 10-8, you'll notice that this behaves as intended and displays only the required columns.

For completeness, I compiled the same code against Microsoft's implementation of .NET and ran this on Windows XP Professional, which yielded similar results to those when run under Mono on Linux. However, the implementation of the DataGrid table styles through its DataGridTableStyle property has not yet been implemented, so the byproduct was that all elements of the ArrayList were displayed. Although different, this does show how Mono is progressing, with version 1.1.9 undergoing heavy work on the Windows Forms elements. Figure 10-8 shows the Windows version, with a full implementation of the DataGrid table-style functionality.

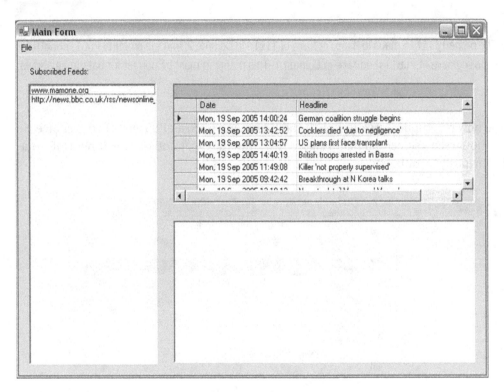

Figure 10-8. *RSS aggregator running on Windows .NET under Windows XP*

■**Note** To overcome the lack of a DataGrid table-style implementation, a possible method is to implement only the get property for those ArrayList elements you want to expose.

Remoting Using .NET

Remoting, while not used directly within the RSS aggregator project, is an important concept to understand and is directly related to some of the network-based technologies I have already discussed. I'll now provide an overview of what .NET remoting is and then show some tangible examples that demonstrate its capability and power.

What Is Remoting?

The .NET remoting feature is implemented through a combination of classes in the `System.Net.Runtime.Remoting` namespace and within the .NET Framework runtime. A piece of code, which I'll call an *application,* can live within several boundaries; these are the physical machine, the process being hosted by that machine, and the application domain that may live within the process. In normal circumstances, applications that live in these boundaries could not call the methods of another remote object without significant thought about the following:

- Communication channels

- Activation

- Lifetime support

The .NET Framework and the remoting classes provide support for all these concepts and more! This removes a lot of the complexity involved in designing and implementing objects that can remotely interact with one another, regardless of their locations but obviously assuming that connectivity exists. I've seen .NET remoting for numerous distributed applications in large organizations, especially to allow multiple applications to communicate with each other. A good example is when you implement several services that need to be available 24×7 and so are hosted on a central server that is contactable by your client application. Your client application can then call the methods on these remote objects as if they were local, accessing the functionality available.

Remote Objects

A key objective of remoting within the .NET Framework is to abstract the complexities involved in calling a remote object. An object is considered remote if it exists on a different physical machine or even if it exists on the same machine but a different application domain. If an object exists within the same application domain, then it's considered a local reference. Figure 10-9 shows the distinction between remote and local objects.

In Figure 10-9, the user invokes a method on Object 1, which then makes a *local* call to Object 2. This is local because the processes share the same application domain. It's then Object 2 that makes a *remote* call to Object 5, which sits on a different physical machine and in a different application domain. Then the call eventually returns to Object 1 where this makes another remote call to Object 3, which is remote despite being on the same machine and because it resides in a different application domain.

To ensure that an object and its attributes can be transferred to a remote object, it must support the `[serializable]` attribute, indicating that the object can be transformed into a format for passing to another process. It must also derive from the `MarshalByRefObject` type, which provides the inherent ability to support the .NET remoting framework. In the case of method calls, these are transferred to the remote message in the form of a message that is deciphered and acted on accordingly.

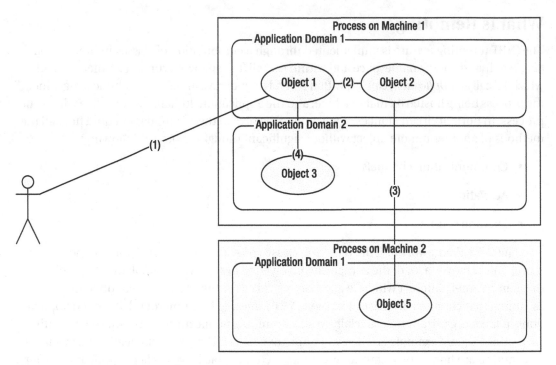

Figure 10-9. *Remote object call invocation examples*

Proxy Objects

Once your client object makes a demand of a remote object through a reference, whether accessing its properties or attributes or calling its methods, these demands are directed through a proxy object that acts as the representative for the remote object. This proxy acts as a shim for the remote object, allowing .NET's CLR to intercept these requests and direct them, if valid, to the remote object. This interception is possible because the framework creates a local instance of the TransparentProxy class that acts as the intermediary between the client and the remote object (see Figure 10-10).

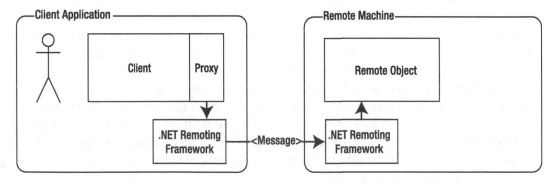

Figure 10-10. *Use of proxy objects*

I'll cover this topic in more detail when I cover some of the other methods used as part of the remoting framework, but in addition to the TransparentProxy class, a RealProxy class is also created that encapsulates the TransparentProxy class. When the client instantiates an instance of a remote object, the TransparentProxy class-based instance is created and returned. It is through this that all further interactions are directed. Subsequent method invocations are directed through the RealProxy class, which ultimately applies to the remote object. The ObjRef class represents the serializable instance of the object that is being called, which holds additional information such as the remote object's location and communication information. The RealProxy class uses this for both exchanging information and making the remote calls (see Figure 10-11).

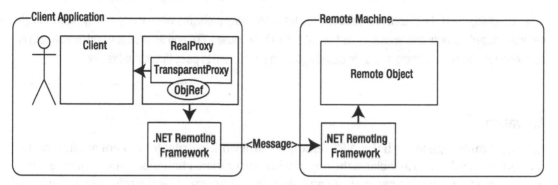

Figure 10-11. *Use of proxy objects using internal .NET remoting classes*

Channels and Sinks

A *channel* is a user-definable mechanism through which messages are transported both to and from remote objects. At least one or more channels are associated with a given application domain; as a result, when the application domain is destroyed, this deletion is cascaded down to the associated channels, and they too are destroyed. The association between a remote object and a channel is handled by the client using the RegisterChannel method. The .NET Framework ensures that this connection is established and correct before any interaction is started. Figure 10-12 illustrates the interactions.

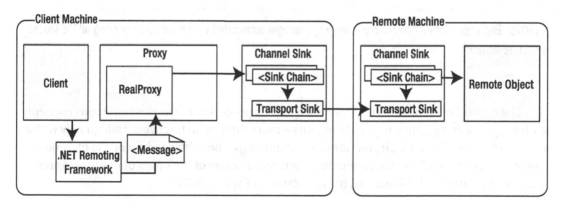

Figure 10-12. *Remoting using channels and sinks*

In the previous example, you can see where the .NET remoting framework, part of the CLR, converts a method call into a message that is then transported to the remote machine by the RealProxy class using a channel. The channel in turn contains several sinks that process the message and pass this on to the next sink until the *transport sink* is hit, at which point the message is sent to the remote machine. The remote machine then has a similar configuration except that the sink is reversed, eventually resolving into the actual method call on the remote object.

Several channels exist, and you can develop your own channels and sinks using the .NET Framework, although an HTTP channel and a TCP channel are both provided by default. The HTTP channel, for example, contains an initial sink that formats the method call into a SOAP XML-based message that is then serialized and transported as appropriate.

Note Using the HTTP channel for remoting results in far fewer problems when trying to negotiate through network-based security concepts such as firewalls. This is because HTTP and its standard port (usually 80) is common for Internet browsing and so is usually granted permission to pass through a firewall.

Activation

An object must register with the .NET remoting framework in order for a client application to reference it, and it also associates the object with one or more channels. These dependencies are so a client application can activate an object, in essence creating the reference using a process termed *activation*. This may be on the client or server side, with the latter usually being used when the state of an object must be maintained. For server activation, the GetObject or new methods are used, with CreateInstance or new being used for client activation objects.

Object Lifetime

The lifetime of an object is controlled in different ways, depending on whether the object is activated on the client or server side. In the case of client-side activation, the life span of an object is controlled by the leasing service provided as part of the .NET remoting framework. In the case of server-side activation, the server governs the lifetime of the object.

Note Each application domain has a leasing manager associated with it for administering all the leases within its domain.

The control of an object's life span is a complex process and involves numerous concepts such as sponsorship, renewing, and timeouts—more than could be covered adequately within a single chapter. Therefore, if you want to find out more about how to handle the lifetime of your object, please refer to the Mono documentation or one of the many books from Apress, such as . *Advanced .NET Remoting*, by Ingo Rammer (Apress, 2002).

.NET Remoting Example

Now that I've provided you with an overview of remoting within the .NET Framework, I'll walk you through an example that demonstrates some of the concepts discussed. I'll show how to create a business object that returns an RSS feed, in this example, a hard-coded string of XML. This service is then exposed by a remoting server and registers with the Tcp channel on a specific port (in this case 8090). A corresponding client application is then presented; this shows how it can request the activation of the remote RSS feed service object and call the GetFeed() method, outputting the results to the console window.

Creating the Service Object

The remoting example begins with the creation of a service object. This is a class that provides the functionality required from the service you will expose but also supports the .NET remoting framework, allowing it to be activated and called remotely. The first step in the example is to include the relevant namespaces required to support a remoting object, as follows:

```
using System;
using System.Runtime.Remoting;
using System.Runtime.Remoting.Channels;
using System.Runtime.Remoting.Channels.Tcp;
```

Once you have imported the relevant namespaces, you're free to use the classes they contain. You can now define the structure for the class, including the declaration of its namespace and the class signature that must inherit from MarshalByRefObject in order to support remoting. This construct is as follows:

```
namespace RSSAggregator
{
  // RSSService - the RSS feed service object
  //
  public class RSSService : MarshalByRefObject
  {
    //TODO: Implementation goes here
  }
}
```

Once the class signature is complete, you can now add the two methods that the class will support. The first is the default constructor for which you've provided an implementation; it simply outputs some text to the console to indicate that the object has been activated. This constructor is as follows:

```
public RSSService()
{
  Console.Out.WriteLine("Activation has occurred");
}
```

Finally, you can provide this class's main method, GetFeed, which will return some arbitrary data that in reality would be data from a specified RSS feed. In this case, you'll simply output some text to the console to show that the method has been invoked. This is as follows:

```
public string GetFeed()
{
  return "Data returned here";
}
```

If you piece this code together, the final source for the service object is as follows:

```
using System;
using System.Runtime.Remoting;
using System.Runtime.Remoting.Channels;
using System.Runtime.Remoting.Channels.Tcp;

namespace RSSAggregator
{
  // RSSService - the RSS feed service object
  //
  public class RSSService : MarshalByRefObject
  {
    public RSSService()
    {
      Console.Out.WriteLine("Activation has occurred");
    }

    public string GetFeed()
    {
      return "Data returned here";
    }
  }
}
```

This service object must exist as a library so that both the client and server applications may reference it. To do this, you use the following command-line syntax:

```
mcs /t:library /out:service.dll /r:System.Runtime.Remoting ch10ex4a.cs
```

This will provide the output file service.dll, which can be referenced from your applications as discussed. You can now define the server application.

Creating the Server Application

Once the service object is available, you can start the definition of the server application. I'll go through the code step by step, highlighting and describing the key elements. The first step, as before, is to ensure that the required namespaces have been included, as follows:

```
using System;
using System.Runtime.Remoting;
using System.Runtime.Remoting.Channels;
using System.Runtime.Remoting.Channels.Tcp;
```

You are now able to define the class signature for the RSSServer class, as follows:

```
namespace RSSAggregator
{
  public class RSSServer
  {
    static void Main()
    {
      //TODO: Implementation goes here
    {
  }
}
```

With the class signature now in place, you can start to focus on the implementation of the server's core code, held within the Main() method as is usual for a console application. The first step is to create a TCP channel that will provide the communication mechanism required for any client connections. In this case you'll bind the channel's sink to port 8090, something that is arbitrary but must not be used and should be communicated to all required client applications. For example:

```
// Create and register the channel
TcpChannel c = new TcpChannel(8090);
ChannelServices.RegisterChannel(c);
```

This calls the static method on the ChannelServices class to register a channel using the instance of the TcpChannel class you just created. Once the channel has been registered, the next stage is to register the service object with the .NET remoting framework, which will require the type information for the service object, as shown here:

```
// Register the remote server object (RSSAggregator.RSSServer) and method
Type t = new RSSService().GetType();

RemotingConfiguration.RegisterWellKnownServiceType(t, "GetFeed",
WellKnownObjectMode.SingleCall);
```

The previous methods first create an instance of the class that returns some of the .NET information required. The object class (from which all classes inherit) provides a method for this called GetType(), and you'll use this for convenience in this example. In addition, a static method within the RemotingConfiguration class registers a reference for the GetFeed() method in a SingleCall model.

Finally, you must ensure that the server keeps running to accept requests, and as such, the following lines of code maintain the operational effectiveness by simply not allowing the server to close until the Enter key is pressed:

```
// Wait for <ENTER> to terminate
Console.Out.WriteLine("ENTER to exit...");
string r = Console.In.ReadLine();
```

If you bring these elements together, the server code looks as follows:

```
using System;
using System.Runtime.Remoting;
using System.Runtime.Remoting.Channels;
using System.Runtime.Remoting.Channels.Tcp;

namespace RSSAggregator
{
  public class RSSServer
  {
    public static void Main(string[] args)
    {
      // Create and register the channel
      TcpChannel c = new TcpChannel(8090);
      ChannelServices.RegisterChannel(c);

      // Register the remote server object (RSSAggregator.RSSServer) and method
      Type t = new RSSService().GetType();

      RemotingConfiguration.RegisterWellKnownServiceType(t, "GetFeed",
      WellKnownObjectMode.SingleCall);


      // Wait for <ENTER> to terminate
      Console.Out.WriteLine("ENTER to exit...");
      string r = Console.In.ReadLine();

    }
  }
}
```

This now needs to be compiled into an RSS project, as follows:

```
mcs ch10ex4s.cs /r:System.Runtime.Remoting /r:Service.dll /out:Server.exe
```

This will provide the output application that runs as a server, which when ready will be able to talk to numerous devices across the world, both at work and privately.

Creating the Client

You have created both the Service.dll business component and the Server.exe application that references it. You can now create the client application to test against the server executable just built. The first step is to build the method signature and import the relevant namespaces, as follows:

```
using System;
using System.Runtime.Remoting;
using System.Runtime.Remoting.Channels;
using System.Runtime.Remoting.Channels.Tcp;

namespace RSSAggregator
{
  public class Client
  {
    public static void Main(string[] args)
    {
    }
  }
}
```

Once the class signature is complete, you're able to provide further implementation. The first task is to create a client-side TCP session (and port number) that can be registered with the remoting channel services, as follows:

```
// Create and register the channel
TcpChannel c = new TcpChannel(1011);
ChannelServices.RegisterChannel(c);
```

Finally, within the client application, you need to activate the remote object and call the GetFeed() method of this object. You can do this using the GetObject() method on the Activator class and passing a reference to a type of the correct class and a URL that points to the service endpoint, which in this case includes the TCP stream on the local machine at port 8090 and the GetFeed() method. For example:

```
RSSService s = (RSSService)Activator.GetObject(typeof(RSSAggregator.RSSService),
"tcp://localhost:8090/GetFeed");
if (s == null)
{
  Console.Out.WriteLine("The Server could not be found");
}
else
{
  Console.Out.WriteLine(s.GetFeed());
}
```

Listing 10-1 shows the full example. After the code, I'll discuss techniques for building and testing the client application.

Listing 10-1. *Example Remoting Client Application*

```
using System;
using System.Runtime.Remoting;
using System.Runtime.Remoting.Channels;
using System.Runtime.Remoting.Channels.Tcp;

namespace RSSAggregator
{
  public class Client
  {
    public static void Main(string[] args)
    {
       // Create and register the channel
       TcpChannel c = new TcpChannel(1011);
       ChannelServices.RegisterChannel(c);

       RSSService s = (RSSService)Activator.GetObject(
       typeof(RSSAggregator.RSSService), "tcp://localhost:8090/GetFeed");
       if (s == null)
       {
           Console.Out.WriteLine("The Server could not be found");
       }
       else
       {
           Console.Out.WriteLine(s.GetFeed());
       }
    }
  }
}
```

The syntax for compiling the client application is as follows, and it provides links to several references required by the application:

```
mcs ch10ex4c.cs /r:System.Runtime.Remoting /r:Service.dll /out:Client.exe
```

Now that both the server and client applications have been built, you can see remoting in action relatively easily. First you start the Server.exe application, and then you start the Client.exe application that creates a service object and calls the GetFeed() method. Figure 10-13 shows the client application window first, with the successful execution of the method and its output.

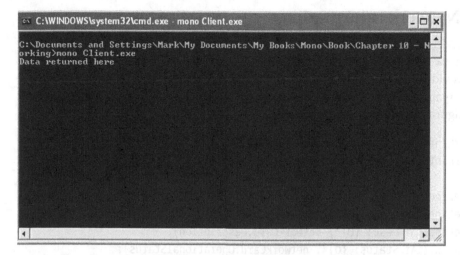

Figure 10-13. *The successful execution of the* Client.exe *application*

Here you can see that the application ran, and by following the code, you can see that it connected to the remote object and invoked the GetFeed() method, which in turn displayed the string "Data returned here" as its implementation. Conversely, you can look at the server window, as shown in Figure 10-14, which shows two Activation events, one when you create the object instance to obtain its type information (using the GetType() method) and one when the client activates the object whilst invoking the GetFeed() method.

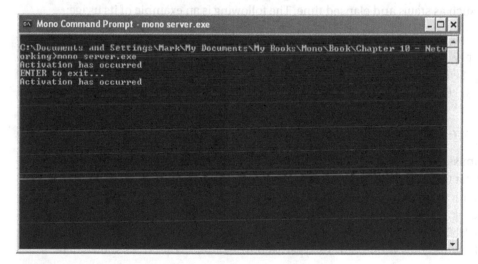

Figure 10-14. *The output from the remoting server application*

What's New in .NET 2.0?

Version 2.0 of the .NET Framework contains some useful enhancements covering network connectivity within .NET. I'll discuss some of these features in the following sections.

Obtaining Network Information

The System.Net.NetworkInformation namespace contains several new classes that allow you to access specific network information about the computer against which the code is run; more specifically, it provides access to NetworkInterface instances that represent each network card in the machine. Against this you can then access properties such as physical addresses, DNS settings, IP configuration, and more. The following is an example of its usage:

```
foreach (NetworkInterface networkCard in
        NetworkInterface.GetAllNetworkInterfaces())
{
  Console.WriteLine("ID: {0}", networkCard.Id);
  Console.WriteLine("\t Name: {0}", networkCard.Name);
  Console.WriteLine("\t Desc: {0}", networkCard.Description);
  Console.WriteLine("\t Status: {0}", networkCard.OperationalStatus);
  Console.WriteLine("\t MAC Addr: {0}",
  networkCard.GetPhysicalAddress().ToString());
}
```

Testing Connectivity

Another useful feature is the System.Net.NetworkInformation.Ping class that allows you to check whether another device is accessible over TCP/IP. You invoke this by using the Send() method on the Ping class, which returns a PingReply instance. This contains various pieces of information such as status and elapsed time. The following is an example of its usage:

```
Ping ping = new Ping();
PingReply reply = null;
reply = ping.Send("192.168.2.2");
Console.Out.WriteLine("The Ping Status was {0}", reply.Status.ToString());
```

File Transfer Protocol (FTP) Support

An obvious omission from earlier versions of the .NET Framework was their lack of support for the File Transfer Protocol (FTP), allowing you to issue FTP commands within your application. This has been rectified with the introduction of the FtpWebRequest object, which now provides managed code support for FTP and is included in the System.Net namespace. Its usage is still based on the WebRequest class's Create() method, as was the HttpWebRequest class shown in Chapter 10. However, this would now be typecast into an FtpWebRequest, as shown here:

```
FtpWebRequest ftpRequest =
        (FtpWebRequest)WebRequest.Create("ftp://localhost/testfile.txt");
```

You can, however, use the WebClient class to encapsulate some of the mundane functionality, such as getting the response and reading the stream. The following example shows how you can use the WebClient to download a file using FTP:

```
WebClient client = new WebClient();
client.Credentials = new NetworkCredential("anonymous",
"mark@mamone.org");
client.DownloadFile("ftp://localhost/afile.txt", "C:\\samplefile.txt");
```

This summary of new 2.0 features is obviously not exhaustive; far more classes exist. Refer to http://www.mono-project.com/Mono_Project_Roadmap for the latest information on Mono's implementation, and refer to http://msdn.microsoft.com/netframework/ for the latest .NET news.

Summary

In this chapter, I covered several important topics that are especially crucial in a connected world. I introduced networking, introduced the different types of networks, and explained how the types fundamentally work. You then looked at the .NET Framework's support for some of the networking concepts described, including protocol support. You explored the intricacies of the request-response method for retrieving data over HTTP (and FTP) because they provide a foundation for the Internet. You saw examples of how some of the .NET classes can download Web pages and XML feeds, a key requirement in the implementation of the RSS aggregator. You then learned about remoting, the features it provides, and how the .NET Framework supports remoting. Finally, you saw some examples that implemented the remoting concepts discussed; you can use these examples when developing your own applications with remoting functionality.

In the next chapter, you'll use this network knowledge to learn how to run applications against your own Web server using Mono.

■ ■ ■

CHAPTER 11

Using ASP.NET

So far I've concentrated on showing you how to write rich, client-side applications that use Mono and its support for .NET's Windows Forms technologies. I've touched on using the networking features of Mono to interact with a network, specifically the Internet. An obvious omission is how Mono supports the development of Web pages and Web sites. Perhaps not surprisingly, Mono does this very well! The .NET Framework includes ASP.NET, which, like the remoting technology discussed in Chapter 10, is implemented by the .NET runtime. ASP.NET includes classes that provide the functionality necessary to create extremely powerful Web pages. In this chapter, I'll provide an overview of the ASP.NET technology, the components it provides, and the functionality that you can embrace when developing powerful Web pages without any client-side requirements other than a Web browser.

Overview of ASP.NET

The following sections give you an overview of ASP.NET and solidify your existing knowledge by clarifying, amongst other things, the history surrounding the Internet and the World Wide Web.

What Is the World Wide Web?

As mentioned in an earlier chapter, the Internet is different from the World Wide Web. The Internet is a collection of networked devices using Transmission Control Protocol/Internet Protocol (TCP/IP), while the World Wide Web is a collection of Web servers that reside on the Internet and typically serve Web pages using HTML over Hypertext Transfer Protocol (HTTP).

What Components Are Required to Build a Web Site?

The ASP.NET technology is built upon several concepts, and I'll provide an overview of them in this chapter. In addition, I'll discuss how you can obtain, install, and configure these components in order to build your own Web site. So, what components does ASP.NET require? The ASP.NET technology depends on several features provided as part of the .NET Framework as well as, arguably the most important component, a Web server. In summary, the following components are required:

Web server: A Web server is required for two reasons. First, the Web server accepts requests for resources such as Web pages and processes them, returning the results to the user. Second, the Web server hosts resources such as Web pages in order to accept and process any user requests for them.

CLR: The CLR processes the .NET code and its associated libraries. The ASP.NET technology stack and your own custom code is built using .NET, with the CLR compiling and executing the code.

.NET Framework: The .NET Framework provides an implementation of not just the ASP.NET technology but also the libraries and associated classes that are required for you to develop your Web pages.

Web applications or pages: Finally, the components mentioned so far support and implement the ASP.NET technology, which lets you design, develop, and run your Web pages and applications. Therefore, you deploy the files and assemblies related to your custom Web application onto the Web server for the end user to access.

What Is ASP.NET?

ASP.NET is the next iteration of ASP, another Microsoft technology; however, it's important to note that although ASP.NET is able to run existing ASP code, it is a total rewrite and has been extensively enhanced. Both technologies are fundamentally focused on processing server-side code as a result of requests from users, predominately from a Web browser; the output, which is usually a Web page, is returned to the user for displaying in a browser. While popular, ASP has its weaknesses, so ASP.NET addresses these, as well as provides numerous other features. These are the key areas of functionality and power that ASP.NET offers:

- Built on the CLR

- Code separation

- Simple configuration

- .NET Framework services

I'll now elaborate on each of these features. ASP.NET is built upon the CLR, which means you can develop code in any of the languages supported by .NET. Not only is your code compiled, but it's also *strongly typed*. (I discussed the benefits of strong typing in earlier chapters.) Also, you separate the user interface's design from the code used to run the application. You achieve this separation first by using markup languages such as HTML for your design view and also by putting your code in a specific *code-behind* file that is referenced from your user interface page within ASP.NET page directives. This allows the user interface to focus on the look and feel, with the business code written in a separate file that could be maintained by someone else on your team. Finally, the relationship with the CLR means that the ASP.NET technology may benefit from calling upon .NET Framework services and features such as the ability to support Web Forms (a Windows Forms–type technology but for Web browsers), its strong support for Web Services, and the XML-based configuration files.

All these features means ASP.NET is great for building Web-based solutions that can be deployed with no software required on a user's machine other than a Web browser (also known as a *zero footprint*) and that can run on multiple operating systems, thanks to its support in

Mono. (You can find more information about Mono and ASP.NET at http://www.mono-project.com/ASP.NET.)

Going Inside ASP.NET

In the following sections, I'll delve a little deeper into the ASP.NET architecture and discuss some of the features I've introduced thus far. However, this isn't a book solely about ASP.NET, so I recommend further research on your part.

Architecture

The ASP.NET architecture is a component within the overall .NET Framework, as shown in Figure 11-1.

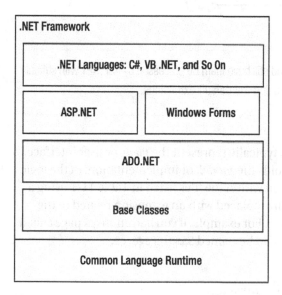

Figure 11-1. *ASP.NET and .NET architecture*

As you can see from Figure 11-1, the ASP.NET component is a fundamental part of the overall .NET Framework and as such benefits from being able to leverage other technologies within the framework (such as ADO.NET for data handling). It also uses the services provided as part of the CLR such as JIT compilation and caching to ensure your application performs as well as possible. I'll describe in more detail some of these architectural components and, in doing so, discuss how some of them are implemented, which will help clarify the relationship between the different layers shown in Figure 11-1.

ASP.NET Page Components

The structure of an ASP.NET page consists of several elements that I'll discuss in more detail in the following sections. Some are mandatory, and some are optional.

File Structure and Naming

You can build an ASP.NET resource construct from several text-based files; the extensions of these files depend on the intent of the file. Table 11-1 shows some of the file extensions known to ASP.NET.

Table 11-1. *ASP.NET Extensions*

Extension	Description
.aspx	Web page holding core user interface
.asmx	Web Service
.ascx	Web control
.asax	Global page

■ **Note** In theory, you could change these extensions and still have them be processed by ASP.NET with suitable configuration changes, but for simplicity I recommend using the default extensions.

In addition to these extensions whose files typically represent the *view*, or user interface, presented to the user, an associated code file holds the *model*, or implementation, of the logic behind the page. This code file is referenced from within the files listed in Table 11-1 using a page directive, but the extension used is typically replaced with an extension related to the .NET language being used, as shown in Table 11-2. For example, if you had an .aspx page called SamplePage.aspx, then the code file using C# would be named SamplePage.cs.

Table 11-2. *Some Common .NET File Extensions by Language*

Extension	Description
.cs	C#
.vb	VB .NET
.jsl	Visual C#

Web Forms

A Web Forms application is a Windows Forms–type user interface that is built from ASP.NET's native controls, custom controls, or a combination of both. The presentation is rendered in HTML by the actual Web controls themselves; this means no software is required on the client other than a Web browser.

ASP.NET Server Controls

An ASP.NET server control is code written to take advantage of ASP.NET's ability to present a user interface in the same way a Windows Forms application would be written but with the output in HTML. ASP.NET includes several powerful native controls, but you also have the option of writing your own controls or using controls from the open-source and commercial marketplaces. This allows you to develop a control specific to your requirements and have an implementation that meets those requirements.

Web Services

A Web Service is a method of providing an implementation that can be exposed over a network such as the Internet or an intranet. This method can then be called, or *consumed*, by a client application, and the results are returned, regardless of the platform on which the Web Service is running and regardless of the client application making the call. This is through the adoption of standards such as SOAP, XML, and HTTP.

Web Page Structure

An ASP.NET page consists of the constructs covered in the following sections. These constructs define the structure of the page, the features to use, and the implementation.

Directive

When the compiler processes an ASP.NET page, it interprets and subsequently compiles the page based on instructions from the directives, which are placed in blocks within the file. You indicate a code *block* by wrapping its content in <%...%> tags, and you denote a *directive* by using the @ symbol immediately after the opening <% tag. This notation is similar to ASP. A directive can also have associated optional attributes that the compiler looks for when interpreting the page. The following example demonstrates this concept:

```
<%@Page Language="C#" Src="SamplePage.cs" %>
```

The directive is indicated as a page directive by using the Page syntax. This directive defines two attributes. The first is Language="C#", which is the default language to use (in this case C#). The second is Src="SamplePage.cs", which is the source attribute that specifies the code for this file is in Sample.cs.

You could add other attributes; for example, ASP.NET pages can support inheritance, so you could specify an attribute that indicates the page from which it should inherit its code and user interface.

HTML

As you would expect, the page will usually include the interface definition using standard HTML elements. You have the option of additionally specifying the runat="server" attribute value, which allows you to request that the HTML is processed at the server rather than on the user's machine. This means that while the server is processing the associated code, the elements—and more specifically, any code, including the code attached to HTML elements—is then able to programmatically access the features of an element from your code by uniquely identifying an HTML element with an ID tag. The following example shows how the code could access the form and its attributes by referring to the MyForm ID:

```
<%@ Page Language="C#" %>
<html>
<body>
<form id="MyForm" runat="server">
This is a Test
</form>
</body>
</html>
```

Another common scenario is when a textbox is placed on the form in HTML and its value is programmatically set by code whilst being processed on the server. For example, you can implement some code to return data from the database and store this in the textbox for the user to then interact with.

Code

Another feature is the ability to include code within the page that is either defined as being executed on the server (by using the server value for the runat attribute) or locally (by simply omitting the attribute altogether). This attribute is used through a combination of a <script> element and the runat attribute. This element has been extended to also allow you to define the language for the code encapsulated within it; for example, the following element defines a function called OutputText() that simply outputs some text:

```
<script language="c#" runat="server">
  void OutputText()
  {
    Response.Write("This is a Test");
  }
</script>
```

You can then either use the function defined earlier or enter code that is executed inline. This shows how to call the previous function:

```
<% OutputText(); %>
```

This shows you how to implement the function's implementation inline:

```
<% Response.Write("This is a test"); %>
```

While the output from these two lines would be the same, the first example that references a method has obvious benefits, such as encouraging code reuse. Also, it is more easily read and therefore understandable (assuming you use meaningful function names).

Custom Controls

It's likely that while designing your user interface you'll encounter components that could be reused across several projects. Indeed, several controls are included as standard within the

.NET Framework that ASP.NET can use. Some examples of these include the Label, TextBox, and ListBox controls.

In addition to using the default controls, you can define your own. You can build custom controls from the ground up, or you can combine existing code and logic to offer specific functionality; in either case, these controls are known as *composite controls*. For example, an Address control could combine several TextBox controls; conversely, an example of a noncomposite control is a custom progress bar with a single graphical bar.

If you find that a control doesn't exist by default and you don't want to go to the trouble of building your own, then you have the option of using an open-source control. (See `http://csharp-source.net/` or `http://www.asp.net` for examples). You can also purchase a commercial control from the numerous vendors that offer such products. (See `http://www.infragistics.com/` for a good example.) Alternatively, if a control already exists but its functionality doesn't match what you require, you can use inheritance to subclass an existing control and extend its functionality to perform exactly the tasks you want. Using this feature allows your control to inherit the existing functionality of the control and allows you to either add your own or modify the behavior of existing methods where possible.

Data Binding

Another type of ASP.NET control provided as part of the .NET Framework is a *data-bound control*, which can take its contents from a database using an appropriate data source. This uses a technique known as *data binding*, discussed in Chapter 6. You can specify the binding information between the server control and the data source using a markup element similar to that used for page directives, as follows:

```
<asp:Label id="label1" runat="server"
    Text='<%# Container.DataItem("CustomerName") %/>'
```

ASP.NET's Execution Model

Figure 11-2 shows the execution model for ASP.NET.

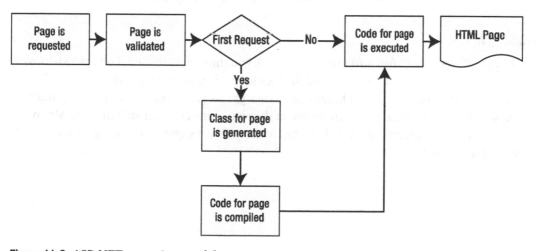

Figure 11-2. *ASP.NET execution model*

As you can see in Figure 11-2, a request for a page is received by the .NET Framework and handled by an ASP.NET *handler*. If this is the first request, a *class file* representing the page (both its user interface and background code) is generated, and this is compiled (using the JIT compiler) to an assembly within the .NET Framework's own cache. Upon successful compilation, the temporary class file is removed, and the assembly is executed, resulting in its output being returned to the client. If this is *not* the first request for the resource, the precompiled assembly is used, and the output is returned to the client as before.

Installing a Web Server

I've covered the architecture of the ASP.NET technology, its relationship with the .NET Framework, and the CLR. I've also discussed the features of ASP.NET and how to utilize them. I'll now describe the available Web servers and how to install them.

You can use one of many open-source and commercial Web servers in conjunction with ASP.NET. The Windows XP Professional and Windows Server operating systems include IIS as standard, but within this book I'll focus on two open-source Web servers, specifically Apache and the XSP Web server. In the next sections, I'll cover how to obtain and install these Web servers.

Obtaining and Installing the XSP Web Server

The XSP Web server is a lightweight Web server that was, and still is, written in the C# language using the System.Web namespace and its classes. The source for this Web server is freely available, and because it was written using the .NET Framework, it will run on any operating system that has the .NET Framework installed.

Obtaining XSP

The XSP binaries and source are freely available on the Mono Web page, with XSP being included as a standard part of the Mono Windows installation. For Linux and other operating systems, you'll need to download a specific package that is then installed using the package manager of your choice. You'll see how to start your Web server in the "Using Your Web Server" section.

Installing XSP

Installing XSP is a straightforward process; I'll walk you through installing it on the two most common operating systems. You can find the files for both (and others) in the Downloads section of the Mono home page at http://www.mono-project.com/downloads. My recommendation is that you install the XSP component at the same time as you install the core Mono packages; if you've already installed Mono but without XSP, I suggest you uninstall Mono and reinstall with XSP selected.

Installing on Windows

As mentioned, you can install XSP on Windows as an individual component if desired; the only other installation question is, what port do want XSP to listen on? Typically, for testing purposes I use 8080 for both Linux and Windows. Figure 11-3 shows the setup window.

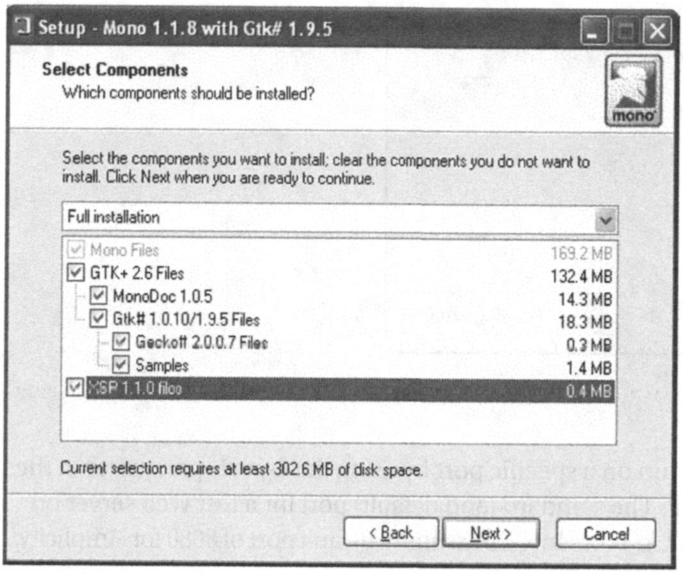

Figure 11-3. *Installing XSP on Windows*

Installing on Linux

You can install XSP from the download package easily by using the package manager of your choice. This can typically involve manually running it from the command line or opening the downloaded package and allowing the association with the .rpm extension to invoke your distribution's package manager automatically. My preference is to use the installer that is provided for all Linux x86–based distributions. Once you've downloaded it, you can invoke with the following commands:

```
chmod +x mono-1.1.8.2_1-installer.bin
./ mono-1.1.8.2_1-installer.bin
```

This will start a graphical-based tool that will install the complete Mono installation, including XSP, into the directory of your choice. If you already have Mono installed, you can either remove this (recommended) or leave this in place and allow it to install the new Mono installation alongside. In this instance, you'll need to ensure that you run all Mono-related binaries (including XSP) from their intended locations. Figure 11-4 shows the installation screen.

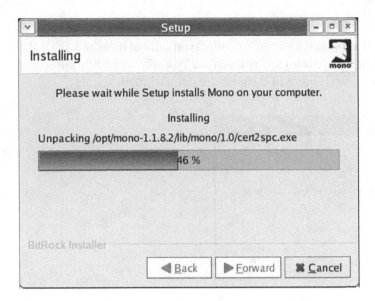

Figure 11-4. *Installing XSP on Linux*

XSP on Linux is configured to run on a specific port by using the `--port` parameter at the command line when executing XSP. The standard (and default) port for a test Web server on Linux or Unix is 8080. Therefore, for Linux or Unix, I'll assume a default port of 8080 for simplicity as your Web server configuration.

Obtaining and Installing Apache

Apache is the standard Web server within the open-source community. This can be attributed to its maturity (it was first publicly released in 1995), its power, and its proven capability in both open-source and commercial installations.

Obtaining Apache

You can obtain the Apache source, binaries, and installer from one of the mirrors identified on Apache's main Web page at `http://httpd.apache.org`. Apache is available for numerous operating systems including Windows and Linux, as you can see from the download page in Figure 11-5.

Once you have obtained the Apache installation files, you will also need to obtain the `mod_mono` module from `http://www.mono-project.com/Mod_mono`. Once you've downloaded and extracted it (using something like `tar -xvzf mod_mono-<version>.tar.gz`), you are then in a position to compile and install the Apache-to-Mono link module using a command line such as this:

```
cd mod_mono-<version>
./configure --prefix=/usr
make install
```

This will build the `mod_mono` module using the files in the install make file and leave you with an Apache module that can be connected to Mono.

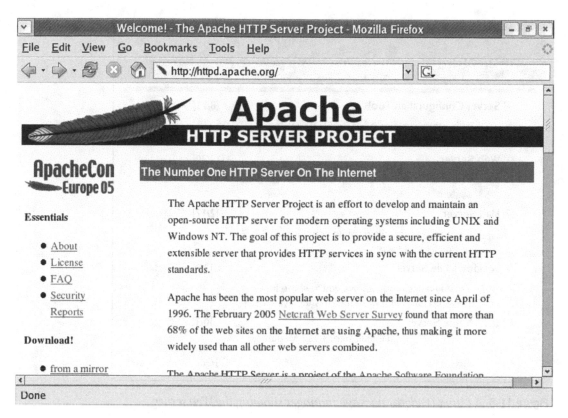

Figure 11-5. *Apache download page*

Note Replace the `<version>` text in the previous code with the Mono version you are using.

Installing Apache

You can find extremely comprehensive instructions for installing Apache on all the platforms it is available for, including Windows and various Linux distributions, at `http://httpd.apache.org/docs/2.0/install.html`. (This link is for version 2.0.) As an alternative, I'll present the method I used to install Apache on both Windows and Linux next.

Installing on Linux

I installed Apache as part of my Fedora Linux distribution because it's simply a case of choosing the Apache option from the package manager. If I hadn't installed this initially, I could start this application afterward and run the package manage manually, navigating to the Web server and verifying the relevant components (obviously including the Apache server). Figure 11-6 shows this screen.

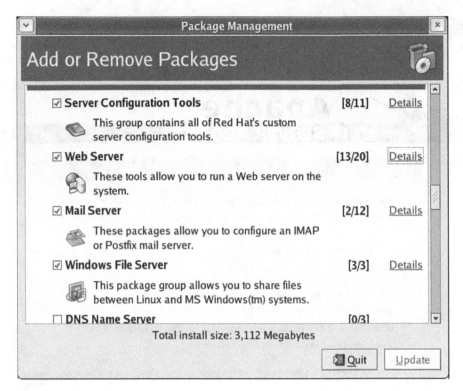

Figure 11-6. *A Linux (Fedora) package manager showing the Web server*

Of course, numerous other methods exist for installing Apache on Linux, either using the package manager as described or using another package manager, such as Yum or RPM, that may be provided with your distribution.

Installing on Windows

When installing Apache on Windows, it's simply a case of downloading the appropriate version from the Apache download site (see `http://httpd.apache.org/download.cgi`). I chose the Windows 32-bit binary with an installer (which requires Microsoft Windows Installer 1.2); then you simply have to execute the installer. Figure 11-7 shows the first startup screen.

You should note that when running on the Windows platform, you also have the option of installing the Apache server as a Windows service, allowing the service to run without the user being logged in. If your server is a dedicated Web server, then this would obviously be the preferred option, but it is optional because the Apache service on Windows is equally at home running within a DOS window as a process. To install Apache as a Windows service, simply type the following command line:

```
apache -k install
```

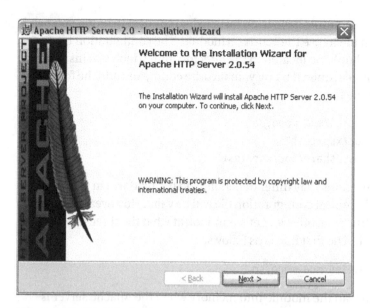

Figure 11-7. *The Windows Apache initial installation screen*

Connecting Mono to Your Web Server

Once you have installed the prerequisite files, including the .NET Framework and your Web server, you can connect the Web server to the Mono environment, allowing you to then build your own Web pages and access them via a browser. This connection takes different forms depending on the Web server you have installed; therefore, I'll provide instructions for both Windows and Linux operating systems. However, at the time of writing, the mod_mono module for connecting Apache to Mono is not available on Windows. It is for this reason that I recommend you use XSP when developing your Mono-based ASP.NET applications for the Windows operating system.

Connecting Mono to XSP

To connect Mono to XSP, you have nothing to configure other than to run the XSP Web server with the appropriate parameters.

Connecting Mono to Apache

To extend Apache to support Mono (and other technologies), you use modules that provide hooks into the Apache framework, which is similar to how Microsoft IIS uses ISAPI filters. These modules register a file extension with a module that is then used to process the file and return the results via the Apache server. In the case of Mono, the mod_mono module redirects the request to an XSP component called mod-mono-server, which is currently implemented only on the Linux operating system.

Once Apache and the mod_mono module have been installed, to connect to Mono you need to modify Apache's configuration file to use the mod_mono module. The configuration file for Apache is called httpd.conf and should be located in the directory into which you installed Apache. Once you have found this file, open it using your favorite editor, and add the following configuration lines to the end of the file:

```
LoadModule mono_module /usr/modules/mod_mono.so
Alias /MySamples "/usr/share/doc/xsp/test"
MonoApplications "/MySamples:/usr/share/doc/xsp/test"
```

The configuration and file locations may differ depending on the platform in which you are installing, but the concept of a central configuration file will be valid. However, ensure you follow any platform-specific instructions offered. Let's now look at what the three lines of configuration actually accomplish. The first line is as follows:

```
LoadModule mono_module /usr/modules/mod_mono.so
```

This line instructs Apache to load the module into memory when the Apache server is either started or restarted. This allows code to be introduced in the form of modules dynamically at runtime using the Dynamic Shared Object (DSO) mechanism. (See http://biocal2.bio. jhu.edu/manual/dso.html.) The next configuration is as follows:

```
Alias /MySamples "/usr/share/doc/xsp/test"
```

This allows documents to be stored in a local file system directory other than the Apache server's root directory. Using the previous Alias directive, the following request, http:// 127.0.0.1:8080/index.html, would resolve to /usr/share/dpc/xsp/test/index.html on the file system. The final line is as follows:

```
MonoApplications "/MySamples:/usr/share/doc/xsp/test"
```

The MonoApplications directive indicates that all requests to either /MySamples or /usr/ share/doc/xsp/test should be also processed by Mono, specifically ASP.NET.

You then need to add some lines that associate the correct handler for requests that come into Apache. This configuration code varies depending on the version of Apache you are using; for version 1.3.x, use this:

```
<Directory /usr/share/doc/xsp/test>
  SetHandler mono
  <IfModule mod_dir.c>
    DirectoryIndex index.aspx
  </IfModule>
</Directory>
```

For version 2.0.x of Apache, use this:

```
<Location /MySamples >
  SetHandler mono
</Location>
```

The previous configuration associates an alias, in this case MySamples, with the location of your ASP.NET files, so you would need to use this in your test URL. If you are unsure, check the documentation provided for mod_mono.

Using Your Web Server

Once you've installed the Web server of your choice and connected it to Mono if required, you are now in a position to test whether it actually works. After I show how to do this, I'll show some of the features of ASP.NET in action with a few practical examples.

Testing Your Web Server

The first task is to check whether your Web server installation and configuration has worked. The most obvious way is to use one of the example files installed as part of ASP.NET.

Starting Your Web Server

For your Web server to process requests, it needs to be running. It will typically be running either as a background or as a foreground process. For example, a background process may be using a Windows service on Windows or a daemon process on Linux/Unix. In this example, I'll be running a Web server as a foreground process by simply executing the appropriate command line in a shell window (or command prompt on Windows). I'll focus purely on XSP because you can find a wealth of information about running Apache on its own Web site within the installation instructions. In addition, you may need to provide a root directory for XSP to look for the Web pages you request. If you fail to specify a directory, XSP will use the current directory by default. Table 11-3 summarizes the key command-line parameters that XSP recognizes.

Table 11-3. *XSP Command-Line Options*

Option	Description
--port	TCP port to listen on. This defaults to 8080.
--address	IP address on which to listen. This defaults to 0.0.0.0.
--root	Root directory to associate with Web server. The default is current directory.
--appconfigfile	Associates application configuration using XML file.
--appconfigdir	Directory of the XML application configuration file.
--applications	Virtual and real directories, separated with colon (:), for Web applications.
--version	Displays the XSP version number.
--verbose	Switches on verbose mode. Recommended for debugging.

Starting XSP on Windows

On Microsoft Windows, the XSP executable is installed within the standard Windows Programs menu as a menu tree that relates specifically to the Mono version installed. You can either choose the XSP Test Web Server item from this menu or open a command-prompt window and type the following command line:

```
xsp --port 8080 --root "C:\Program Files\Mono-1.1.8\share\doc\xsp\test"
```

■ **Note** The previous --root command obviously depends on the directory you specified existing. The example is pointing to the examples supplied with XSP under Mono version 1.1.8.

After successful execution, you should see a window similar to Figure 11-8.

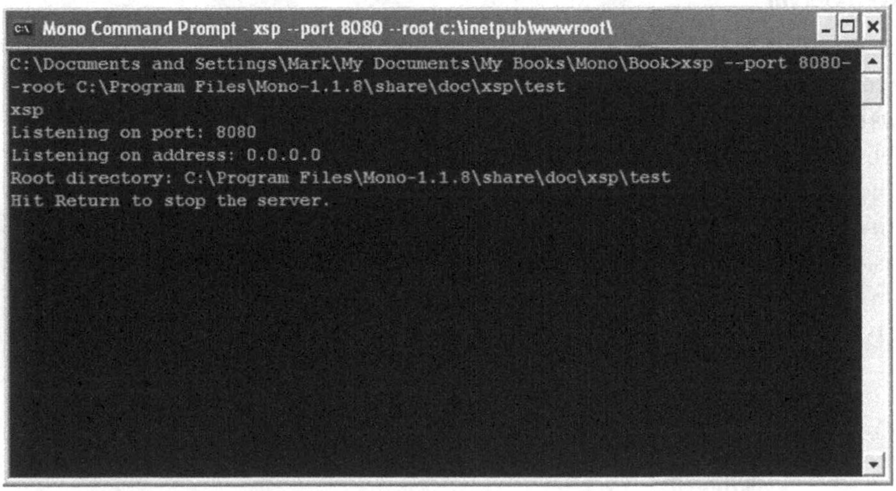

Figure 11-8. *XSP running on Windows*

Starting XSP on Linux/Unix

If using Linux, you need to open a terminal window and at the command line run the XSP service simply by moving to the root directory where your ASP.NET pages are held and running the xsp executable. On Linux, the ASP.NET samples are installed in /opt/Mono<version>/share/doc/xsp/test within the root directory in which XSP is installed. By default, XSP installs into the /opt directory, so the command line is as follows (using the default directory syntax this time):

```
cd /opt/Mono<version> /share/doc/xsp/test
xsp --port 8080
```

Alternatively, you can use the --root command to specify the root directory where your ASP.NET pages are held, as follows:

```
xsp --port 8080 --root /share/doc/xsp/test
```

Note You'd need to modify the previous path to reflect the Mono version installed and therefore the directory path in which it was placed.

If successful, you should see a terminal window similar to Figure 11-9.

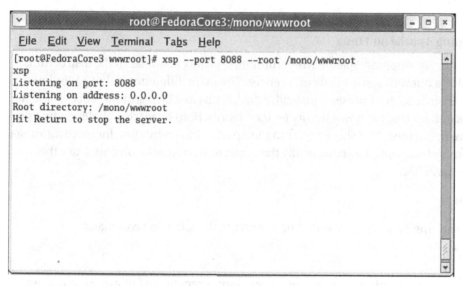

Figure 11-9. *XSP running on Linux*

Starting/Stopping Apache on Windows

To start, stop, or restart Apache when running on the Windows platforms, you have several options that are in part based on how you've installed Apache. I won't cover the process for performing these tasks against Apache when running as a Windows service through the Services option of the Windows Control Panel, because it's pretty straightforward. I will, however, focus on starting, restarting, or stopping Apache from the command line; the options are virtually the same as on Linux.

To start the Apache Web server under Windows, execute the following command:

```
apache
```

To start the Apache Web server running as a Windows service, execute the following command:

```
apache -k start
```

To stop the Apache Web server running as a process, you simply close down the process using the Ctrl+C keyboard combination. If you want to stop Apache running as a Windows service, execute the following command:

```
apache -k stop
```

Finally, restarting Apache is available only when running it as a Windows service; execute the following command:

```
apache -k restart
```

Starting/Stopping Apache on Linux

Starting, restarting, or stopping Apache when running on Linux is similar to the instructions given for Windows but with some subtle differences. The main difference is that a Windows service option is obviously not present; instead, Apache runs as a background process, and its binary name is either httpd (as it was for my Fedora distribution) or apachectl, depending on the distribution being used. You should refer to the Apache documentation for more information. The command-line options are basically the same; to start Apache on Linux, use the following command line:

```
apachectl start
```

To stop a running Apache process on Linux, execute the following command:

```
apachectl stop
```

Finally, to restart a running Apache process on Linux, execute the following command:

```
apachectl restart
```

Browsing a Sample Page

After you have successfully started your Web server, you can open the browser of your choice and browse to one of the example ASP.NET Web pages, taking note to include the correct port number on which your Web server was configured to listen. The default page for the samples directory is a page that displays a Web page with links for all the sample pages included with ASP.NET; you can access it by entering a URL of http://localhost:<port>. If you want to be more specific, you can enter a URL that details the specific ASP.NET page to open such as http://localhost:<port>/1.1/Webcontrols/calendar.aspx when using XSP as your Web server or http://localhost:<port>/MySamples/1.1/webcontrols/calendar.aspx when using Apache as your Web server (the subtle difference being where your Web server searches from). This page should process and render the ASP.NET page within your Web browser, as shown in Figure 11-10.

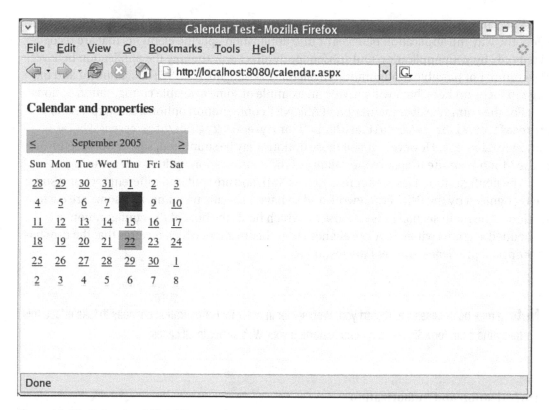

Figure 11-10. *Calendar ASP.NET sample running against a Web server*

If a screen similar to Figure 11-10 displays, then the test was successful. You can now proceed to building your own Web sites!

Building Your Own Web Site

At this point in the chapter, you should have installed and started a Web server—preferably XSP to keep within the spirit of Mono, but you could have installed Apache or any other Web server available that can be connected to Mono. You are now ready to start developing your own applications using ASP.NET.

Configuring Your Web Application

One of the early tasks when building your own Web site is configuring your application and ASP.NET. You can do this in one of two ways: providing a configuration for your application alone or modifying a global configuration that affects all applications running on your Web server. In either case, the configuration details are held in a file with an .xml extension, and this file's location changes depending on whether the configuration is to be applied locally or globally.

To configure a *local* application, create or modify a file called web.config, which should be placed within the root directory of your Web application. The *global* settings are held in a file called machine.config, which is in a directory called CONFIG under the installation folder of the .NET Framework. If a local web.config file is not present, the settings within the global machine.config file take effect.

You can split the configuration files into elements that are ASP.NET specific and therefore affect the way the application behaves or into application-specific elements that are recognized only by your application and subsequently affect only the way the application behaves. The number of possible configurations available to configure ASP.NET is significant and too large to focus on here, but I will provide an example of some available configuration options.

For the complete documentation of ASP.NET configuration options, see `http://msdn.microsoft.com/library/default.asp?url=/library/en-us/cpguide/html/cpconASPNET➡ Configuration.asp`. However, not all these options may be supported, so it is worth returning to the Mono Web site to ensure the validity of the configuration options you are using.

The configuration files are represented as XML and are split into different sections; some are recognized by the .NET Framework and so have a specific meaning, and some are custom sections. The main section is `<system.web>`, which holds the bulk of the configuration in embedded sections within it. A key element is authentication, which ensures that the user has appropriate privileges to access the resource.

Note It may be necessary to restart your Web server in order for configuration changes to take effect; this is certainly the case for XSP. I recommend restarting your Web server in all cases.

Authentication and Authorization

The following example configuration section shows how to specify the authentication mechanism that will be used by your application:

```
<?xml version="1.0" encoding="utf-8"?>
<configuration>
  <system.web>
    <authorization>
      <deny users="?"/>
    </authorization>
  </system.web>
</configuration>
```

The previous section will switch on authorization for all resources within the Web page by denying access to *all* unauthenticated users and will invoke the authentication method specified; the following code shows the configuration section for this authentication method. Alternatively, you can use the `<allow>` tag to allow specific users or groups of users, but in this case you want all users to be authenticated.

```
<authentication mode="Forms">
  <forms name="login" loginUrl="login.aspx">
    <credentials passwordFormat="Clear">
      <user name="mark" password="password"/>
    </credentials>
  </forms>
</authentication>
```

The previous configuration element starts by defining the authentication mode used; this must be from the list of valid values shown in Table 11-4.

Table 11-4. *ASP.NET Authentication Modes*

Value	Description
Windows	Uses the Windows authentication model in IIS. This is valid for IIS only.
Forms	ASP.NET forms authentication.
Passport	Microsoft Passport authentication.
None	Anonymous users only.

In this case, I'll show how to use forms authentication and will provide an ASP.NET page for specifically handing the authentication required. This is indicated by the following <forms> element, which in this case specifies an arbitrary name and an ASP.NET page called login.aspx to handle the authentication:

```
<forms name="login" loginUrl="login.aspx">
</forms>
```

Finally, you have the option of specifying the credentials used by the authentication mechanism directly within the configuration file, or you can programmatically obtain and verify them from an external source such as a database or directory service. In this case, the following explicitly specifies the credential list using the configuration entries:

```
<credentials passwordFormat="Clear">
  <user name="mark" password="password"/>
</credentials>
```

This defines that the password will be sent in clear format, although you can use one of the valid encryption mechanisms available such as SHA1 or MD5. However, if you use HTTP, the encrypted password will still be clearly visible. If you need to encrypt all traffic being sent using HTTP, you'll need to use HTTPS. It also provides a list (a single entry in this case) of valid usernames and passwords.

■**Note** The mechanism for specifying credentials in the configuration file is a valid and acceptable one, but beware that you must secure your Web server, which provides administration overhead if the number of users is significant.

The final step is to provide an implementation for the login.aspx page, which will provide the user with the ability to enter a username and password and verify this against the stored credentials by either accepting the request and redirecting the user to the resource requested or providing an "access denied" page.

Securing a Web Page

In this section, you'll actually be developing two pages, one for the login page represented within login.aspx and another for the home page, represented in home.aspx, that will be protected from unauthenticated access. Listing 11-1 shows the login page.

Listing 11-1. *Login Page*

```
<%@ Page Language="C#" %>
<%@ Import Namespace="System.Web.Security" %>
<html>
<body>
<form runat="server">
  <h3><font face="Verdana">Login Page</font></h3>
  <table>
    <tr>
      <td>Username:</td>
      <td><asp:TextBox id="Username" type="text" runat="server"/></td>
    </tr>
    <tr>
      <td>Password:</td>
      <td><asp:TextBox id="Password" type=password runat="server"/></td>
    </tr>
  </table>
</form>
</body>
</html>
```

After entering the code in Listing 11-1, save this to disk as a file named login.aspx. You can then access this from a Web browser using the URL http://localhost:8080/login.aspx, after which you should see a screen similar to Figure 11-11.

Alternatively, the more likely scenario is that a user accesses another resource such as the home page, and with the authentication mechanism you've put in place (to deny all anonymous users), any request to a page in this directory from an unauthenticated user will result in them being redirected to the login.aspx page for authentication. Try it! Add a home.aspx or similar page, and try to access it directly; the results will be the same.

Examining the code in Listing 11-1, you'll notice that most of the text within the .aspx file is HTML. The only entries for which this is not true are the page directive and some of the elements marked as running on the server. The <form> element submits its values to the server—for example, when you click the login button (not inserted into the page yet)—and the input fields for which you'll need to extract the data.

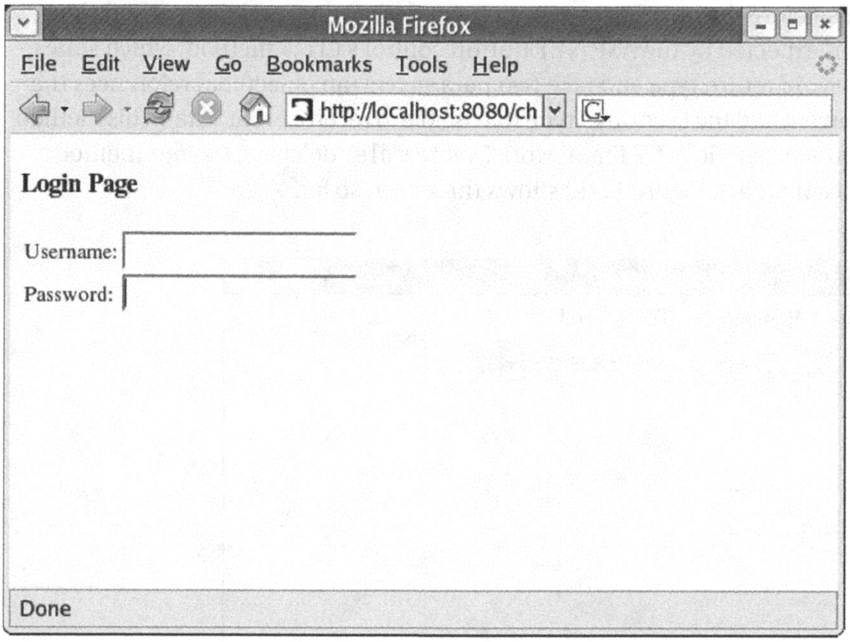

Figure 11-11. *login.aspx user interface*

The screen looks fine, pretty much like most login pages, but it doesn't actually do anything other than prompt you for a username and password. Let's add a button that allows the user to actually perform the login. This will require you to add a login button after the text input boxes but still within the <form> element. So, you'll need to add the following text immediately after the closing <table> element.

```
<asp:button text="Login" OnClick="Login_Click" runat="server"/>
```

You'll notice an immediate change in the syntax; this isn't a normal button—it's an ASP.NET Button control as indicated by the prefix I've highlighted in bold. This is because submitting the form data is not enough; you want to be able to invoke a method on the server that can act on the login request. You do this by adding an attribute against the button for the OnClick event (it's actually the Click method in the button class) that points to a method name; I've highlighted this too. So, you'll need to add this method's signature to the page using the following code:

```
<script language="C#" runat="server">
  void Login_Click (object sender, EventArgs e)
  {
  // TODO: Implementation
  }
</script>
```

You can add this before the opening <body> element declaration, and the method signature must match that expected by the ASP.NET Button control's Click method, which states that it should have a void return type and take two parameters (an object that references the object that fired the event and the EventArgs type that is able to receive event data). This method signature is based on the generic .NET Framework EventHandler delegate, so your method implementation must match it. Figure 11-12 shows the screen so far.

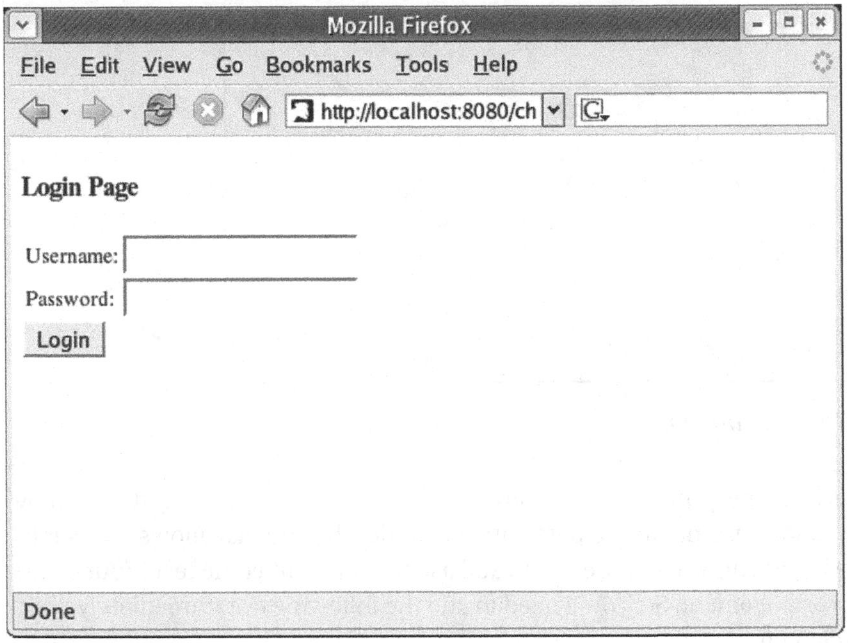

Figure 11-12. *Login.aspx user interface with login button*

So, the button is present, and the event is being invoked, but you have yet to implement what actually takes place when the button is clicked. The implementation needs to check that the username and password combination is valid and, if so, redirect the user to the resource they initially tried and that was protected. If the validation fails, you'll need some means of telling the user this, so you'll add a simple Label control that displays the error text. For the additional label, add the following text after the button's definition:

```
<asp:Label id="Msg" ForeColor="red" Font-Name="Verdana"
 Font-Size="8" runat="server" />
```

Now you can wire up the login event handler with some appropriate code and use the label you just added to report any login failures. The System.Web.Security namespace provides a class called FormsAuthentication. This class has a static method called Authenticate, which takes the username and password as parameters, returning true if the user is authenticated against the credentials provided (in the web.config file). You can use this to check whether the user is valid and redirect the user as appropriate. You could validate the credentials against a database or corporate directory, but for this example you'll use ASP.NET's built-in credentials method. The implementation therefore looks like this:

```
void Login_Click(object sender, EventArgs e) {

  if (FormsAuthentication.Authenticate(Username.Text, Password.Text))
    FormsAuthentication.RedirectFromLoginPage(Username.Text, true);
  else
    Msg.Text = "Error: Invalid username and/or password.";
}
```

This implementation will redirect the user to the page they originally requested by using the RedirectFromLoginPage method and passing the username. The implementation will also indicate whether to persist the login credentials in a cookie. (You can modify this to be driven by the user if you want.) If the authentication fails, then it simply returns an error message using the label provided, as shown in Figure 11-13.

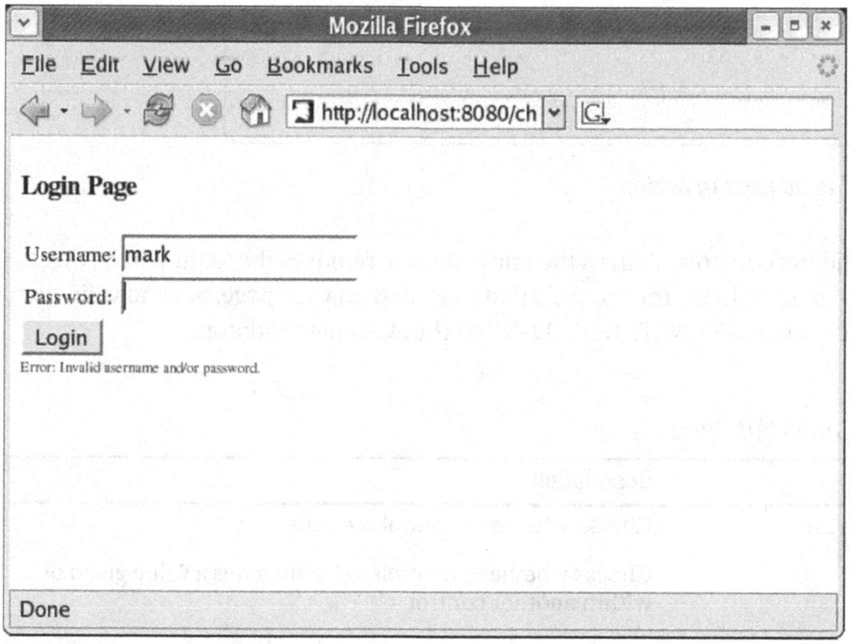

Figure 11-13. *Invalid login attempt*

Finally, let's add some validation to the username and password fields. You can use another ASP.NET control to perform validation against an ASP.NET-based control. In this case, you want to check for blank values because both fields are required; the RequiredFieldValidator control is ideal for this because it allows you to check for a field being null and display an error message if true. Embed the code for this next to the control you want to check, which will put the error message next to the offending control. The implementation is as follows:

```
<td><ASP:RequiredFieldValidator ControlToValidate="Username"
 Display="Static" ErrorMessage="*" runat="server"/></td>
```

If you enter blank values for the username and/or password, you'll see a screen similar to Figure 11-14.

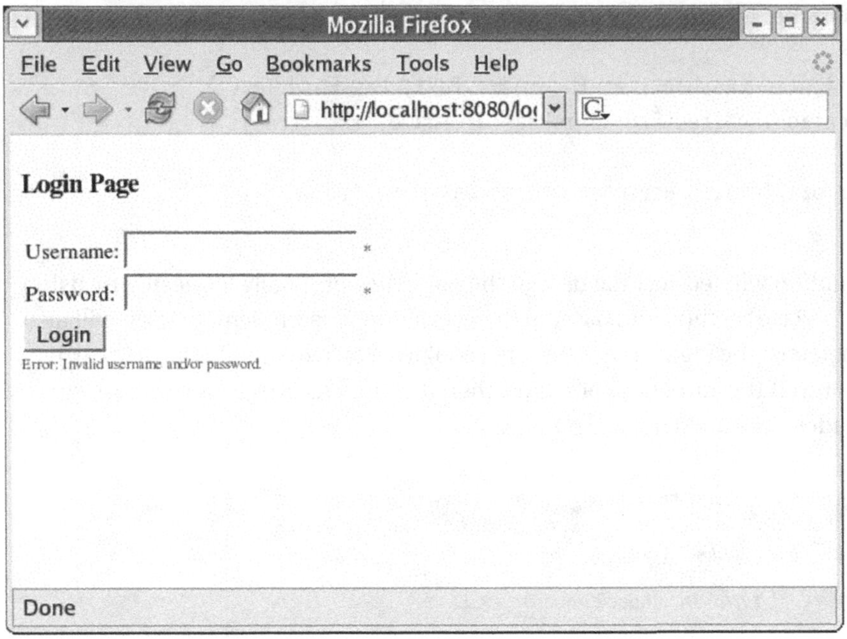

Figure 11-14. *Control validators in action*

Using input validator controls, such as the one just used, removes the tedium of having to write your own validation code for the controls that may exist on your page. Several validator controls are available within ASP.NET. Table 11-5 lists the available validators.

Table 11-5. *ASP.NET Input Validators*

Validator Control	Description
RequiredFieldValidator	Checks whether a control is empty
CompareValidator	Checks whether a controls value matches a value given or within another control
RegularExpressionValidator	Checks whether a control matches the regular expression provided
RangeValidator	Checks whether a controls value is within a given range
CustomValidator	Allows you to provide your own validation within a function
ValidationSummary	Displays a summary of all validation errors

You've taken a look at using ASP.NET to secure a Web page and to create a home page that can be protected. You'll now learn how a Web Service can provide business logic that is exposed across the Internet using standard protocols and how your application can consume these methods to provide client-server interaction.

Using ASP.NET to Write a Dynamic Web Page

In this section, you'll learn how to write a typical ASP.NET page that has dynamic elements. This is obviously something that I have already touched on through the implementation of the login page, but you can take this a step further and include a page that is not only dynamic in the data it displays but also dynamic in the way the user can interact with it. Because the RSS aggregator project is Windows Forms based and not Web based, I'll use an example that is included within Mono and ASP.NET as an illustration and briefly discuss its implementation. I'll show an example that uses data binding to represent dynamic content and then displays a user selection. The example I'll use is databind-arraylist.aspx, which is provided as one of the ASP.NET examples. The page looks like Figure 11-15 when running.

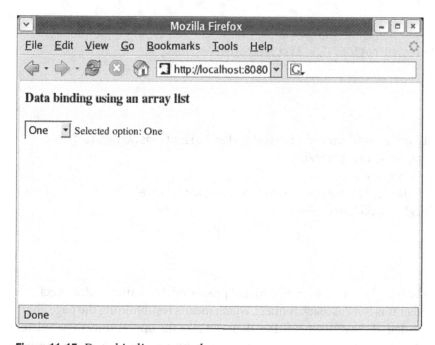

Figure 11-15. *Data binding example*

Listing 11-2 shows the code for this example.

Listing 11-2. *Dynamic Web Page Example*

```
<%@ Page Language="C#" %>
<html>
<head>
<script runat="server">
  private void Page_Load (object sender, EventArgs e)
  {
    if (!IsPostBack)
    {
      optionsList.Add ("One");
      optionsList.Add ("Two");
      optionsList.Add ("Three");
      optionsList.Add ("Four");
      optionsList.Add ("Five");
      list.DataSource = optionsList;
      list.DataBind();
    }
    else
      msg.Text = "Selected option: " + list.SelectedItem.Text;
  }
</script>
</head>
<body>
<object id="optionsList" runat="server" class="System.Collections.ArrayList" />
<h3>Data binding using an array list</h3>
<form id="form" runat="server">
    <asp:DropDownList id="list" runat="server" autopostback="true" />
    <asp:Label id="msg" runat="server" />
</form>
</body>
</html>
```

In this example, the Page_Load event is trapped and processed. In Listing 11-2, a check takes place to see whether this is a PostBack request, which means resubmitting the page after it has first been downloaded. If the answer is false, then you take the opportunity to populate an array with entries (One, Two, and so on) and bind this to the drop-down list control using its DataSource property and the DataBind() method. The following code extract shows how to do this:

```
if (!IsPostBack){
  optionsList.Add ("One");
  optionsList.Add ("Two");
  optionsList.Add ("Three");
  optionsList.Add ("Four");
  optionsList.Add ("Five");
  list.DataSource = optionsList;
  list.DataBind();
}
```

I've already shown what to do if the answer to PostBack() is true. However, a subsequent submission must mean the user has selected an entry from the drop-down control, as this is ASP.NET's default behavior. In this case, you show the text for the item chosen, as shown here:

```
else
  msg.Text = "Selected option: " + list.SelectedItem.Text;
```

The data is held within an ArrayList object that is referenced as such using some HTML that creates a server-side object of this type, which you can then reference in your ASP.NET code. This is shown in the following code:

```
<object id="optionsList" runat="server" class="System.Collections.ArrayList" />
```

Finally, within the standard ASP.NET <form> element, you can create two visible controls—one for the DropDownList control with automatic postback (invoked on selection) set to true and the other a Label control for displaying the text of the selected entry. The following code shows how to do this:

```
<asp:DropDownList id="list" runat="server" autopostback="true" />
<asp:Label id="msg" runat="server" />
```

Although this is a simple example, when combined with the login page, you should now have a grasp of how you can use ASP.NET to generate two-way, dynamic Web pages.

Writing a Web Service

A Web Service is a method for which its implementation is exposed across a network, such as the Internet or an intranet, using standard protocols and technologies such as HTTP and XML. This allows you to write business logic that may exist on one machine and have it be accessed (also known as *consumed*) by another program that is running on a different physical machine. A Web Service allows you to expose your API across the Internet to be called by another application; a good example of this is the Google search engine that exposes an API as a Web Service that you can use in your own application. (See http://www.google.com/apis/ for more details.)

Overview of Web Service Terminology and Concepts

All traffic sent to and from a Web Service is represented in XML, which is used to define protocols and languages that Web Service–aware applications can understand. One protocol is SOAP, and related technologies are WSDL and Universal Description, Discovery, and Integration (UDDI):

SOAP: SOAP is an XML-based messaging protocol that was created to encapsulate a Web Service request and response in a lightweight manner across a network. These requests and responses are encapsulated into an XML document known as an *envelope*. Using an open standard such as XML means that the SOAP envelopes are platform agnostic and represent a package or message (also referred to as a *payload*) that is sent from one device to another. For example, you might request the latest stock share price for a company (a SOAP request), and the Web Service may look this up and return the value (a SOAP response). The .NET Framework encapsulates this work for you, so you simply need to provide the declaration and implementation of your methods, as you have always done by marking the method with a Web Service attribute. You'll learn more about this in the "Creating Your Web Service" section.

WSDL: WSDL is an XML file whose structure is defined in a standard XML schema. It describes the attributes and capabilities of a Web Service, its methods, their parameters, and so on. A client application knows how to communicate with a Web Service by using the WSDL returned by a Web Service, which in turn can be used to form part of the world-wide yellow pages that detail registered Web Services.

UDDI: UDDI is a language that allows you to represent your Web Services in a standard manner to be published in a UDDI repository that can be searched and queried. This is similar to the way a telephone directory lists the services of companies and their contact information. You can find an example repository at `http://www.uddi.org`.

Creating Your Web Service

As you may have guessed, a Web Service has a similar structure to an `.aspx` page, in that the file contains the code processed by the Web server and a directive indicating to ASP.NET what sort of files you're dealing with. The Web Service implementation is placed in a file with an extension of `.asmx`, which then starts with a directive, as follows:

```
<%@ WebService Language="C#" Codebehind="webservice.asmx.cs"
Class="MyWebService.RSSFeed" %>
```

The `WebService` directive has similar parameters to that of an ASP.NET page directive, `language` and `Codebehind`, but it also has a `Class` parameter that defines the name of the class (including a namespace if required) that provides the implementation. This example defines a class called `RSSFeed` within the `MyWebService` namespace; therefore, the code must match this. Here is the skeleton Web Service implementation:

```
<%@ WebService Language="c#" Codebehind="webservice.asmx.cs"
 Class="MyWebService.RSSFeed" %>

using System;
using System.Web.Services;
using System.Web.Services.Protocols;

namespace MyWebService
{
  public class RSSFeed : System.Web.Services.WebService
  {
    //TODO: Implementation
  }
}
```

If you point your browser to this Web Service, it should return a user-friendly screen describing the Web Service's capability, which at the moment is nothing, as shown in Figure 11-16.

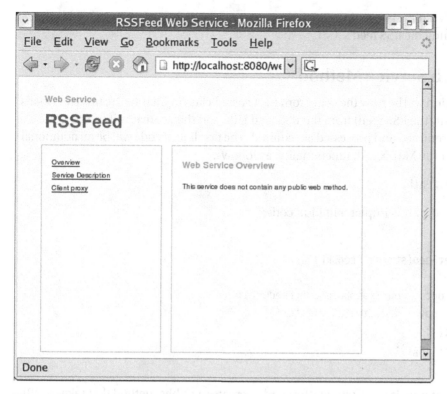

Figure 11-16. *Web Service description page*

You can return the WSDL associated with the Web Service by simply adding ?wsdl to the
end of the URL, such as http://localhost:8080/webservice.asmx?wsdl. Depending on the
browser, this will either return the WSDL within an XML view (as is the case with Microsoft's
Internet Explorer) or return a blank page, which has the WSDL as its source (as is the case with
Firefox under Linux, although Firefox under Windows behaves in a similar fashion to Internet
Explorer), in which case you'll need to view the page's source from the View menu. You'll see
WSDL like the following:

```
<?xml version="1.0" encoding="utf-8"?>
<definitions xmlns:soap="http://schemas.xmlsoap.org/wsdl/soap/"
  xmlns:soapenc="http://schemas.xmlsoap.org/soap/encoding/"
  xmlns:s="http://www.w3.org/2001/XMLSchema"
  xmlns:http="http://schemas.xmlsoap.org/wsdl/http/"
  xmlns:mime="http://schemas.xmlsoap.org/wsdl/mime/"
  xmlns:tm="http://microsoft.com/wsdl/mime/textMatching/"
  xmlns:s0="http://tempuri.org/"
  name="RSSFeed"
  targetNamespace="http://tempuri.org/"
  xmlns="http://schemas.xmlsoap.org/wsdl/">
  <types />
  <service name="RSSFeed" />
</definitions>
```

This obviously isn't very exciting and makes for a useless Web Service, so let's add a method for returning the RSS feed's XML.

Adding a Web Service Method

This implementation will borrow the code from the Channel class in Chapter 10; this class loads the XML document (the RSS feed) from the RSS feed URL and then converts it into an XML string that can be returned and processed as required. The first line of code will be an additional include to support the XML XPath functionality, as follows:

```
using System.Xml.XPath;
```

This is followed by this implementation code:

```
[WebMethod]
public string GetFeed(string FeedURL)
{
  XPathDocument doc = new XPathDocument(FeedURL);
  XPathNavigator nav = doc.CreateNavigator();
  nav.MoveToRoot();
  return nav.ToString();
}
```

The implementation is pretty straightforward; it creates a public method that takes a URL as a string and returns a string value. This is public and marked as [WebMethod], which enables ASP.NET to publish this as a Web Service method for external parties to call. The implementation simply creates an XPath document from which a navigation object is created. You can then use this to move to the root of the document and return the string value, in effect returning the whole RSS feed as XML. If you save this to a disk and load the webservice.asmx file in the browser, you'll see the overview screen but this time with the GetFeed method available. You can then choose this link, which will show you details of the GetFeed method; also, this will allow you to test it using the Test Form link. If you enter your favorite RSS URL (as a fully qualified URL using an http:// prefix) in the box and click the Invoke button, you'll see a screen similar to Figure 11-17.

This example shows the test form and the output from invoking the GetFeed method, which in this case is the RSS feed as represented as XML. This example uses Microsoft Internet Explorer running on Windows XP and calls the Web Service running on Fedora Linux using XSP and ASP.NET on Mono! The possibility for writing complex business logic is endless, and with the adoption of open standards, you can remove the boundaries normally associated with running on a specific operating system.

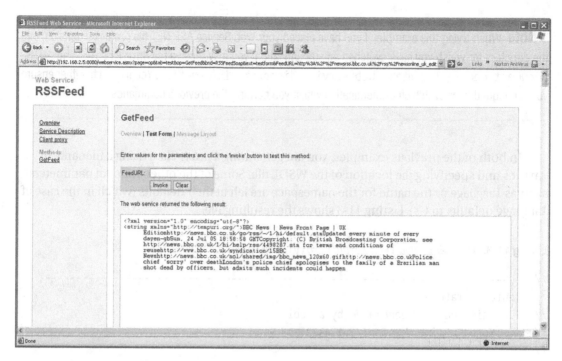

Figure 11-17. *Web method output*

Consuming a Web Service

As I mentioned previously, a Web Service is a class and its methods are exposed over a network (most often the Internet or an intranet); these methods can then be consumed by an external application that in the previous example was a Web browser. Obviously, you'll want to consume these methods in your own applications, which could be either a Windows Forms application or an ASP.NET-based application—the choice is yours. However, you obviously need to write some code to consume the Web Service and present this in the form of a class whose methods match the Web Service methods.

You can do this in a few ways; you could write this code by hand or use an IDE to do the hard work for you. An easy method in Mono is to use the command-line application called wsdl that can query, interpret, and process Web Services through the use of command-line parameters. You'll use this to generate a proxy class, implemented in C#, by simply pointing it at your Web Service. You can then include this proxy class in your application for accessing the Web Service and its methods, taking the manual effort out of generating it!

To generate the proxy class, you'll need to invoke the command-line application. If you want to generate the proxy class from a running Web Service, the command line is as follows:

```
wsdl /out:mark.cs http://localhost:8080/Webservice.asmx?wsdl
```

However, if you have generated the WSDL manually or you have downloaded it to a file, then you would specify the file path instead of the URL as shown here:

```
wsdl /out:mark.cs ./wsdl.xml
```

■**Note** When trying this example, if you have placed your Web Service ASP.NET file (.asmx extension) into the directory for which you have switched on authentication, you may receive the error `Error: The HTML document does not contain Web service discovery information.` You'll need to either ensure you are logged in or switch off authentication whilst you perform the previous commands.

In both of the previous examples, you are generating a proxy class using a filename of `mark.cs` and specifying the location of the WSDL file. Some of the other optional parameters such as language or the name for the namespace are left at their defaults (which in the case of language defaults to C#). Listing 11-3 shows the resulting file.

Listing 11-3. *Autogenerated Web Service Proxy Code*

```
// ---------------------------------------------------------------------------
// <autogenerated>
//     This code was generated by a tool.
//     Mono Runtime Version: 1.1.4322.573
//
//     Changes to this file may cause incorrect behavior and will be lost if
//     the code is regenerated.
// </autogenerated>
// ---------------------------------------------------------------------------

//
// This source code was autogenerated by Mono Web Services Description
 Language Utility
//

/// <remarks/>
[System.Web.Services.WebServiceBinding(Name="RSSFeedSoap",
Namespace="http://tempuri.org/"),
System.Diagnostics.DebuggerStepThroughAttribute(),
System.ComponentModel.DesignerCategoryAttribute("code")]
public class RSSFeed: System.Web.Services.Protocols.SoapHttpClientProtocol {

    public RSSFeed () {
        this.Url = "http://localhost:8080/webservice.asmx";
    }

    [System.Web.Services.Protocols.SoapDocumentMethodAttribute(
"http://tempuri.org/GetFeed",RequestNamespace="http://tempuri.org/",
ResponseNamespace="http://tempuri.org/",ParameterStyle=System.
Web.Services.Protocols.SoapParameterStyle.Wrapped,Use=
```

```
System.Web.Services.Description.SoapBindingUse.Literal)]
    public string GetFeed(string FeedURL) {
        object[] results = this.Invoke("GetFeed", new object[] {
            FeedURL});
        return ((string)(results[0]));
    }

    public System.IAsyncResult BeginGetFeed(string FeedURL,
System.AsyncCallback callback, object asyncState) {
        return this.BeginInvoke("GetFeed", new object[] {
            FeedURL}, callback, asyncState);
    }

    public string EndGetFeed(System.IAsyncResult asyncResult) {
        object[] results = this.EndInvoke(asyncResult);
        return ((string)(results[0]));
    }
}
```

I won't discuss the implementation line by line but will highlight some of the key areas that are worthy of consideration. The first thing to notice is that the resulting class, called RSSFeed, inherits its functionality from the SoapHttpClientProtocol class, which is part of the .NET Framework. This has several attributes and methods; the first of which you'll encounter is Url, which is initialized within its constructor to point to the URL of the Web Service. If your Web Service has moved, you could simply change this value.

The next thing to notice is that several methods basically can be attributed to a synchronous or asynchronous calling model. The synchronous method, called GetFeed (matching the Web Service method), makes a request of the Web Service (using the inherited Invoke method) and waits for a response (see Figure 11-18).

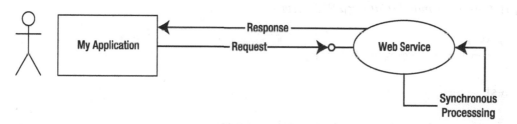

Figure 11-18. *Synchronous Web Service call*

Alternatively, the asynchronous method relies on the initial invocation using the BeginGetFeed method that accepts a callback method for which an instance of the EndGetFeed method is passed, ultimately returning the result (see Figure 11-19).

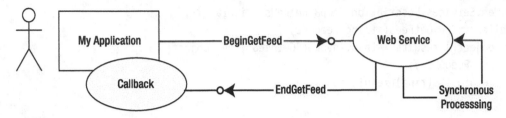

Figure 11-19. *Asynchronous Web Service call*

So, if you were to include the RSSFeed class created in the mark.cs file (which could have been compiled into a library and its namespace referenced), the programmatic invocation of the Web Service using the synchronous model would look like the following:

```
using System;
using RSSAggregator;

class Test
{
  public static void Main(string[] args)
  {
    RSSFeed rs = new RSSFeed();
    Console.Out.WriteLine(rs.GetFeed("http://newsrss.bbc.co.uk/rss/
    newsonline_uk_edition/front_page/rss.xml"));
  }
}
```

As you would expect, this would call the Web Service, passing the RSS feed URL as a parameter, and the XML RSS feed would be returned to the console. If you were to invoke the method asynchronously, the code would look like Listing 11-4.

Listing 11-4. *Asynchronously Calling a Web Service*

```
using System;
using System.Runtime.Remoting.Messaging;

class Test
{
  // Indicator as to whether the Async call is finished
  public static bool bFinished = false;

  // Callback method
  //
  public static void GetFeed_Callback(IAsyncResult result)
  {
    RSSFeed rs = (RSSFeed)result.AsyncState;
    Console.Out.WriteLine(rs.EndGetFeed(result));
    bFinished = true;
  }
```

```
public static void Main(string[] args)
{
  RSSFeed rs = new RSSFeed();
  AsyncCallback callback = new AsyncCallback(Test.GetFeed_Callback);

  rs.BeginGetFeed("http://newsrss.bbc.co.uk/rss/newsonline_uk_edition/
  front_page/rss.xml", callback, rs);

  Console.Out.WriteLine("Waiting for web service to finish");
  while (!bFinished);
  Console.Out.WriteLine("Web service has finished!");

}
}
```

As you can see, this is slightly more complex. It starts by declaring a *callback* method that is passed as a parameter and is automatically called by the Web Service when its processing is complete. In this case, this calls the EndGetFeed method to display the results, as follows:

```
public static void GetFeed_Callback(IAsyncResult result)
{
  RSSFeed rs = (RSSFeed)result.AsyncState;
  Console.Out.WriteLine(rs.EndGetFeed(result));
  bFinished = true;
}
```

The asynchronous method is invoked by creating a delegate that points to the callback method, as shown here:

```
AsyncCallback callback = new AsyncCallback(Test.GetFeed_Callback);
```

You are then able to call the method to invoke the asynchronous method that takes the URL, a callback method, and a reference to the proxy as parameters. This method call is as follows:

```
rs.BeginGetFeed("http://newsrss.bbc.co.uk/rss/newsonline_uk_edition/
front_page/rss.xml", callback, rs);
```

You are then in a position to perform other processing whilst the Web Service is working; in this case, you simply look until a flag is set within the Web Service callback method, at which point you come out of the loop and terminate the application with a suitable message. This is as follows:

```
Console.Out.WriteLine("Waiting for web service to finish");
while (!bFinished);
Console.Out.WriteLine("Web service has finished!");
```

In this example, the Web Service calls are made easy with the proxy class being automatically generated using the wsdl command-line application, and this significantly reduces the amount of effort required to consume and interact with Web Services.

What's New in ASP.NET 2.0?

The new features that have been incorporated into ASP.NET are numerous; far too many exist to list them individually within this section of the chapter. As a result, I'll present the key areas in which improvements have been made. Here are the key new features:

Master pages: Master pages allow you to significantly reduce the time it takes to develop complex pages, and they provide far greater control. A master page consists of a *template* on which you base other ASP.NET pages, all of which inherit the template page's core functionality. You are then free to implement page-specific content that combines the functionality of the template page with your individual content to provide a fully functional page. This is great for implementing common navigation options on your Web pages!

Themes: In addition to providing far greater control over the layout and structure of your Web pages, themes allow you to heavily customize the look and feel of your controls, pages, and Web sites. A theme contains standard HTML style sheets and images to represent the style that should be associated with the theme; you can then reference the theme to modify the look of your ASP.NET pages.

Rich data controls: The existing data controls, which include the ability to bind to a data source and save you from significant programming, have been extended. A new GridView control allows you to sort, view, and edit the data presented without writing a single line of code! A new DetailsView control allows you to quickly build master/detail forms from your data, again with virtually no code.

Enhanced authentication support: The ability to control authentication to your ASP.NET pages was always fairly straightforward, but you would typically still need to write the standard logon screen. This is no longer the case! Various authentication-related controls, such as Login and CreateUserWizard, allow you to create simple login pages, and you can add user maintenance and persistent data storage simply by adding new controls.

Web Part controls: Web Parts originated with Microsoft's SharePoint product, and these have now been brought into ASP.NET 2.0. ASP.NET allows you to configure a WebPartZone control to act as a container for Web Parts, which can then encapsulate functionality and inherit behavior associated with Windows Forms controls. For example, you can minimize them, maximize them, and so on. This core functionality is all provided through these new controls.

Breadcrumb trail control: A new control that is useful is the ability to leave a breadcrumb trail for you users, allowing them to see the path they have taken through the Web site and provide them with the ability to return to a known point without having to guess how many times they need to click a browser's back button.

Mobile support: The ASP.NET controls now all provide mobile support, something that previously required a completely separate set of controls. The ASP.NET 2.0 controls all know how to render themselves to a mobile device, outputting various mobile markup languages such as Compact HTML (CHTML) or Wireless Markup Language (WML), depending on the device.

Enhanced configuration support: Certain classes have been introduced that provide far greater flexibility when reading or updating configuration files within ASP.NET. The new `System.Configuration.Configuration` class provides you with a strongly typed view of the existing configuration files and allows you to access this information in a variety of ways.

As you can imagine, this is the tip of the iceberg when it comes to new features in ASP.NET 2.0. For more information, I recommend always looking at the Mono Web site. In addition, watch Microsoft's developer site (`http://msdn.microsoft.com/asp.net/`). Apress has several good books, including *Pro ASP.NET 2.0 in C# 2005*, by Matthew MacDonald and Mario Szpuszta (Apress, 2005), and *ASP.NET 2.0 Revealed*, by Patrick Lorenz (Apress, 2003). In the more recent versions of Mono, version 2.*x* of the XSP Web server is available (called `xsp2`); this allows you to use the new features found in ASP.NET here and now! You can find some examples that demonstrate these new features in the `\doc\xsp\test\2.0` directory under your Mono installation directory.

Summary

As you can see, the ASP.NET technology is a large subject and is the sole topic of numerous books. It's an extremely powerful feature of Mono and can lead to feature-rich, thin-client applications that are relatively simple to develop but do not suffer from the client-side requirement of typical fat-client applications such as those based on Windows Forms. The chapter provided an overview of ASP.NET concepts and why features such as Web Services are important when dealing with heterogeneous environments. You looked briefly at the architecture behind the ASP.NET runtime and how it uses JIT compilation and caching to achieve good performance. You then looked at obtaining, installing, and configuring the required components, including using some of the leading Web servers on the market. This allowed you to use a Web server to see a number of ASP.NET's powerful features in action, including the following:

- Securing Web resources
- Creating a login page
- Creating a Web Service
- Writing a dynamic Web page

You now have the foundation necessary to start experimenting and discovering some of the other fantastic features that ASP.NET has to offer.

Using Advanced Mono Techniques

Having reached the end of the book, you're now armed with sufficient knowledge to start designing and developing your own solutions using Mono and the .NET Framework. For those areas that I didn't have time to cover completely, you've been provided with guidance to explore the relevant features in more detail yourself. However, this doesn't mean that you've learned all there is to know about the .NET Framework, its technologies, and the Mono implementation! In this final chapter, I'll guide you through some of the more advanced concepts within Mono and uncover how you can enhance your applications by taking advantage of these advanced topics available within the framework. In this chapter, we'll specifically look at the following:

- Performance

- Monitoring

- Reflection

- Multithreading

- Interoperability tips

This again still leaves a wealth of other features to explore, but these topics are the ones most Mono programmers often asked about once they've gained experience and arguably yield the most return for your effort in applications.

Monitoring Your Performance

Monitoring application performance is crucial to its success, and in this section we'll examine various solutions for doing exactly that. If you're new to this concept, the idea of measuring software efficiency may seem a tad odd; after all, how can you measure such an abstract thing? But if you look around, you'll see we're surrounded by everyday objects that inform you of their performance and provide feedback; for example, cars, microwaves, and cookers all have instrumentation for reporting their performance, and computers are the same! Here, you'll learn the ways in which the performance of your application or its components can be measured and displayed, providing the information you need to quantify any improvements you may make.

So what can help measure performance? One popular solution is WBEM, the Web-Based Enterprise Management standard. If you are working with the Microsoft Windows operating system, you can use Microsoft's implementation of this standard, known as Windows Management Instrumentation (WMI), available for Windows 2000, XP, and 2003. (See http://msdn. microsoft.com/library/default.asp?url=/library/en-us/dnhcvs04/html/vs04d6a.asp for more details.) If you're working on the Linux operating system, then available to you are open implementations of the WBEM standard such as OpenWBEM (http://www.openwbem.org/). We're going to examine another solution, however, one provided by Mono's own profiling tool that is built into the common language runtime. This is more than sufficient, but in case you feel that you need further profiling information, I will also mention some of mechanisms available to you on operating systems such as Linux within the "Other Profiling Tools" section.

Using the Mono Profiler

The Mono profiler is provided as part of the Mono installation and supported within the runtime system. It is invoked by specifying the --profile flag when using the mono command-line command to execute your application. If you were to use the HelloWorld application created in Chapter 1 as an example:

```
using System;
namespace HelloWorld
{
  class Hello
  {
    static void Main(string[] args)
    {
      Console.Out.WriteLine("Hello World!");
    }
  }
}
```

and you were to compile (assuming this application was saved to a file called helloworld.cs) and execute it using the --profile flag as shown in the following command lines:

```
mcs helloworld.cs
mono --profile helloworld.exe
```

The output is significant, even for small programs, and just an extract of this is shown next to avoid filling the chapter with profiling output. You may wish to send this output to a file, however, rather than attempt to view this on screen; this can be achieved by simply piping the output to a file of your choice by using the following command line instead:

```
mono --profile helloworld.exe > profileText.txt
```

In either case, take some time to examine the output as shown here:

```
Hello World!
Total time spent compiling 401 methods (sec): 0.09375
Slowest method to compile (sec): 0.01563:
```

```
System.Object::runtime_invoke_void(object,intptr,intptr
,intptr)
Time(ms) Count    P/call(ms) Method name
#########################
 109.375    22    4.972    System.Object::
runtime_invoke_void(object,intptr,intptr,intptr)
   Callers (with count) that contribute at least for 1%:
            3  13 % I18N.Common.Manager::.ctor()
            2   9 % System.Int32::ToString()
            1   4 % .Test::Main(string[])
            1   4 % System.Console::.cctor()
            1   4 % System.Text.Encoding::GetEncoding(string)
            1   4 % System.String::ToLowerInvariant()
            1   4 % System.MonoType::InvokeMember(string,BindingFlags,
         Binder,object,object[],ParameterModifier[],CultureInfo,string[])
            1   4 % System.Reflection.MonoMethodInfo::get_parameter_info(intptr)
            1   4 % System.Reflection.MonoMethod::Invoke(object,BindingFlags,
         Binder,object[],CultureInfo)
            1   4 % System.Collections.CaseInsensitiveHashCodeProvider::.ctor()
            1   4 % System.Globalization.CultureInfo::get_CurrentCulture()
            1   4 % System.Globalization.CultureInfo::ConstructInvariant(bool)
            1   4 % System.Collections.Hashtable::Add(object,object)
            1   4 % System.Collections.Hashtable::KeyEquals(object,object)
            1   4 % System.Console::OpenStandardError(int)
            1   4 % System.IO.FileStream::.ctor(intptr,FileAccess,bool,int,bool,bool)
            1   4 % System.IO.UnexceptionalStreamWriter::.ctor(Stream,Encoding)
            1   4 % System.IO.StreamWriter::.ctor(Stream,Encoding,int)
            1   4 % System.IO.UnexceptionalStreamReader::.ctor(Stream,Encoding)
#########################
 109.375     1  109.375    .Test::Main(string[])
   Callers (with count) that contribute at least for 1%:
      1.  100 % System.Object::runtime_invoke_void_string[]
      2.  (object,intptr,intptr,intptr)

** Extract from output removed for clarity**

#########################
  15.625    165   0.095    System.Collections.Hashtable::Find(object)
   Callers (with count) that contribute at least for 1%:
          165  100 % System.Collections.Hashtable::Contains(object)
Total number of calls: 17742

Allocation profiler
Total mem Method
Total memory allocated: 79 KB
```

If you examine the output, you can see that 17,742 calls were made while executing the `helloworld.exe` application, with a number of methods being called more than once. The output breaks the results down into method calls with the following information shown for each:

- *Time (ms or milliseconds)*: The time taken in milliseconds to execute the code

- *Count*: The number of times the code has been executed

- *P/call (ms)*: Average time spent each time this code is called

- *Method name*: The name of the method being called

As you can see, the profiler displays quite a bit of information; if you want to delve into the depths of the profiling output, you can determine which methods are your most expensive in terms of resources, either as method calls or elapsed time, or both. The profiler also displays the memory usage for the application and the total number of calls made.

A very simple test of the profiler feature under the Mono runtime is to run your application using a normal string representation. The line that outputs the string is shown here:

```
Console.Out.WriteLine("Hello World!");
```

Then you can modify this to present a concrete string for output, because this enables the JIT compiler to profile the code, knowing that the string is fixed in sized and cannot be changed. You can then profile the difference by modifying the code as follows:

```
using System;
namespace HelloWorld
{
  class Hello
  {
    static void Main(string[] args)
    {
      Console.Out.WriteLine(@"Hello World!");
    }
  }
}
```

Recompile the application and execute it with the command lines that follow, using the profiler as you did previously:

```
mcs helloworld.cs
mono --profile helloworld.exe
```

You'll see from using the profiler that the second example actually requires two fewer calls, *17740* as opposed to *17742*, and is on average *20 to 30 ms* faster. This is obviously a negligible difference (unlike if the method is called thousands of times, in which case it would mean a difference!), but by using the profiler, you can obtain a better understanding of your code and streamline your methods for maximum performance. If you find interpreting the textual output of the profiler difficult, consider trying one of the number of graphical applications that work with the profiler and make life far easier for interpreting the data. Some examples are Exemplar Profiler (see http://fizmez.com/?useCase=viewProduct&product=exemplarProfiler) and the Mono Profile Viewer (see http://forge.novell.com/modules/xfmod/project/?monoprof). The latter is shown in Figure 12-1 interpreting the HelloWorld output that was redirected to a file.

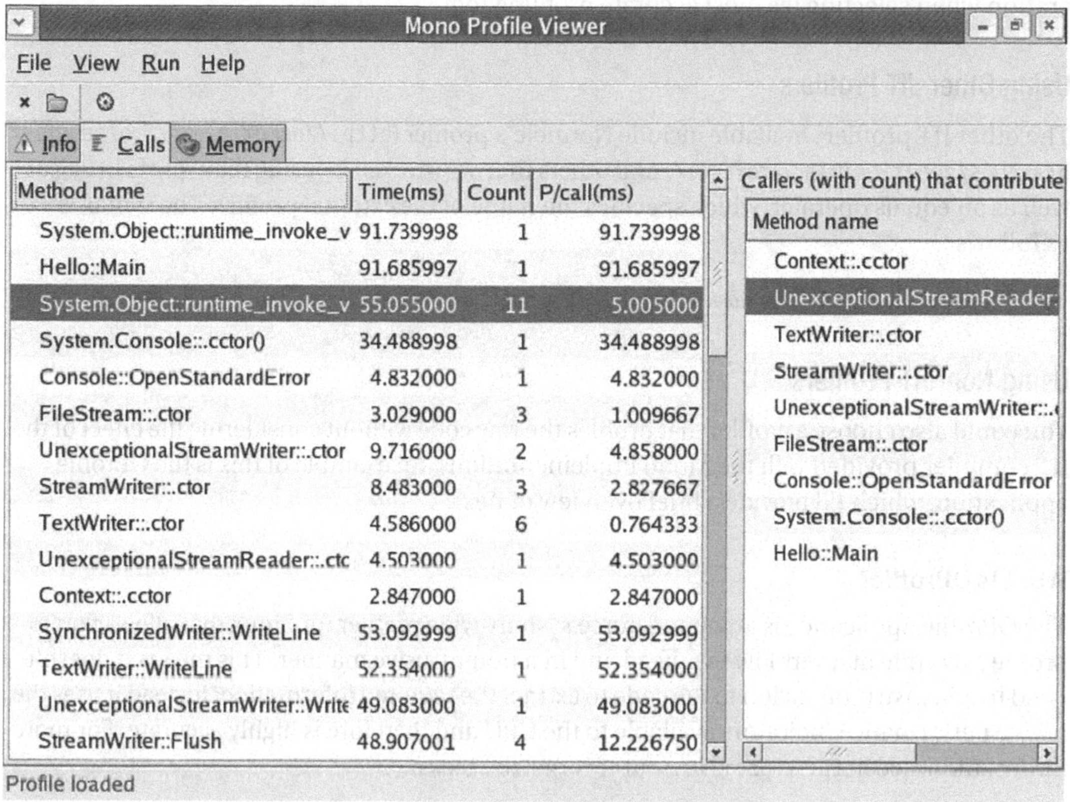

Figure 12-1. *The Mono Profile Viewer application*

So far, we've taken a look at how you can profile your application and view the data produced to measure your application's performance. Now let's take a look at some common ways you can improve your application's performance, analyzing the output of other profiling tools as a pointer to your potential performance problems.

Other Profiling Tools

In addition to Mono's own profiling tool, you have the option of using other profiling tools available both commercially and on the open-source market. These tools typically fall into two camps: the first consists of the JIT profilers like the one provided with Mono, and others are native profilers that profile your code without considering JIT overhead, although such overhead is only incurred once because of the CLR's ability to cached precompiled code. As you may recall, the JIT compiler does incur certain overheads through extra tasks, such as the need to check for compilation at runtime. Other factors that affect performance are related to an application running within a managed environment (the CLR) and the services this offers. This is obviously something that compiled applications don't suffer from and that the JIT and the CLR try to reduce, but they are overheads nonetheless. Therefore, profilers are available that either consider the implications of JIT and CLR or don't, and you'll find this worthy of consideration when selecting the most accurate profiling tool.

Using Other JIT Profilers

The other JIT profilers available include Nermele's profiler (`http://nemerle.org/svn/nemerle/branches/generics/misc/profiler/`) and others that are invoked by using the `--profile` flag as well as an equals operator, which specifies the name of the external profiler. The syntax is as follows:

```
mono --profile=<profiler name> helloworld.exe
```

Using Non-JIT Profilers

You could also choose a profiler that profiles the raw code without considering the effect of the JIT compiler provided with the Mono implementations. An example of this is the OProfile application, which I'll provide a brief overview of next.

What Is OProfile?

The OProfile application is an open-source system-wide profiler for Linux that allows you to profile raw code at a very low overhead and in a nonintrusive manner. This means it doesn't need to add instrumentation to the code to extract the required information; instead it uses the native performance indicators available to the CPU and therefore is highly accurate. For more information, see `http://oprofile.sourceforge.net/news/`.

How Can I Use OProfile with Mono?

The first step to using OProfile is to use the Ahead Of Time compiler option, indicated by the flag `--aot` that compiles the application to native code, which can then be used by the OProfile application for profiling. For the HelloWorld application, the command line would look like this:

```
mono --aot helloworld.exe
```

This will invoke the native assembler and linker, resulting in a new shared object file that can be used by the OProfile application. The results of the executed commands and the generated files are shown in Figure 12-2.

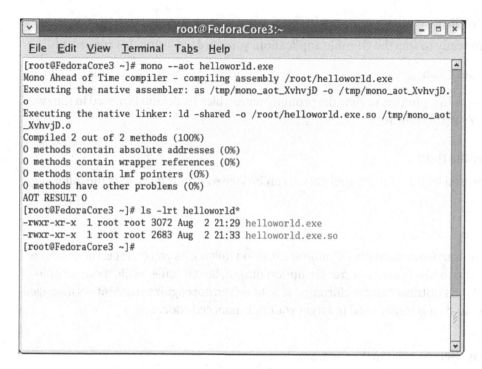

Figure 12-2. *Compiling using the Ahead-Of-Time compilation option*

You are now in a position to run the resulting executable using the OProfile profiling tool.

Initializing OProfile

The first step in being able to profile your code is to initialize the OProfile application using the following command line:

```
opcontrol --no-vmlinux
```

This informs the profiler to not capture performance data on the actual Linux kernel itself, although if you do want this information, it is possible to obtain it using the following command:

```
opcontrol --vmlinux=/boot/vmlinux-`uname -r`
```

However, it's worth pointing out that the preceding example requires you to point the profiler at the location of the vmlinux file.

Starting OProfile

Once the OProfile application has been initialized, you're then able to switch on the profiler by using this command:

```
opcontrol --start
```

At this point, you would execute the application or perform tasks that you want the profiler to capture. When finished, you must then stop the OProfile application.

Stopping OProfile

When you are ready to stop the OProfile application, you can do so using this command:

```
opcontrol --shutdown
```

You are now in a position to view the profiling data, which by default is placed in the /var/lib/oprofile/samples directory.

Viewing OProfile Data

The data captured by the OProfile application can be viewed simply by issuing the following command:

```
opreport
```

Sample output from using the OProfile application follows. As you can see, the output is similar in nature to Mono's own --profile option output, but OProfile, while more complicated to use, is less obtrusive and performant. It is, however, not cognizant of Mono's managed environment, and so is ideally used to target your nonmanaged code.

```
Cpu type: PIII
Cpu speed was (MHz estimation) : 699.667
Counter 0 counted CPU_CLK_UNHALTED events (clocks processor is not halted) with
a unit mask of 0x00 (No unit mask) count 10000
vma        samples   %            symbol name
080483d0 0         0            _start
080483f4 0         0            call_gmon_start
08048420 0         0            __do_global_dtors_aux
08048480 0         0            fini_dummy
08048490 0         0            frame_dummy
080484c0 0         0            init_dummy
08048640 0         0            __do_global_ctors_aux
08048670 0         0            init_dummy
08048680 0         0            _fini
080484d0 40317     49.9356      main
080485bc 40421     50.0644      func1
```

Clearing OProfile Data

If you wish to clear any existing OProfile data, you achieve this by using the --reset command as follows:

```
opcontrol --reset
```

To summarize, the OProfile application is perfect for when you want a detailed but nonobtrusive profiling solution. However, due to its complexity, I'd recommend only using this tool under certain conditions:

- Performance is paramount.

- Mono's profiling is not providing you with sufficient detail.

- You are using a native language such as C or C++.

A comprehensive guide for using this tool is beyond the scope of this chapter, but for full instructions on how to using OProfile, see http://oprofile.sourceforge.net/docs/.

Enhancing Your Performance

The performance of your application will often be one of the first things a user notices, and how unfortunate it would be if it topped the list of annoying idiosyncrasies for your application or even resulted in system failure. The unfortunate thing about performance is that sometimes you're not to blame, especially as you get further away from the actual implementation of key concepts. What do I mean by this? Consider the diagram shown in Figure 12-3.

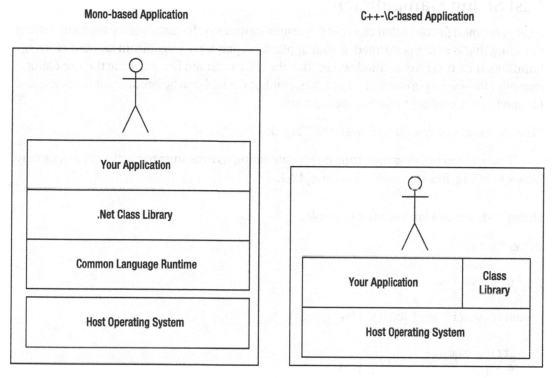

Figure 12-3. *.NET and "traditional" application runtime stacks*

The diagram shows the layers of abstraction involved when running a typical Mono-based application, compared with typical C- or C++-based application. These layers of abstraction are your friend when it comes to speed of development, but at a cost! So how bad is it? The efficiency in the technologies used such as JIT compilation, caching features, and optimization all mean that more often than not, the application scenarios presented previously are comparable, but there is room for improvement, which comes in the form of two different approaches:

1. Understanding and respecting the runtime technologies used

2. Ensuring that your code is performant by design, not by accident

The first point relates to runtime components such as the garbage collector (GC), which handles all of the memory management for your application. If you understand and appreciate how this works, you can optimize your code to take advantage of it, and not leave it working so hard that your application's performance fails. The second point relates to the breadth of the technologies available, especially within the class library, where you can implement a piece of functionality in several different ways, though they aren't all equal in performance.

In the following section, we'll look at both respecting the managed environment in which your applications run and profiling the code as a result, accompanied by examples of how these can be taken into account when designing and implementing your application. To provide a demonstrable difference in speed, we're going to loop around an example piece of code a significant number of times; otherwise, as the inefficiency is so small, the difference would be difficult to gauge. However, while the improvements are small in isolation, when looking at the whole application, the speed improvements can make a noticeable difference.

Fast String Manipulation

A very common problem that can affect your application's performance is the amount of string handling that is being performed. If your application performs a significant amount of string handling, then there are methods other than the concatenation feature using the + operator that offer increased performance. Let's take a look at the problem before an option is presented for solving it. Consider the following sentence:

```
"The quick brown fox jumped over the lazy dog"
```

If we were to building this string by concatenating its constitute parts, the code in C# may look something like that shown in Listing 12-1.

Listing 12-1. *String Manipulation Example*

```
using System;

public class Test
{
  public static void Main(string[] args)
  {
    string example="";
    for (int i=1; i<100000; i++)
    {
      example = "The ";
      example = example + "quick ";
      example = example + "brown ";
      example = example + "fox ";
      example = example + "jumped ";
      example = example + "over ";
      example = example + "the ";
      example = example + "lazy ";
      example = example + "dog";
    }
  }
}
```

This involves concatenating nine individual string values incrementally into a single string whose value is held in a string variable called example. This concatenation is repeated such that the concatenation is completed 100,000 times! The .NET compiler treats string objects as *immutable* (that is, they cannot be changed), and so for each statement, the previous string value is thrown away and left for the garbage collector to clean up, and a new string value is assigned. In the preceding example, this ultimately results in the garbage collector holding a single string value pointed to by the variable example and nine temporary strings that are byproducts of the concatenation.

The execution time for the Main() method in this simple application is 2,312.500 ms, with 55,272KB of memory being consumed by the garbage collector. This overhead is associated with the way in which .NET handles its string manipulation, something that is similar to other languages such as Java. It is therefore recommended that you use the StringBuilder class in such instances, as it can deal with changing strings far more efficiently resulting in faster code. Let's consider the revised example shown in Listing 12-2.

Listing 12-2. *Faster String Manipulation Example*

```
using System;
using System.Text;

public class Test
{
  public static void Main(string[] args)
  {

    StringBuilder example = new StringBuilder();
    for (int i=1; i<100000; i++)
    {
      example.Append("The ");
      example.Append("quick ");
      example.Append("brown ");
      example.Append("fox ");
      example.Append("jumped ");
      example.Append("over ");
      example.Append("the ");
      example.Append("lazy ");
      example.Append("dog");
    }
  }
}
```

In this example, the execution time for the Main() method is 781.250 ms, with 32,768KB of memory being consumed by the garbage collector. This is approximately 33% faster, although such speed increases are anticipated only in methods that are called repeatedly or within loops.

Avoid Boxing to Increase Performance

Through its class library and the common language runtime, the .NET Framework provides comprehensive support for various different object types, which in the case of .NET all inherit from the System.Object base class. In this respect, it's not dissimilar to a number of other object-oriented languages, but it can become pretty tedious to treat all types as reference types, even when you're using their values, as is often the case with common data types such as integers. In this case, compilers such as that in the .NET Framework provide a number of commonly used data types known as *primitives*, which allow you to remove some of the additional syntax normally associated with these types of reference types. For example, these two statements are semantically the same:

```
int a = new int(10);
int a=10;
```

The second example, which shows a direct assignment of the integer value to the variable, is not only simpler to use, but also the compiled code generated will be exactly the same. This is because the compiler maps all *primitive* types to base class types that exist within the framework, which in the case of an int is the System.Int32 type. The mappings are shown in Table 12-1.

Table 12-1. *Primitive Type to Base Class Type Mappings*

C# Primitive Type	Class Type	Description
sbyte	System.SByte	Signed 8-bit value
byte	System.Byte	Unsigned 8-bit value
short	System.Int16	Signed 16-bit value
ushort	System.UInt16	Unsigned 16-bit value
int	System.Int32	Signed 32-bit value
uint	System.UInt32	Unsigned 32-bit value
long	System.Int64	Signed 64-bit value
ulong	System.UInt64	Unsigned 64-bit value
char	System.Char	16-bit Unicode character
float	System.Single	32-bit float
double	System.Double	64-bit float
bool	System.Boolean	A true/false value
decimal	System.Decimal	96-bit signed integer times 100 through 1028
object	System.Object	Base of all types
string	System.String	String type

When your code is expecting a reference type, and you pass a value type, the compiler performs an action called *boxing*. This involves converting the value type into a reference type by first allocating sufficient memory to hold both the value and the object that will represent it, and then copying the value type into the reference type. This is obviously costly in terms of heap memory used (as it's a value type first) and the processing time taken to perform the conversion. I'll demonstrate by example. Consider the following value type definition:

```
Int32 val = 10;
```

If you were to assign this to a reference type, such as an Object, the compiler would need to box this in order to perform the conversion. An example of boxing is shown here:

```
Int32 val = 10;
Object o = val;  // This assigns 'o' a boxed version of 'val'
```

Therefore, to avoid boxing, you should understand in which instances the compiler will need to perform boxing or unboxing, and thus avoid it in your code by using native assignment or passing operations.

Using structs When Class Features Are Not Required

You may remember that in the earlier C# chapters we discussed the subtle differences between a *class* and a *struct*. The overhead associated with the common language runtime supporting functionality found in classes can be very costly to performance, so if you simply wish to use a class as a collection of attributes, then I recommend using a struct instead with the general rule of thumb being as follows:

- Only use a struct when you have fields totaling 32 bytes or less of data.

- You need to pass the item by *value only*.

However, special care should be taken that you don't inadvertently box the struct by passing it to a method signature expecting it to be or assigning it to a System.Object type. For example, the code in Listing 12-3 would box.

Listing 12-3. *An Example of Boxing*

```
struct MyStruct
{
  public int a;
}

public class Test
{
  public static void Main(string[] args)
  {
    MyStruct e;
    e.a=0;
    BoxIt(e);
  }
```

```
  public static void BoxIt(object val)
  {
    // Do nothing, but val is now a boxed version of the struct MyStruct
  }
}
```

Helping Your Friend the Garbage Collector

Although the GC will do the right thing in terms of releasing and finalizing objects on time, you can assist the GC by clearing the fields that point to objects. This means that some objects might be eligible for collection earlier than they would be; this can help reduce the memory consumption and reduce the work that the GC has to do.

When you are finished with an object, release it back to the garbage collector as soon as possible by calling the Close() method and then Dispose() method if your class implements one. In all cases, the garbage collector reclaims the memory allocated by the object; this is part of the memory management features it offers.

■ **Note** Setting an object to null has no benefit unless it means that you're releasing an object reference. In all cases, when an object is no longer referenced, the garbage collector will reclaim its memory when next executed, or if the object that is no longer referenced has a Dispose() method, then it will be reclaimed immediately. As a point of reference, Java garbage collection works in a very similar fashion with the concept of unreachable objects (those that are no longer referenced) and objects that have the Finalize() method rather than the Dispose() method.

Performance Interactions Using foreach

If your application requires you to traverse a collection of objects either held in an array or in a collection reference type, you have a number of options. You could either walk through this array\collection by its index value or you can use the foreach C# feature. As a general rule of thumb, the foreach statement generates more performant code and ensures that objects that provide an implementation for the IDispose interface (to clean up) call it, and thus is more memory efficient. Consider the use of foreach in Listing 12-4.

Listing 12-4. *Iteration Example*

```
using System;

public class Test
{
  public static void Main(string[] args)
  {
    string s = "This is a Test";
    foreach(char c in s)
      Console.Out.WriteLine(c);
  }
}
```

However, for simple character arrays, an index-based loop will often be faster because the compiler doesn't have the overhead of the objects contained within and the need to create enumerator objects. Therefore, for your string, the example shown in Listing 12-5 would be faster.

Listing 12-5. *Faster Iteration Example*

```
using System;

public class Test
{
  public static void Main(string[] args)
  {
    string s = "This is a Test";
    for(int i=0;i<s.Length;i++)
      Console.Out.WriteLine(s[i]);
  }
}
```

As is the case with all performance tips, the key to ensuring your code is running at optimal speed is to use real-world profiling as discussed earlier.

Other Quick-Fire Tips

I've also included some other performance tips in the following simple list that you may wish to explore:

- *Use chunky calls rather than chatty calls*: It's better that your functions perform an optimal amount of work while still being well defined, rather than lots of fine granular calls that must be repeated often.

- *Appropriate exception handling*: Exception handling is expensive in terms of performance and memory, so only use exceptions when your code encounters an *exceptional* error. Otherwise, use other error indicators such as numeric values as return values.

- *Good assembly management*: Avoid the overhead of loading assemblies that may only contain one method that is used; instead, look to consolidate assemblies while taking care to maintain a sensible structure.

- *ASP.NET*: Switch off the View State feature in ASP.NET unless you need it. An ASP.NET page stores the values held in its controls in a hidden field called ViewState; this takes up space and incurs a performance hit when being transferred. If you don't need it, switch it off in the ASP.NET configuration file.

- *Use jagged arrays where appropriate*: The JIT compiler is more efficient at dealing with jagged (irregularly shaped) arrays rather than rectangular arrays.

▪ **Note** For more tips on performance within Mono, see `http://www.mono-project.com/` `FAQ:_Technical#Performance`, and for more tips on writing scalable applications, see `http://` `msdn.microsoft.com/library/default.asp?url=/library/en-us/dnpag/html/` `scalenetcheck06.asp`.

Understanding Reflection

The concept of reflection, as its name suggests, allows you to discover information about objects at runtime, regardless of whether these objects are *assemblies* or *reference data types*. Such information is typically available only to the compiler, but in the case of runtime-based environments such as .NET (and Java), it is available through a specific API, which in .NET's case is called *reflection*. While this is a very advanced topic, reflection is an extremely powerful feature, and so in this section of the chapter I'll provide an overview of what reflection actually is and some examples of how you can use it.

The application programming interface available for calling the reflection framework is found within the `System.Reflection` namespace, and so you should remember to use this within your application before attempting to make use of its API. Let's see its usage through some examples, starting by considering the data type declaration found in Listing 12-6.

Listing 12-6. *Reflection Data Type Declaration Example*

```
using System;

public class Person
{
  private int age;
  public Person()
  {
    age = 0;
  }

  public Person(int age)
  {
    this.age = age;
  }

  public void WhatsMyAge()
  {
    Console.Out.WriteLine("My age is " + this.age.ToString());
  }
}
```

We can write a test harness that demonstrates this data type as shown here:

```
public class Test
{
  static void Main(string[] args)
  {
    Person p1 = new Person();
    p1.WhatsMyAge();
  }
}
```

Using the Reflection API

You can also discover information about a class by using the reflection API previously mentioned. The first task is to get a reference to a Type class by using the GetType() method; this then opens the doors for obtaining other information through reflection. The statement that follows achieves this based on using an instance of the data type called p1 as created in the previous example:

```
Type obj = p1.GetType();
```

Once you have your Type class reference, you can call reflection-based methods on this object to find out more information about your class. A good example is that you can return a collection of ConstructorInfo objects that provide information about the constructors defined within your class. I'll demonstrate this with an example: Listing 12-7 extends the Main() method of the previous example to output the method signature for all constructors in the class.

Listing 12-7. *Reflection Example*

```
public class Test
{
  static void Main(string[] args)
  {
    Person p1 = new Person();

    Type obj = p1.GetType();
    ConstructorInfo [] info = obj.GetConstructors();
    foreach( ConstructorInfo c in info )
    {
      Console.WriteLine(c);
    }
  }
}
```

The output for the example should look like this:

```
Void .ctor()
Void .ctor(Int32)
```

This shows that the class has two constructors: one is the default constructor that takes no parameters, and the other is your custom constructor that takes an integer value as a parameter.

What Else Can Reflection Show?

You could use a similar approach to display information about the methods defined or display attributes about a particular objects, whether this pertains to the object itself or the members contained within it. Some examples of the attributes that can be found within the Type class are listed in Table 12-2.

Table 12-2. *An Example of Type Properties Available*

Property	Description
Name	Gives name of the type
FullName	Gives fully qualified name of the type
Namespace	Gives namespace name
IsClass	Defines the object as a class
IsInterface	Defines the object as an interface
IsAbstract	Defines the object as abstract
IsCOMObject	Defines the object as a COM object
IsEnum	Defines the object as an enumeration
IsSealed	Defines the object as sealed
IsPublic	Defines the object as public

This is only the tip of the iceberg, but you can reflect on assemblies and the objects within assemblies, and you can create instances and invoke methods or access attributes and properties purely by using the reflection API. Table 12-3 presents a list of the areas for which reflection can be used to return information.

Table 12-3. *Reflection Classes Supported in .NET*

Class	Description
Assembly	Provides information on assemblies
Module	Provides information on modules
ConstructorInfo	Provides information on constructors
MethodInfo	Provides information on methods
FieldInfo	Provides information on fields
EventInfo	Provides information on events
PropertyInfo	Provides information on properties
ParameterInfo	Provides information on parameters

Some examples of where reflection is used is within debuggers, JIT compilers, syntax highlighting in editors, and more. Explore the possibilities and experiment using the methods discussed and the example provided.

Processing Asynchronously Using Threads

I've touched on how to assess the performance of your applications and even suggested some tips for increasing it by using either good programming principles or electively using more performant classes. However, there is another way of achieving an increase in performance, although it does require significantly more effort. This method takes advantage of the fact your computer can process more than one instruction at a time using a concept known as *threading*.

What Are Processes and Threads?

A computer typically contains one or more central processing units, which in turn process a number of instructions per second. The number of instructions it can process per second is typically dependent on the type of processor and its speed, although more recently dual-core processors have been introduced into the marketplace that allow simultaneous processing from a single chip. Your operating system, whether it is Linux or Windows (or some other), will typically run your application within a boundary known as a *process*. A process can be thought of as a fence around your application in which the application's code and resources such as memory are associated. The operating system also supports *threads*, which are concurrent streams of activity that also can contain code and resources such as memory, but are shared by a process. It is at the thread level that an operating system will typically schedule its processing time, granting a finite amount of time to each thread in turn for processing. Where a machine has more than one processing unit or a CPU capable of handling more than one instruction simultaneously, the operating system will typically utilize this. This is why multiple processor machines are ideally for high processing requirements—providing the application uses threads!

.NET's Threading Support

The .NET Framework provides comprehensive support for threads and related topics such as synchronization within the System.Threading namespace. The key areas you'll need to be aware of when dealing with threads include the following:

- Creating and starting a thread

- Suspending, resuming, or terminating a thread

- Processing within a thread

Let's work through these one by one using examples.

How Threads Are Used in Applications

At the lowest level, a thread is a central processing unit property that the operating system will usually use to schedule processing against. This means that individual threads can be assigned to multiple processors in a single machine, should the hardware support this feature (that is, it has more than one processor). A graphical user interface is often assigned its own dedicated thread to ensure that your application is perceived as being fast when executing, because other threads handle any background processing required.

How you use threads is, of course, your own decision. You may choose to create a number of threads that are managed by a single *main* thread—a common approach for many applications such as those that involve graphical user interfaces.

Creating Your Thread

The first step in creating a thread is preparing a function that will actually perform any processing you require; after all, there's not much use in a thread that does nothing! This is achieved by defining a function that will be doing your work such that it has the same method signature as the ThreadStart delegate, which is a delegate used to represent the function called by your thread. First consider the example shown in Listing 12-8, in which the ThreadStart delegate is highlighted in bold.

Listing 12-8. *Thread Creation and Execution Example*

```
using System;
using System.Threading;

public class Worker
{
  private Thread thread = null;
  private int delay;

  // Constructor
  //
  public Worker(int val)
  {
    delay = val;
  }

  // Main 'worker' function
  //
  protected void process()
  {

    while (1==1)
    {
      Console.Out.WriteLine(thread.Name + " " + DateTime.Now.ToString());
      Thread.Sleep(delay*1000);
    }
  }
}
```

```
// Start the thread
//
public void Start()
{
  //TODO
}

// Terminate the thread
//
public void Terminate()
{
  //TODO
}
}
```

You can use this class to encapsulate your work; alternatively, you could have used a method within any class, providing it has the same signature, in this case meaning it takes no parameters and returns no parameters. I'll walk through the preceding class briefly before moving on to its missing implementation. The first thing to notice is that you're providing a constructor that takes an integer value, as shown here:

```
// Constructor
//
public Worker(int val)
{
  delay = val;
}
```

This is so you can pass and store (in a member variable) a value that represents the number of seconds to wait before outputting a value to the console in the main working function. You can use this to show how more than one thread is running simultaneously by outputting its assigned Name and the current date and time frequency, showing the number of seconds elapsed. We will then provide a suitable "worker" method to actually represent the work required by the thread, as shown here:

```
// Main "worker" function
//
protected void process()
{
  while (1==1)
  {
    Console.Out.WriteLine(thread.Name + " " + DateTime.Now.ToString());
    Thread.Sleep(delay*1000);
  }
}
```

Its implementation is arbitrary, as you'll complete this with the processing you require for your application. In this case, it outputs its name and the date and time, after which the thread then sleeps (or pauses) for the number of seconds indicated by the value passed to the Worker class constructor, and continues. Finally, you'll see two placeholders for methods that create and start the threads processing using the Start() method and terminates the thread using the Terminate() method. Let's walk through the implementation of these methods before testing this in a suitable test harness.

Starting Your Thread

First we'll focus on the Start() method, which needs to create a thread that is local to the Worker class and associate it with the process() function defined within that class. After this has completed successfully, we can then start the thread running, which should start to invoke the process() method's code. The implementation for the Start() method is shown here:

```
// Start the thread
//
public void Start()
{
  thread = new Thread(new ThreadStart(process));
  if (thread != null)
  {
    thread.Name = delay.ToString();
    thread.Start();
  }
}
```

In the preceding example, you assign a new instance of a Thread class to the thread member variable, creating an instance of a ThreadStart class that points to your process function. Then after first checking that the thread object is not null, you assign it an arbitrary name (use the count passed) and start it running by calling Start(). You can actually start to write an application to test your code by creating two instances of your worker class, each with different delay rates, and start them processing. Do this using the following test harness and examine the output:

```
public class Test
{
  static void Main(string[] args)
  {

    Worker w1 = new Worker(5);
    Worker w2 = new Worker(2);

    w1.Start();
    w2.Start();

  }
}
```

After leaving it for a number of seconds to run (I suggest longer than 20 seconds) and examining the output, you should see something similar to the following:

```
5 03/08/2005 22:42:51
2 03/08/2005 22:42:51
2 03/08/2005 22:42:53
2 03/08/2005 22:42:55
5 03/08/2005 22:42:56
2 03/08/2005 22:42:57
2 03/08/2005 22:42:59
5 03/08/2005 22:43:01
2 03/08/2005 22:43:01
2 03/08/2005 22:43:03
2 03/08/2005 22:43:05
5 03/08/2005 22:43:06
2 03/08/2005 22:43:07
```

After the threads initially starting (see that both output the same date and time), you can then see that the threads are running in parallel, but the different delays in each show by the thread with the short delay (beginning with 2) outputting values more regularly than the one with the longer delay (beginning with 5). This is as expected, but you'll also notice that the output is directly related to the number of seconds you wait. However, to stop the thread, you'll need to kill the running process—*not a good programming practice*. So, add the implementation for the Terminate() method as shown here:

```
// Terminate the thread
//
public void Terminate()
{
  if (thread != null)
    if (thread.IsAlive)
      thread.Abort();
}
```

Its implementation is straightforward; it first performs a series of defensive checks, specifically that the thread attribute has been assigned and that the thread is running or alive! If both of these conditions are satisfied, you can safely call the Abort() method, which will kill the thread. If you add these calls to your test application's implementation, as shown here, you can then examine the output.

```
public class Test
{
  static void Main(string[] args)
  {
```

```
    // Create instances
    Worker w1 = new Worker(5);
    Worker w2 = new Worker(2);

    // Start threads
    w1.Start();
    w2.Start();

    // Terminate the threads
    w1.Terminate();
    w2.Terminate();

  }
```

The output after running the preceding test application is as follows:

---

2 03/08/2005 22:48:45

This is because the first thread starts but is terminated immediately, as is the second, even before it has time to execute. Let's add a delay in between the processing to allow the threads to run as shown here:

```
public class Test
{
  static void Main(string[] args)
  {

    Worker w1 = new Worker(5);
    Worker w2 = new Worker(2);

    w1.Start();
    w2.Start();

    Thread.Sleep(20000);

    w1.Terminate();
    w2.Terminate();

  }
}
```

I've highlighted the statement that causes the delay; this calls the Sleep() method on the current thread passing in 20 seconds (20×1,000 milliseconds) as the delay. Notice that the Main() function is running on a separate thread from the ones you've created; you know this because the two worker threads continue to output values at their appropriate points. This default thread is created automatically by the compiler and the common language runtime.

You can do other things, such as add methods to suspend or resume a thread, the implementations for which are shown in the next sections.

Suspending a Thread

The suspension of a thread is straightforward: you simply need to do similar defensive checks as those when terminating the thread, except that in this instance you query the ThreadState property, which must be in the ThreadState.Running state. The implementation for this method is shown here:

```
// Suspend the thread
//
public void Suspend()
{
  if (thread != null)
    if (thread.ThreadState != ThreadState.Suspended)
      thread.Suspend();
}
```

Let's extend the example to demonstrate the functionality to suspend a running thread. First, modify your Main() function so that you create your threads (albeit with slightly shorter delays) and terminate them as before, but introduce a main loop that will keep running until the q key is pressed, followed by a carriage return. Once the user has chosen to quit, a boolean flag called bQuit will be set to true, and the loop will terminate. This enables the threads to running indefinitely until the user decides to quit the application, but it also allows you to add some further functionality to suspend or resume a thread, depending on a key combination. So, the first thing you'll do is introduce the ability to suspend one of the threads by pressing the 1 key followed by a carriage return. This is trapped, and the Suspend() method introduced previously is called on thread 1, referenced by the w1 variable. Listing 12-9 demonstrates this with the new Main() method and its suspend functionality in bold.

Listing 12-9. *Thread Suspend and Resume Demonstration*

```
static void Main(string[] args)
{
  Worker w1 = new Worker(1);
  Worker w2 = new Worker(2);

  w1.Start();
  w2.Start();

  Console.Out.WriteLine("Press 'q' to quit, '1' to Suspend Thread
  1, '2' to Resume Thread 1 - Followed by Enter ");

  bool bQuit = false;
  while (!bQuit)
  {
    int i = Console.Read();
```

```
    // 'q' Pressed
    if (i==113)
      bQuit = true;

    // '1' Pressed
    if (i==49)
    {
      w1.Suspend();
      Console.Out.WriteLine("*Thread 1 Suspended...");
    }
  }

  w1.Terminate();
  w2.Terminate();
}
```

If you compile and execute the preceding example, and, after letting the threads execute for a few seconds, choose to suspend thread 1 by pressing the 1 key, output similar to that shown here should be displayed:

```
Press 'q' to quit, '1' to Suspend Thread 1, '2' to Resume Thread 1 - Followed
by Enter
1 9/27/2005 11:14:05 PM State:Running
2 9/27/2005 11:14:05 PM State:Running
1 9/27/2005 11:14:06 PM State:Running
2 9/27/2005 11:14:07 PM State:Running
1 9/27/2005 11:14:07 PM State:Running
1
*Thread 1 Suspended...
2 9/27/2005 11:14:09 PM State:Running
2 9/27/2005 11:14:11 PM State:Running
2 9/27/2005 11:14:13 PM State:Running
```

You should notice that after thread 1 has been suspended, the only output produced is from thread 2; this is because thread 1 is in a suspended state. Next, let's look at how you can resume a suspend thread.

Resuming a Thread

The resumption of a suspended thread is again straightforward; the same defensive checks are performed, except that in this instance you query the ThreadState property, which must be in the ThreadState.Suspended state. The implementation for this method is as follows:

```
// Resume the thread
//
public void Resume()
{
```

```
  if (thread != null)
    if (thread.ThreadState != ThreadState.Running)
      thread.Resume();
}
```

So you can extend your Main() method to also trap the 2 key and resume thread 1, as shown in this example code:

```
// 2 key pressed
if (i==50)
{
  w1.Resume();
    Console.Out.WriteLine("*Thread 1 Resumed...");
}
```

If you again compile and execute your code, and then wait for a few seconds before suspending thread 1 by pressing the 1 key, and, after waiting a few more seconds, resume thread 1 by pressing the 2 key, the output should look similar to the following:

```
Press 'q' to quit, '1' to Suspend Thread 1, '2' to Resume Thread 1 - Followed
by Enter
2 9/27/2005 10:00:46 PM State:Running
1 9/27/2005 10:00:46 PM State:Running
1 9/27/2005 10:00:47 PM State:Running
1 9/27/2005 10:00:48 PM State:Running
2 9/27/2005 10:00:48 PM State:Running
1
*Thread 1 Suspended...
2 9/27/2005 10:00:50 PM State:Running
2 9/27/2005 10:00:52 PM State:Running
2 9/27/2005 10:00:54 PM State:Running
2
*Thread 2 Resumed...
1 9/27/2005 10:00:54 PM State:Running
1 9/27/2005 10:00:55 PM State:Running
2 9/27/2005 10:00:56 PM State:Running
1 9/27/2005 10:00:56 PM State:Running
1 9/27/2005 10:00:57 PM State:Running
2 9/27/2005 10:00:58 PM State:Running
```

This clearly shows that thread 1 is being suspended and then later resumed as a result of the user interacting with the application via the keyboard.

Once again, these are significant topics, and a number of areas such as using objects to synchronize more than one thread, the protection of resources that may be accessed by more than one thread simultaneously, and storing data locally within a thread, have not been covered. These topics and more are left for you to research and explore on your own.

Enhancing Interoperability

This section covers the concept of interoperability: what it is and why it's important. In addition, I'll provide a list of key areas in which care should be taken in order to achieve it.

What Is Interoperability?

The term *interoperability* means *hardware and software on different machines sharing functionality and data.* In this section, we'll be focusing on achieving the software aspects of interoperability only.

If you're working on your machine, and everything you will ever want in terms of software and hardware is on it, interoperability isn't important! However, I doubt whether this is ever going to be the case; for example, you may want to access something on the Internet, plug in a new device, or load some software. All of these could have implications in terms of interoperability. If you imagine the world of online business—the communication between businesses and the sharing of data—is almost mandatory, then achieving interoperability is paramount. Therefore, in the following section, I'll present and discuss some considerations to take into account.

Achieving Interoperability

I've covered a vast array of information within this book, and I've touched on one of the key reasons why Mono was ported to operating systems other than Microsoft Windows—interoperability. The Linux operating system is a commercially sound choice in the world of commerce, as is Mac OS X and others, but these operating systems, until recently, haven't had the ability to run the .NET Framework. Now, thanks to Mono, that's not the case any more; you can comfortably write applications that utilize the .NET Framework and simply ask that your user be running an implementation of the CLR for your application to work. This offers a key step towards interoperability: applications written to the .NET Framework will now work *unchanged* on other operating systems with the caveats mentioned. For more information on portability, see `http://www.mono-project.com/FAQ:_Technical`. Here I'll list some of the areas to be cognizant of when building your application.

Client Footprint

When deciding how to write an application, the first consideration is whether your application is going to have a *client footprint*, that is, whether it requires certain resources or technologies to be present on the host machine in order for it to run. For example, if you develop a Windows Forms–based application, this will require as a minimum the CLR and dependent assemblies to be present. If, however, you develop a Web-based application using ASP.NET, then you will only need a suitable Web browser on the client machine. This is an important consideration, so make your choice carefully. Another consideration is, when your application is deployed locally, whether it has the processing power available to the local machine. This may be more than adequate, but then again, it may not! By contrast, a *thin-client* application is processed centrally on a server whose specification you can usually influence, and so the demands on the client machine are minimal—thus potentially improving performance.

.NET Framework Conformance

When writing your Mono-based application, be aware that your target platform must contain the dependent technologies. For example, if you use an OdbcConnection class, then the .NET Framework will expect a compatible ODBC driver to be installed on the machine it is running against. In the case of the .NET Framework, you should ensure that the .NET Class Library objects you use have been implemented on the target implementation of the CLR. This is especially true when dealing with the open-source .NET implementation, i.e., Mono, and the Windows .NET implementation. You should also note that there are currently a number of versions of the .NET Framework—versions 1.0, 1.1, and the new 2.0—that are all backward compatible but *not* forward compatible. A key consideration here is that your code only implement features available on the target platform; it would be pointless to write an application against Microsoft version 2.0's of the .NET Framework and then deploy it against Mono framework implementations, as in all likelihood Mono will be trailing behind (if only for a limited period!) Microsoft's implementation of version 2.0 of the .NET Framework and so would not work.

Avoiding Proprietary Extensions

When developing your application, avoid using proprietary extensions such as .NET's ability to perform COM Interop calls or using technologies that aren't available on your target platform. For example, you may decide to use the GTK+ toolkit, but you will need to ensure that this is present on the target platform, and if it's not, arrange for this to be installed as part of your applications deployment.

Sharing Data

When sharing data, you need to keep in mind a couple of key considerations. The first is that you are using an encoding mechanism that both platforms understand, and this is known as *encoding interoperability*. For example, UTF-8 is well known on most operating systems, but if you're deploying to a geographical location whose language requires 16 bits for representation (such as China), then UTF-8 will be insufficient. Therefore, in these instances, the recommendation is UTF-16.

Another consideration when sharing data is *data model interoperability*, which ensures that both parties understand the format of the data. This is usually enforced by sharing a schema, the metadata for your data that indicates the format of the data.

To ensure data interoperability, my recommendation is to use the XML, as long as the appropriate encoding mechanism is used and you ensure data integrity by also applying and sharing the XML Schema.

Interprocess Communication

Finally, when sharing data, you'll probably encounter the problem of how to actually exchange it. When direct communication between processes is required, this is known as *interprocess communication* (also called a Remote Procedure Call, or RPC); but when dealing with processes that may be on different physical machines (also know as Remote Method Invocation, or RMI, in Java or DCOM on Windows), this presents complications. In this instance, the universal mechanism for exchanging data and making calls is via the Simple Object Access Protocol

(SOAP) or using a technology known as Web Services. This isn't without its complications, but it's a relatively painless mechanism for sharing functionality and is fast promoting a series of standards (see `http://msdn.microsoft.com/webservices/webservices/understanding/specs/default.aspx`) that will help make *service-oriented architecture* (SOA), the collaboration of components exposing functionality, a reality.

Summary

To conclude this book, I've presented some of the more advanced topics found within the .NET Framework and Mono. First, you saw how to assess the performance of your application using both built-in and additional *profilers*. This followed with a discussion on how to address performance, assuming that you have first diagnosed the problem(s) using profiling. I then introduced the topic of reflection, showing how you can obtain introspective information on your assemblies and classes at runtime using the reflection application programming interface. You also looked at increasing your application's response time yet further by tapping into the power of multithreaded applications, allowing (what often appears to be) simultaneous processing of code. Finally, I provided some tips on how to work toward the utopia of true interoperability between your applications running on different operating systems.

Index

Printed in the United States
By Bookmasters